Philosophers Speak for Themselves

From Thales to Plato

Edited by
T. V. SMITH

Phoenix Books

THE UNIVERSITY OF CHICAGO PRESS

This book, together with

FROM ARISTOTLE TO PLOTINUS (Phoenix Book P 9)

is also available in a one-volume, clothbound edition from

THE UNIVERSITY OF CHICAGO PRESS

THE UNIVERSITY OF CHICAGO PRESS, CHICAGO 37
Cambridge University Press, London, N.W. 1, England
The University of Toronto Press, Toronto 5, Canada

PHILOSOPHIC OVERTONES

A PHILOSOPHER'S FAITH

That we shall be better and braver and less helpless if we think that we ought to enquire, than we should have been if we indulged in the idle fancy that there was no knowing and no use in seeking to know what we do not know;—that is a theme upon which I am ready to fight, in word and deed, to the utmost of my power.—PLATO.

A PHILOSOPHER'S CAUTION

It is the mark of an educated man to look for precision in each class of things just so far as the nature of the subject admits; it is evidently equally foolish to accept probable reasoning from a mathematician and to demand from a rhetorician scientific proofs.—ARISTOTLE.

A PHILOSOPHER'S PRAYER

Beloved Pan, and all ye other gods who haunt this place, give me beauty in the inward soul; and may the outward and inward man be at one. May I reckon the wise to be the wealthy, and may I have such a quantity of gold as a temperate man and he only can bear and carry.—SOCRATES.

A PHILOSOPHER'S ADVICE

Absorb not all that you wish, but all that you can hold. Only be of sound mind, and then you will be able to hold all that you wish. For the more the mind receives, the more does it expand.

"What then?" you say, "do we not know certain men who have sat for many years at the feet of a philosopher and yet have not acquired the slightest tinge of wisdom?" Of course I know such men. There are indeed persevering gentlemen who stick at it; I do not call them pupils of the wise, but merely "squatters." . . . . This class, as you will see, constitutes a large part of the listeners,—who regard the philosopher's lecture-room merely as a sort of lounging-place for their leisure. They do not set about to lay aside any faults there, or to receive a rule of life, by which they may test their characters; they merely wish to enjoy to the full the delights of the ear. . . . . But the true hearer is ravished and stirred by the beauty of the subject matter, not by the jingle of empty words. When a bold word has been uttered in defiance of death, or a saucy fling in defiance of Fortune, we take delight in acting straightway upon that which we have heard. Men are impressed by such words, and become what they are bidden to be. . . . . It is easy to rouse a listener so that he will crave righteousness; for Nature has laid the foundations and planted the seeds of virtue in us all.—SENECA.

ACKNOWLEDGMENTS

TO PERSONS

To colleagues, Charles W. Morris, Charles Hartshorne, Charner M. Perry, and Clifford P. Osborne—thanks, all. To the latter two special acknowledgments: to Professor Perry for proofreading, an onerous job done at home at a difficult time while I dreamed in modern Athens of the scenes and thoughts which this book commemorates, and to Dr. Osborne for critical aid on the introductions throughout, particularly on Aristotle; for translating into English the intricate turns of Gorgias' skepticism as reported by Sextus Empiricus; and for aid on the proof.

TO PUBLISHERS

To Kegan Paul, Trench, Trubner and Company and Charles Scribner's Sons, respectively, the English and the American publishers of Fairbanks' *The First Philosophers of Greece*, from which all selections from the pre-Socratics are taken, save as otherwise indicated. To the latter, also, for the material on Democritus. To the Open Court Publishing Company for A. E. Taylor's translation of the first book of Aristotle's *Metaphysics*. To the Macmillan Company for Welldon's translation of Aristotle's *Ethics*, and the few excerpts, indicated in the text, from the Davies and Vaughan translation of Plato's *Republic*.

But most of all to Professor Edward Capps, the American editor of the "Loeb Classical Library" series, from which the majority of my selections are taken. Acknowledgment is made in each several case and at the proper place. But neither that nor this can begin to indicate my debt to this magnificent library. The editor has not only done the handsome thing, which exact justice would not have required, of

v

letting me use a large body of material without charge, but has made it possible in this way for me to call attention in fashion exemplary to the greatest storehouse in English of classic wisdom from Greece and Rome. Every student who uses this book will, I hope, treasure for present and later use the knowledge of where he can get more, much more, of such mellow reflection as he has here sampled from this ever growing Loeb series.

TABLE OF CONTENTS

A PANORAMA

In ancient Greece a speculative sophistication, once initiated by Thales, developed so rapidly that Plato was able out of the back window of his mind, as it were, to find still verdant for gorgeous myth the primitive plains of animism. We are to trace out of a religious—not to say superstitious—background the emergence of questions that demanded real rather than fanciful answers. And though the answers were not at hand for a long time, the questions were so sincerely and so persistently put that they kept a quest for answers alive until from Greece stems much of the spirit of science as well as no little of what passes for philosophy. The questions before Socrates chiefly concerned the nature of reality, falling easily into two parts: the nature of the unchanging and the nature of the changing. Classical Greek philosophy culminated as an attempt to answer these two questions in such a way as to furnish guidance, and in a pinch consolation, for the human venture. Socrates as a stalwart personality refracts all inherited influences in fruitful directions, being himself all the while different from, and much more than, his opinions and doctrines. Plato maximized, Aristotle minimized, the discrepancy between change and permanence, both alike enhancing the joys of pure speculation with the fertility of projected action informed by thought. Stoicism and Epicureanism, though with somewhat different emphases, sought practically to lessen the discrepancy by moderation if not by renunciation of desire.

Our Panorama is broken but not greatly impaired by the new two-volume arrangement of what was originally a single large book. Whoever has caught the vision which intoxicated Plato will wish to pursue in *From Aristotle to Plotinus* Aristotle's efforts to correct and to systematize that vision. And to remember that Alexander the Great was Aristotle's student and subsequent collaborator in collecting materials for research from all over the world will mean a launching through curiosity into Roman thought and civilization, with which the next volume closes.

THE PRE-SOCRATICS

But for the other, each of these two problems would have been prime in early Greek speculation: permanence displacing change, change displacing permanence. If there is something to change, it must remain itself while it is changing; otherwise there is literally nothing to change, but only change itself. Yet if what changes remains literally itself, then is not change an illusion? The senses are dispraised from both these camps as leading to deception; and reason is played up from the diverse sectors as correcting sense and achieving finality. Out of the emphatic process, however, contradictories are set up in the name of reason; and Parmenides and Heraclitus, as representing the two camps, present able answers to each other: either Being alone *is* without any possibility of change, or change *is* and is the only Being. A method that can prove opposites as cogently as Greek rationalism early proved both that change alone is permanent and that the permanent alone is real must be supplanted by its very success.

Pluralists arose, as mediators, to show how the unchanging can itself change, if it but be diverse and be furnished with a field of motion. Change passes from the meaning of internal transformation into that of transposition of elements in space. But as early animism disappears, the pluralistic elements are left too inert to initiate change. Outside forces, mythical or abstract, arise to motivate change. Then comes atomism as a culmination of the mediation of these early incompatibles. Atoms are inanimate but they are indigenously mobile, and in their natural movements combinations occur, new bodies and new qualities arise, and the pluralistic elements take on order and inevitability as out of chance a cosmos is born.

Meantime, life goes on and practical demands multiply

with the extension of citizenship and the spread of divers opportunities. Curiosity about nature passes into concern with human nature; and the proper vocation of some becomes the political management of others. Sophists arise as rhetoricians to teach, in short, the fine art of how men may become citizens to their own advantage.

CHAPTER I
THE MILESIAN DOCTRINE OF BASIC STUFF AND CHANGE

THE MILESIAN SCHOOL
THALES, ANAXIMANDER, ANAXIMENES

Early in Greece certain thinkers, particularly at Miletus, attempted to pick out the common identical elements from the various processes of nature and thus to arrive at a universal first principle to which all changes and diversities could be referred. This led to the conception of a world-substance, something fundamental which persists throughout all change. Thales, Anaximander, and Anaximenes recognized, respectively, water, the infinite, and air as the single underlying principle.

As to the exact process whereby this fundamental substance gets transformed into its various derivatives, Thales seems to have been silent; Anaximander spoke of change in two directions—the hot and the cold—suggesting therefor a type of moral explanation (a giving of satisfaction for some injustice); and Anaximenes maintained that the process was one of rarefaction and condensation. Their several attempts to account for the causes of these changes mark a transition from polytheistic mythology to a self-moving monism. The traditional notion of the world, which regarded all change as caused by the activities of spirits, was discounted if not discarded; and all changes apparently came to be regarded by these thinkers as derived from the spontaneous activity of some one ultimate reality, whatever the "stuff" be called.

* * *

THALES

According to Aristotle, the founder of the Ionic physical philosophy, and therefore the founder of Greek philosophy, was Thales of Miletus. According to Diogenes Laertius, Thales was born in the first year of the thirty-fifth Olympiad

(640 B.C.), and his death occurred in the fifty-eighth Olympiad (548–545 B.C.). He attained note as a scientific thinker and was regarded as the founder of Greek philosophy because he discarded mythical explanations of things, and asserted that a physical element, water, was the first principle of all things. There are various stories of his travels, and in connection with accounts of his travels in Egypt he is credited with introducing into Greece the knowledge of geometry. Tradition also claims that he was a statesman, and as a practical thinker he is classed as one of the Seven Wise Men. A work entitled *Nautical Astronomy* was ascribed to him, but it was recognized as spurious even in antiquity.

Some say that the earth rests on water. We have ascertained that the oldest statement of this character is the one accredited to Thales the Milesian, to the effect that it rests on water, floating like a piece of wood or something else of that sort.[1]

And Thales, according to what is related of him, seems to have regarded the soul as something endowed with the power of motion, if indeed he said that the loadstone has a soul because it moves iron.[2]

ANAXIMANDER

Anaximander of Miletus was a companion or pupil of Thales. According to Apollodorus, he was born in the second or third year of the forty-second Olympiad (611–610 B.C.). Of his life little is known; Zeller infers from the statement of Aelian to the effect that he led the Milesian colony into Apollonia that he was a man of influence in Miletus. He was a student of geography and astronomy; and various inventions, such as the sundial, are attributed to him. His book, which was referred to as the first philosophical treatise in Greece, may not have received the title *Concerning Nature* until after his death. It soon became rare, and Simplicius does not seem to have had access to it.

The beginning of that which is, is the boundless but whence that which is arises, thither must it return again of necessity; for the things give satisfaction and reparation to one another for their injustice, as is appointed according to the ordering of time.[3]

---

[1] Aristotle, *De Caelo*, ii. 13; 294 a 28.

[2] Aristotle, *De Anima*, i. 2; 405 a 19.

[3] The translation of this fragment is taken from Zeller, *Outlines of the History of Greek Philosophy* (13th ed., revised by Nestle and translated by Palmer), p. 28. Burnet says: "This conception of justice and injustice recurs more than once in Ionic natural philosophy, and always in the same connection. It refers to the encroachment of one opposite or 'element' upon another. It is in consequence of this that they are both absorbed once more in their common ground." (*Greek Philosophy*. Part I. Thales to Plato, pp. 22–23.)

For some who hold that the real, the underlying substance, is a unity, either one of the three [elements] or something else that is denser than fire and more rarefied than air, teach that other things are generated by condensation and rarefaction. .... And others believe that existing opposites are separated from the unity, as Anaximander says. ....[4]

There is no beginning of the infinite, for in that case it would have an end. But it is without beginning and indestructible, as being a sort of first principle; for it is necessary that whatever comes into existence should have an end, and there is a conclusion of all destruction. Wherefore as we say, there is no first principle of this [i.e., the infinite], but it itself seems to be the first principle of all other things and to surround all and to direct all, as they say who think that there are no other causes besides the infinite (such as mind, or friendship), but that it itself is divine; for it is immortal and indestructible, as Anaximander and most of the physicists say.[5]

ANAXIMENES

Anaximenes of Miletus was a pupil or companion of Anaximander. According to Apollodorus, quoted by Diogenes, he flourished from about 585 to 524 B.C. Of his life nothing is known.

Anaximenes arrived at the conclusion that air is the one, movable, infinite, first principle of all things. For he speaks as follows: Air is the nearest to an immaterial thing; for since we are generated in the flow of air, it is necessary that it should be infinite and abundant, because it is never exhausted.[6]

Anaximenes regarded air as the first principle.[7]

Anaximenes says that air is the first principle of all things, and that it is infinite in quantity but is defined by its qualities; and all things are generated by a certain condensation or rarefaction

[4] Aristotle, *Physics*, i. 4; 187 a 12.

[5] *Ibid.*, iii. 4; 203 b 7.

[6] *Collection des anciens alchimistes grecs*, Livre i, Paris, 1887, p. 83, ll. 7-10, Olympiodorus.

[7] Aristotle, *Metaphysics*, i. 3; 984 a 5.

of it. Motion also exists from eternity. And by compression of the air the earth was formed, and it is very broad; accordingly he says that this rests on air; and the sun and the moon and the rest of the stars were formed from earth. He declared that the sun is earth because of its swift motion, and it has the proper amount of heat.[8]

[8] Plutarch, *Strom.* 3; Diels' *Doxographic Graeci* 579.

CHAPTER II
THE METAPHYSICAL PROBLEM—FROM CHANGE TO CHANGELESSNESS

THE FLOWING PHILOSOPHY
HERACLITUS, CRATYLUS

THE ELEATIC SCHOOL
XENOPHANES, PARMENIDES, ZENO, MELISSUS

Heraclitus of Ephesus took over one phase of the Milesian doctrine, namely, eternal motion, and made it the central point of his philosophy. Nothing abides, the whole world is involved in ceaseless change, and the fact of change is itself the only changeless. The appearance of stability is a mere illusion of the senses and must be corrected by the understanding. Fire whose becoming and ceasing is its very being is the ever ready symbol for this unending flux which constitutes reality. Cratylus, the disciple, made bold to the point of paradox this doctrine of the flux. If the master taught, as according to one of the fragments he did teach, that we cannot step twice into the same river, the disciple declares that we cannot step into it even once; for not only does the river change while we are stepping, but we ourselves change also.

Xenophanes, who is reputed to have founded the Eleatic school, disseminated a critical view of deity, which came to metaphysical maturity in Parmenides. The latter opposed to Heracliteanism the view that reality excludes all difference and hence admits of no change. Starting with the concept of Being, which he identified with thought, Parmenides arrived at his fundamental postulate—Only Being Is. According to this thesis, substantial change is impossible. For if Being has originated, it must have come from Being or from Not-Being; in the latter case it has come from nothing, which is impossible, and in the former case it has come from itself, which means that it always was. The same

9

arguments apply to its passing away. Change of place, or mo-
tion, is also excluded, because if Being moved it must move into
empty space, but empty space does not exist.

Parmenides' pupil, Zeno, attempted to defend the Eleatic doc-
trine by showing the absurdities of those who believed in change
to be greater than the difficulties that attended the doctrine of his
master. If an object moves, it must move either where it is or
where it is not; but it cannot move where it is, for it is already
there; and it cannot move where it is not, because it is not there
to do the moving. Another disciple, Melissus, argued that Being
is infinite rather than, according to Parmenides, finite; for since
there is no empty space, there is nothing to prevent the unlimited
extension of Being.

.   .   .

HERACLITUS

According to Apollodorus, Heraclitus, son of Blyson, flourished in the sixty-
ninth Olympiad (504–501 B.C.). An attempt to fix the date from his reference to the
expulsion from Ephesus of his friend Hermodorus (Frag. 114) has resulted in a somewhat later date, though it is by no means impossible that Hermodorus was expelled
during Persian rule in the city. Beyond the fact that Heraclitus lived in Ephesus we
know nothing of his life; of the many stories related about him, most can be proved
false, and there is no reason for crediting the remainder. His philosophic position is
clear, however, since he refers to Pythagoras and Xenophanes (Frags. 16–17), and
Parmenides (vss. 46 ff.) seems to refer to him. His book is said to have been divided
into three parts: (1) concerning the All, (2) political, (3) theological. Even in antiquity he was surnamed "The Dark" or "The Obscure."

1. Not on my authority, but on that of truth, it is wise for you
to accept the fact that all things are one.

2. This truth, though it always exists, men do not understand,
as well before they hear it as when they hear it for the first time.
For although all things happen in accordance with this truth, men
seem unskilled indeed when they make trial of words and matters
such as I am setting forth, in my effort to discriminate each thing
according to its nature, and to tell what its state is. But other men
fail to notice what they do when awake, in the same manner that
they forget what they do when asleep.

4. Eyes and ears are bad witnesses for men, since their souls
lack understanding.

7. If you do not hope, you will not find that which is not hoped for; since it is difficult to discover and impossible to attain.

15. Eyes are more exact witnesses than ears.

16. Much learning does not teach one to have understanding; else it would have taught Hesiod, and Pythagoras, and again Xenophanes, and Hecataeus.

17. Pythagoras, son of Mnesarchus, prosecuted investigations more than any other man, and [selecting these treatises] he made a wisdom of his own—much learning and bad art.

20. This order, the same for all things, no one of gods or men has made, but it always was, and is, and ever shall be, an ever-living fire, kindling according to fixed measure, and extinguishing according to fixed measure.

21. The transformations of fire are, first of all, sea; and of the sea one half is earth, and the other half is lightning flash.

22. All things are exchanged for fire, and fire for all things; as wares are exchanged for gold, and gold for wares.

25. Fire lives in the death of earth, and air lives in the death of fire; water lives in the death of air, and earth in that of water.

29. The sun will not overstep his bounds; if he does, the Erinnyes, allies of justice, will find him out.

32. The sun is new every day.

35. Hesiod is the teacher of most men; they suppose that his knowledge was very extensive, when in fact he did not know night and day, for they are one.

36. God is day and night, winter and summer, war and peace, satiety and hunger; but he assumes different forms, just as when incense is mingled with incense; every one gives him the name he pleases.

38. Souls smell in Hades.

41–42. You could not step twice in the same rivers; for other and yet waters are ever flowing on.

44. War is father of all and king of all; and some he made gods and some men, some slaves and some free.

46. Opposition unites. From what draws apart results the most beautiful harmony. All things take place by strife.[1]

57. Good and bad are the same.

---

[1] Quoted by Aristotle as an illustration of the search for a deeper principle, more in accordance with nature.

62. Men should know that war is general and that justice is strife; all things arise and [pass away] through strife.

68. For to souls it is death to become water, and for water it is death to become earth; but water is formed from earth, and from water, soul.

69. Upward, downward, the way is one and the same.

71. The limits of the soul you could not discover, though traversing every path.

72. It is a delight to souls to become wet.

73. Whenever a man gets drunk, he is led about by a beardless boy, stumbling, not knowing whither he goes, for his soul is wet.

74. The dry soul is wisest and best.

78. Life and death, and waking and sleeping, and youth and old age, are the same; for the latter change and are the former, and the former change back to the latter.

81. In the same rivers we step and we do not step; we are and we are not.

91. Understanding is common to all. It is necessary for those who speak with intelligence to hold fast to the common element of all, as a city holds fast to law, and much more strongly. For all human laws are nourished by one which is divine, and it has power so much as it will; and it suffices for all things and more than suffices.

104. It is not good for men to have whatever they want. Disease makes health sweet and good; hunger, satiety; toil, rest.

109. It is better to conceal ignorance than to put it forth into the midst.

110. It is law to obey the counsel of one.

111. For what sense or understanding have they? They follow the bards and employ the crowd as their teacher, not knowing that many are bad and few good. For the very best choose one thing before all others, immortal glory among mortals, while the masses eat their fill like cattle.

113. To me one man is ten thousand if he be the best.

114. The Ephesians deserve to be hanged, every one that is a man grown, and the youth to abandon the city, for they cast out Hermodorus the best man among them, saying:—Let no one among us be best, and if one be best, let him be so elsewhere and among others.

119. (He used to say that) Homer deserved to be cast out of the lists and flogged, and Archilochus likewise.

122. There awaits men at death what they do not expect or think.

130. They purify themselves by defiling themselves with blood, as if one who had stepped into the mud were to wash it off with mud. If any one of men should observe him doing so, he would think he was insane. And to these images they pray, just as if one were to converse with men's houses, for they know not what gods and heroes are.

131. All things are full of souls and of divine spirits.

134. False opinion of progress is the stoppage of progress.

CRATYLUS

About the life of Cratylus we know next to nothing. He seems to have been an Athenian. That he was a disciple of Heraclitus and an early teacher of Plato we learn upon the authority of Aristotle. There are many legends of the excesses to which he carried his Heracliteanism. His influence upon Plato can perhaps be better estimated by a perusal of Plato's dialogue of the same name. A fragment of that dialogue will be found below, pp. 153–55.

. . . . Observing that all this indeterminate substance is in motion, and that no true predication can be made of that which changes, they supposed that it is impossible to make any true statement about that which is in all ways and entirely changeable. For it was from this supposition that there blossomed forth the most extreme view of those which we have mentioned, that of the professed followers of Heraclitus, and such as Cratylus held, who ended by thinking that one need not say anything, and only moved his finger; and who criticized Heraclitus for saying that one cannot enter the same river twice, for he himself held that it cannot be done even once.[2]

In his youth Plato first became acquainted with Cratylus and the Heraclitean doctrines—that the whole sensible world is always in a state of flux, and that there is no scientific knowledge of it—and in after years he still held these opinions.[3]

[2] Aristotle, *Metaphysics*, 1010a.

[3] *Ibid.*, 987a.

XENOPHANES

Xenophanes of Colophon, son of Dexias (Apollodorus says of Orthomenes), was the founder of the Eleatic school. After a careful review of the evidence, Zeller concludes that he was born about 580 B.C.; it is agreed by all writers that he lived to a great age. The stories of his travels and adventures are numerous. He speaks of the way between the Ionic colonies and the Persians as beginning in his youth. According to Diogenes, he sang the founding of Elea in two thousand hexameter verses. The reference to him by Heraclitus (Frag. 16) indicates the general respect for his philosophy. He composed poetry of all varieties, and is said to have recited his own poems. His philosophic views were embodied in a poem which was early lost, and to which later ages gave the name *Concerning Nature*.

1. God is one, supreme among gods and men, and not like mortals in body or mind.

2. The whole [of god] sees, the whole perceives, the whole hears.

3. But without effort he sets in motion all things by mind and thought.

4. It [i.e., being] always abides in the same place, not moves at all, nor is it fitting that it should move from one place to another.

5. But mortals suppose that the gods are born (as they themselves are), and that they wear man's clothing and have human voice and body.

6. But if cattle or lions had hands, so as to paint with their hands and produce works of art as men do, they would paint their gods and give them bodies in form like their own—horses like horses, cattle like cattle.

7. Homer and Hesiod attributed to the gods all things which are disreputable and worthy of blame when done by men; and they told of them many lawless deeds, stealing, adultery, and deception of each other.

8. For all things come from earth, and all things end by becoming earth.

9. For we are all sprung from earth and water.

14. Accordingly there has not been a man, nor will there be, who knows distinctly what I say about the gods or in regard to all things, for even if one chances for the most part to say what is true, still he would not know; but every one thinks he knows.

15. These things have seemed to me to resemble the truth.

16. In the beginning the gods did not at all reveal all things clearly to mortals, but by searching men in the course of time find them out better.

18. Now, however, I come to another topic, and I will show the way. . . . . They say that once on a time when a hound was badly treated a passer-by pitied him and said, 'Stop beating him, for it is the soul of a dear friend; I recognised him on hearing his voice.'

19. Already now sixty-seven years my thoughts have been tossed restlessly up and down Greece, but then it was twenty and five years from my birth, if I know how to speak the truth about these things.

PARMENIDES

Parmenides, the son of Pyres (or Pyrrhes), of Elea, was born about 515 B.C.; his family was of noble rank and rich, but Parmenides devoted himself to philosophy. He was associated with members of the Pythagorean society, and is himself called a Pythagorean by later writers. In the formulation of his philosophic system, however, he was most influenced by his aged fellow-townsman, Xenophanes; the doctrines of Xenophanes he developed into a system which was embodied in a poetic work *On Nature*. The statement that he made laws for the citizens may have reference to some connection with the Pythagorean society.

CONCERNING TRUTH

Come now I will tell thee—and do thou hear my word and heed it—what are the only ways of enquiry that lead to knowledge. The one way assuming that being is and that it is impossible for it not to be, is the trustworthy path, for truth attends it. The other, that non-being is and that it necessarily is, I call a wholly incredible course, since thou canst not recognise not-being (for this is impossible), nor couldst thou speak of it, for thought and being are the same thing.

It makes no difference to me at what point I begin, for I shall always come back again to this.

It is necessary both to say and to think that being is; for it is possible that being is, and it is impossible that not-being is; this is what I bid thee ponder. I restrain thee from this first course of investigation; and from that course also along which mortals knowing nothing wander aimlessly, since helplessness directs the roaming thought in their bosoms, and they are borne on deaf and likewise blind, amazed, headstrong races, they who consider being and not-being as the same and not the same; and that all things follow a back-turning course.

There is left but this single path to tell thee of: namely, that being is. And on this path there are many proofs that being is without beginning and indestructible; it is universal, existing alone, immovable and without end; nor ever was it nor will it be, since it now *is*, all together, one, and continuous. For what generating of it wilt thou seek out? From what did it grow, and how? I will not permit thee to say or to think that it came from not-being; for it is impossible to think or to say that not-being is. What thing would then have stirred it into activity that it should arise from not-being later rather than earlier? So it is necessary that being either is absolutely or is not. Nor will the force of the argument permit that anything spring from being except being itself. Therefore justice does not slacken her fetters to permit generation or destruction, but holds being firm.

Either being exists or it does not exist. It has been decided in accordance with necessity to leave the unthinkable, unspeakable path, as this is not the true path, but that the other path exists and is true. How then should being suffer destruction? How come into existence? If it came into existence, it is not being, nor will it be if it ever is to come into existence. . . . . So its generation is extinguished, and its destruction is proved incredible.

Nor is it subject to division, for it is all alike; nor is anything more in it, so as to prevent its cohesion, nor anything less, but all is full of being; therefore the all is continuous, for being is continuous to being.

Farther it is unmoved, in the hold of great chains, without beginning or end, since generation and destruction have completely disappeared and true belief has rejected them. It lies the same, abiding in the same state and by itself; accordingly it abides fixed in the same spot. For powerful necessity holds it in confining bonds, which restrain it on all sides. Therefore divine right does not permit being to have any end; but it is lacking in nothing, for if it lacked anything it would lack everything.

Nevertheless, behold steadfastly all absent things as present to thy mind; for thou canst not separate being in one place from contact with being in another place; it is not scattered here and there through the universe, nor is it compounded of parts.

Therefore thinking and that by reason of which thought exists are one and the same thing, for thou wilt not find thinking without the *being* from which it receives its name. Nor is there nor will there be anything apart from being; for fate has linked it together, so that it is a whole and immovable. Wherefore all these things will be but a name, all these things which mortals determined in the belief that they were true, viz. that things arise and perish, that they are and are not, that they change their position and vary in colour.

But since there is a final limit, it is perfected on every side, like the mass of a rounded sphere, equally distant from the centre at every point. For it is necessary that it should neither be greater at all nor less anywhere, since there is no not-being which can prevent it from arriving at equality, nor is being such that there may ever be more than what is in one part and less in another, since the whole is inviolate. For if it is equal on all sides, it abides in equality within its limits.

ZENO

Zeno of Elea, son of Teleutagoras, was born early in the fifth century B.C. He was the pupil of Parmenides, and his relations with him were so intimate that Plato calls him Parmenides's son (*Sophist* 241D). Strabo applies to him as well as to his master the name Pythagorean, and gives him the credit of advancing the cause of law and order in Elea. Several writers say that he taught in Athens for a while. There are numerous accounts of his capture as party to a conspiracy; these accounts differ widely from each other, and the only point of agreement between them has reference to his determination in shielding his fellow-conspirators. We find reference to one book which he wrote in prose (Plato, *Parmenides* 127C), each section of which showed the absurdity of some element in the popular belief.

a) SIMPLICIUS'S ACCOUNT OF ZENO'S ARGUMENTS, INCLUDING THE TRANSLATION OF THE FRAGMENTS

For Eudemus says in his *Physics*, 'Then does not this exist, and is there any *one*? This was the problem. He reports Zeno as saying that if any one explains to him the *one*, what it is, he can tell him what things are. But he is puzzled, it seems, because each of the senses declares that there are many things, both absolutely, and as the result of division, but no one establishes the mathematical point. He thinks that what is not increased by receiving additions, or decreased as parts are taken away, is not one of the things that are.' It was natural for Zeno, who, as if for the sake of exercise, argued both sides of a case (so that he is called double-tongued), to utter such statements raising difficulties about the one; but in his book which has many arguments in regard to each point, he shows that a man who affirms multiplicity naturally falls into contradictions. Among these arguments is one by which he shows that if there are many things, these are both small and great—great enough to be infinite in size, and small enough to be nothing in size. By this he shows that what has neither greatness nor thickness nor bulk could not even be. (FRAGMENT 1) *'For if,'* he says, *'anything were added to another being, it could not make it any greater; for since greatness does not exist, it is impossible to increase the greatness of a thing by adding to it. So that which is added would be nothing. If when something is taken away that which is left is no less, and if it becomes no greater by receiving additions, evidently that which has been added or taken away is nothing.'*[4] These things Zeno says, not denying the one, but holding that each thing has the greatness of many and infinite things, since there is always something before that which is apprehended, by reason of its infinite divisibility; and this he proves by first showing that nothing has any greatness because each thing of the many is identical with itself and is one.

And why is it necessary to say that there is a multiplicity of things when it is set forth in Zeno's own book? For again in showing that, if there is a multiplicity of things, the same things are both finite and infinite, Zeno writes as follows, to use his own words: (FRAGMENT 2) *'If there is a multiplicity of things, it is necessary that these should be just as many as exist, and not more nor fewer. If there are just as many as there are, then the number would be finite. If there is a multiplicity at all, the number is infinite, for there are always others between any two, and yet others between each pair of these. So the number of things is infinite.'* So by the process of division he shows that their number is infinite. And as to magnitude, he begins with this same argument. For first showing that (FRAGMENT 3) *'if being did not have magnitude, it would not exist at all,'* he goes on, *'if anything exists, it is necessary that each thing should have some magnitude and thickness, and that one part of it should be separated from another. The same argument applies to the thing that precedes this. That also will have magnitude and will have something before it. The same may be said of each thing once for all,*

---

[4] Italics mine in this and subsequent Zeno fragments.—T. V. S.

for there will be no such thing as last, nor will one thing differ from another. So if there is a multiplicity of things, it is necessary that these should be great and small—small enough not to have any magnitude, and great enough to be infinite.'

Zeno's argument seems to deny that place exists, putting the question as follows: (FRAGMENT 4) *'If there is such a thing as place, it will be in something, and that which is in something is in some place. Then this place will be in a place, and so on indefinitely. Accordingly there is no such thing as place.'*

Eudemus' account of Zeno's opinion runs as follows:—'Zeno's problem seems to come to the same thing. For it is natural that all being should be somewhere, and if there is a place for things, where would this place be? In some other place, and that in another, and so on indefinitely.'

Zeno's argument that when anything is in a space equal to itself, it is either in motion or at rest, and that nothing is moved in the present moment, and that the moving body is always in a space equal to itself at each present moment, may, I think, be put in a syllogism as follows: The arrow which is moving forward is at every present moment in a space equal to itself, accordingly it is in a space equal to itself in all time; but that which is in a space equal to itself in the present moment is not in motion. Accordingly it is in a state of rest, since it is not moved in the present moment, and that which is not moving is at rest, since everything is either in motion or at rest. So the arrow which is moving forward is at rest while it is moving forward, in every moment of its motion.

The Achilles argument is so named because Achilles is named in it as the example, and the argument shows that if he pursued a tortoise it would be impossible for him to overtake it.

Aristotle accordingly solves the problem of Zeno the Eleatic, which he propounded to Protagoras the Sophist.[5] Tell me, Protagoras, said he, does one grain of millet make a noise when it falls, or does the ten-thousandth part of a grain? On receiving the answer that it does not, he went on: Does a measure of millet grains make a noise when it falls, or not? He answered, it does make a noise. Well, said Zeno, does not the statement about the measure of millet apply to the one grain and the ten-thousandth part of a grain? He assented, and Zeno continued, Are not the statements

[5] Aristotle, *Physics*, vii. 5, 250 a 20.

as to the noise the same in regard to each? For as are the things that make a noise, so are the noises. Since this is the case, if the measure of millet makes a noise, the one grain and then ten-thousandth part of a grain make a noise.

b) ZENO'S ARGUMENTS AS DESCRIBED BY ARISTOTLE

Zeno's problem demands some consideration; if all being is in some place, evidently there must be a place of this place, and so on indefinitely.[6]

It is not difficult to solve Zeno's problem, that if place is anything, it will be in some place; there is no reason why the first place should not be in something else, not however as in that place, but just as health exists in warm beings as a state while warmth exists in matter as a property of it. So it is not necessary to assume an indefinite series of places.[7]

(Time and space are continuous . . . . the divisions of time and space are the same.) Accordingly Zeno's argument is erroneous, that it is not possible to traverse infinite spaces, or to come in contact with infinite spaces successively in a finite time. Both space and time can be called infinite in two ways, either absolutely as a continuous whole, or by division into the smallest parts. With infinites in point of quantity, it is not possible for anything to come in contact in a finite time, but it is possible in the case of the infinites reached by division, for time itself is infinite from this standpoint. So the result is that it traverses the infinite in an infinite, not a finite time, and that infinites, not finites, come in contact with infinites.[8]

And Zeno's reasoning is fallacious. For if, he says, everything is at rest [or in motion] when it is in a space equal to itself, and the moving body is always in the present moment < in a space equal to itself, > then the moving arrow is still. This is false; for time is not composed of present moments that are indivisible, nor indeed is any other quantity. Zeno presents four arguments concerning motion which involve puzzles to be solved, and the first of these shows that motion does not exist because the moving body must go half the distance before it goes the whole distance; of this we

[6] *Ibid.*, iv. 1; 209 a 23.

[7] *Ibid.*, iv. 3; 210 b 22.   [8] *Ibid.*, vi. 2; 233 a 21.

have spoken before (*Physics*, viii. 8; 263 a 5). And the second is
called the Achilles argument; it is this:—The slow runner will never
be overtaken by the swiftest, for it is necessary that the pursuer
should first reach the point from which the pursued started, so
that necessarily the slower is always somewhat in advance. This
argument is the same as the preceding, the only difference being
that the distance is not divided each time into halves. . . . . His
opinion is false that the one in advance is not overtaken; he is not
indeed overtaken while he is in advance; but nevertheless he is
overtaken, if you will grant that he passes through the limited
space. These are the first two arguments, and the third is the one
that has been alluded to, that the arrow in its flight is stationary.
This depends on the assumption that time is composed of present
moments; there will be no syllogism if this is not granted. And the
fourth argument is with reference to equal bodies moving in opposite directions past equal bodies in the stadium with equal speed,
some from the end of the stadium, others from the middle; in which
case he thinks half the time equal to twice the time. The fallacy
lies in the fact that while he postulates that bodies of equal size
move forward with equal speed for an equal time, he compares
the one with something in motion, the other with something at
rest.[9]

MELISSUS

Melissus of Samos, son of Ithagenes, was a contemporary of Zeno, though he
may have been slightly younger. Parmenides is said to have been his teacher, and it
is possible that he may have made the acquaintance of Heraclitus. According to
Diogenes, he was a respected statesman, and there seems to be good evidence (Plutarch *Pericles* 26 [after Aristotle]) that he commanded the Samian fleet at its victory
over the Athenians, 440 B.C. He wrote a book which later writers refer to under
various titles.

a) SIMPLICIUS'S ACCOUNT OF MELISSUS, INCLUDING THE
TRANSLATION OF THE FRAGMENTS

Melissus, making use of the axioms of the physicists, in regard to
generation and destruction, begins his book as follows: (FRAG-
MENT I) *If nothing is, how could this be spoken of as though something
is? And if anything is, either it has come into being, or else it always*

[9] *Ibid.*, vi. 9; 239 b 5.

has been. If it came into being, it sprung either from being or from not-being; but it is impossible that any such thing should have sprung from not-being (for nothing else that is could have sprung from it, much less pure being); nor could it have sprung from being, for in that case it <would simply be, and> would not have come into existence. So then being is not generated; being always is, nor will it be destroyed. For being could not be changed into not-being (this also is conceded by the physicists) nor into being; for then it would abide as it is, and would not be destroyed. Accordingly being was not generated, nor will it be destroyed; so it always was and always will be.[10] (FRAGMENT 2) But while that which comes into existence has a beginning, that which does not come into existence does not have a beginning, and being which did not come into existence would not have a beginning. Farther, that which is destroyed has an end; but if anything is not subject to destruction, it does not have an end; and that which has neither beginning nor end is of course infinite; so being is infinite. (FRAGMENT 3) And if it is infinite, it is one; for if being were two, both parts could not be infinite, but each would be limited by the other. But being is infinite; there could not be several beings; accordingly being is one. (FRAGMENT 4) Farther, if being is one it does not move; for the one is always homogeneous [lit. like itself]; and that which is homogeneous could not perish or become greater or change its arrangement or suffer pain or annoyance. If it experienced any of these things it would not be one; for that which is moved with any sort of motion changes something from one thing into something different; but there is nothing else except being, so this will not be moved. (FRAGMENT 5) To follow another line of argument: there is no place void of being, for the void is nothing; but that which is nothing could not exist; so then being is not moved: it is impossible for it to go anywhere, if there is no void. Nor is it possible for it to contract into itself, for in that case different degrees of density would arise, and this is impossible; for it is impossible that the rare should be as full as the dense; but the rare is more empty than the dense, and there is no such thing as emptiness. It is necessary to judge whether being is full or not by its capacity to receive something else: if it will not receive anything it is full; if it will receive something it is not full. Now if the void does not exist, it must of necessity be full; and if this is the case it does not move, not because it is impossible

---

[10] Italics mine for this and subsequent fragments of Melissus.—T. V. S.

for it to move through space already filled, as we say of bodies, but because all being cannot be moved into being (for there is nothing besides itself), nor can being be moved into not-being, for not-being does not exist.

Melissus also is blamed because in his frequent references to the beginning he does not use the word to mean a beginning in time which applies to that which comes into existence, but rather to mean a logical beginning which does not apply to the things that are changing collectively. He seems to have seen clearly before Aristotle that all matter, even that which is eternal, being limited has a limited capacity, and in itself is always at the end of time, and because of the ever-moving beginning of that which passes, it is always at the beginning, and remains eternal, so that that which has beginning and end in quantity has also beginning and end in time, and the reverse; for that which has beginning and end in time is not everything simultaneously. So he bases his proof on beginning and end in time. Accordingly he says that that which is not everything—*i.e.* which is not the whole simultaneously—is not without beginning or end; what applies to things that are indivisible and infinite in their being, applies so much the more to pure being; and that all applies to being. Melissus puts it as follows: (FRAGMENT 7) *Since then it did not come into being but is, it always was and always will be, and has neither beginning nor end, but is infinite. For if it had come into existence it would have had a beginning (for that which once came into existence would have a beginning) and an end (for that which once came into existence would come to an end); if it neither had a beginning nor came to an end, it always was and always will be; it has not beginning or end; but it is impossible that anything which is not the whole should always exist. . . . .* (FRAGMENT 8) *But as it always exists, so it is necessary also that it be always infinite in magnitude.* (FRAGMENT 15) *If being is separated it moves; and that which moves could not exist simultaneously.*

(FRAGMENT 16) *If being exists it must be one, and being one it is necessary that it should not itself have body; and if it should have thickness, it would have parts and would no longer be a unity.* (FRAGMENT 9) *Nothing which has beginning and end is either eternal or infinite.* (FRAGMENT 10) *If it were not one, it would be bounded by something else.*

Melissus bringing his previous topic to a conclusion goes on to consider motion. (FRAGMENT 11) *So then the all is eternal and in-finite and homogeneous; and it could neither perish nor become greater nor change its arrangement nor suffer pain or distress. If it experienced any of these things it would no longer be one; for if it becomes different, it is necessary that being should not be homogeneous, but that which was before must perish, and that which was not must come into existence. If then the all should become different by a single hair in ten thousand years, it would perish in the whole of time.* (FRAGMENT 12) *And it is impossible for its order to change, for the order existing before does not perish, nor does another which did not exist come into being; and since nothing is added to it or subtracted from it or made different, how could any of the things that are change their order? But if anything became different its order would already have been changed.* (FRAGMENT 13) *Nor does it suffer pain, for the all could not be pained; it would be impossible for anything suffering pain always to be; nor does it have power equal to the power of what is healthy. It would not be homogeneous if it suffered pain; it would suffer pain whenever anything was added or taken away, and it would no longer be homogeneous. Nor could what is healthy suffer a pang of pain, for both the healthy and being would perish, and not-being would come into existence. The same reasoning that applies to pain applies also to distress.* (FRAGMENT 14) *Nor is there any void, for the void is nothing, and that which is nothing could not be. Nor does it move, for it has nowhere to go to, since it is full; for if there were a void it could go into the void, but since there is no void it has nowhere to go to. It could not be rare and dense, for it is not possible for the rare to be as full as the dense, but the rare is already more empty than the dense. This is the test of what is full and what is not full: if it has room for anything, or admits anything into it, it is not full; if it does not have room for anything, or admit anything into it, it is full. If no void exists it must be full; if then it is full it does not move.* These are the doctrines of Melissus.

(FRAGMENT 6) *What was, always was and always will be; for if it had come into existence, it necessarily would have been nothing before it came into existence. If now there were nothing existing, nothing would ever have come into existence from nothing.*

(FRAGMENT 17) *This argument is the strongest proof that being is one only. And the proofs are as follows: For if a multiplicity of things existed it would be necessary that these things should be just such as I* say the one is. For if earth exists, and water and air and iron and gold and fire and the living and the dead and black and white, and everything else which men say is real,—if these things exist and we see and hear them correctly, it is necessary that each thing should be such as we first determined, namely, it should not change its character or become different, but should always be each thing what it is. Now we say that we see and hear and understand correctly; but it seems to us that hot becomes cold and cold hot, that hard becomes soft and soft hard, that the living being dies and life comes from what is not living; and that all these things become different, and what they are is not like what they were. It seems to us that iron, being hard to the touch, wastes away becoming liquefied, and so does gold and rock, and whatever else seems to be strong, so that we conclude that we do not see or know things that are. And earth and rock arise from water. These things then do not harmonise with each other. Though we said that many things are eternal, and have forms and strength, it seems that they all become different and change their character each time they are seen. Evidently we do not see correctly, nor is the appearance of multiplicity correct; for they would not change their character if they were real, but would remain each thing as it seemed, for nothing is nobler than that which is real. But if they change their character, being perishes and not-being comes into existence. So then if a multiplicity of things exist, it is necessary that they should be such as the one is.

b) ARISTOTLE'S ACCOUNT OF MELISSUS

Both Melissus and Parmenides argue fallaciously, and they make false assumptions and their reasonings are not logical; but the argument of Melissus is the more wearisome, for it sets no problem, but granted one strange thing, others follow; and there is no difficulty in this. The error in the reasoning of Melissus is plain, for he thinks that if everything which has come into being has a beginning, he can assume that that which has not come into being does not have a beginning. This, then, is strange, that he should think that everything has a beginning except time, and this does not, and that simple generation has no beginning but change alone begins, as though change as a whole did not come into being. Even if the all is a unity, why then should it not move? Why should not the whole be moved even as a part of it which is a unity, namely water, is moved in itself? Then why should there not be change?

It is not possible that being should be one in form, but only in its source.[11]

The same is true of syllogisms, as for instance in the case of Melissus' argument that the all is infinite; in this he assumes that the all is not generated (for nothing is generated from not-being), and that that which is generated, is generated from a beginning. If then the all was not generated, it does not have a beginning, so it is infinite. It is not necessary to assent to this, for even if everything which is generated has a beginning, it does not follow that if anything has a beginning it was generated, as a man with a fever is warm, but one who is warm may not have a fever.[12]

Or again, as Melissus assumes in his argument that generation and having a beginning are the same thing, or that that which is generated from equals has the same size. The two statements, that what is generated has a beginning, and that what has a beginning is generated, he deems equivalent, so that the generated and the limited are both the same in that they each have a beginning. Because what is generated has a beginning, he postulates that what has a beginning is generated, as though both that which is generated and that which is finite were the same in having a beginning.[13]

[11] *Physics*, i. 9; 186 a 6.

[12] Aristotle, *Sophistic Elenchi* 5; 163 b 13.

[13] *Ibid.*, 6; 164 b 35.

CHAPTER III

ACCOMMODATIONS TO CHANGE: METAPHYSICAL PLURALISM

THE MEDIATORS
EMPEDOCLES, ANAXAGORAS

Parmenides had developed the notion of permanence in such a way as to deny all change, and Heraclitus had carried the idea of change to a point where permanence was impossible. Subsequent philosophers attempted to reconcile these two views by assuming a plurality of original elements which in themselves are substantially unchangeable, but which can alter their relations with respect to one another. Empedocles, Anaxagoras, and the atomists all adopted this general approach to the problem, but they differed among themselves as to the number and quality of the elements of reality, and as to the cause of their motion. Empedocles postulated four qualitatively determined elements—earth, air, fire, and water—and explained the fact of change by the attractive power of Love and the repulsive power of Strife. According to Anaxagoras, there is a countless number of original elements, qualitatively unchangeable, which are combined and separated by the ubiquitous power of Mind. The atomists maintained that there is an infinite number of original particles, without quality, moving in a void, and that the cause of their motion is inherent in the elements themselves. Change of the unchanging will thus be fully explained, when we look at the atomists more in detail; but it is a relative and not an absolute change which arises from the explanation—a transposition rather than a transformation.

. . .

EMPEDOCLES

Empedocles, son of Meton, grandson of an Empedocles who was a victor at Olympia, made his home at Acragas in Sicily. He was born about 494 B.C., and lived to the age of sixty. The only sure date in his life is his visit to Thurii soon after its foundation (444). Various stories are told of his political activity, which may be genuine traditions; these illustrate a democratic tendency. At the same time he claimed almost the homage due to a god, and many miracles are attributed to him. His writings in some parts are said to imitate Orphic verses, and apparently his religious activity was in line with this sect. His death occurred away from Sicily—probably in the Peloponnesus.

BOOK I

1. And do thou hear me, Pausanias, son of wise Anchites.

2. For scant means of acquiring knowledge are scattered among the members of the body; and many are the evils that break in to blunt the edge of studious thought. And gazing on a little portion of life that is not life, swift to meet their fate, they rise and are borne away like smoke, persuaded only of that on which each one chances as he is driven this way and that, but the whole he vainly boasts he has found. Thus these things are neither seen nor heard distinctly by men, nor comprehended by the mind. And thou, now that thou hast withdrawn hither, shalt learn no more than what mortal mind has seen.

19. But come, examine by every means each thing how it is clear, neither putting greater faith in anything seen than in what is heard, nor in a thundering sound more than in the clear assertions of the tongue, nor keep from trusting any of the other members in which there lies means of knowledge, but know each thing in the way in which it is clear.

33. Hear first the four roots of all things: bright Zeus, life-giving Hera (air), and Aidoneus (earth), and Nestis who moistens the springs of men with her tears.

36. And a second thing I will tell thee: There is no origination of anything that is mortal, nor yet any end in baneful death; but only mixture and separation of what is mixed, but men call this 'origination.'

40. But when light is mingled with air in human form, or in form like the race of wild beasts or of plants or of birds, then men say that these things have come into being; and when they are separated, they call them evil fate; this is the established practice, and I myself also call it so in accordance with the custom.

45. Fools! for they have no far-reaching studious thoughts who think that what was not before comes into being or that anything dies and perishes utterly.

48. For from what does not exist at all it is impossible that any-thing come into being, and it is neither possible nor perceivable that being should perish completely; for things will always stand wherever one in each case shall put them.

51. A man of wise mind could not divine such things as these, that so long as men live what indeed they call life, so long they exist and share what is evil and what is excellent, but before they are formed and after they are dissolved, they are really nothing at all.

60. Twofold is the truth I shall speak; for at one time there grew to be one alone out of many, and at another time, however, it sepa-rated so that there were many out of the one. Twofold is the com-ing into being, twofold the passing away, of perishable things; for the latter (*i.e.* passing away) the combining of all things both be-gets and destroys, and the former (*i.e.* coming into being), which was nurtured again out of parts that were being separated, is itself scattered.

66. And these (elements) never cease changing place continu-ally, now being all united by Love into one, now each borne apart by the hatred engendered of Strife, until they are brought together in the unity of the all, and become subject to it. Thus inasmuch as one has been wont to arise out of many and again with the sepa-ration of the one the many arise, so things are continually coming into being and there is no fixed age for them; and farther inasmuch as they (the elements) never cease changing place continually, so they always exist within an immovable circle.

74. But come, hear my words, for truly learning causes the mind to grow. For as I said before in declaring the ends of my words: Twofold is the truth I shall speak; for at one time there grew to be the one alone out of many, and at another time it separated so that there were many out of the one; fire and water and earth and boundless height of air, and baneful Strife apart from these, bal-ancing each of them, and Love among them, their equal in length and breadth. 81. Upon her do thou gaze with thy mind, nor yet sit dazed in thine eyes; for she is wont to be implanted in men's members, and through her they have thoughts of love and accom-plish deeds of union, and call her by the names of Delight, and Aphrodite; no mortal man has discerned her with them (the ele-ments) as she moves on her way. But do thou listen to the un-deceiving course of my words. . . . .

87. For these (elements) are equal, all of them, and of like ancient race; and one holds one office, another another, and each has his own nature. . . . . For nothing is added to them, nor yet does anything pass away from them; for if they were continually perishing they would no longer exist. . . . . Neither is any part of this all empty, nor over full. For how should anything cause this all to increase, and whence should it come? And whither should they (the elements) perish, since no place is empty of them? And in their turn they prevail as the cycle comes round, and they disappear before each other, and they increase each in its allotted turn. But these (elements) are the same; and penetrating through each other they become one thing in one place and another in another, while ever they remain alike (*i.e.* the same).

110. For they two (Love and Strife) were before and shall be, nor yet, I think, will there ever be an unutterably long time without them both.

96. But come, gaze on the things that bear farther witness to my former words, if in what was said before there be anything defective in form. Behold the sun, warm and bright on all sides, and whatever is immortal and is bathed in its bright ray, and behold the rain-cloud, dark and cold on all sides; from the earth there proceed the foundations of things and solid bodies. In Strife all things are, endued with form and separate from each other, but they come together in Love and are desired by each other. 104. For from these (elements) come all things that are or have been or shall be; from these there grew up trees and men and women, wild beasts and birds and water-nourished fishes, and the very gods, long-lived, highest in honour.

139. But when mighty Strife was nurtured in its members and leaped up to honour at the completion of the time, which has been driven on by them both in turn under a mighty oath. . . . .

169. But now I shall go back over the course of my verses, which I set out in order before, drawing my present discourse from that discourse. When Strife reached the lowest depth of the eddy and Love comes to be in the midst of the whirl, then all these things come together at this point so as to be one alone, yet not immediately, but joining together at their pleasure, one from one place, another from another. And as they were joining together Strife departed to the utmost boundary. But many things remained un-

mixed, alternating with those that were mixed, even as many as Strife, remaining aloft, still retained; for not yet had it entirely departed to the utmost boundaries of the circle, but some of its members were remaining within, and others had gone outside.

180. But, just as far as it is constantly rushing forth, just so far there ever kept coming in a gentle immortal stream of perfect Love; and all at once what before I learned were immortal were coming into being as mortal things, what before were unmixed as mixed, changing their courses. And as they (the elements) were mingled together there flowed forth the myriad species of mortal things, patterned in every sort of form, a wonder to behold.

195. In this way, by the good favour of Tyche, all things have power of thought.

196. And in so far as what was least dense came together as they fell.

197. For water is increased by water, primeval fire by fire, and earth causes its own substance to increase, and air, air.

BOOK II

210. And if your faith be at all lacking in regard to these (elements), how from water and earth and air and sun (fire) when they are mixed, arose such colours and forms of mortal things, as many as now have arisen under the uniting power of Aphrodite. . . . .

236. Hair and leaves and thick feathers of birds are the same thing in origin, and reptiles' scales, too, on strong limbs.

247. This is indeed remarkable in the mass of human members; at one time all the limbs which form the body, uniting into one by Love, grow vigorously in the prime of life; but yet at another time, separated by evil Strife, they wander each in different directions along the breakers of the sea of life. Just so it is with plants and with fishes dwelling in watery halls, and beasts whose lair is in the mountains, and birds borne on wings.

262. But come now, hear of these things; how fire separating caused the hidden offspring of men and weeping women to arise, for it is no tale apart from our subject, or witless. In the first place there sprang up out of the earth forms grown into one whole, having a share of both, of water and of fire. These in truth fire caused to grow up, desiring to reach its like; but they showed as yet no

lovely body formed out of the members, nor voice nor limb such as is natural to men.

333. For it is by earth that we see earth, and by water water, and by air glorious air; so, too, by fire we see destroying fire, and love by love, and strife by baneful strife. For out of these (elements) all things are fitted together and their form is fixed, and by these men think and feel both pleasure and pain.

BOOK III

338. Would that in behalf of perishable beings thou, immortal Muse, mightest take thought at all for our thought to come by reason of our cares! Hear me now and be present again by my side, Kalliopeia, as I utter noble discourse about the blessed gods.

342. Blessed is he who has acquired a wealth of divine wisdom, but miserable he in whom there rests a dim opinion concerning the gods.

344. It is not possible to draw near (to god) even with the eyes, or to take hold of him with our hands, which in truth is the best highway of persuasion into the mind of man; for he has no human head fitted to a body, nor do two shoots branch out from the trunk, nor has he feet, nor swift legs, nor hairy parts, but he is sacred and ineffable mind alone, darting through the whole world with swift thoughts.

366. Friends, I know indeed when truth lies in the discourses that I utter; but truly the entrance of assurance into the mind of man is difficult and hindered by jealousy.

369. There is an utterance of Necessity, an ancient decree of the gods, eternal, sealed fast with broad oaths: whenever any one defiles his body sinfully with bloody gore or perjures himself in regard to wrong-doing, one of those spirits who are heir to long life, thrice ten thousand seasons shall he wander apart from the blessed, being born meantime in all sorts of mortal forms, changing one bitter path of life for another. For mighty Air pursues him Seaward, and Sea spews him forth on the threshold of Earth, and Earth casts him into the rays of the unwearying Sun, and Sun into the eddies of Air; one receives him from the other, and all hate him. One of these now am I too, a fugitive from the gods and a wanderer, at the mercy of raging Strife.

383. For before this I was born once a boy, and a maiden, and a plant, and a bird, and a darting fish in the sea.

385. And I wept and shrieked on beholding the unwonted land where are Murder and Wrath, and other species of Fates, and wasting diseases, and putrefaction and fluxes.

ANAXAGORAS

Anaxagoras of Clazomenae, son of Hegesiboulus, was born in the seventieth Olympiad (500–497) and died in the first year of the eighty-eighth Olympiad (428), according to the chronicles of Apollodorus. It is said that he neglected his possessions in his pursuit of philosophy; he began to teach philosophy in the archonship of Callias at Athens (480). The fall of a meteoric stone at Aegus Potamui (467 or 469) influenced profoundly his views of the heavenly bodies. Pericles brought him to Athens, and tradition says he remained there thirty years. His exile (434–432) was brought about by the enemies of Pericles, and he died at Lampsacus. He wrote but one book according to Diogenes, and the same authority says this was written in a pleasing and lofty style.

1. All things were together, infinite both in number and in smallness; for the small also was infinite. And when they were all together, nothing was clear and distinct because of their smallness; for air and aether comprehended all things, both being infinite; for these are present in everything, and are greatest both as to number and as to greatness.

2. For air and aether are separated from the surrounding mass; and the surrounding (mass) is infinite in quantity.

4. But before these were separated, when all things were together, not even was any colour clear and distinct; for the mixture of all things prevented it, the mixture of moist and dry, of the warm and the cold, and of the bright and the dark (since much earth was present), and of germs infinite in number, in no way like each other; for none of the other things at all resembles the one the other.

3. And since these things are so, it is necessary to think that in all the objects that are compound there existed many things of all sorts, and germs of all objects, having all sorts of forms and colours and tastes.

11. So these things rotate and are separated by force and swiftness. And the swiftness produces force; and their swiftness is in no way like the swiftness of the things now existing among men, but it is certainly many times as swift.

5. In all things there is a portion of everything except mind; and there are things in which there is mind also.

6. Other things include a portion of everything, but mind is infinite and self-powerful and mixed with nothing, but it exists alone itself by itself. For if it were not by itself, but were mixed with anything else, it would include parts of all things, if it were mixed with anything; for a portion of everything exists in everything, as has been said by me before, and things mingled with it would prevent it from having power over anything in the same way that it does now that it is alone by itself. For it is the most rarefied of all things and the purest, and it has all knowledge in regard to everything and the greatest power; over all that has life, both greater and less, mind rules. And mind ruled the rotation of the whole, so that it set it in rotation in the beginning. First it began the rotation from a small beginning, then more and more was included in the motion, and yet more will be included. Both the mixed and the separated and distinct, all things mind recognised. And whatever things were to be, and whatever things were, as many as are now, and whatever things shall be, all these mind arranged in order; and it arranged that rotation, according to which now rotate stars and sun and moon and air and aether, now that they are separated. Rotation itself caused the separation, and the dense is separated from the rare, the warm from the cold, the bright from the dark, the dry from the moist. And there are many portions of many things. Nothing is absolutely separated nor distinct, one thing from one another, except mind. All mind is of like character, both the greater and the smaller. But nothing different is like anything else, but in whatever object there are the most, each single object is and was most distinctly these things.

7. And when mind began to set things in motion, there was separation from everything that was in motion, and however much mind set in motion, all this was made distinct. The rotation of the things that were moved and made distinct caused them to be yet more distinct.

8. The dense, the moist, the cold, the dark, collected there where now is the earth; the rare, the warm, the dry, the bright, departed toward the farther part of the aether.

9. Earth is condensed out of these things that are separated. For water is separated from the clouds, and earth from the water;

and from the earth stones are condensed by cold; and these are separated farther from water.

12. But mind, as it always has been, especially now also is where all other things are, in the surrounding mass, and in the things that were separated, and in the things that are being separated.

13. Things in the one universe are not divided from each other, nor yet are they cut off with an axe, neither hot from cold, nor cold from hot.

15. For neither is there a least of what is small, but there is always a less. For being is not non-being. But there is always a greater than what is great. And it is equal to the small in number; but with reference to itself each thing is both small and great.

16. And since the portions of the great and the small are equal in number, thus also all things would be in everything. Nor yet is it possible for them to exist apart, but all things include a portion of everything. Since it is not possible for the least to exist, nothing could be separated, nor yet could it come into being of itself, but as they were in the beginning so they are now, all things together. And there are many things in all things, and of those that are separated there are things equal in number in the greater and the lesser.

17. The Greeks do not rightly use the terms 'coming into being' and 'perishing.' For nothing comes into being nor yet does anything perish, but there is mixture and separation of things that are. So they would do right in calling the coming into being 'mixture,' and the perishing 'separation.'

CHAPTER IV
GREEK ATOMISM

THE ATOMISTS
LEUCIPPUS, DEMOCRITUS

Leucippus was the founder and Democritus the greatest representative of Greek atomism. The basic principle of atomism is the same in all cases, that of an infinite number of homogeneous elements without qualitative distinction moving in an infinite void. It was thus devised as a theory that would admit both permanence and change as real. The physical character of the atoms accounts for the fact of permanence, and their motion in the void accounts for the fact of change. Thus in Democritus there came to full fruition the earlier attempts to reconcile the theories of Heraclitus and Parmenides. As a result of the presuppositions of atomism, all of the qualities of things depend upon the size, shape, and spatial relations of the atoms, and all changes are due to altered combinations of atoms. An object originates when a complex of atoms is formed, and perishes when the complex is dissolved. Even the soul and the mind are composed of atoms. The soul atoms, however, are distributed over the whole body, while the thought atoms are concentrated at one place in the body, unmixed. Sensation is caused by changes in the soul atoms produced by effluences from external objects. The effluences that are too fine to disturb the soul atoms pass on to the mind and cause thought. Sensation and thought thus have the same origin, but they do not have the same epistemological value. Real knowledge, that is, knowledge of atoms and the void, can be obtained only by thought; sensation, on the other hand, is concerned with changeable phenomena, and cannot yield a true knowledge of reality. We have here the real antithesis of Plato's idealism and the deepest opposition to the dominant mood of Greek classical thought. On the basis of this materialism, however, Democritus raised an ethics in which happiness is taken as the highest good and a theology in which the gods are allowed to exist to account for the ideas we have of them and to perform whatever functions they do perform. The moral appeal of the philosophy of Democritus was great, inexplicably great for those who believe that morality cannot be built upon lowly materialism.

. . .

LEUCIPPUS

Leucippus lives largely in the fame of Democritus. His birthplace is disputed as between Miletus, Abdera, and Elea; his dates are not known, though they apparently fall in the fifth century B.C.; his identity was disputed in the Epicurean school; and as early as Aristotle he was merged as a thinker with Democritus, supposed to have been his disciple. Diogenes says that Leucippus was a pupil of Zeno.

Nothing occurs at random, but everything for a reason and by necessity.[1]

a) ARISTOTLE ON LEUCIPPUS[2]

Leucippus and Democritus have decided about all things practically by the same method and on the same theory, taking as their starting-point what naturally comes first. . . . . Leucippus, however, thought he had a theory which was in harmony with sense-perception, and did not do away with coming into being and passing away, nor motion, nor the multiplicity of things. He made this concession to experience, while he conceded, on the other hand, to those who invented the One that motion was impossible without the void, that the void was not real, and that nothing of what was real was not real. "For," said he, "that which is, strictly speaking, real is an absolute *plenum;* but the *plenum* is not one. On the contrary, there are an infinite number of them, and they are invisible owing to the smallness of their bulk. They move in the void (for there is a void); and by their coming together they effect coming into being; by their separation, passing away."

[1] Cyril Bailey (trans.), *The Greek Atomists and Epicurus,* p. 85. This is the only aphorism attributed to Leucippus.—T. V. S.

[2] *De Generatione et Corruptione* A, 8. 324b, 35. The translation is Burnet's (*Early Greek Philosophy,* pp. 354–355). See also Aristotle's further characterization of the doctrine of the two atomists in his survey of his contemporaries, *Metaphysics,* Book I, 985b 5–25; see below, chap. ix.

Atoms Fall
In Vortex

Get Content

b) DIOGENES LAERTIUS ON THE DOCTRINE OF LEUCIPPUS[3]

The sum of things is unlimited, and they all change into one another. The All includes the empty as well as the full. The worlds are formed when atoms fall into the void and are entangled with one another; and from their motion as they increase in bulk arises the substance of the stars. The sun revolves in a larger circle round the moon. The earth rides steadily, being whirled about the centre; its shape is like that of a drum. Leucippus was the first to set up atoms as first principles. Such is a general summary of his views; on particular points they are as follows.

He declares the All to be unlimited, as already stated; but of the All part is full and part empty,[4] and these he calls elements. Out of them arise the worlds unlimited in number and into them they are dissolved. This is how the worlds are formed. In a given section many atoms of all manner of shapes are carried from the unlimited into the vast empty space. These collect together and form a single vortex, in which they jostle against each other and, circling round in every possible way, separate off, by like atoms joining like. And, the atoms being so numerous that they can no longer revolve in equilibrium, the light ones pass into the empty space outside, as if they were being winnowed; the remainder keep together and, becoming entangled, go on their circuit together, and form a primary spherical system. This parts off like a shell, enclosing within it atoms of all kinds; and, as these are whirled round by virtue of the resistance of the centre, the enclosing shell becomes thinner, the adjacent atoms continually combining when they touch the vortex. In this way the earth is formed by portions brought to the centre coalescing. And again, even the outer shell grows larger by the influx of atoms from outside, and, as it is carried round in the vortex, adds to itself whatever atoms it touches. And of these some portions are locked together and form a mass, at first damp and miry, but, when they have dried and revolve with the universal vortex, they afterwards take fire and form the substance of the stars.

The orbit of the sun is the outermost, that of the moon nearest

---

[3] Hicks's translation ("Loeb Classical Library" series, II, 439–43). Save for some opening sentences, the entire discussion of Leucippus is given.—T. V. S.

[4] By the "full" is meant matter, atoms; by the "empty," space.

to the earth; the orbits of the other heavenly bodies lie between these two. All the stars are set on fire by the speed of their motion; the burning of the sun is also helped by the stars; the moon is only slightly kindled. The sun and the moon are eclipsed < when . . . . , but the obliquity of the zodiacal circle is due > to the inclination of the earth to the south; the regions of the north are always shrouded in mist, and are extremely cold and frozen. Eclipses of the sun are rare; eclipses of the moon constantly occur, and this because their orbits are unequal. As the world is born, so, too, it grows, decays and perishes, in virtue of some necessity, the nature of which he does < not > specify.

DEMOCRITUS

Democritus, like Protagoras, was a citizen of Abdera, in Thrace. His life extended from about 460 to about 370 B.C. There are stories of a patrimony wasted in travel and observation and of nights spent in research. Then he settled at Abdera for teaching and study. He was certainly widely known in ancient times as a learned man, having versed himself, as Diogenes says, "in every department of philosophy." Unlike Socrates, a contemporary, he wrote voluminously, though none of his writings have come directly to us. Aristotle is not without debt to Democritus in the field of natural studies. If this learned citizen of Abdera traveled to Athens, as is both alleged and denied, he did not make the impression upon the Athenians that Protagoras had made there. "I came to Athens," so Diogenes reports him, "and no one knew me." It is a curious fact, however explained—ignorance of him, jealousy of him, disrespect for his doctrine have all been suggested as explanations— that Plato, who mentions so many men, never unambiguously refers to Democritus, the chief contemporary opponent of Plato's whole way of thought and the destined father, indeed, of metaphysical atomism.

These selections from Democritus are reprinted from Bakewell's *Source Book in Ancient Philosophy* with permission by the publishers, Charles Scribner's Sons.— T. V. S.

6.[5] Man should know from this rule that he is cut off from truth.

7. This argument too shows that in truth we know nothing about anything, but every man shares the generally prevailing opinion.

8. And yet it will be obvious that it is difficult to really know of what sort each thing is.

10. Now, that we do not really know of what sort each thing is, or is not, has often been shown.

[5] The numbering of the fragments is that of Diels.

117. Verily we know nothing. Truth is buried deep.

9. In fact we do not know anything infallibly, but only that which changes according to the condition of our body and of the [influences] that reach and impinge upon it.

11. There are two forms of knowledge, one genuine, one obscure. To the obscure belong all of the following: sight, hearing, smell, taste, feeling. The other form is the genuine, and is quite distinct from this. (And then distinguishing the genuine from the obscure, he continues:) Whenever the obscure [way of knowing] has reached the *minimum sensible* of hearing, smell, taste, and touch, and when the investigation must be carried farther into that which is still finer, then arises the genuine way of knowing, which has a finer organ of thought.

0. [Democritus][6] says: By convention sweet is sweet, by convention bitter is bitter, by convention hot is hot, by convention cold is cold, by convention color is color. But in reality there are atoms and the void. That is, the objects of sense are supposed to be real and it is customary to regard them as such, but in truth they are not. Only the atoms and the void are real.

2. Of practical wisdom these are the three fruits: to deliberate well, to speak to the point, to do what is right.

3. He who intends to enjoy life should not be busy about many things, and in what he does should not undertake what exceeds his natural capacity. On the contrary, he should have himself so in hand that even when fortune comes his way, and is apparently ready to lead him on to higher things, he should put her aside and not o'erreach his powers. For a being of moderate size is safer than one that bulks too big.

THE GOLDEN SAYINGS OF DEMOCRITUS

35. If any one hearken with understanding to these sayings of mine many a deed worthy of a good man shall he perform and many a foolish deed be spared.

37. If one choose the goods of the soul, he chooses the diviner [portion]; if the goods of the body, the merely mortal.

38. 'Tis well to restrain the wicked, and in any case not to join him in his wrong-doing.

[6] Sext. Emp. *Math.* vii. 135.

40. 'Tis not in strength of body nor in gold that men find happiness, but in uprightness and in fulness of understanding.

41. Not from fear but from a sense of duty refrain from your sins.

43. Repentance for one's evil deeds is the safeguard of life.

45. He who does wrong is more unhappy than he who suffers wrong.

49. 'Tis a grievous thing to be subject to an inferior.

53. Many who have not learned wisdom live wisely, and many who do the basest deeds can make most learned speeches.

54. Fools learn wisdom through misfortune.

55. One should emulate works and deeds of virtue, not arguments about it.

57. Strength of body is nobility in beasts of burden, strength of character is nobility in men.

58. The hopes of the right-minded may be realized, those of fools are impossible.

59. Neither art nor wisdom may be attained without learning.

60. It is better to correct your own faults than those of another.

61. Those who have a well-ordered character lead also a well-ordered life.

62. Good means not [merely] not to do wrong, but rather not to desire to do wrong.

64. There are many who know many things, yet are lacking in wisdom.

77. Fame and wealth without wisdom are unsafe possessions.

78. Making money is not without its value, but nothing is baser than to make it by wrong-doing.

68. You can tell the man who rings true from the man who rings false, not by his deeds alone, but also by his desires.

82. False men and shams talk big and do nothing.

89. My enemy is not the man who wrongs me, but the man who means to wrong me.

90. The enmity of one's kindred is far more bitter than the enmity of strangers.

98. The friendship of one wise man is better than the friendship of a host of fools.

99. No one deserves to live who has not at least one good-man-and-true for a friend.

108. Seek after the good, and with much toil shall ye find it; the evil turns up of itself without your seeking it.

111. For a man petticoat government is the limit of insolence.

118. (Democritus said he would rather discover a single demonstration than win the throne of Persia.)

119. Men have made an idol of luck as an excuse for their own thoughtlessness. Luck seldom measures swords with wisdom. Most things in life quick wit and sharp vision can set right.

154a. In the weightiest matters we must go to school to the animals, and learn spinning and weaving from the spider, building from the swallow, singing from the birds,—from the swan and the nightingale, imitating their art.

160. An evil and foolish and intemperate and irreligious life should not be called a bad life, but rather, dying long drawn out.

176. Fortune is lavish with her favors, but not to be depended on. Nature on the other hand is self-sufficing, and therefore with her feebler but trustworthy [resources] she wins the greater [meed] of hope.

174. The right-minded man, ever inclined to righteous and lawful deeds, is joyous day and night, and strong, and free from care. But if a man take no heed of the right, and leave undone the things he ought to do, then will the recollection of no one of all his transgressions bring him any joy, but only anxiety and self-reproaching.

175. Now as of old the gods give men all good things, excepting only those that are baneful and injurious and useless. These, now as of old, are not gifts of the gods: men stumble into them themselves because of their own blindness and folly.

178. Of all things the worst to teach the young is dalliance, for it is this that is the parent of those pleasures from which wickedness springs.

231. A sensible man takes pleasure in what he has instead of pining for what he has not.

230. A life without a holiday is like a long journey without an inn to rest at.

232. The pleasures that give most joy are the ones that most rarely come.

233. Throw moderation to the winds, and the greatest pleasures bring the greatest pains.

234. Men in their prayers beg the gods for health, not knowing that this is a thing they have in their own power. Through their incontinence undermining it, they themselves become, because of their passions, the betrayers of their own health.

191. Men achieve tranquillity through moderation in pleasure and through the symmetry of life. Want and superfluity are apt to upset them and to cause great perturbations in the soul. The souls that are rent by violent conflicts are neither stable nor tranquil. One should therefore set his mind upon the things that are within his power, and be content with his opportunities, nor let his memory dwell very long on the envied and admired of men, nor idly sit and dream of them. Rather, he should contemplate the lives of those who suffer hardship, and vividly bring to mind their sufferings, so that your own present situation may appear to you important and to be envied, and so that it may no longer be your portion to suffer torture in your soul by your longing for more. For he who admires those who have, and whom other men deem blest of fortune, and who spends all his time idly dreaming of them, will be forced to be always contriving some new device because of his [insatiable] desire, until he ends by doing some desperate deed forbidden by the laws. And therefore one ought not to desire other men's blessings, and one ought not to envy those who have more, but rather, comparing his life with that of those who fare worse, and laying to heart their sufferings, deem himself blest of fortune in that he lives and fares so much better than they. Holding fast to this saying you will pass your life in greater tranquillity and will avert not a few of the plagues of life—envy and jealousy and bitterness of mind.

235. All who delight in the pleasures of the belly, exceeding all measure in eating and drinking and love, find that the pleasures are brief and last but a short while—only so long as they are eating and drinking—but the pains that come after are many and endure. The longing for the same things keeps ever returning, and whenever the objects of one's desire are realized forthwith the pleasure vanishes, and one has no further use for them. The pleasure is brief, and once more the need for the same things returns.

252. We ought to regard the interests of the state as of far greater moment than all else, in order that they may be adminis-

tered well; and we ought not to engage in eager rivalry in despite
of equity, nor arrogate to ourselves any power contrary to the common welfare. For a state well administered is our greatest safeguard. In this all is summed up: When the state is in a healthy
condition all things prosper; when it is corrupt, all things go to
ruin.

THE ATOMISTS ON THE SOUL, ACCORDING TO ARISTOTLE

DEMOCRITIST EXPLAINS SOUL

There[7] are some who maintain that fundamentally and primarily
the soul is the principle of movement. They reasoned that that
which is not itself in motion cannot move anything else, and thus
they regarded the soul as one of those objects which were in motion.
Democritus, whose view agrees with that of Leucippus, consequently maintained soul to be a sort of fire and heat. For as the
forms of the atoms are as the atoms themselves unlimited, he declares that those which are spherical in shape constitute fire and
soul, these atoms being like the so-called motes which are seen in
the sunbeams that enter through doorways, and it is in such a
mixed heap of seeds that he finds the elements of the whole natural
world. The reason why they maintain that the spherical atoms
constitute the soul, is that atoms of such configuration are best
able to penetrate through everything, and to set the other things
in motion at the same time as they are moved themselves, the assumption here being that the soul is that which supplies animals
with motion. This same assumption led them to regard respiration
as the boundary with which life was coterminous. It was, they
held, the tendency of the encircling atmosphere to cause contrac-
tion in the animal body and to expel those atomic forms, which,
from never being at rest themselves, supply animals with movement. This tendency, however, was counteracted by the reënforce-
ment derived from the entrance from outside in the act of respiration of new atoms of a similar kind. These last in fact—such was
their theory—as they united to repel the compressing and solidify-
ing forces prevented those atoms already existing in animals from
being expelled from them: and life, they thought, continued so
long as there was strength to carry on this process.

[7] Aristotle, *De Anima*, I. 2, 403 b 30. The passages from Aristotle's *Psychology*
are given in Wallace's translation.

[Democritus held][8] that the soul and reason were the same thing, and that this belonged to the class of primary and indivisible bodies, and had the capacity of motion because of the smallness of its parts and because of its shape. Now the most mobile shape is the spherical, and such is the shape of reason and of fire.

DIOGENES LAERTIUS ON THE DOCTRINE OF DEMOCRITUS[9]

The first principles of the universe are atoms and empty space; everything else is merely thought to exist. The worlds are unlimited; they come into being and perish. Nothing can come into being from that which is not nor pass away into that which is not. Further, the atoms are unlimited in size and number, and they are borne along in the whole universe in a vortex, and thereby generate all composite things—fire, water, air, earth; for even these are conglomerations of given atoms. And it is because of their solidity that these atoms are impassive and unalterable. The sun and the moon have been composed of such smooth and spherical masses, i.e. atoms, and so also the soul, which is identical with reason. We see by virtue of the impact of images upon our eyes.

All things happen by virtue of necessity, the vortex being the cause of the creation of all things, and this he calls necessity. The end of action is tranquillity, which is not identical with pleasure, as some by a false interpretation have understood, but a state in which the soul continues calm and strong, undisturbed by any fear or superstition or any other emotion. This he calls well-being and many other names; the qualities of things exist merely by convention; in nature there is nothing but atoms and void space. These, then, are his opinions.

[8] Aristotle, *ibid.*, 405 a 8.

[9] Hicks's translation ("Loeb Classical Library" series, II, 453–55). This is a small portion of Diogenes' discussion of Democritus, though the remainder is given over to gossip about his life and to a list of his books which runs well over half a hundred titles.—T. V. S.

CHAPTER V

ORACLES, MYSTERY CULTS, AND PYTHAGOREANISM

PYTHAGORAS AND THE PYTHAGOREANS

It is clear that the early Greek philosophers, while raising questions of their own, were limited as regards answers by many inherited concepts. Such, for instance, were those of the four elements—earth, air, fire, and water. Moreover, there operated vaguely some inherited notion of a proper, or moral, relationship between these elements. The moral fragment from Anaximander we have already noted. Xenophanes also we have remarked as an apostle of some divine pervasiveness. The generalized notion of Fate as arbiter, or that of Necessity as marking the boundary of fruitful effort, is worthy of careful note. Cornford makes out a sociological genesis of these inheritances. The Eleusinian mysteries and the Orphic rites are on the scene when philosophy begins. The oracles became the local voices of pervasive divinity. As divinity disperses, however, to reassemble grandly on Mount Olympus, the oracles consolidate until a few mouthpieces, like Delphi, speak authoritatively for the gods.

But Delphi grew at last too worldly wise; the prestige of the Persians terrified Apollo himself. And in a crucial moment, when consulted before Salamis, he struck a debilitating blow at orthodoxy by advising the Athenians thus: "Fly to the ends of the earth, leaving your houses and the high citadel of your wheel-shaped city. . . . . Go from the sanctuary, and steel your hearts to meet misfortunes." Human courage, however, won in the event over divine timidity; and mysticism took a form more compatible with ensuing Greek glory than ambiguous oracles had proved to be.

The religious motif, however, persisted intellectualized in Pythagorean numerology, a doctrine that maintained a high in-

fluence even through the classical period. Socrates' deference to his divine "voice," and Plato's growing attention to numbers and his habitual reliance in a pinch upon factors doubtfully rational, are illustrative of the fact that Greek philosophy arose with Thales as hylozoistic and subsided with Plotinus as silently mystical.

. . .

PYTHAGORAS

Pythagoras, son of Mnesarchus, a native of Samos, left his fatherland to escape the tyranny of Polycrates (533/2 or 529/8 B.C.). He made his home for many years in Croton in Southern Italy, where his political views gained control in the city. At length he and his followers were banished by an opposing party, and he died at Metapontum. Many stories are told of his travels into Egypt and more widely, but there is no evidence on which the stories can be accepted. He was a mystic thinker and religious reformer quite as much as a philosopher, but there is no reason for denying that the doctrines of the school originated with him. Of his disciples, Archytas, in Southern Italy, and Philolaus and Lysis, at Thebes, are the best known. It is the doctrine of the school, not the teaching of Pythagoras himself, which is known to us through the writings of Aristotle.

a) DIOGENES LAERTIUS ON PYTHAGORAS[1]

This is what Heraclides of Pontus tells us he [Pythagoras] used to say about himself: that he had once been Aethalides and was accounted to be Hermes' son, and Hermes told him he might choose any gift he liked except immortality: so he asked to retain through life and through death a memory of his experiences. Hence in life he could recall everything, and when he died he still kept the same memories. Afterwards in course of time his soul entered into Euphorbus and he was wounded by Menelaus. Now Euphorbus used to say that he had once been Aethalides and obtained this gift from Hermes, and then he told of the wanderings of his soul, how it migrated hither and thither, into how many plants and animals it had come, and all that it underwent in Hades, and all that the other souls there have to endure. When Euphorbus died, his soul passed into Hermotimus, and he also, wishing to authenticate the story, went up to the temple of Apollo at Branchidae, where he

---

[1] This account is taken directly from the Hicks's translation ("Loeb Classical Library" series) of Diogenes Laertius (II, 323–31 and 335–37). It takes Diogenes to do Pythagoras justice, and this is but a fragment of the story.—T. V. S.

identified the shield which Menelaus, on his voyage home from Troy, had dedicated to Apollo, so he said; the shield being now so rotten through and through that the ivory facing only was left. When Hermotimus died, he became Pyrrhus, a fisherman of Delos, and again remembered everything, how he was first Aethalides, then Hermotimus, and then Pyrrhus. But when Pyrrhus died, he became Pythagoras, and still remembered all the facts mentioned.

There are some who insist, absurdly enough, that Pythagoras left no writings whatever. At all events Heraclitus, the physicist, almost shouts in our ear, "Pythagoras, son of Mnesarchus, practised inquiry beyond all other men, and in this selection of his writings made himself a wisdom of his own, showing much learning but poor workmanship." The occasion of this remark was the opening words of Pythagoras' treatise *On Nature*, namely, "Nay, I swear by the air I breathe, I swear by the water I drink, I will never suffer censure on account of this work." Pythagoras in fact wrote three books, *On Education*, *On Statesmanship*, and *On Nature*. But the book which passes as the work of Pythagoras is by Lysis of Tarentum, a Pythagorean, who fled to Thebes and taught Epaminondas. . . . .

The contents in general of the aforesaid three treatises of Pythagoras are as follows. He forbids us to pray for ourselves, because we do not know what will help us. Drinking he calls, in a word, a snare, and he discountenances all excess, saying that no one should go beyond due proportion either in drinking or in eating. Of sexual indulgence, too, he says, "Keep to the winter for sexual pleasures, in summer abstain; they are less harmful in autumn and spring, but they are always harmful and not conducive to health." Asked once when a man should consort with a woman, he replied, "When you want to lose what strength you have."

He divided man's life into four quarters thus: "Twenty years a young man, twenty years an old man; and these four periods correspond to the four seasons, the boy to spring, the youth to summer, the young man to autumn, and the old man to winter," meaning by youth one not yet grown up and by a young man a man of mature age. According to Timaeus, he was the first to say, "Friends have all things in common" and "Friendship is equality"; indeed, his disciples did put all their possessions into one common stock.

For five whole years they had to keep silence, merely listening to his discourses without seeing him,[2] until they passed an examination, and thenceforward they were admitted to his house and allowed to see him. . . . .

The following were his watchwords or precepts: don't stir the fire with a knife, don't step over the beam of a balance, don't sit down on your bushel, don't eat your heart, don't help a man off with a load but help him on, always roll your bed-clothes up, don't put God's image on the circle of a ring, don't leave the pan's imprint on the ashes, don't wipe up a mess with a torch, don't commit a nuisance towards the sun, don't walk the highway, don't shake hands too eagerly, don't have swallows under your own roof, don't keep birds with hooked claws, don't make water on nor stand upon your nail- and hair-trimmings, turn the sharp blade away, when you go abroad don't turn round at the frontier.

This is what they meant. Don't stir the fire with a knife: don't stir the passions or the swelling pride of the great. Don't step over the beam of a balance: don't overstep the bounds of equity and justice. Don't sit down on your bushel: have the same care of to-day and the future, a bushel being the day's ration. By not eating your heart he meant not wasting your life in troubles and pains. By saying do not turn round when you go abroad, he meant to advise those who are departing this life not to set their hearts' desire on living nor to be too much attracted by the pleasures of this life. The explanations of the rest are similar and would take too long to set out.

b) PASSAGES IN PLATO REFERRING TO THE PYTHAGOREANS

The saying that is uttered in secret rites, to the effect that we men are in a sort of prison, and that one ought not to loose himself from it nor yet to run away, seems to me something great and not easy to see through; but this at least I think is well said, that it is the gods who care for us, and we men are one of the possessions of the gods.[3]

For some say that it (the body) is the tomb of the soul—I think it was the followers of Orpheus in particular who introduced this

---

[2] Because he lectured at night.　　　[3] *Phaedo* 62.

word—which has this enclosure like a prison in order that it may be kept safe.[4]

I once heard one of the wise men say that now we are dead and the body is our tomb, and that that part of the soul where desires are, it so happens, is open to persuasion, and moves upward or downward. And, indeed, a clever man—perhaps some inhabitant of Sicily or Italy—speaking allegorically, and taking the word from 'credible' and 'persuadable,' called this a jar; and he called those without intelligence uninitiated, and that part of the soul of uninitiated persons where the desires are, he called its intemperateness, and said it was not water-tight, as a jar might be pierced with holes—using the simile because of its insatiate desires.[5]

And the wise men say that one community embraces heaven and earth and gods and men and friendship and order and temperance and righteousness, and for that reason they call this whole a universe, my friend, for it is not without order nor yet is there excess. It seems to me that you do not pay attention to these things, though you are wise in regard to them. But it has escaped your notice that geometrical equality prevails widely among both gods and men.[6]

c) PASSAGES IN ARISTOTLE REFERRING TO
THE PYTHAGOREANS

For all who think they have worthily applied themselves to such philosophy, have discoursed concerning the infinite, and they all have asserted some first principle of things—some, like the Pythagoreans and Plato, a first principle existing by itself, not connected with anything else, but being itself the infinite in its essence. Only the Pythagoreans found it among things perceived by sense (for they say that number is not an abstraction), and they held that it was the infinite outside the heavens.[7]

(The Pythagoreans) both hold that the infinite is being, and divide it.[8]

And the Pythagoreans say that there is a void, and that it enters into the heaven itself from the infinite air, as though it (the heaven) were breathing; and this void defines the natures of things, inas-

[4] *Cratylus* 400.   [6] *Ibid.* 507.

[5] *Gorgias* 493.   [7] *Physics*, iii. 4; 203 a 1.   [8] *Ibid.*, iii. 4; 204 a 33.

much as it is a certain separation and definition of things that lie together; and this is true first in the case of numbers, for the void defines the nature of these.[9]

For as the Pythagoreans say, the all and all things are defined by threes; for end and middle and beginning constitute the number of the all, and also the number of the triad.[10]

And since there are some who say that there is a right and left of the heavens, as, for instance, those that are called Pythagoreans (for such is their doctrine), we must investigate whether it is as they say.[11]

Wherefore one of the Pythagoreans might be surprised in that they say that there are only these two first principles, the right and the left, and they pass over four of them as not having the least validity; for there is no less difference up and down, and front and back than there is right and left in all creatures.[12]

And some are dwelling in the upper hemisphere and to the right, while we dwell below and to the left, which is the opposite to what the Pythagoreans say; for they put us above and to the right, while the others are below and at the left.[13]

Some think it necessary that noise should arise when so great bodies are in motion, since sound does arise from bodies among us which are not so large and do not move so swiftly; and from the sun and moon and from the stars in so great number, and of so great size, moving so swiftly, there must necessarily arise a sound inconceivably great. Assuming these things and that the swiftness has the principle of harmony by reason of the intervals, they say that the sound of the stars moving on in a circle becomes musical. And since it seems unreasonable that we also do not hear this sound, they say that the reason for this is that the noise exists in the very nature of things, so as not to be distinguishable from the opposite silence; for the distinction of sound and silence lies in their contrast with each other, so that as blacksmiths think there is no difference between them because they are accustomed to the sound, so the same thing happens to men.[14]

What occasions the difficulty and makes the Pythagoreans say

[9] *Ibid.*, iv. 6; 213 b 22.

[10] *De Caelo*, i. 1; 268 a 10.

[11] *Ibid.*, ii. 2; 284 b 6.

[12] *Ibid.*, ii. 2; 285 a 10.

[13] *Ibid.*, ii. 2; 285 b 23.

[14] *Ibid.*, ii. 9; 290 b 15.

that there is a harmony of the bodies as they move, is a proof. For whatever things move themselves make a sound and noise; but whatever things are fastened in what moves or exist in it as the parts in a ship, cannot make a noise, nor yet does the ship if it moves in a river.[15]

They say that the whole heaven is limited, the opposite to what those of Italy, called the Pythagoreans, say; for these say that fire is at the centre and that the earth is one of the stars, and that moving in a circle about the centre it produces night and day. And they assume yet another earth opposite this which they call the counter-earth, not seeking reasons and causes for phenomena, but stretching phenomena to meet certain assumptions and opinions of theirs and attempting to arrange them in a system. . . . . And farther the Pythagoreans say that the most authoritative part of the All stands guard, because it is specially fitting that it should, and this part is the centre; and this place that the fire occupies, they call the guard of Zeus, as it is called simply the centre, that is, the centre of space and the centre of matter and of nature.[16]

The same holds true for those who construct the heaven out of numbers; for some construct nature out of numbers, as do certain of the Pythagoreans.[17]

With these and before them (Anaxagoras, Empedocles, Atomists) those called Pythagoreans applying themselves to the sciences, first developed them; and being brought up in them they thought that the first principles of these (*i.e.* numbers) were the first principles of all things. And since of these (sciences) numbers are by nature the first, in numbers rather than in fire and earth and water they thought they saw many likenesses to things that are and that are coming to be, as, for instance, justice is such a property of numbers, and soul and mind are such a property, and another is opportunity, and of other things one may say the same of each one.

And further, discerning in numbers the conditions and reasons of harmonies also; since, moreover, other things seemed to be like numbers in their entire nature, and numbers were the first of every nature, they assumed that the elements of numbers were the elements of all things, and that the whole heavens were harmony and number. And whatever characteristics in numbers and harmonies

---

[15] *Ibid.*, ii. 9; 291 a 7.   [16] *Ibid.*, ii. 13; 293 a 19.   [17] *Ibid.*, iii. 1; 300 a 15.

they could show were in agreement with the properties of the heavens and its parts and with its whole arrangement, these they collected and adapted; and if there chanced to be any gap anywhere, they eagerly sought that the whole system might be connected with these (stray phenomena). To give an example of my meaning: inasmuch as ten seemed to be the perfect number and to embrace the whole nature of numbers, they asserted that the number of bodies moving through the heavens were ten, and when only nine were visible, for the reason just stated they postulated the counter-earth as the tenth. We have given a more definite account of these thinkers in other parts of our writings. But we have referred to them here with this purpose in view, that we might ascertain from them what they asserted as the first principles and in what manner they came upon the causes that have been enumerated. They certainly seem to consider number as the first principle and as it were the matter in things and in their conditions and states; and the odd and the even are elements of number, and of these the one is infinite and the other finite, and unity is the product of both of them, for it is both odd and even, and number arises from unity, and the whole heaven, as has been said, is numbers.

A different party in this same school say that the first principles are ten, named according to the following table:—finite and infinite, even and odd, one and many, right and left, male and female, rest and motion, straight and crooked, light and darkness, good and bad, square and oblong. After this manner Alkmaeon of Kroton seems to have conceived them, and either he received this doctrine from them or they from him; for Alkmaeon arrived at maturity when Pythagoras was an old man, and his teachings resembled theirs. For he says that most human affairs are twofold, not meaning opposites reached by definition, as did the former party, but opposites by chance—as, for example, white-black, sweet-bitter, good-bad, small-great. This philosopher let fall his opinions indefinitely about the rest, but the Pythagoreans declared the number of the opposites and what they were. From both one may learn this much, that opposites are the first principles of things; but from the latter he may learn the number of these, and what they are. But how it is possible to bring them into relation with the causes of which we have spoken they have not clearly worked out; but they seem to range their elements under the category of matter, for they say that being is compounded and formed from them, and that they inhere in it.[18]

Down to the Italian philosophers and with the exception of them the rest have spoken more reasonably about these principles, except that, as we said, they do indeed use two principles, and the one of these, whence is motion, some regard as one and others as twofold. The Pythagoreans, however, while they in similar manner assume two first principles, add this which is peculiar to themselves: that they do not think that the finite and the infinite and the one are certain other things by nature, such as fire or earth or any other such thing, but the infinite itself and unity itself are the essence of the things of which they are predicated, and so they make number the essence of all things. So they taught after this manner about them, and began to discourse and to define what being is, but they made it altogether too simple a matter. For they made their definitions superficially, and to whatever first the definition might apply, this they thought to be the essence of the matter; as if one should say that twofold and two were the same, because the twofold subsists in the two. But undoubtedly the two and the twofold are not the same; otherwise the one will be many—a consequence which even they would not draw. So much then may be learned from the earlier philosophers and from their successors.[19]

And Plato only changed the name, for the Pythagoreans say that things exist by imitation of numbers, but Plato, by sharing the nature of numbers.[20]

But that the one is the real essence of things, and not something else with unity as an attribute, he affirms, agreeing with the Pythagoreans; and in harmony with them he affirms that numbers are the principles of being for other things. But it is peculiar to him that instead of a single infinite he posits a double infinite, an infinite of greatness and of littleness; and it is also peculiar to him that he separates numbers from things that are seen, while they say that numbers are the things themselves, and do not interpose mathematical objects between them. This separation of the one and numbers from things, in contrast with the position of the

---

[18] *Metaphysics*, i. 5; 985 b 23—986 b 8.

[19] *Ibid.*, 987 a 9–27.   [20] *Ibid.*, i. 6; 987 b 10.

Pythagoreans, and the introduction of ideas, are the consequence of his investigation by concepts.[21]

Those, however, who carry on their investigation with reference to all things, and divide things into what are perceived and what are not perceived by sense, evidently examine both classes, so one must delay a little longer over what they say. They speak correctly and incorrectly in reference to the questions now before us. Now those who are called Pythagoreans use principles and elements yet stranger than those of the physicists, in that they do not take them from the sphere of sense, for mathematical objects are without motion, except in the case of astronomy. Still, they discourse about everything in nature and study it; they construct the heaven, they observe what happens in its parts and their states and motions; they apply to these their first principles and causes, as though they agreed entirely with the other physicists that being is only what is perceptible and what that which is called heaven includes. But their causes and first principles, they say, are such as to lead up to the higher parts of reality, and are in harmony with this rather than with the doctrines of nature. In what manner motion will take place when finite and infinite, odd and even, are the only underlying realities, they do not say; nor how it is possible for genesis and destruction to take place without motion and change, or for the heavenly bodies to revolve. Farther, if one grant to them that greatness arises from these principles, or if this could be proved, nevertheless, how will it be that some bodies are light and some heavy? For their postulates and statements apply no more to mathematical objects than to things of sense; accordingly they have said nothing at all about fire or earth or any such objects, because I think they have no distinctive doctrine about things of sense. Farther, how is it necessary to assume that number and states of number are the causes of what is in the heavens and what is taking place there from the beginning and now, and that there is no other number than that out of which the world is composed? For when opinion and opportune time are at a certain point in the heavens, and a little farther up or down are injustice and judgment or a mixture of them, and they bring forward as proof that each one of these is number, and the result then is that at this place there is already a multitude

[21] *Ibid.*, i. 6; 987 b 22.

of compounded quantities because those states of number have each their place—is this number in heaven the same which it is necessary to assume that each of these things is, or is it something different? Plato says it is different; still, he thinks that both these things and the causes of them are numbers; but the one class are ideal causes, and the others are sense causes.[22]

And the most difficult and perplexing question of all is whether unity and being are not, as Plato and the Pythagoreans say, something different from things but their very essence, or whether the underlying substance is something different, friendship, as Empedocles says, or as another says, fire, or water, or air.[23]

Plato and the Pythagoreans assert that neither being nor yet unity is something different from things, but that it is the very nature of them, as though essence itself consisted in unity and existence.[24]

So it turns out that many things of which the forms appear different have one form, as the Pythagoreans discovered; and one can say that there is one form for everything, and the others are not forms; and thus all things will be one.[25]

Whether the one itself is a sort of essence, as first the Pythagoreans and later Plato affirmed. . . . .[26]

And they are wrong who assume, as do the Pythagoreans and Speusippos, that the most beautiful and the best is not in the first principle, because the first principles of plants and animals are indeed causes; for that which is beautiful and perfect is in what comes from these first principles.[27]

The Pythagoreans (before Democritus) only defined a few things, the concepts of which they reduced to numbers, as for instance opportunity or justice or marriage. . . . .[28]

The Pythagoreans say that there is but one number, the mathematical, but things of sense are not separated from this, for they are composed of it; indeed, they construct the whole heaven out of numbers, but not out of unit numbers, for they assume that the

[22] Ibid., i. 8; 989 b 32—990 a 32.

[23] Ibid., ii. 1; 996 a 4.

[24] Ibid., ii. 4; 1001 a 9.

[25] Ibid., 1036 b 17.

[26] Ibid., ix. 2; 1053 b 11.

[27] Ibid., xi. 7; 1072 b 31.

[28] Ibid., xii. 4; 1078 b 21.

unities have quantity; but how the first unity was so constituted as to have quantity, they seem at a loss to say.[29] All, as many as regard the one as the element and first principle of things, except the Pythagoreans, assert that numbers are based on the unit; but the Pythagoreans assert, as has been remarked, that numbers have quantity.[30]

The Pythagorean standpoint has on the one hand fewer difficulties than those that have been discussed, but it has new difficulties of its own. The fact that they do not regard number as separate, removes many of the contradictions; but it is impossible that bodies should consist of numbers, and that this number should be mathematical. Nor is it true that indivisible elements have quantity; but, granted that they have this quality of indivisibility, the units have no quantity; for how can quantity be composed of indivisible elements? but arithmetical number consists of units. But these say that things are number; at least, they adapt their speculations to such bodies as consist of elements which are numbers.[31]

On the other hand the Pythagoreans, because they see many qualities of numbers in bodies perceived by sense, regard objects as numbers, not as separate numbers, but as derived from numbers. And why? Because the qualities of numbers exist in harmony both in the heaven and in many other things. But for those who hold that number is mathematical only, it is impossible on the basis of their hypothesis to say any such thing; and it has already been remarked that there can be no science of these numbers. But we say, as above, that there is a science of numbers. Evidently the mathematical does not exist apart by itself, for in that case its qualities could not exist in bodies. In such a matter the Pythagoreans are restrained by nothing; when, however, they construct out of numbers physical bodies—out of numbers that have neither weight nor lightness, bodies that have weight and lightness—they seem to be speaking about another heaven and other bodies than those perceived by sense.[32]

[29] *Ibid.*, xii, 6; 1080 b 16.
[30] *Ibid.*, xii. 6; 1080 b 31.
[31] *Ibid.*, xii. 8; 1083 b 9.
[32] *Ibid.*, xiii. 3; 1090 a 20.

And the Pythagoreans seem to speak more persuasively about it, putting the unity in the co-ordination of good things.[33]

The evil partakes of the nature of the infinite, the good of the finite, as the Pythagoreans conjectured.[34]

Reciprocity seems to some to be absolutely just, as the Pythagoreans say; for these defined the just as that which is reciprocal to another.[35]

First Pythagoras attempted to speak concerning virtue, but he did not speak correctly; for bringing virtues into correspondence with numbers, he did not make any distinct.[36]

[33] *Ethics*, i. 4; 1096 b 5.
[34] *Ibid.*, ii. 5; 1106 b 29.
[35] *Ibid.*, v. 8; 1132 b 21.
[36] *Magna Moralia*, i. 1; 1182 a 11.

CHAPTER VI
THE GREEK ENLIGHTENMENT
THE SOPHISTS
Protagoras, Gorgias

The Greek Enlightenment was characterized by a spirit of independent reflection and criticism. The leaders in this movement, the Sophists, substituted the right of private judgment for the authority of existing institutions, which latter they regarded as contracts between the mutually selfish or as dominance of the weak by the strong. The contradiction of Greek reason by itself (Heraclitus–Parmenides) motivated a turn to the practical; and the results of physical speculation gave a low-lying foundation for duties of a rising democratic citizenship. The Sophists based their ethical theory upon an epistemological relativism in which, according to Protagoras, man becomes the measure of everything. This relativism easily became a skepticism, excused by Protagoras in the theological field by "the obscurity of the question and the shortness of human life."

Gorgias, another eminent representative, is credited with this gem of agnosticism, not to say of nihilism: "First, nothing exists; second, if anything did exist we could never know it; third, if perchance a man should come to know it, it would remain a secret, he would be unable to describe it to his fellow-men."

Plato is our chief informant upon these popular teachers of an awakening Greece; and though he has honored these two great representatives of the movement with a dialogue named after each, it is clear that his dislike was grounded on more than purely rational considerations. They took pay for their work, as he did not; and they were not, as he assumed himself to be, clairvoyant of something eternal. Whatever the complete grounds for Plato's suspicions of them, it is fairly clear that they did much to turn the course of speculation from nature to man. In this regard

*they were the successors of the Seven (or more) Wise Men, and
the predecessors of Socrates, who himself was made by Aristophanes in the "Clouds" to be the ringleader of them all. With
these remarks and cautions we shall know how to take Plato's
(and Aristotle's) picture of the Sophists. To transcend the relativism of Protagoras and the nihilism of Gorgias and to reach
more universal standards of truth and value was a worthy task—
a task worthy, indeed, of any and every Socrates.*

. . .

PROTAGORAS

Protagoras is identified as a citizen of Abdera, and his life covers approximately
the period 481–411. Independent of the none too sympathetic picture Plato gives
of him in the *Protagoras* and the *Theaetetus*, we know that he frequented Athens,
that he lived for a time in the circle of Pericles, and that the latter asked his aid in
drawing up a constitution for the pan-Hellenic colony of Thurii, founded in the
year 444. His was a name to conjure with in his age; even Plato makes this clear.
His religious agnosticism got him in trouble with the Athenians. But his fame is
bright as one who turned from nature to man and thus created a symbol of the not
infrequently recurring concern with the subject rather than the object of knowledge.

Man is the measure of all things, of things that are that they are,
and of things that are not that they are not.

As to the gods, I have no means of knowing either that they
exist or that they do not exist. For many are the obstacles that
impede knowledge, both the obscurity of the question and the
shortness of human life.

Education needs natural gifts and practice; a man must begin
to learn in his youth; education does not spout in the soul unless
a great depth is reached.[1]

We [Socrates speaking] came upon Protagoras as he was walking round in the cloister [of Callias' house in Athens], and close
behind him two companies were walking round also; on the one

[1] The translation of these three snatches from the educational philosophy of
Protagoras is from Zeller, *Outlines of the History of Greek Philosophy* (13th ed. revised by Nestle and translated by Palmer), p. 83.

[2] From the dialogue *Protagoras* 314E–315B, Lamb translation (Loeb Classical
Library).

side Callias, son of Hipponicus and his brother on the mother's side, Paralus, son of Pericles, and Charmides, son of Glaucon, while the other troop consisted of Pericles' other son Xanthippus, Philippides, son of Philomelus, and Antimoerus of Mende, who is the most highly reputed of Protagoras' disciples and is taking the course professionally with a view to becoming a sophist. The persons who followed in their rear, listening to what they could of the talk, seemed to be mostly strangers, brought by the great Protagoras from the several cities which he traverses, enchanting them with his voice like Orpheus, while they follow where the voice sounds, enchanted; and some of our own inhabitants were also dancing attendance. As for me, when I saw their evolutions I was delighted with the admirable care they took not to hinder Protagoras at any moment by getting in front; but whenever the master turned about and those with him, it was fine to see the orderly manner in which his train of listeners split up into two parties on this side and on that, and wheeling round formed up again each time in his rear most admirably.

DIOGENES LAERTIUS ON PROTAGORAS[3]

Protagoras was the first to maintain that there are two sides to every question, opposed to each other, and he even argued in this fashion, being the first to do so. Furthermore he began a work thus: "Man is the measure of all things, of things that are that they are, and of things that are not that they are not." He used to say that soul was nothing apart from the senses, as we learn from Plato in the *Theaetetus*, and that everything is true. In another work he began thus: "As to the gods, I have no means of knowing either that they exist or that they do not exist. For many are the obstacles that impede knowledge, both the obscurity of the question and the shortness of human life." For this introduction to his book the Athenians expelled him; and they burnt his works in the market-place, after sending round a herald to collect them from all who had copies in their possession.

He was the first to exact a fee of a hundred minae and the first to distinguish the tenses of verbs, to emphasize the importance of seizing the right moment, to institute contests in debating, and to

---

[3] From the Hicks's translation ("Loeb Classical Library" series), II, 463–69. But for opening and closing remarks irrelevant for our purpose, we quote all that Laertius has to say on Protagoras.—T. V. S.

teach rival pleaders the tricks of their trade. Furthermore, in his dialectic he neglected the meaning in favour of verbal quibbling, and he was the father of the whole tribe of eristical disputants now so much in evidence; insomuch that Timon too speaks of him as

> Protagoras, all mankind's epitome,
> Cunning, I trow, to war with words.

He too first introduced the method of discussion which is called Socratic. Again, as we learn from Plato in the Euthydemus, he was the first to use in discussion the argument of Antisthenes which strives to prove that contradiction is impossible, and the first to point out how to attack and refute any proposition laid down; so Artemidorus the dialectician in his treatise *In Reply to Chrysippus*. He too invented the shoulder-pad on which porters carry their burdens, so we are told by Aristotle in his treatise *On Education;* for he himself had been a porter, says Epicurus somewhere. This was how he was taken up by Democritus, who saw how skilfully his bundles of wood were tied. He was the first to mark off the parts of discourse into four, namely, wish, question, answer, command;[4] others divide into seven parts, narration, question, answer, command, rehearsal, wish, summoning; these he called the basic forms of speech. Alcidamas made discourse fourfold, affirmation, negation, question, address.

The first of his books he read in public was that *On the Gods*, the introduction to which we quoted above; he read it at Athens in Euripides' house, or, as some say, in Megaclides'; others again make the place the Lyceum and the reader his disciple Archagoras, Theodotus's son, who gave him the benefit of his voice. His accuser was Pythodorus, son of Polyzelus, one of the four hundred; Aristotle, however, says it was Euathlus.

The works of his which survive are these:[5]

The Art of Controversy	Of the Ancient Order of Things
Of Wrestling	On the Dwellers in Hades
On Mathematics	Of the Misdeeds of Mankind
Of the State	A Book of Precepts
Of Ambition	Of Forensic Speech for a Fee,
Of Virtues	two books of opposing arguments

[4] These answer roughly to the optative, the indicative, and the imperative.

[5] It is clear, of course, that this list omits the book *On the Gods*, from which Laertius has just quoted, if not also the book from which his first quotation is taken. —T. V. S.

This is the list of his works. Moreover there is a dialogue which Plato wrote upon him.

Philochorus says that, when he was on a voyage to Sicily, his ship went down, and that Euripides hints at this in his *Ixion*. According to some his death occurred, when he was on a journey, at nearly ninety years of age, though Apollodorus makes his age seventy, assigns forty years for his career as a sophist, and puts his floruit in the 84th Olympiad.

There is an epigram of my own on him as follows:

> Protagoras, I hear it told of thee
> Thou died'st in eld when Athens thou didst flee;
> Cecrops' town chose to banish thee; but though
> Thou 'scap'dst Athene, not so Hell below.

The story is told that once, when he asked Euathlus his disciple for his fee, the latter replied, "But I have not won a case yet." "Nay," said Protagoras, "if I win this case against you I must have the fee, for winning it; if you win, I must have it, because *you* win it."

GORGIAS

Gorgias of Leontini (483–375) was a pupil of Zeno. Carrying the Eleatic doctrine to its logical limit, he doubted himself out of philosophy, and became a rhetorician. As a public figure he was often in Athens, it appears, and represented his native city there in 427, asking for help against Syracuse. His appearances at Olympi, Delphi, and particularly at Athens were used to spread the spirit of pan-Hellism, to which he was devoted. Plato named an important dialogue after Gorgias.

FUNERAL ORATION[6]

For what was absent in these men which should be present in men, and what was present of things which should be absent? Would that I could say what I wish and wish what I should, evading displeasure and eluding human jealousy. For the virtue of these men was a divine possession; their mortality was human. Frequently they preferred the clemency of equity to the harshness of law; frequently, too, the righteousness of reason to the rigidity of codes. For this they held to be the most godlike and most uni-

---

[6] Cited from Gomperz, *Greek-Thinkers*, I, 478, as an example of the rhetoric for which Gorgias was (in)famous. To sense the rhythm of those sentences, which roll even in English, may help to make more intelligible the reputation of Gorgias.—T. V. S.

versal code: in the right place to do aright and to speak aright, to keep silence aright, and to bear aright.

It is a law of nature that the strong shall not be hindered by the weak, but that the weak shall be ruled and led by the strong; that the strong shall go before and the weak shall follow after.[7]

PLATO ON GORGIAS[8]

GORGIAS: Well, I will try, Socrates, to reveal to you clearly the whole power of rhetoric. . . . . You know, I suppose, that these great arsenals and walls of Athens, and the construction of your harbours, are due to the advice of Themistocles, and in part to that of Pericles, not to your craftsmen.

SOCRATES: So we are told, Gorgias, of Themistocles; and as to Pericles I heard him myself when he was advising us about the middle wall.

GORGIAS: So whenever there is an election . . . . , Socrates, you see it is the orators who give the advice and get resolutions carried in these matters.

SOCRATES: That is just what surprises me, Gorgias, and has made me ask you . . . . what in the world the power of rhetoric can be. For, viewed in this light, its greatness comes over me as something supernatural.

GORGIAS: Ah yes, if you knew all, Socrates,—how it comprises in itself practically all powers at once! And I will tell you a striking proof of this; many and many a time have I gone with my brother or other doctors to visit one of their patients, and have found him unwilling either to take medicine or submit to the surgeon's knife or cautery; and when the doctor failed to persuade him I succeeded, by no other art than that of rhetoric. And I further declare that, if a rhetorician and a doctor were to enter any city you please, and there had to contend in speech before the Assembly or some other meeting as to which of the two should be appointed physician, you would find the physician was nowhere, while the master of speech would be appointed if he wished. And if he had to contend with a member of any other profession whatsoever, the rhetorician

---

[7] The translation of this quotation, which Isocrates in his *Praise of Helen* (10.2) attributes to Gorgias, is from Zeller, *Outline of the History of Greek Philosophy* (13th ed. revised by Nestle and translated by Palmer), p. 89.

[8] *Gorgias* 455-457. The translation is Lamb's (Loeb Classical Library).

would persuade the meeting to appoint him before anyone else in the place: for there is no subject on which the rhetorician could not speak more persuasively than a member of any other profession whatever, before a multitude. So great, so strange, is the power of this art. At the same time, Socrates, our use of rhetoric should be like our use of any other sort of exercise. For other exercises are not to be used against all and sundry; just because one has learnt boxing or wrestling or fighting in armour so well as to vanquish friend and foe alike: this gives one no right to strike one's friends, or stab them to death. Nor, in all conscience, if a man took lessons at a wrestling-school, and having got himself into good condition and learnt boxing he proceeded to strike his father and mother, or some other of his relations or friends, should that be reason for hating athletic trainers and teachers of fighting in armour, and expelling them from our cities. For they imparted their skill with a view to its rightful use against enemies and wrongdoers, in self-defence, not provocation; whereas the others have perverted their strength and art to an improper use. So it is not the teachers who are wicked, nor is the art either guilty or wicked on this account, but rather, to my thinking, those who do not use it properly. Now the same argument applies also to rhetoric: for the orator is able, indeed, to speak against every one and on every question in such a way as to win over the votes of the multitude, practically in any matter he may choose to take up: but he is no whit the more entitled to deprive the doctors of their credit, just because he could do so, or other professions of theirs; he must use his rhetoric fairly, as in the case of athletic exercise. And, in my opinion, if a man becomes a rhetorician and then uses this power and this art unfairly, we ought not to hate his teacher and cast him out of our cities. For he imparted that skill to be used in all fairness, whilst this man puts it to an opposite use. Thus it is the man who does not use it aright who deserves to be hated and expelled and put to death, not his teacher.

SEXTUS EMPIRICUS ON GORGIAS[9]

Gorgias of Leontini was also one of those who deny that there is any criterion, but he does not attack this problem in the

---

[9] *Adversus Mathematicos*, Book VII, 65 ff. Translated from the Greek by Clifford P. Osborne.

same way as the followers of Pythagoras do. For in his work on *Not-Being and Nature* there are three consecutive steps in his argument. In the first of these he maintains that nothing exists; in the second he holds that even if something does exist it is incomprehensible to man; and in the third he argues that even if it is comprehensible it cannot be communicated or explained to anybody else.

To prove that nothing exists he reasons in the following manner. If something exists it is either Being, or Not-Being, or both Being and Not-Being. But it is neither Being, nor Not-Being, nor Being and Not-Being, as he goes on to show; hence it is nothing.

Surely Not-Being does not exist. For if Not-Being does exist it will both be and not be at the same time. In so far as it is considered as not being it will not be, and in so far as it is considered as Not-Being it will be. But it is absolutely absurd that anything should both be and not be at the same time. Therefore Not-Being does not exist. To put it another way, if Not-Being does exist then Being would not exist, for these are opposites and hence are contrary to one another. For if it should happen that that which is not is, then it would also happen that that which is is not. But it is not true that that which is is not, and neither is it true that that which is not is.

Moreover, Being does not exist either. For if Being does exist, it either has come into being, or always was, or both has come into being and always was. But it neither has come into being, nor always was, nor both has come into being and always was, as we shall show. Being, then, does not exist. For if Being always was (and we must start from this point) it does not have any beginning, for everything which comes into existence has a beginning, but that which always was, not having come into existence, does not have any beginning, and not having any beginning it is infinite. If, moreover, it is infinite, it is nowhere. For if it is anywhere, it will be different from that Being in which it is, and thus, being enclosed by something, Being will not be infinite, because the container is greater than the contained. But there is nothing greater than infinity. Hence infinity is nowhere. And indeed it is not enclosed within itself, for in that case the contained and the container would be the same thing, and Being would become two things, place and body, for the container is place and the contained is body. But this is absurd. Therefore Being is not enclosed within itself. Hence, if Being is eternal it is infinite, and if it is infinite it is nowhere, and if it is nowhere it does not exist. If, therefore, Being is eternal it certainly does not exist.

Neither is it possible that Being has come to be. For if it has come to be, it has come either from Being or from Not-Being. But it has not come from Being, for if Being exists it has not come to be, but already is. Neither has it come from Not-Being, for what is not is not able to produce anything, because that which produces something must necessarily be. Hence Being has not come to be.

In like manner it is impossible that Being both has come to be and always was, for these two things are contradictory to one another, and if Being always was it has not come to be, and if it has come to be it is not true that it always was. If, therefore, Being neither has come to be nor always was, nor both has come to be and always was, it does not exist. In another way, if anything exists it is either one or many. But it is neither one nor many as will be shown. Hence Being does not exist. For if it is one it is either a quantum or a continuum, and either extension or body. Whichever of these it may be it is not one. For if it is a quantum it may be divided and if it is a continuum it may be separated. Similarly, if it is extended it is separable, and if it should happen to be a body it would be triple, for it would have length, breadth, and thickness. But it is absurd to say that Being is not any of these. Hence Being is not one. But neither is Being many. For if it is not one it is not many, for many is a synthesis of ones. Therefore, if the one is rejected the many must be rejected also.

From these arguments, then, it is apparent that if anything exists it is neither Being nor Not-Being. And it is also easy to show that it is not both Being and Not-Being. For if it is Being and also Not-Being, then Not-Being would be the same as Being as far as existence is concerned. And for that reason it is neither of these. For it is agreed that Not-Being does not exist. And the same thing has been proved about Being. Therefore it (both Being and Not-Being) does not exist. But even if Being were the same as Not-Being, it cannot be both. For if it is both it is not the same, and if it is the same it is not both. Consequently it is nothing. For if it is neither Being, nor Not-Being, nor both Being and Not-Being, nothing can be known about it: it is nothing.

But if something does exist it is unknown and incomprehensible to man, as he goes on to show. For if, says Gorgias, what is thought is not reality, then Being is not thought. And this is according to reason. Suppose, for example, that what is thought should happen to be white, then it would happen that what is white is thought. Similarly, if it should happen that what is thought is not reality then it would happen that reality is not thought. It is a safe and sound conclusion, then, that if what is thought is not reality, Being is not thought. But what is thought (this has already been assumed) is not reality, as we shall show. Therefore Being is not thought. But it is evident that what is thought is not reality. For if what is thought is reality, then everything that is thought exists, and in whatever manner anybody may think it, which is absurd and silly. For if anybody should think that a man is flying or that chariots are racing over the sea, that does not mean that straightway a man is flying or that chariots are racing over the sea. Therefore what is thought is not reality.

Moreover if what is thought is reality, then what is not real will not be thought. For contraries are true of contraries. But if Not-Being is contrary to Being, surely then if it happens that Being is thought, it will also happen that Not-Being will not be thought. But this is absurd. For both Scylla and the Chimera and many such things that are not real are thought. It is not true, then, that what is thought is reality. Just as things that are seen are said to be visible because they are seen, and things which are heard are said to be audible because they are heard, and as we do not reject visible things because they are not heard, nor dismiss audible things because they are not seen (each necessarily being judged by its appropriate faculty and not by any other),—thus also with what is thought. Even if it is not seen with the eyes nor heard with the ears, it will exist, since it is apprehended by the appropriate faculty. If, then, anybody thinks that chariots are racing over the sea, even if he does not see them, he must believe that chariots are racing over the sea. But this is absurd. Being, therefore, is neither thought nor comprehended.

But if it can be comprehended it cannot be communicated to anybody else. For if reality is visible and audible and generally perceptible, that is, if reality is what is presented to our sense organs from without, then the visible presentations will be apprehended by the sense of sight, and the audible presentations will be apprehended by the sense of hearing, and not contrarywise. But how can these things be communicated to others? The means of communication is language. But language is neither sense data nor reality. Therefore, we do not communicate reality to others, but only language, which is quite different from the presentations, just as the visible is different from the audible and vice versa. Thus, since reality is presented to us from without, it cannot be our language. And not being language, it cannot be communicated to others. Language, he says, originates from those things which strike us from without, that is, from things perceived by the senses. For the mixture of chyle produces in us the language which expresses quality itself, and the influx of color determines what is said about color. And thus language does not explain what lies outside, but what lies outside indicates and reveals language. So language can never show how visible and audible things are presented, and thus cannot communicate presentations and reality. For, he says, even though language is presented, nevertheless it differs from the other presentations. Visible bodies differ very much from what is said about them. For the visible is apprehended by one sense organ and language by another. Language then does not indicate many of the presentations, just as they do not indicate their nature to one another. Because of these perplexities, according to Gorgias, the criterion of truth is destroyed. There is no criterion, then, either of Being, or of the possibility of its being known or communicated to others.

THE BIG THREE OF CLASSICAL PHILOS-
OPHY: SOCRATES, PLATO, ARISTOTLE

Like a splendid sonnet sequence in literature, the moral and metaphysical moment of Greek life at its height passes from the quest of Socrates through the faith of Plato to the systematization of Aristotle. Starting from a vivid and massive personality, as such things often if not always start, the philosophic enterprise comes to speculative maturity in Plato. The transfer of interest from nature to man, which Socrates consummated, Plato celebrates by turning all the resources of nature and mind into the creation through eugenic selection and rigorous education of philosopher-kings, with a single eye upon those goods which for one man to have more of does not mean for another man to have less of. Plato is diverse in interest, and the most significant unity of his thought is this singleness of ultimate aim. His search for standards as final bulwark of knowledge against skepticism and of virtue in practice against Sophism in theory took him so far afield, however, that he was never able with complete assurance to retrace his flight from facts. The path of that dialectical flight, nevertheless, marks in myth and allegory and irony the majestic curve of man's highest imaginative splendor. Aristotle, biologist rather than poet, colonized in the world of fact the finest children of Platonic fancy. *Patterns* of things become patterns of *things*, and the quest for the ideal may now, but for an aberrant diversion, center its attention on the natural, and thus make one again the world of mind and the world of nature. The field of fact becomes thus dynamic, and mind the principle of development by which all things move from the less formed to the more formed. This high moment of Greek genius culminates in an ethics which orients man in nature, save for an anomalous undertow in Aristotle toward a transcendent deity, and makes the duties of citizenship the finest opportunities for self-realization. Man appears a child of nature, and nature through man becomes a teleological system with man himself the mediator and chief beneficiary.

For purposes of dividing one large tome into two more convenient volumes we have deferred Aristotle to *From Aristotle to Plotinus*. He comes as logically at the beginning of the new as he does at the close of the old: for Aristotle is a genuine connecting link between the work of Plato, his outgrown master, and Roman civilization, consolidated at the point of the sword by Aristotle's student, Alexander the Great.

CHAPTER VII
SOCRATES

PERSONALITY AND PROBABLE DOCTRINE
PLATO ON SOCRATES' LIFE AND DOCTRINE
PLATO'S *Apology:* SOCRATES AT HIS TRIAL
XENOPHON ON SOCRATES' DEFENCE TO THE JURY

Socrates (469–399), one of the heroes of humanity, is an equivocal character. Perhaps that is the reason he has become a hero. Like Jesus, whom we shall presently characterize, Socrates wrote nothing; and those who wrote about him, even more than those who wrote about Jesus, differed in their pictures of his character. To dramatize their diversity: Xenophon makes of him a stupid, good man; Aristophanes (in the "Clouds"), a clever, bad man; and Plato, a wise, good man. The Platonic picture has tended historically to command the field; and Socrates and Plato are so intertwined in that picture that biography would be easier if we could roll the two into one and call the composite "Plocrates." But each has grown too great to be absorbed by the other, and both together too great to be bound by a single character. Weaving the accounts of Aristophanes and Xenophon as best we may around the Platonic Socrates in order to make a single character, we see immortalized a sort of secular saint who outsophisticated the Sophists and raised a structure of knowledge, or confidence of knowledge, upon a foundation too weak in other hands to support more than changing opinion. His probable teaching may be summarized in three propositions, with a possible if not probable fourth proposition added: (1) all skills, goods, and values appear on analysis to reduce to just one virtue; (2) this single virtue is knowledge; (3) virtue, since it is one and knowledge, can be taught; and a Platonic if not Socratic final thesis (4) the knowledge which virtue consists of is not knowledge of just anything but of the good, i.e., of virtue itself. In person both repellent and seductive, the gadfly of Athens, the exciting teacher (whose enemies said corrupter) of youth, Socrates believed himself the possessor of an "inner monitor" which gave him the authority of the gods for the correction of men. Ironic and persistent in his moral mission, he was tried for impiety and immorality and condemned to death. How he took the whole dramatic matter you may soon see from both Xenophon and Plato: he lectured his judges, flouted covert offers of clemency, rejected easy chances of escape ("Crito"), jested with the jailer, and reproached his friends for their little faith in his future and their grief over his approaching death. He lived to argue and died to prove that it is better to suffer than to inflict injustice.

.   .   .

PLATO ON SOCRATES' LIFE AND DOCTRINE

Phaedo 96–100. Lamb translation ("Loeb Classical Library" series).

". . . . When I was young, Cebes, I was tremendously eager for the kind of wisdom which they call investigation of nature. I thought it was a glorious thing to know the causes of everything, why each thing comes into being and why it perishes and why it exists; and I was always unsettling myself with such questions as these: Do heat and cold, by a sort of fermentation, bring about the organization of animals, as some people say? Is it the blood, or air, or fire by which we think? Or is it none of these, and does the brain furnish the sensations of hearing and sight and smell, and do memory and opinion arise from these, and does knowledge come from memory and opinion in a state of rest? And again I tried to find out how these things perish, and I investigated the phenomena of heaven and earth until finally I made up my mind that I was by nature totally unfitted for this kind of investigation. And I will give you a sufficient proof of this. I was so completely blinded by these studies that I lost the knowledge that I, and others also, thought I had before; I forgot what I had formerly believed I knew about many things and even about the cause of man's growth. For I had thought previously that it was plain to everyone that man grows through eating and drinking; for when, from the food he eats, flesh is added to his flesh and bones to his bones, and in the same way the appropriate thing is added to each of his other parts, then the small bulk becomes greater and the small man large. That is what I used to think. Doesn't that seem to you reasonable?"

"Yes," said Cebes.

"Now listen to this, too. I thought I was sure enough, when I saw a tall man standing by a short one, that he was, say, taller by a head than the other, and that one horse was larger by a head than another horse; and, to mention still clearer things than those, I thought ten were more than eight because two had been added to the eight, and I thought a two-cubit rule was longer than a one-cubit rule because it exceeded it by half its length."

"And now," said Cebes, "what do you think about them?"

"By Zeus," said he, "I am far from thinking that I know the cause of any of these things, I who do not even dare to say, when one is added to one, whether the one to which the addition was made has become two, or the one which was added, or the one which was added and the one to which it was added became two by the addition of each to the other. I think it is wonderful that when each of them was separate from the other, each was one and they were not then two, and when they were brought near each other this juxtaposition was the cause of their becoming two. And I cannot yet believe that if one is divided, the division causes it to become two; for this is the opposite of the cause which produced two in the former case; for then two arose because one was brought near and added to another one, and now because one is removed and separated from another. And I no longer believe that I know by this method even how one is generated or, in a word, how anything is generated or is destroyed or exists, and I no longer admit this method, but have another confused way of my own.

"Then one day I heard a man reading from a book, as he said, by Anaxagoras, that it is the mind that arranges and causes all things. I was pleased with this theory of cause, and it seemed to me to be somehow right that the mind should be the cause of all things, and I thought, 'If this is so, the mind in arranging things arranges everything and establishes each thing as it is best for it to be. So if anyone wishes to find the cause of the generation or destruction or existence of a particular thing, he must find out what sort of existence, or passive state of any kind, or activity is best for it. And therefore in respect to that particular thing, and other things too, a man need examine nothing but what is best and most excellent; for then he will necessarily know also what is inferior, since the science of both is the same.' As I considered these things I was delighted to think that I had found in Anaxagoras a teacher of the cause of things quite to my mind, and I thought he would tell me whether the earth is flat or round, and when he had told me that, would go on to explain the cause and the necessity of it, and would tell me the nature of the best and why it is best for the earth to be as it is; and if he said the earth was in the centre, he would proceed to show that it is best for it to be in the centre; and I had made up my mind that if he made those things clear to me, I would no longer yearn for any other kind of cause. And I had determined that I would find out in the same way about the sun and the moon and the other stars, their relative speed, their revolutions, and their other changes, and why the active or passive condition of each of them is for the best. For I never imagined that, when he said they were ordered by intelligence, he would introduce any other cause for these things than that it is best for them to be as they are. So I thought when he assigned the cause of each thing and of all things in common he would go on and explain what is best for each and what is good for all in common. I prized my hopes very highly, and I seized the books very eagerly and read them as fast as I could, that I might know as fast as I could about the best and the worst.

"My glorious hope, my friend, was quickly snatched away from me. As I went on with my reading I saw that the man made no use of intelligence, and did not assign any real causes for the ordering of things, but mentioned as causes air and ether and water and many other absurdities. And it seemed to me it was very much as if one should say that Socrates does with intelligence whatever he does, and then, in trying to give the causes of the particular thing I do, should say first that I am now sitting here because my body is composed of bones and sinews, and the bones are hard and have joints which divide them and the sinews can be contracted and relaxed and, with the flesh and the skin which contains them all, are laid about the bones; and so, as the bones are hung loose in their ligaments, the sinews, by relaxing and contracting, make me able to bend my limbs now, and that is the cause of my sitting here with my legs bent. Or as if in the same way he should give voice and air and hearing and countless other things of the sort as causes for our talking with each other, and should fail to mention the real causes, which are, that the Athenians decided that it was best to condemn me, and therefore I have decided that it was best for me to sit here and that it is right for me to stay and undergo whatever penalty they order. For, by Dog, I fancy these bones and sinews of mine would have been in Megara or Boeotia long ago, carried thither by an opinion of what was best, if I did not think it was better and nobler to endure any penalty the city may inflict rather than to escape and run away. But it is most absurd to call things of that sort causes. If anyone were to say that I could not have done what I thought proper if I had not bones and sinews and other things that I have, he would be right. But to say that those things are the cause of my doing what I do, and that I act with intelligence but not from the choice of what is best, would be an extremely careless way of talking. Whoever talks in that way is unable to make a distinction and to see that in reality a cause is one thing, and the thing without which the cause could never be a cause is quite another thing. And so it seems to me that most people, when they give the name of cause to the latter, are groping in the dark, as it were, and are giving it a name that does not belong to it. And so one man makes the earth stay below the heavens by putting a vortex about it, and another regards the earth as a flat trough supported on a foundation of air; but they do not look for the power which causes things to be now placed as it is best for them to be placed, nor do they think it has any divine force, but they think they can find a new Atlas more powerful and more immortal and more all-embracing than this, and in truth they give no thought to the good, which must embrace and hold together all things. Now I would gladly be the pupil of anyone who would teach me the nature of such a cause; but since that was denied me and I was not able to discover it myself or to learn of it from anyone else, do you wish me, Cebes," said he, "to give you an account of the way in which I have conducted my second voyage in quest of the cause?"

"I wish it with all my heart," he replied.

"After this, then," said he, "since I had given up investigating realities, I decided that I must be careful not to suffer the misfortune which happens to people who look at the sun and watch it during an eclipse. For some of them ruin their eyes unless they

look at its image in water or something of the sort. I thought of
that danger, and I was afraid my soul would be blinded if I looked
at things with my eyes and tried to grasp them with any of my
senses. So I thought I must have recourse to conceptions and examine in them the truth of realities. Now perhaps my metaphor is
not quite accurate; for I do not grant in the least that he who
studies realities by means of conceptions is looking at them in
images any more than he who studies them in the facts of daily
life. However, that is the way I began. I assume in each case
some principle which I consider strongest, and whatever seems to
me to agree with this, whether relating to cause or to anything
else, I regard as true, and whatever disagrees with it, as untrue.
But I want to tell you more clearly what I mean; for I think you do
not understand now."

"Not very well, certainly," said Cebes.

"Well," said Socrates, "this is what I mean. It is nothing new,
but the same thing I have always been saying, both in our previous
conversation and elsewhere. I am going to try to explain to you
the nature of that cause which I have been studying, and I will revert to those familiar subjects of ours as my point of departure and
assume that there are such things as absolute beauty and good and
greatness and the like. If you grant this and agree that these exist,
I believe I shall explain cause to you and shall prove that the soul
is immortal."

"You may assume," said Cebes, "that I grant it, and go on."

"Then," said he, "see if you agree with me in the next step. I
think that if anything is beautiful it is beautiful for no other
reason than because it partakes of absolute beauty; and this applies
to everything. Do you assent to this view of cause?"

"I do," said he.

"Now I do not yet, understand," he went on, "nor can I perceive those other ingenious causes. If anyone tells me that what
makes a thing beautiful is its lovely colour, or its shape or anything
else of the sort, I let all that go, for all those things confuse me,
and I hold simply and plainly and perhaps foolishly to this, that
nothing else makes it beautiful but the presence or communion
(call it which you please) of absolute beauty, however it may have
been gained; about the way in which it happens, I make no positive statement as yet, but I do insist that beautiful things are

made beautiful by beauty. For I think this is the safest answer I
can give to myself or to others, and if I cleave fast to this, I think
I shall never be overthrown, and I believe it is safe for me or anyone else to give this answer, that beautiful things are beautiful
through beauty. Do you agree?"

"I do."

PLATO'S *APOLOGY:* SOCRATES AT HIS TRIAL[1]

Fowler translation ("Loeb Classical Library" series).

How you, men of Athens, have been affected by my accusers, I
do not know; but I, for my part, almost forgot my own identity, so
persuasively did they talk; and yet there is hardly a word of truth
in what they have said. But I was most amazed by one of the
many lies that they told—when they said that you must be on your
guard not to be deceived by me, because I was a clever speaker.
For I thought it the most shameless part of their conduct that

[1] In the spring of 399 B.C., when Socrates was seventy years old, he was accused
of impiety and of corrupting the youth. The chief accuser was Meletus, who was
seconded by Anytus and Lycon. In the *Euthyphro* Meletus is spoken of as an insig-
nificant youth, and in the *Apology* he is said to have been incensed by Socrates' criticism of the poets. Nothing further is known of him, though he may be identical with
the Meletus mentioned in the *Frogs* of Aristophanes as a poet of *Skolia.* The
statement of Diodorus Siculus, that the Athenians, overcome by repentance for
their injustice to Socrates, put Meletus and Anytus to death, deserves no credence.
Anytus, who is one of the characters in the *Meno*, was a man of substance,
who had served as general of the Athenian armies and had recently been active
in expelling the Thirty Tyrants. He was a bitter enemy of all the sophists,
and, according to the author of the *Apology* attributed to Xenophon, he had been
irritated by Socrates' criticism of his conduct in employing his son in his tannery,
when the young man was fitted for higher things. Lycon was charged by the comic
poet Eupolis with being of foreign descent, and the comic poet Cratinus refers to his
poverty and effeminacy, though Aristophanes (*Wasps*, 1301) mentions him among
aristocrats. He seems to have been a person of no great importance.

Cases involving religion came under the jurisdiction of the King Archon, to whom
Meletus submitted his indictment of Socrates (see the beginning of the *Euthyphro*),
and such cases, like others, were tried before the heliastic court, which consisted
altogether of six thousand citizens chosen by lot, six hundred from each of the ten
tribes. The court did not, however, usually sit as a whole, but was divided, so that
cases were tried before smaller bodies, consisting generally of five hundred jurymen
or judges, though sometimes the number was less, as four hundred or two hundred,
and sometimes more, as one thousand. One additional judge was added to these even
numbers to avoid a tie. Socrates was tried before a court of 501 (*Apology*, 36 A). If
the accuser did not receive a fifth part of the votes cast in a case of this kind, he was
subject to a fine of 1000 drachmae (about £35 or $175). No penalty was prescribed

they are not ashamed because they will immediately be convicted
by me of falsehood by the evidence of fact, when I show myself to
be not in the least a clever speaker, unless indeed they call him a
clever speaker who speaks the truth; for if this is what they mean,
I would agree that I am an orator—not after their fashion. Now
they, as I say, have said little or nothing true; but you shall hear
from me nothing but the truth. Not, however, men of Athens,
speeches finely tricked out with words and phrases, as theirs are,
nor carefully arranged, but you will hear things said at random
with the words that happen to occur to me. For I trust that what
I say is just; and let none of you expect anything else. For surely
it would not be fitting for one of my age to come before you like a
youngster making up speeches. And, men of Athens, I urgently
beg and beseech you if you hear me making my defence with the
same words with which I have been accustomed to speak both
in the market place at the bankers' tables, where many of you
have heard me, and elsewhere, not to be surprised or to make a dis-

---

by law for the offence with which Socrates was charged. After Socrates was found
guilty the penalty still remained to be determined. The rule was that the accused,
after conviction, should propose a counter penalty, the court being obliged to choose
one of the two penalties proposed (*Apology*, 36 B–38 B); no compromise was permitted.

The question has frequently been asked, whether the *Apology* is substantially
the speech made by Socrates before the court or a product of Plato's imagination.
In all probability it is essentially the speech delivered by Socrates, though it may
well be that the actual speech was less finished and less charming than that which
Plato has reported. The legal procedure is strictly followed, and the manner of
speech is that which was, as we know from Plato and also from Xenophon, usual
with Socrates. There is nothing inconsistent with what we know of Socrates, and no
peculiarly Platonic doctrine is suggested. The purpose of the dialogue, or rather, of
the speech, for it is hardly a dialogue, is to present Socrates in a true and favourable
light to posterity, and that end could hardly be gained by publishing a fiction as the
speech which many Athenians must have remembered at the time of publication,
which was, in all probability, not long after the trial.

In form the *Apology*, if we disregard the two short addresses after the conviction
and the condemnation, follows the rules in vogue for public speeches. A brief introduction is followed by the narrative and argument, after which the speech closes with
a brief appeal to the judges and to God (36 D). It conforms to Plato's own rule
(*Phaedrus*, 264 C), that every discourse should, like a living being, have its middle
parts and its members, all in proper agreement with each other and with the whole,
which is, after all, the rule of common sense, followed for the most part even by those
teachers of rhetoric whose elaborate subdivisions and high-sounding nomenclature
Plato ridicules in the *Phaedrus* (266 E–267 D). The two shorter addresses after the
case had been decided against Socrates cannot be expected to stand as independent
and complete speeches; they are, and must be, treated as supplementary and sub-

turbance on this account. For the fact is that this is the first time I have come before the court, although I am seventy years old; I am therefore an utter foreigner to the manner of speech here. Hence, just as you would, of course, if I were really a foreigner, pardon me if I spoke in that dialect and that manner in which I had been brought up, so now I make this request of you, a fair one, as it seems to me, that you disregard the manner of my speech—for perhaps it might be worse and perhaps better—and observe and pay attention merely to this, whether what I say is just or not; for that is the virtue of a judge, and an orator's virtue is to speak the truth.

First then it is right for me to defend myself against the first false accusations brought against me, and the first accusers, and then against the later accusations and the later accusers. For many accusers have risen up against me before you, who have been speaking for a long time, many years already, and saying nothing true; and I fear them more than Anytus and the rest, though these also are dangerous; but those others are more dangerous, gentle-

---

ordinate to the speech delivered before the first adverse vote. Yet they are symmetrically arranged and their topics are skilfully presented. A peroration would hardly be appropriate before the last of these and the last itself needs no formal introduction; it serves as a fitting conclusion for the entire discourse. As such it is a brilliant example of oratorical composition.

The high moral character and genuine religious faith of Socrates are made abundantly clear throughout this whole discourse. It would seem almost incredible that the Athenian court voted for his condemnation, if we did not know the fact. His condemnation is to be explained by the general hostility to the sophists. Socrates was, to be sure, not a sophist, though Aristophanes in the *Clouds* selects him as the representative of that profession to be ridiculed. He did not teach for pay and did not promise any definite result from his instruction. He did not investigate natural phenomena or claim to ensure the political or financial success of his hearers; his aim was to show the way to righteousness, to the perfection of the individual soul. This seems harmless enough, but Socrates endeavoured to lead men to righteousness by making them think, and thinking, especially on matters of religion, is not welcomed by the slothful or the conservative. The mere fact that he was a leader of thought caused Socrates to be confounded with the sophists who were also leaders of thought, and were, chiefly, perhaps, for that reason, regarded with suspicion and hostility. Moreover, Socrates claimed to possess a *daimonion*, or spiritual monitor, which guided his actions. He did not, so far as we know, attribute a distinct personality to this inner voice, but his belief in it caused him to be accused of introducing "new spiritual beings" or divinities and of disbelieving in the gods of the state, although he was apparently punctilious in religious observances. His method had also, without doubt, aroused many personal antagonisms (*Apology*, 21 c–23 a). Probably Meletus and the judges who voted for the condemnation of Socrates believed that they were acting in the interest of religion and piety, though their verdict has not been approved by later generations.

men, who gained your belief, since they got hold of most of you in childhood, and accused me without any truth, saying, "There is a certain Socrates, a wise man, a ponderer over the things in the air and one who has investigated the things beneath the earth and who makes the weaker argument the stronger." These, men of Athens, who have spread abroad this report, are my dangerous enemies. For those who hear them think that men who investigate these matters do not even believe in gods. Besides, these accusers are many and have been making their accusations already for a long time, and moreover they spoke to you at an age at which you would believe them most readily (some of you in youth, most of you in childhood), and the case they prosecuted went utterly by default, since nobody appeared in defence. But the most unreasonable thing of all is this, that it is not even possible to know and speak their names, except when one of them happens to be a writer of comedies. And all those who persuaded you by means of envy and slander—and some also persuaded others because they had been themselves persuaded—all these are most difficult to cope with; for it is not even possible to call any of them up here and cross-question him, but I am compelled in making my defence to fight, as it were, absolutely with shadows and to cross-question when nobody answers. Be kind enough, then, to bear in mind, as I say, that there are two classes of my accusers—one those who have just brought their accusation, the other those who, as I was just saying, brought it long ago, and consider that I must defend myself first against the latter; for you heard them making their charges first and with much greater force than these who made them later. Well, then, I must make a defence, men of Athens, and must try in so short a time to remove from you this prejudice which you have been for so long a time acquiring. Now I wish that this might turn out so, if it is better for you and for me, and that I might succeed with my defence; but I think it is difficult, and I am not at all deceived about its nature. But nevertheless, let this be as is pleasing to god, the law must be obeyed and I must make a defence.

Now let us take up from the beginning the question, what the accusation is from which the false prejudice against me has arisen, in which Meletus trusted when he brought this suit against me. What did those who aroused the prejudice say to arouse it? I must, as it were, read their sworn statement as if they were plaintiffs: "Socrates is a criminal and a busybody, investigating the things beneath the earth and in the heavens and making the weaker argument stronger and teaching others these same things." Something of that sort it is. For you yourselves saw these things in Aristophanes' comedy, a Socrates being carried about there, proclaiming that he was treading on air and uttering a vast deal of other nonsense, about which I know nothing, either much or little. And I say this, not to cast dishonour upon such knowledge, if anyone is wise about such matters (may I never have to defend myself against Meletus on so great a charge as that!),—but I, men of Athens, have nothing to do with these things. And I offer as witnesses most of yourselves, and I ask you to inform one another and to tell, all those of you who ever heard me conversing—and there are many such among you—now tell, if anyone ever heard me talking much or little about such matters. And from this you will perceive that such are also the other things that the multitude say about me.

But in fact none of these things are true, and if you have heard from anyone that I undertake to teach people and that I make money by it, that is not true either. Although this also seems to me to be a fine thing, if one might be able to teach people, as Gorgias of Leontini and Prodicus of Ceos and Hippias of Elis are. For each of these men, gentlemen, is able to go into any one of the cities and persuade the young men, who can associate for nothing with whomsoever they wish among their own fellow citizens, to give up the association with those men and to associate with them and pay them money and be grateful besides.

And there is also another wise man here, a Parian, who I learned was in town; for I happened to meet a man who has spent more on sophists than all the rest, Callias, the son of Hipponicus; so I asked him—for he has two sons—"Callias," said I, "if your two sons had happened to be two colts or two calves, we should be able to get and hire for them an overseer who would make them excellent in the kind of excellence proper to them; and he would be a horse-trainer or a husbandman; but now, since they are two human beings, whom have you in mind to get as overseer? Who has knowledge of that kind of excellence, that of a man and a citizen? For I think you have looked into the matter, because you have the sons.

Is there anyone," said I, "or not?" "Certainly," said he. "Who," said I, "and where from, and what is his price for his teaching?" "Evenus," he said, "Socrates, from Paros, five minae." And I called Evenus blessed, if he really had this art and taught so reasonably. I myself should be vain and put on airs, if I understood these things; but I do not understand them, men of Athens.

Now perhaps someone might rejoin: "But, Socrates, what is the trouble about you? Whence have these prejudices against you arisen? For certainly this great report and talk has not arisen while you were doing nothing more out of the way than the rest, unless you were doing something other than most people; so tell us what it is, that we may not act unadvisedly in your case." The man who says this seems to me to be right, and I will try to show you what it is that has brought about my reputation and aroused the prejudice against me. So listen. And perhaps I shall seem to some of you to be joking; be assured, however, I shall speak perfect truth to you.

The fact is, men of Athens, that I have acquired this reputation on account of nothing else than a sort of wisdom. What kind of wisdom is this? Just that which is perhaps human wisdom. For perhaps I really am wise in this wisdom; and these men, perhaps, of whom I was just speaking, might be wise in some wisdom greater than human, or I don't know what to say; for I do not understand it, and whoever says I do, is lying and speaking to arouse prejudice against me. And, men of Athens, do not interrupt me with noise, even if I seem to you to be boasting; for the word which I speak is not mine, but the speaker to whom I shall refer it is a person of weight. For of my wisdom—if it is wisdom at all— and of its nature, I will offer you the god of Delphi as a witness. You know Chaerephon, I fancy. He was my comrade from a youth and the comrade of your democratic party, and shared in the recent exile and came back with you. And you know the kind of man Chaerephon was, how impetuous in whatever he undertook. Well, once he went to Delphi and made so bold as to ask the oracle this question; and, gentlemen, don't make a disturbance at what I say; for he asked if there were anyone wiser than I. Now the Pythia replied that there was no one wiser. And about these things his brother here will bear you witness, since Chaerephon is dead.

But see why I say these things; for I am going to tell you whence the prejudice against me has arisen. For when I heard this, I thought to myself: "What in the world does the god mean, and what riddle is he propounding? For I am conscious that I am not wise either much or little. What then does he mean by declaring that I am the wisest? He certainly cannot be lying, for that is not possible for him." And for a long time I was at a loss as to what he meant; then with great reluctance I proceeded to investigate him somewhat as follows.

I went to one of those who had a reputation for wisdom, thinking that there, if anywhere, I should prove the utterance wrong and should show the oracle "This man is wiser than I, but you said I was wisest." So examining this man—for I need not call him by name, but it was one of the public men with regard to whom I had this kind of experience, men of Athens—and conversing with him, this man seemed to me to seem to be wise to many other people and especially to himself, but not to be so; and then I tried to show him that he thought he was wise, but was not. As a result, I became hateful to him and to many of those present; and so, as I went away, I thought to myself, "I am wiser than this man; for neither of us really knows anything fine and good, but this man thinks he knows something when he does not, whereas I, as I do not know anything, do not think I do either. I seem, then, in just this little thing to be wiser than this man at any rate, that what I do not know I do not think I know either." From him I went to another of those who were reputed to be wiser than he, and these same things seemed to me to be true; and there I became hateful both to him and to many others.

After this then I went on from one to another, perceiving that I was hated, and grieving and fearing, but nevertheless I thought I must consider the god's business of the highest importance. So I had to go, investigating the meaning of the oracle, to all those who were reputed to know anything. And by the Dog, men of Athens—for I must speak the truth to you—this, I do declare, was my experience: those who had the most reputation seemed to me to be almost the most deficient, as I investigated at the god's behest, and others who were of less repute seemed to be superior men in the matter of being sensible. So I must relate to you my wandering as I performed my Herculean labours, so to speak, in order that the oracle might be proved to be irrefutable. For after the public men I went to the poets, those of tragedies, and those of dithyrambs, and the rest, thinking that there I should prove by actual test that I was less learned than they. So, taking up the poems of theirs that seemed to me to have been most carefully elaborated by them, I asked them what they meant, that I might at the same time learn something from them. Now I am ashamed to tell you the truth, gentlemen; but still it must be told. For there was hardly a man present, one might say, who would not speak better than they about the poems they themselves had composed. So again in the case of the poets also I presently recognised this, that what they composed they composed not by wisdom, but by nature and because they were inspired, like the prophets and givers of oracles; for these also say many fine things, but know none of the things they say; it was evident to me that the poets too had experienced something of this same sort. And at the same time I perceived that they, on account of their poetry, thought that they were the wisest of men in other things as well, in which they were not. So I went away from them also thinking that I was superior to them in the same thing in which I excelled the public men.

Finally then I went to the hand-workers. For I was conscious that I knew practically nothing, but I knew I should find that they knew many fine things. And in this I was not deceived; they did know what I did not, and in this way they were wiser than I. But, men of Athens, the good artisans also seemed to me to have the same failing as the poets; because of practising his art well, each one thought he was very wise in the other most important matters, and this folly of theirs obscured that wisdom, so that I asked myself in behalf of the oracle whether I should prefer to be as I am, neither wise in their wisdom nor foolish in their folly, or to be in both respects as they are. I replied then to myself and to the oracle that it was better for me to be as I am.

Now from this investigation, men of Athens, many enmities have arisen against me, and such as are most harsh and grievous, so that many prejudices have resulted from them and I am called a wise man. For on each occasion those who are present think I am wise in the matters in which I confute someone else; but the fact is, gentlemen, it is likely that the god is really wise and by his oracle means this: "Human wisdom is of little or no value." And it appears that he does not really say this of Socrates, but merely uses my name, and makes me an example, as if he were to say: "This one of you, O human beings, is wisest, who, like Socrates, recognises that he is in truth of no account in respect to wisdom."

Therefore I am still even now going about and searching and investigating at the god's behest anyone, whether citizen or foreigner, who I think is wise; and when he does not seem so to me, I give aid to the god and show that he is not wise. And by reason of this occupation I have no leisure to attend to any of the affairs of the state worth mentioning, or of my own, but am in vast poverty on account of my service to the god.

And in addition to these things, the young men who have the most leisure, the sons of the richest men, accompany me of their own accord, find pleasure in hearing people being examined, and often imitate me themselves, and then they undertake to examine others; and then, I fancy, they find a great plenty of people who think they know something, but know little or nothing. As a result, therefore, those who are examined by them are angry with me, instead of being angry with themselves, and say that "Socrates is a most abominable person and is corrupting the youth."

And when anyone asks them "by doing or teaching what?" they have nothing to say, but they do not know, and that they may not seem to be at a loss, they say these things that are handy to say against all the philosophers, "the things in the air and the things beneath the earth" and "not to believe in the gods" and "to make the weaker argument the stronger." For they would not, I fancy, care to say the truth, that it is being made very clear that they pretend to know, but know nothing. Since, then, they are jealous of their honour and energetic and numerous and speak concertedly and persuasively about me, they have filled your ears both long ago and now with vehement slanders. From among them Meletus attacked me, and Anytus and Lycon, Meletus angered on account of the poets, and Anytus on account of the artisans and the public men, and Lycon on account of the orators; so that, as I said in the beginning, I should be surprised if I were able to remove this prejudice from you in so short a time when it has grown so great. There you have the truth, men of Athens, and I speak without hiding anything from you, great or small or prevaricating. And yet I know pretty well that I am making myself hated by just that conduct; which is also a proof that I am speaking the truth and that this is the prejudice against me and these are its causes. And whether you investigate this now or hereafter, you will find that it is so.

Now so far as the accusations are concerned which my first accusers made against me, this is a sufficient defence before you; but against Meletus, the good and patriotic, as he says, and the later ones, I will try to defend myself next. So once more, as if these were another set of accusers, let us take up in turn their sworn statement. It is about as follows: it states that Socrates is a wrongdoer because he corrupts the youth and does not believe in the gods the state believes in, but in other new spiritual beings.

Such is the accusation. But let us examine each point of this accusation. He says I am a wrongdoer because I corrupt the youth. But I, men of Athens, say Meletus is a wrongdoer, because he jokes in earnest, lightly involving people in a lawsuit, pretending to be zealous and concerned about things for which he never cared at all. And that this is so I will try to make plain to you also.

Come here, Meletus, tell me: don't you consider it of great importance that the youth be as good as possible? "I do." Come now, tell these gentlemen who makes them better? For it is evident that you know, since you care about it. For you have found the one who corrupts them, as you say, and you bring me before these gentlemen and accuse me; and now, come, tell who makes them better and inform them who he is. Do you see, Meletus, that you are silent and cannot tell? And yet does it not seem to you disgraceful and a sufficient proof of what I say, that you have never cared about it? But tell, my good man, who makes them better? "The laws." But that is not what I ask, most excellent one, but what man, who knows in the first place just this very thing, the laws. "These men, Socrates, the judges." What are you saying, Meletus? Are these gentlemen able to instruct the youth, and do they make them better? "Certainly." All, or some of them and others not? "All." Well said, by Hera, and this is a great plenty of helpers you speak of. But how about this? Do these listeners make them better, or not? "These also." And how about the senators? "The senators also." But, Meletus, those in the assembly, the assembly-men, don't corrupt the youth, do they? or

do they also all make them better? "They also." All the Athenians, then, as it seems, make them excellent, except myself, and I
alone corrupt them. Is this what you mean? "Very decidedly,
that is what I mean." You have condemned me to great unhappi-
ness! But answer me; does it seem to you to be so in the case of
horses, that those who make them better are all mankind, and he
who injures them some one person? Or, quite the opposite of this,
that he who is able to make them better is some one person, or very
few, the horse-trainers, whereas most people, if they have to do
with and use horses, injure them? Is it not so, Meletus, both in the
case of horses and in that of all other animals? Certainly it is,
whether you and Anytus deny it or agree; for it would be a great
state of blessedness in the case of the youth if one alone corrupts
them, and the others do them good. But, Meletus, you show clearly
enough that you never thought about the youth, and you exhibit
plainly your own carelessness, that you have not cared at all for
the things about which you hale me into court.

But besides, tell us, for heaven's sake, Meletus, is it better to
live among good citizens, or bad? My friend, answer; for I am not
asking anything hard. Do not the bad do some evil to those who are
with them at any time and the good some good? "Certainly." Is
there then anyone who prefers to be injured by his associates
rather than benefited? Answer, my good man; for the law orders
you to answer. Is there anyone who prefers to be injured? "Of
course not." Come then, do you hale me in here on the ground
that I am corrupting the youth and making them worse voluntarily or involuntarily? "Voluntarily I say." What then, Meletus?
Are you at your age so much wiser than I at my age, that you have
recognized that the evil always do some evil to those nearest them,
and the good some good; whereas I have reached such a depth of
ignorance that I do not even know this, that if I make anyone of
my associates bad I am in danger of getting some harm from him,
so that I do this great evil voluntarily, as you say? I don't believe
this, Meletus, nor do I think anyone else in the world does! but
either I do not corrupt them, or if I corrupt them, I do it involuntarily, so that you are lying in both events. But if I corrupt them
involuntarily, for such involuntary errors the law is not to hale
people into court, but to take them and instruct and admonish
them in private. For it is clear that if I am told about it, I shall

stop doing that which I do involuntarily. But you avoided associating with me and instructing me, and were unwilling to do so, but you hale me in here, where it is the law to hale in those who need punishment, not instruction.

But enough of this, for, men of Athens, this is clear, as I said, that Meletus never cared much or little for these things. But nevertheless, tell us, how do you say, Meletus, that I corrupt the youth? Or is it evident, according to the indictment you brought, that it is by teaching them not to believe in the gods the state believes in, but in other new spiritual beings? Do you not say that it is by teaching this that I corrupt them? "Very decidedly that is what I say." Then, Meletus, for the sake of these very gods about whom our speech now is, speak still more clearly both to me and to these gentlemen. For I am unable to understand whether you say that I teach that there are some gods, and myself then believe that there are some gods, and am not altogether godless and am not a wrong-doer in that way, that these, however, are not the gods whom the state believes in, but others, and this is what you accuse me for, that I believe in others; or you say that I do not myself believe in gods at all and that I teach this unbelief to other people. "That is what I say, that you do not believe in gods at all." You amaze me, Meletus! Why do you say this? Do I not even believe that the sun or yet the moon are gods, as the rest of mankind do? "No, by Zeus, judges, since he say that the sun is a stone and the moon earth." Do you think you are accusing Anaxagoras, my dear Meletus, and do you so despise these gentlemen and think they are so unversed in letters as not to know that the books of Anaxagoras the Clazomenian are full of such utterances? And forsooth the youth learn these doctrines from me, which they can buy sometimes (if the price is high) for a drachma in the orchestra and laugh at Socrates, if he pretends they are his own, especially when they are so absurd! But for heaven's sake, do you think this of me, that I do not believe there is any god? "No, by Zeus, you don't, not in the least." You cannot be believed, Meletus, not even, as it seems to me, by yourself. For this man appears to me, men of Athens, to be very violent and unrestrained, and actually to have brought this indictment in a spirit of violence and unrestraint and rashness. For he seems, as it were, by composing a puzzle to be making a test: "Will Socrates, the wise man, recognize that I am joking and contradicting myself, or shall I deceive him and the others who hear me?" For he appears to me to contradict himself in his speech, as if he were to say, "Socrates is a wrongdoer, because he does not believe in gods, but does believe in gods." And yet this is the conduct of a jester.

Join me, then, gentlemen, in examining how he appears to me to say this; and do you, Meletus, answer; and you, gentlemen, as I asked you in the beginning, please bear in mind not to make a disturbance if I conduct my argument in my accustomed manner.

Is there any human being who believes that there are things pertaining to human beings, but no human beings? Let him answer, gentlemen, and not make a disturbance in one way or another. Is there anyone who does not believe in horses, but does believe in things pertaining to horses? or who does not believe that flute-players exist, but that things pertaining to flute-players do? There is not, best of men; if you do not wish to answer, I say it to you and these others here. But answer at least the next question. Is there anyone who believes spiritual things exist, but does not believe in spirits? "There is not." Thank you for replying reluctantly when forced by these gentlemen. Then you say that I believe in spiritual beings, whether new or old, and teach that belief; but then I believe in spiritual beings at any rate, according to your statement, and you swore to that in your indictment. But if I believe in spiritual beings, it is quite inevitable that I believe also in spirits; is it not so? It is; for I assume that you agree, since you do not answer. But do we not think the spirits are gods or children of gods? Yes, or no? "Certainly." Then if I believe in spirits, as you say, if spirits are a kind of gods, that would be the puzzle and joke which I say you are uttering in saying that I, while I do not believe in gods, do believe in gods again, since I believe in spirits; but if, on the other hand, spirits are a kind of bastard children of gods, by nymphs or by any others, whoever their mothers are said to be, what man would believe that there are children of gods, but no gods? It would be just as absurd as if one were to believe that there are children of horses and asses, namely mules, but no horses and asses. But, Meletus, you certainly must have brought this suit either to make a test of us or because you were at a loss as to what true wrongdoing you could accuse me of; but there is no way for you to persuade any man who has even a little sense that it is possible for the same person to believe in spiritual and divine existences and again for the same person not to believe in spirits or gods or heroes.

Well then, men of Athens, that I am not a wrongdoer according to Meletus's indictment, seems to me not to need much of a defence, but what has been said is enough. But you may be assured that what I said before is true, that great hatred has arisen against me and in the minds of many persons. And this it is which will cause my condemnation, if it is to cause it, not Meletus or Anytus, but the prejudice and dislike of the many. This has condemned many other good men, and I think will do so; and there is no danger that it will stop with me. But perhaps someone might say: "Are you then not ashamed, Socrates, of having followed such a pursuit, that you are now in danger of being put to death as a result?" But I should make to him a just reply: "You do not speak well, Sir, if you think a man in whom there is even a little merit ought to consider danger of life or death, and not rather regard this only, when he does things, whether the things he does are right or wrong and the acts of a good or a bad man. For according to your argument all the demigods would be bad who died at Troy, including the son of Thetis, who so despised danger, in comparison with enduring any disgrace, that when his mother (and she was a goddess) said to him, as he was eager to slay Hector, something like this, I believe, 'My son, if you avenge the death of your friend Patroclus and kill Hector, you yourself shall die; "for straightway," ' she says, ' "after Hector, is death appointed unto thee" '; he, when he heard this, made light of death and danger, and feared much more to live as a coward and not to avenge his friends, and 'Straightway,' said he, 'may I die, after doing vengeance upon the wrongdoer, that I may not stay here, jeered at beside the curved ships, a burden of the earth.' Do you think he considered death and danger?"

For thus it is, men of Athens, in truth; wherever a man stations himself, thinking it is best to be there, or is stationed by his commander, there he must, as it seems to me, remain and run his risks, considering neither death nor any other thing more than disgrace.

So I should have done a terrible thing, if, when the commanders whom you chose to command me stationed me, both at Potidaea and at Amphipolis and at Delium, I remained where they stationed me, like anybody else, and ran the risk of death, but when the god gave me a station, as I believed and understood, with orders to spend my life in philosophy and in examining myself and others, then I were to desert my post through fear of death or anything else whatsoever. It would be a terrible thing, and truly one might then justly hale me into court, on the charge that I do not believe that there are gods, since I disobey the oracle and fear death and think I am wise when I am not. For to fear death, gentlemen, is nothing else than to think one is wise when one is not; for it is thinking one knows what one does not know. For no one knows whether death be not even the greatest of all blessings to man, but they fear it as if they knew that it is the greatest of evils. And is not this the most reprehensible form of ignorance, that of thinking one knows what one does not know? Perhaps, gentlemen, in this matter also I differ from other men in this way, and if I were to say that I am wiser in anything, it would be in this, that not knowing very much about the other world, I do not think I know. But I do know that it is evil and disgraceful to do wrong and to disobey him who is better than I, whether he be god or man. So I shall never fear or avoid those things concerning which I do not know whether they are good or bad rather than those which I know are bad. And therefore, even if you acquit me now and are not convinced by Anytus, who said that either I ought not to have been brought to trial at all, or since I was brought to trial, I must certainly be put to death, adding that if I were acquitted your sons would all be utterly ruined by practising what I teach—if you should say to me in reply to this: "Socrates, this time we will not do as Anytus says, but we will let you go, on this condition, however, that you no longer spend your time in this investigation or in philosophy, and if you are caught doing so again you shall die"; if you should let me go on this condition which I have mentioned, I should say to you, "Men of Athens, I respect and love you, but I shall obey the god rather than you, and while I live and am able to continue, I shall never give up philosophy or stop exhorting you and pointing out the truth to any one of you whom I may meet, saying in my accustomed way: "Most excellent man, are you who are a citizen of Athens, the greatest of cities and the most famous for wisdom and power, not ashamed to care for the acquisition of wealth and for reputation and honour, when you neither care nor take thought for wisdom and truth and the perfection of your soul?" And if any of you argues the point, and says he does care, I shall not let him go at once, nor shall I go away, but I shall question and examine and cross-examine him, and if I find that he does not possess virtue, but says he does, I shall rebuke him for scorning the things that are of most importance and caring more for what is of less worth. This I shall do to whomever I meet, young and old, foreigner and citizen, but most to the citizens, inasmuch as you are more nearly related to me. For know that the god commands me to do this, and I believe that no greater good ever came to pass in the city than my service to the god. For I go about doing nothing else than urging you, young and old, not to care for your persons or your property more than for the perfection of your souls, or even so much; and I tell you that virtue does not come from money, but from virtue comes money and all other good things to man, both to the individual and to the state. If by saying these things I corrupt the youth, these things must be injurious; but if anyone asserts that I say other things than these, he says what is untrue. Therefore I say to you, men of Athens, either do as Anytus tells you, or not, and either acquit me, or not, knowing that I shall not change my conduct even if I am to die many times over.

Do not make a disturbance, men of Athens; continue to do what I asked of you, not to interrupt my speech by disturbances, but to hear me; and I believe you will profit by hearing. Now I am going to say some things to you at which you will perhaps cry out; but do not do so by any means. For know that if you kill me, I being such a man as I say I am, you will not injure me so much as yourselves; for neither Meletus nor Anytus could injure me; that would be impossible, for I believe it is not god's will that a better man be injured by a worse. He might, however, perhaps kill me or banish me or disfranchise me; and perhaps he thinks he would thus inflict great injuries upon me, and others may think so, but I do not; I think he does himself a much greater injury by doing what he is doing now—killing a man unjustly. And so, men of Athens, I am now making my defence not for my own sake, as one might imagine, but far more for yours, that you may not by condemning me err in your treatment of the gift the god gave you. For if you put me to death, you will not easily find another, who, to use a rather absurd figure, attaches himself to the city as a gadfly to a horse, which, though large and well bred, is sluggish on account of his age and needs to be aroused by stinging. I think the god fastened me upon the city in some such capacity, and I go about arousing, and urging and reproaching each one of you, constantly alighting upon you everywhere the whole day long. Such another is not likely to come to you, gentlemen; but if you take my advice, you will spare me. But you, perhaps, might be angry, like people awakened from a nap, and might slap me, as Anytus advises, and easily kill me; then you would pass the rest of your lives in slumber, unless god, in his care for you, should send someone else to sting you. And that I am, as I say, a kind of gift from the god, you might understand from this; for I have neglected all my own affairs and have been enduring the neglect of my concerns all these years, but I am always busy in your interest, coming to each one of you individually like a father or an elder brother and urging you to care for virtue; now that is not like human conduct. If I derived any profit from this and received pay for these exhortations, there would be some sense in it; but now you yourselves see that my accusers, though they accuse me of everything else in such a shameless way, have not been able to work themselves up to such a pitch of shamelessness as to produce a witness to testify that I ever exacted or asked pay of anyone. For I think I have a sufficient witness that I speak the truth, namely, my poverty.

Perhaps it may seem strange that I go about and interfere in other people's affairs to give this advice in private, but do not venture to come before your assembly and advise the state. But the reason for this, as you have heard me say at many times and places, is that something divine and spiritual comes to me, the very thing which Meletus ridiculed in his indictment. I have had this from my childhood; it is a sort of voice that comes to me, and when it comes it always holds me back from what I am thinking of doing, but never urges me forward. This it is which opposes my engaging in politics. And I think this opposition is a very good thing; for you may be quite sure, men of Athens, that if I had undertaken to go into politics, I should have been put to death long ago and should have done no good to you or to myself. And do not be angry with me for speaking the truth; the fact is that no man will save his life who nobly opposes you or any other populace and prevents many unjust and illegal things from happening in the state.

A man who really fights for the right, if he is to preserve his life for even a little while, must be a private citizen, not a public man.

I will give you powerful proofs of this, not mere words, but what you honour more—actions. And listen to what happened to me, that you may be convinced that I would never yield to any one, if that was wrong, through fear of death, but would die rather than yield. The tale I am going to tell you is ordinary and commonplace, but true. I, men of Athens, never held any other office in the state, but I was a senator; and it happened that my tribe held the presidency when you wished to judge collectively, not severally, the ten generals who had failed to gather up the slain after the naval battle; this was illegal, as you all agreed afterwards. At that time I was the only one of the prytanes who opposed doing anything contrary to the laws, and although the orators were ready to impeach and arrest me, and though you urged them with shouts to do so, I thought I must run the risk to the end with law and justice on my side, rather than join with you when your wishes were unjust, through fear of imprisonment or death.[2] That was when the democracy still existed; and after the oligarchy was established, the Thirty sent for me with four others to come to the rotunda and ordered us to bring Leon the Salaminian from Salamis to be put to death. They gave many such orders to others also, because they wished to implicate as many in their crimes as they could. Then I, however, showed again, by action, not in word only, that I did not care a whit for death if that be not too rude an expression, but that I did care with all my might not to do anything unjust or unholy. For that government, with all its power, did not frighten me into doing anything unjust, but when we came out of the rotunda, the other four went to Salamis and arrested Leon, but I simply went home; and perhaps I should have been put to death for it, if the government had not quickly been put down. Of these facts you can have many witnesses.

Do you believe that I could have lived so many years if I had been in public life and had acted as a good man should act, lending my aid to what is just and considering that of the highest importance? Far from it, men of Athens; nor could any other man. But you will find that through all my life, both in public, if I en-

---

[2] Xenophon, *Mem.* iv. 4. 2, states that Socrates, as presiding officer, refused to put the question to vote.

gaged in any public activity, and in private, I have always been the same as now, and have never yielded to any one wrongly, whether it were any other person or any of those who are said by my traducers to be my pupils. But I was never any one's teacher. If any one, whether young or old, wishes to hear me speaking and pursuing my mission, I have never objected, nor do I converse only when I am paid and not otherwise, but I offer myself alike to rich and poor; I ask questions, and whoever wishes may answer and hear what I say. And whether any of them turns out well or ill, I should not justly be held responsible, since I never promised or gave any instruction to any of them; but if any man says that he ever learned or heard anything privately from me, which all the others did not, be assured that he is lying.

But why then do some people love to spend much of their time with me? You have heard the reason, men of Athens; for I told you the whole truth; it is because they like to listen when those are examined who think they are wise and are not so; for it is amusing. But, as I believe, I have been commanded to do this by the God through oracles and dreams and in every way in which any man was ever commanded by divine power to do anything whatsoever. This, Athenians, is true and easily tested. For if I am corrupting some of the young men and have corrupted others, surely some of them who have grown older, if they recognise that I ever gave them any bad advice when they were young, ought now to have come forward to accuse me. Of if they did not wish to do it themselves, some of their relatives—fathers or brothers or other kinsfolk— ought now to tell the facts. And there are many of them present, whom I see; first Crito here, who is of my own age and my own deme and father of Critobulus, who is also present; then there is Lysanias the Sphettian, father of Aeschines, who is here; and also Antiphon of Cephisus, father of Epigenes. Then here are others whose brothers joined in my conversations, Nicostratus, son of Theozotides and brother of Theodotus (now Theodotus is dead, so he could not stop him by entreaties), and Paralus, son of Demod-ocus; Theages was his brother; and Adimantus, son of Aristo, whose brother is Plato here; and Aeantodorus, whose brother Apollodorus is present. And I can mention to you many others, some one of whom Meletus ought certainly to have produced as a witness in his speech; but if he forgot it then, let him do so now; I yield the floor to him, and let him say, if he has any such testimony. But you will find that the exact opposite is the case, gentlemen, and that they are all ready to aid me, the man who corrupts and injures their relatives, as Meletus and Anytus say. Now those who are themselves corrupted might have some motive in aiding me; but what reason could their relatives have, who are not corrupted and are already older men, unless it be the right and true reason, that they know that Meletus is lying and I am speaking the truth?

Well, gentlemen, this, and perhaps more like this, is about all I have to say in my defence. Perhaps some one among you may be offended when he remembers his own conduct, if he, even in a case of less importance than this, begged and besought the judges with many tears, and brought forward his children to arouse compassion, and many other friends and relatives; whereas I will do none of these things, though I am, apparently, in the very greatest danger. Perhaps some one with these thoughts in mind may be harshly disposed toward me and may cast his vote in anger. Now if any one of you is so disposed—I do not believe there is such a person—but if there should be, I think I should be speaking fairly if I said to him, My friend, I too have relatives, for I am, as Homer has it, "not born of an oak or a rock," but of human parents, so that I have relatives and, men of Athens, I have three sons, one nearly grown up, and two still children; but nevertheless I shall not bring any of them here and beg you to acquit me. And why shall I not do so? Not because I am stubborn, Athenians, or lack respect for you. Whether I fear death or not is another matter, but for the sake of my good name and yours and that of the whole state, I think it is not right for me to do any of these things in view of my age and my reputation, whether deserved or not; for at any rate the opinion prevails that Socrates is in some way superior to most men. If then those of you who are supposed to be superior either in wisdom or in courage or in any other virtue whatsoever are to behave in such a way, it would be disgraceful. Why, I have often seen men who have some reputation behaving in the strangest manner, when they were on trial, as if they thought they were going to suffer something terrible if they were put to death, just as if they would be immortal if you did not kill them. It seems to me that they are a disgrace to the state and that any stranger might say that those of the Athenians who excel in virtue, men whom they themselves honour with offices and other marks of esteem, are no better than women. Such acts, men of Athens, we who have any reputation at all ought not to commit, and if we commit them you ought not to allow it, but you should make it clear that you will be much more ready to condemn a man who puts before you such pitiable scenes and makes the city ridiculous than one who keeps quiet.

But apart from the question of reputation, gentlemen, I think it is not right to implore the judge or to get acquitted by begging; we ought to inform and convince him. For the judge is not here to grant favours in matters of justice, but to give judgment; and his oath binds him not to do favours according to his pleasure, but to judge according to the laws; therefore, we ought not to get you into the habit of breaking your oaths, nor ought you to fall into that habit; for neither of us would be acting piously. Do not, therefore, men of Athens, demand of me that I act before you in a way which I consider neither honourable, nor right nor pious, especially when impiety is the very thing for which Meletus here has brought me to trial. For it is plain that if by persuasion and supplication I forced you to break your oaths I should teach you to disbelieve in the existence of the gods and in making my defence should accuse myself of not believing in them. But that is far from the truth; for I do believe in them, men of Athens, more than any of my accusers, and I entrust my case to you and to god to decide it as shall be best for me and for you.

I am not grieved, men of Athens, at this vote of condemnation you have cast against me, and that for many reasons, among them the fact that your decision was not a surprise to me. I am much more surprised by the number of votes for and against it; for I did not expect so small a majority, but a large one. Now, it seems, if only thirty votes had been cast the other way, I should have been acquitted. And so, I think, so far as Meletus is concerned, I have even now been acquitted, and not merely acquitted, but anyone can see that, if Anytus and Lycon had not come forward to accuse me, he would have been fined a thousand drachmas for not receiving a fifth part of the votes.

And so the man proposes the penalty of death. Well, then, what shall I propose as an alternative? Clearly that which I deserve, shall I not? And what do I deserve to suffer or to pay, because in my life I did not keep quiet, but neglecting what most men care for—money-making and property, and military offices, and public speaking, and the various offices and plots and parties that come up in the state—and thinking that I was really too honourable to engage in those activities and live, refrained from those things by which I should have been of no use to you or to myself, and devoted myself to conferring upon each citizen individually what I regard as the greatest benefit? For I tried to persuade each of you to care for himself and his own perfection in goodness and wisdom rather than for any of his belongings, and for the state itself rather than for its interests, and to follow the same method in his care for other things. What, then, does such a man as I deserve? Some good thing, men of Athens, if I must propose something truly in accordance with my deserts; and the good thing should be such as is fitting for me. Now what is fitting for a poor man who is your benefactor, and who needs leisure to exhort you? There is nothing, men of Athens, so fitting as that such a man be given his meals in the prytaneum. That is much more appropriate for me than for any of you who has won a race at the Olympic games with a pair of horses or a four-in-hand. For he makes you seem to be happy, whereas I make you happy in reality; and he is not at all in need of sustenance, but I am needy. So if I must propose a penalty in accordance with my deserts, I propose maintenance in the prytaneum.

Perhaps some of you think that in saying this, as in what I said about lamenting and imploring, I am speaking in a spirit of bravado; but that is not the case. The truth is rather that I am convinced that I never intentionally wronged any one; but I cannot convince you of this, for we have conversed with each other only a little while. I believe if you had a law, as some other people have, that capital cases should not be decided in one day, but only after several days, you would be convinced; but now it is not easy to rid you of great prejudices in a short time. Since, then, I am convinced that I never wronged any one, I am certainly not going to wrong myself, and to say of myself that I deserve anything bad, and to propose any penalty of that sort for myself. Why should I?

Through fear of the penalty that Meletus proposes, about which I say that I do not know whether it is a good thing or an evil? Shall I choose instead of that something which I know to be an evil? What penalty shall I propose? Imprisonment? And why should I live in prison a slave to those who may be in authority? Or shall I propose a fine, with imprisonment until it is paid? But that is the same as what I said just now, for I have no money to pay with. Shall I then propose exile as my penalty? Perhaps you would accept that. I must indeed be possessed by a great love of life if I am so irrational as not to know that if you, who are my fellow citizens, could not endure my conversation and my words, but found them too irksome and disagreeable, so that you are now seeking to be rid of them, others will not be willing to endure them. No, men of Athens, they certainly will not. A fine life I should lead if I went away at my time of life, wandering from city to city and always being driven out! For well I know that wherever I go, the young men will listen to my talk, as they do here; and if I drive them away, they will themselves persuade their elders to drive me out, and if I do not drive them away, their fathers and relatives will drive me out for their sakes.

Perhaps someone might say, "Socrates, can you not go away from us and live quietly, without talking?" Now this is the hardest thing to make some of you believe. For if I say that such conduct would be disobedience to the god and that therefore I cannot keep quiet, you will think I am jesting and will not believe me; and if again I say that to talk every day about virtue and the other things about which you hear me talking and examining myself and others is the greatest good to man, and that the unexamined life is not worth living, you will believe me still less. This is as I say, gentlemen, but it is not easy to convince you. Besides, I am not accustomed to think that I deserve anything bad. If I had money, I would have proposed a fine, as large as I could pay; for that would have done me no harm. But as it is—I have no money, unless you are willing to impose a fine which I could pay. I might perhaps pay a mina of silver. So I propose that penalty; but Plato here, men of Athens, and Crito and Critobulus, and Aristobulus tell me to propose a fine of thirty minas, saying that they are sureties for it. So I propose a fine of that amount, and these men, who are amply sufficient, will be my sureties.

It is no long time, men of Athens, which you gain, and for that those who wish to cast a slur upon the state will give you the name and blame of having killed Socrates, a wise man; for, you know, those who wish to revile you will say I am wise, even though I am not. Now if you had waited a little while, what you desire would have come to you of its own accord; for you see how old I am, how far advanced in life and how near death. I say this not to all of you, but to those who voted for my death. And to them also I have something else to say. Perhaps you think, gentlemen, that I have been convicted through lack of such words as would have moved you to acquit me, if I had thought it right to do and say everything to gain an acquittal. Far from it. And yet it is through a lack that I have been convicted, not however a lack of words, but of impudence and shamelessness, and of willingness to say to you such things as you would have liked best to hear. You would have liked to hear me wailing and lamenting and doing and saying many things which are, as I maintain, unworthy of me—such things as you are accustomed to hear from others. But I did not think at the time that I ought, on account of the danger I was in, to do anything unworthy of a free man, nor do I now repent of having made my defence as I did, but I much prefer to die after such a defence than to live after a defence of the other sort. For neither in the court nor in war ought I or any other man to plan to escape death by every possible means. In battles it is often plain that a man might avoid death by throwing down his arms and begging mercy of his pursuers; and there are many other means of escaping death if one is willing to do and say anything. But, gentlemen, it is not hard to escape death; it is much harder to escape wickedness, for that runs faster than death. And now I, since I am slow and old, am caught by the slower runner, and my accusers, who are clever and quick, by the faster, wickedness. And now I shall go away convicted by you and sentenced to death, and they go convicted by truth of villainy and wrong. And I abide by my penalty, and they by theirs. Perhaps these things had to be so, and I think they are well.

And now I wish to prophesy to you, O ye who have condemned me; for I am now at the time when men most do prophesy, the time just before death. And I say to you, ye men who have slain me, that punishment will come upon you straightway after my death, far more grievous in sooth than the punishment of death which you have meted out to me. For now you have done this to me because you hoped that you would be relieved from rendering an account of your lives, but I say that you will find the result far different. Those who will force you to give an account will be more numerous than heretofore; men whom I restrained, though you knew it not; and they will be harsher, inasmuch as they are younger, and you will be more annoyed. For if you think that by putting men to death you will prevent anyone from reproaching you because you do not act as you should, you are mistaken. That mode of escape is neither possible at all nor honourable, but the easiest and most honourable escape is not by suppressing others, but by making yourselves as good as possible. So with this prophecy to you who condemned me I take my leave.

But with those who voted for my acquittal I should like to converse about this which has happened, while the authorities are busy and before I go to the place where I must die. Wait with me so long, my friends; for nothing prevents our chatting with each other while there is time. I feel that you are my friends, and I wish to show you the meaning of this which has now happened to me. For, judges—and in calling you judges I give you your right name—a wonderful thing has happened to me. For hitherto the customary prophetic monitor always spoke to me very frequently and opposed me even in very small matters, if I was going to do anything I should not; but now this thing which might be thought, and is generally considered, the greatest of evils has come upon me; but the divine sign did not oppose me either when I left my home in the morning, or when I came here to the court, or at any point of my speech, when I was going to say anything; and yet on other occasions it stopped me at many points in the midst of a speech; but now, in this affair, it has not opposed me in anything I was doing or saying. What then do I suppose is the reason? I will tell you. This which has happened to me is doubtless a good thing, and those of us who think death is an evil must be mistaken. A convincing proof of this has been given me; for the accustomed sign would surely have opposed me if I had not been going to meet with something good.

Let us consider in another way also how good reason there is to hope that it is a good thing. For the state of death is one of two things: either it is virtually nothingness, so that the dead has no consciousness of anything, or it is, as people say, a change and migration of the soul from this to another place. And if it is unconsciousness, like a sleep in which the sleeper does not even dream, death would be a wonderful gain. For I think if any one were to pick out that night in which he slept a dreamless sleep and, comparing with it the other nights and days of his life, were to say, after due consideration, how many days and nights in his life had passed more pleasantly than that night,—I believe that not only any private person, but even the great King of Persia himself would find that they were few in comparison with the other days and nights. So if such is the nature of death, I count it a gain; for in that case, all time seems to be no longer than one night. But on the other hand, if death is, as it were, a change of habitation from here to some other place, and if what we are told is true, that all the dead are there, what greater blessing could there be, judges? For if a man when he reaches the other world, after leaving behind these who claim to be judges, shall find those who are really judges who are said to sit in judgment there, Minos and Rhadamanthus, and Aeacus and all the other demigods who were just men in their lives, would the change of habitation be undesirable? Or again, what would any of you give to meet with Orpheus and Musaeus and Hesiod and Homer? I am willing to die many times over, if these things are true; for I personally should find the life there wonderful, when I met Palamedes or Ajax, the son of Telamon, or any other men of old who lost their lives through an unjust judgment, and compared my experience with theirs. I think that would not be unpleasant. And the greatest pleasure would be to pass my time in examining and investigating the people there, as I do those here, to find out who among them is wise and who thinks he is when he is not. What price would any of you pay, judges, to examine him who led the great army against Troy, or Odysseus, or Sisyphus, or countless others, both men and women, whom I might mention? To converse and associate with them and examine them would be immeasurable happiness. At any rate, the folk there do not kill people for it; since, if what we are told is true, they are immortal for all future time, besides being happier in other respects than men are here.

But you also, judges, must regard death hopefully and must

bear in mind this one truth, that no evil can come to a good man either in life or after death, and god does not neglect him. So, too, this which has come to me has not come by chance, but I see plainly that it was better for me to die now and be freed from troubles. That is the reason why the sign never interfered with me, and I am not at all angry with those who condemned me or with my accusers. And yet it was not with that in view that they condemned and accused me, but because they thought to injure me. They deserve blame for that. However, I make this request of them; when my sons grow up, gentlemen, punish them by troubling them as I have troubled you; if they seem to you to care for money or anything else more than for virtue, and if they think they amount to something when they do not, rebuke them as I have rebuked you because they do not care for what they ought, and think they amount to something when they are worth nothing. If you do this, both I and my sons shall have received just treatment from you.

But now the time has come to go away. I go to die, and you to live; but which of us goes to the better lot, is known to none but god.

XENOPHON ON SOCRATES' *DEFENCE TO THE JURY*[3]

Todd translation ("Loeb Classical Library" series).

It seems to me fitting to hand down to memory, furthermore, how Socrates, on being indicted, deliberated on his defence and on his end. It is true that others have written about this, and that all of them have reproduced the loftiness of his words,—a fact

[3] In the year 399 B.C., Socrates, then about seventy years old, was brought to trial by Anytus, Meletus, and Lycon on an indictment charging him with subversion of religion and morals. The fullest account of Socrates at this crisis is to be found in Plato's *Euthyphro*, *Apology of Socrates*, *Crito*, and *Phaedo*. Apparently other admirers also of the great man had described the trial and the last days of his life, but Xenophon, who at that time was with the conglomerate army of Cyrus the Younger on its memorable trip into the heart of Persia, seems to have felt that these various accounts left out one essential point, which he proceeds to develop in the *Apology* or *Defence*.

The first sentence of this composition suggests an intimate connection with something preceding; but this connection is now broken, and whether the *Defence*, as Mahaffy thought, is the original conclusion to Xenophon's *Memoirs of Socrates*, where, in the last chapter, we find practically the same material in smaller compass, or was meant to be part of some other writing, we have no means to determine.

which proves that his utterance really was of the character inti-
mated;—but they have not shown clearly that he had now come to
the conclusion that for him death was more to be desired than life;
and hence his lofty utterance appears rather ill-considered. Hermogenes, the son of Hipponicus, however, was a companion of his
and has given us reports of such a nature as to show that the sub-
limity of his speech was appropriate to the resolve he had made.
For he stated that on seeing Socrates discussing any and every
subject rather than the trial, he had said: "Socrates, ought you
not to be giving some thought to what defence you are going to
make?" That Socrates had at first replied, "Why, do I not seem
to you to have spent my whole life in preparing to defend myself?"
Then when he asked, "How so?" he had said, "Because all my
life I have been guiltless of wrong-doing; and that I consider the

---

Almost equally indeterminate is the date. It is clear that when the *Defence* was
written, both Socrates and Anytus (whose death occurred we know not when) had
been gone several years, and that several accounts of the trial had already appeared.
But there is nothing to show how late the work was written, nor whether it preceded
or followed the *Apology* of Plato.

Hermogenes, the authority on whom Xenophon relied, the indigent brother of
the rich Callias, appears, both from Xenophon's *Defence* and *Symposium* and from
Plato, to have been an intimate in the Socratic circle. Although he is not mentioned
in the doubtless incomplete list given in Plato's *Apology* (33 D–34 A) of friends and
disciples present at the trial, he is named (in Plato's *Phaedo* 59B) as one of those who
were with Socrates at the time of his execution, and so may be presumed to have
been cognizant of what happened in those tragic days.

Xenophon's design in writing the present account was not to give a full report of
the trial or even of Socrates' address to the jury, but to show that because Socrates
believed it time for him to die he had a common-sense basis for his sublime attitude
before the court; but while Plato, the only eye-witness whose work is extant, represents Socrates as telling the jury that he can face death calmly because of his confidence in a life hereafter,—a doctrine greatly elaborated in the *Phaedo*,—Xenophon
does not even mention this faith either in this partial report of the trial or in his
Memoirs of Socrates, but says that in conversation with Hermogenes before the trial
as well as with other friends after it Socrates founded his contentment on the pros-
pect of avoiding the disabilities of old age. Dread of such ills had doubtless filled
many a Greek's heart; at any rate the theme comes out a number of times in poetry,
from the haunting elegy of Mimnermus on. And it seems quite likely that in conversation Socrates had mentioned this commonplace comfort as one reason for his
willingness to die; but whether Plato did not hear it, or thought it not worth record-
ing beside more spiritual thoughts, at any rate he nowhere reports it, and it is certain that in the publicity of the court-room Socrates dwelt rather on his hope of immortality and of communion with the great men of the past. The reader who wishes
to get a true picture of this great man at the climax of his life should therefore not
fail to supplement Xenophon's professedly incomplete account by the fuller one of
Plato.

finest preparation for a defence." Then when Hermogenes again asked, "Do you not observe that the Athenian courts have often been carried away by an eloquent speech and have condemned innocent men to death, and often on the other hand the guilty have been acquitted either because their plea aroused compassion or because their speech was witty?" "Yes, indeed!" he had answered; "and I have tried twice already to meditate on my defence, but my divine sign interposes." And when Hermogenes observed, "That is a surprising statement," he had replied, "Do you think it surprising that even god holds it better for me to die now? Do you not know that I would refuse to concede that any man has lived a better life than I have up to now? For I have realized that my whole life has been spent in righteousness toward god and man,— a fact that affords the greatest satisfaction; and so I have felt a deep self-respect and have discovered that my associates hold corresponding sentiments toward me. But now, if my years are prolonged, I know that the frailties of old age will inevitably be realized,—that my vision must be less perfect and my hearing less keen, that I shall be slower to learn and more forgetful of what I have learned. If I perceive my decay and take to complaining, how," he had continued, "could I any longer take pleasure in life? Perhaps," he added, "god in his kindness is taking my part and securing me the opportunity of ending my life not only in season but also in the way that is easiest. For if I am condemned now, it will clearly be my privilege to suffer a death that is adjudged by those who have superintended this matter to be not only the easiest but also the least irksome to one's friends and one that implants in them the deepest feeling of loss for the dead. For when a person leaves behind in the hearts of his companions no remembrance to cause a blush or a pang, but dissolution comes while he still possesses a sound body and a spirit capable of showing kindliness, how could such a one fail to be sorely missed? It was with good reason," Socrates had continued, "that the gods opposed my studying up my speech at the time when we held that by fair means or foul we must find some plea that would effect my acquittal. For if I had achieved this end, it is clear that instead of now passing out of life, I should merely have provided for dying in the throes of illness or vexed by old age, the sink into which all distresses flow, unrelieved by any joy. As Heaven is my witness, Hermogenes," he had gone on, "I shall never court that fate; but if I am going to offend the jury by declaring all the blessings that I feel gods and men have bestowed on me, as well as my personal opinion of myself, I shall prefer death to begging meanly for longer life and thus gaining a life far less worthy in exchange for death."

Hermogenes stated that with this resolve Socrates came before the jury after his adversaries had charged him with not believing in the gods worshipped by the state and with the introduction of new deities in their stead and with corruption of the young, and replied: "One thing that I marvel at in Meletus, gentlemen, is what may be the basis of his assertion that I do not believe in the gods worshipped by the state; for all who have happened to be near at the time, as well as Meletus himself,—if he so desired,—have seen me sacrificing at the communal festivals and on the public altars. As for introducing 'new divinities' how could I be guilty of that merely in asserting that a voice of god is made manifest to me indicating my duty? Surely those who take their omens from the cries of birds and the utterances of men form their judgments on 'voices.' Will any one dispute either that thunder utters its 'voice,' or that it is an omen of the greatest moment? Does not the very priestess who sits on the tripod at Delphi divulge the god's will through a 'voice'? But more than that, in regard to god's foreknowledge of the future and his forewarning thereof to whomsoever he will, these are the same terms, I assert, that all men use, and this is their belief. The only difference between them and me is that whereas they call the sources of their forewarning 'birds,' 'utterances,' 'chance meetings,' 'prophets,' I call mine a 'divine' thing; and I think that in using such a term I am speaking with more truth and deeper religious feeling than do those who ascribe the gods' power to birds. Now that I do not lie against god I have the following proof: I have revealed to many of my friends the counsels which god has given me, and in no instance has the event shown that I was mistaken."

Hermogenes further reported that when the jurors raised a clamour at hearing these words, some of them disbelieving his statements, others showing jealousy at his receiving greater favours even from the gods than they, Socrates resumed: "Hark ye; let me tell you something more, so that those of you who feel so inclined may have still greater disbelief in my being honoured of

Heaven. Once on a time when Chaerephon made inquiry at the Delphic oracle concerning me, in the presence of many people Apollo answered that no man was more free than I, or more just, or more prudent."

When the jurors, naturally enough, made a still greater tumult on hearing this statement, he said that Socrates again went on: "And yet, gentlemen, the god uttered in oracles greater things of Lycurgus, the Lacedaemonian law-giver, than he did of me. For there is a legend that, as Lycurgus entered the temple, the god thus addressed him: 'I am pondering whether to call you god or man.' Now Apollo did not compare me to a god; he did, however, judge that I far excelled the rest of mankind. However, do not believe the god even in this without due grounds, but examine the god's utterance in detail. First, who is there in your knowledge that is less a slave to his bodily appetites than I am? Who in the world more free,—for I accept neither gifts nor pay from any one? Whom would you with reason regard as more just than the one so reconciled to his present possessions as to want nothing beside that belongs to another? And would not a person with good reason call me a wise man, who from the time when I began to understand spoken words have never left off seeking after and learning every good thing that I could? And that my labour has not been in vain do you not think is attested by this fact, that many of my fellow-citizens who strive for virtue and many from abroad choose to associate with me above all other men? And what shall we say is accountable for this fact, that although everybody knows that it is quite impossible for me to repay with money, many people are eager to make me some gift? Or for this, that no demands are made on me by a single person for the repayment of benefits, while many confess that they owe me a debt of gratitude? Or for this, that during the siege, while others were commiserating their lot, I got along without feeling the pinch of poverty any worse than when the city's prosperity was at its height? Or for this, that while other men get their delicacies in the markets and pay a high price for them, I devise more pleasurable ones from the resources of my soul, with no expenditure of money? And now, if no one can convict me of misstatement in all that I have said of myself, do I not unquestionably merit praise from both gods and men? But in spite of all, Meletus, do you maintain that I corrupt the young by such practices? And yet surely we know what kinds of corruption affect the young; so you tell us whether you know of any one who under my influence has fallen from piety into impiety, or from sober into wanton conduct, or from moderation in living into extravagance, or from temperate drinking into sottishness, or from strenuousness into effeminacy, or has been overcome of any other base pleasure." "But, by Heaven!" said Meletus: "there is one set of men I know,—those whom you have persuaded to obey you rather than their parents." "I admit it," he reports Socrates as replying, "at least so far as education is concerned; for people know that I have taken an interest in that. But in a question of health, men take the advice of physicians rather than that of their parents; and moreover, in the meetings of the legislative assembly all the people of Athens, without question, follow the advice of those whose words are wisest rather than that of their own relatives. Do you not also elect for your generals, in preference to fathers and brothers,—yes, by Heaven! in preference to your very selves,—those whom you regard as having the greatest wisdom in military affairs?" "Yes," Meletus had said; "for that is both expedient and conventional." "Well, then," Socrates had rejoined, "does it not seem to you an amazing thing that while in other activities those who excel receive honours not merely on a parity with their fellows but even more marked ones, yet I, because I am adjudged by some people supreme in what is man's greatest blessing,—education,—am being prosecuted by you on a capital charge?"

More than this of course was said both by Socrates himself and by the friends who joined in his defence. But I have not made it a point to report the whole trial; rather I am satisfied to make it clear that while Socrates' whole concern was to keep free from any act of impiety toward the gods or any appearance of wrong-doing toward man, he did not think it meet to beseech the jury to let him escape death; instead, he believed that the time had now come for him to die. This conviction of his became more evident than ever after the adverse issue of the trial. For, first of all, when he was bidden to name his penalty, he refused personally and forbade his friends to name one, but said that naming the penalty in itself implied an acknowledgment of guilt. Then, when his companions wished to remove him clandestinely from prison, he would not accompany them, but seemed actually to banter them, asking them whether they knew of any spot outside of Attica that was inaccessible to death.

When the trial was over, Socrates (according to Hermogenes) remarked: "Well, gentlemen, those who instructed the witnesses that they must bear false witness against me, perjuring themselves to do so, and those who were won over to do this must feel in their hearts a guilty consciousness of great impiety and iniquity; but as for me, why should my spirit be any less exalted now than before my condemnation, since I have not been proved guilty of having done any of the acts mentioned in the indictment? For it has not been shown that I have sacrificed to new deities in the stead of Zeus and Hera and the gods of their company, or that I have invoked in oaths or mentioned other gods. And how could I be corrupting the young by habituating them to fortitude and frugality? Now of all the acts for which the laws have prescribed the death-penalty—temple robbery, burglary, enslavement, treason to the state—not even my adversaries themselves charge me with having committed any of these. And so it seems astonishing to me how you could ever have been convinced that I had committed an act meriting death. But further, my spirit need not be less exalted because I am to be executed unjustly; for the ignominy of that attaches not to me but to those who condemned me. And I get comfort from the case of Palamedes, also, who died in circumstances similar to mine; for even yet he affords us far more noble themes for song than does Odysseus, the man who unjustly put him to death. And I know that time to come as well as time past will attest that I, too, far from ever doing any man a wrong or rendering him more wicked, have rather profited those who conversed with me by teaching them, without reward, every good thing that lay in my power."

With these words he departed, blithe in glance, in mien, in gait, as comported well indeed with the words he had just uttered. When he noticed that those who accompanied him were in tears, "What is this?" Hermogenes reports him as asking. "Are you just now beginning to weep? Have you not known all along that from the moment of my birth nature had condemned me to death? Verily, if I am being destroyed before my time while blessings are still pouring in upon me, clearly that should bring grief to me and to my

well-wishers; but if I am ending my life when only troubles are in
view, my own opinion is that you ought all to feel cheered, in the
assurance that my state is happy."

A man named Apollodorus, who was there with him, a very
ardent disciple of Socrates, but otherwise simple, exclaimed, "But,
Socrates, what I find it hardest to bear is that I see you being put
to death unjustly!" The other, stroking Apollodorus' head, is said
to have replied, "My beloved Apollodorus, was it your preference
to see me put to death justly?" and smiled as he asked the question.

It is said also that he remarked as he saw Anytus passing by:
"There goes a man who is filled with pride at the thought that he
has accomplished some great and noble end in putting me to death,
because, seeing him honoured by the state with the highest offices, I
said that he ought not to confine his son's education to hides.[4]
What a vicious fellow," he continued, "not to know, apparently,
that whichever one of us has wrought the more beneficial and
noble deeds for all time, *he* is the real victor. But," he is reported
to have added, "Homer has attributed to some of his heroes at
the moment of dissolution the power to foresee the future; and so
I too wish to utter a prophecy. At one time I had a brief association with the son of Anytus, and I thought him not lacking in
firmness of spirit; and so I predict that he will not continue in the
servile occupation that his father has provided for him; but through
want of a worthy adviser he will fall into some disgraceful pro-
pensity and will surely go far in the career of vice." In saying this
he was not mistaken; the young man, delighting in wine, never
left off drinking night or day, and at last turned out worth nothing
to his city, his friends, or himself. So Anytus, even though dead,
still enjoys an evil repute for his son's mischievous education and
for his own hard-heartedness. And as for Socrates, by exalting himself before the court, he brought ill-will upon himself and made his
conviction by the jury all the more certain. Now to me he seems to
have met a fate that the gods love; for he escaped the hardest part
of life and met the easiest sort of death. And he displayed the
stalwart nature of his heart; for having once decided that to die
was better for him than to live longer, he did not weaken in the

[4] The tanning trade had been in the family from at least the time of the boy's
grandfather.

presence of death (just as he had never set his face against any other thing, either, that was for his good), but was cheerful not only in the expectation of death but in meeting it.

And so, in contemplating the man's wisdom and nobility of character, I find it beyond my power to forget him or, in remembering him, to refrain from praising him. And if among those who make virtue their aim any one has ever been brought into contact with a person more helpful than Socrates, I count that man worthy to be called most blessed.

CHAPTER VIII

PLATO

PERSPECTIVE ON THE MAN AND HIS WORK

Apologia pro vita sua (EPISTLE VII)

Plato (427–347) was descended on his father's side from King Codrus and on his mother's side from Solon. A legend more beautiful than most made him the son of Apollo. He was a disciple of Socrates at the time of the latter's condemnation by the Athenian democracy, living thereafter in the memory of the Golden Age of Pericles and Socrates. He not only discouragedly left Athens after the death of Socrates for a season of travel, but he was made distrustful of democracy for the remainder of his life. But the Tyranny of the Thirty, in which he had an uncle, Charmides, and a cousin, Critias, and under which it appears that he could have had, or perhaps did have, a political job, left him disillusioned also as to the wisdom and honor of an oligarchy. There remained one form of government, a monarchy; and hopefully he journeyed (almost commuted) to Syracuse to see what a single, youthful ruler could be helped to achieve if informed by mathematical and philosophic training. With the culminating failure of this sustained mission, Plato's last hope disappeared for the full realization on earth of political wisdom. But the dream remained to comfort his age as it stayed to motivate his entire life—the dream of intelligence ruling the world for the common good. Plato's more technical writings, if any, were lost; and only his literary productions have come down to us. About two dozen of these in dialogue form remain, plus some thirteen letters, the longest and most authentic of which latter we reproduce. His dialogues touch upon every subject known to Greek intelligence and upon most general subjects known to us—always to illuminate and beautify, though seldom to settle, the issue involved. Some dialogues commemorate the life and death of his martyred master ("Euthyphro," "Apology," "Crito," and "Phaedo"); others give Socrates the chief rôle in a search for enlightenment by discussion of basic questions ("Hippias Major," "Hippias Minor," "Ion," "Protagoras," "Charmides," "Laches," "Lysis," "Cratylus," "Euthydemus," "Menexenus," "Gorgias," "Meno"); still others represent the dominance of thought over the play of personality and show Plato approaching intellectual maturity preoccupied with his own problems and master of himself ("Symposium," "Republic," "Phaedrus," "Theaetetus," "Parmenides"); and finally there are critical investigations of abstruse questions with diminishing regard to anything save the argument itself ("Sophist," "Statesman," "Timaeus," "Critias," "Philebus," "Laws"). The dominant note throughout is belief in a rational order, the possibility of discovering that order, and the desirability of using that discovery for the improvement of government and the enhancement of individual life. Arising from this persistent faith in the efficacy of intellectual effort, problems of method of both thought and social management grow central and become at last crucial.

. . .

APOLOGIA PRO VITA SUA: EPISTLE VII

PLATO TO DION'S ASSOCIATES AND FRIENDS WISHES
WELL-DOING

[Bury translation and introduction, "Loeb Classical Library" series—T. V. S.]. This is the longest and most important of the Platonic *Epistles*, and has the best claims to authenticity. From internal evidence we may infer that it was written after the murder of Dion (in 353 B.C.) and before the overthrow of the usurper Callippus in the following year.

While the letter purports to be a message of "counsel" to Dion's friends, it really contains a description and a defence of the whole course of Plato's participation in the political affairs of Sicily, and thus constitutes an elaborate *Apologia pro vita sua*. . . . . Its professed object, to offer "counsel" to Dion's friends, is obviously not its chief object, since only one page (336E–337E) out of nearly thirty is devoted to the actual statement of that "counsel." The chief object can be only that of pleading justification for the part played by Plato in the internal affairs of Sicily and in the struggle between the rival leaders Dionysius and Dion. The main points of the argument, as derived from the personal experiences narrated, would seem to be these: first, a strong reassertion of his political creed, namely, that it is only under the rule of the philosopher-kings, or, failing that, under the rule of just laws in a constitutional republic, that any State can hope to flourish. Plato's conviction of this was the outcome of his early experiences in Athens, and all that he saw later, both at home and abroad, only served to confirm it. Next, he wished to make it clear that this conviction, this political philosophy, was one of the main principles which had governed all his actions in regard to Sicilian affairs. He felt himself forced, as he puts it, to have dealings with Dionysius "lest he should be betraying Philosophy." When Providence seemed to be offering a splendid opportunity of realizing the philosopher's dream of the Ideal State, he felt it incumbent upon him to seize that opportunity: his conscience compelled him. Another reason for his actions which is strongly emphasized throughout the letter was his close friendship with Dion, a friendship based on community of conviction. Dion was a convert to Plato's ethical system and shared his political creed. Therefore Dion's cause and the cause of Philosophy were inextricably intertwined; and the claims of friendship came to reinforce the claims of creed.

These are the main points pressed as supplying a justification of Plato's actions and their motives. But his actions, however well-intentioned, were not successful. Therefore much of the narrative, and of the underlying argument, is framed with the view of explaining this ill-success. The main cause lay in the character of Dionysius, who was fickle, treacherous and vain. Others who should share the blame are Dion's enemies at the Court of Syracuse, who set the tyrant against him. Instance after instance is given of the suspicion and the treachery of Dionysius in his dealings with Dion and with Plato, and of the prevalence of calumny at the Court of Syracuse. Nor was Dion himself wholly blameless, for it was against Plato's advice that he set out on the final enterprise against Dionysius which cost him his life.

These, then, are the main points—apart from the philosophical digression—which emerge from this lengthy, and somewhat confused, narrative. And from a consideration of these points we may gather something of the reasons which moved Plato to write this letter of self-justification. Evidently he is trying to meet hostile criticism; and we may fairly suppose that the main points of the attack corresponded to the main points of his defence. After Dion's failure and death in 353 B.C. no doubt his supporters were ready enough to throw the blame on someone, and Plato, as his most influential adviser, was the most obvious person to blame. He, like the murderer Callippus (they would say), was an Athenian; he, very likely, had helped to embroil Dion with Dionysius; all his pretended influence at the Court of Syracuse had only proved mischievous, judged by results; and, in fact, if only this Athenian had not come meddling with Sicilian affairs everything might have turned out much better. Possibly also they accused Plato of fraud in connexion with Dion's property.

It is easy enough to understand how such attacks might be made at such a crisis on the probity and good sense and consistency of Plato, and how he might have felt himself driven to defend himself against such baseless charges. But it is rather more difficult to see the relevance of what is known as "the philosophical digression" —a passage which some critics have condemned (not unnaturally) as a spurious insertion. [Ritter says, for instance, that "only the philosophical section . . . .

cannot be from the pen of Plato" (*The Essence of Plato's Philosophy*, p. 26 n.).—T. V. S.] It may be suggested that Plato's purpose in stressing the abstruse and difficult nature of philosophy is to rebut the charge that he had failed to convert Dionysius to views shared by himself and Dion. We may also conjecture that his exposition of the nature of Reality, on which he bases his denial that metaphysics can be explained in writing, is inserted with the object of exploding the notion that Dionysius, or any of his other teachers, were philosophers at all in any true sense of the word. For it appears that Dionysius claimed to be a competent exponent of Idealism, and that many were inclined to accept his claims; and doing so, they might be tempted to ascribe Plato's quarrel with the tyrant to professional jealousy. Or else they might argue that if Dionysius could master the subject so easily and quickly, what need can there be for the prolonged course of training prescribed by Plato? And it is to correct such ignorance of the true nature of philosophy, and to expose the hollowness of the claims of philosophic impostors, and thereby to justify his own attitude towards Dionysius, that Plato writes at such length on the subject. He writes, also, with something like passion, because he feels that the criticisms levelled at him are levelled at Philosophy herself, and that her honour is at stake.

As regards the philosophical exposition itself, there is little or nothing that is not either expressed or implied in the statements of Idealism contained in Plato's Dialogues. Two points only need here be indicated, to supplement the paraphrase given in our summary [section analyses], and the references in the footnotes. For one thing, the use of the term "knowledge" is somewhat confusing, since it sometimes seems to be equated with intellectual apprehension in general, and at other times with pure cognition by the reason. As applied to Reality, or the Ideas, it can, of course, only be used in this latter sense of "scientific knowledge."

The other point of technical interest is that here Ideas are postulated of artificial as well as natural objects, contrary to what Aristotle says about the Platonic theory, as well as to some well-known recent expositions of "the later Platonism." Without entering upon this controverted subject, it is enough to say here that, whether or not Plato ever adopted a later theory of the kind described, the Idealism propounded in this letter is, in all essentials, the same as "the earlier theory" of the *Phaedo* and *Republic*. The Idea is the inexpressible and incommunicable Real which lies behind all existence, objective or subjective.

Now while the apologetic character of this letter is sufficiently clear, doubts have been raised as regards its historical setting. Is it really likely that Dion's followers, whether at Syracuse or at Leontini, would have written to Plato for advice, and put in writing also the criticisms and charges implied in this written answer? And can we easily imagine Plato penning this long narrative of events in Sicily for the benefit of people who must have been perfectly familiar with Sicilian history for years past? Moreover it is difficult to suppose that the tyrant Callippus would allow the dispatch of any non-official communications between Syracuse and foreign ports. These considerations seem to render it more probable that not only is this letter an "open" letter addressed rather to the general public than to the parties named in the superscription, but that superscription itself is merely a literary device. The letter was never meant to be sent to Sicily at all. And, this being so, the natural corollary is that the hypothetical letter from Dion's party asking for advice is equally imaginary. So that what Plato is doing in this letter is to indulge in a literary fiction which enables him to publish in epistolary form what is at once a history, an apology and a manifesto. For what public, then, was this intended, if we rule out the Sicilians? There can be little doubt as to the answer: it was the public opinion of his own countrymen which Plato was chiefly concerned to influence: the ignorant gossip, the malicious rumours, the damaging misrepresentations current at Athens, were what annoyed him most and what he was most anxious to disprove.

It may be noticed, further, that this view of the letter is supported by the points of contact it has with the *Antidosis* of Isocrates, a speech contemporary with the letter and, like it, largely autobiographical and apologetic. The way in which Isocrates there criticizes Plato and tries to belittle his work as a writer and teacher is sufficient to show the kind of misrepresentation and professional jealousy against which Plato had to contend at home. And in the defence contained in this letter there is probably much of pointed reference to those domestic critics—pseudo-philosophers of the Dionysian type, sophistical quibblers, and rhetors and writers the dupes of unstable words.

Lastly, the severity with which Sicilian luxury is condemned, combined with the care taken to exculpate Athens from any complicity in the murder of Dion, helps to confirm the view that this seventh letter was published, in the first instance at least, for circulation in Athens and not in Syracuse.

[Plato's policy the same as Dion's. History of Plato's early life, and how he came to form his political creed, and to stand aloof from public life at Athens owing ot its corrupt state.]

You wrote to me that I ought to consider that your policy was the same as that which Dion had; and moreover you charged me to support it, so far as I can, both by deed and word. Now if you really hold the same views and aims as he, I consent to support them, but if not, I will ponder the matter many times over. And what was his policy and his aim I will tell you, and that, as I may say not from mere conjecture but from certain knowledge. For when I originally arrived at Syracuse, being about forty years old, Dion was of the age which Hipparinus has now reached, and the views which he had then come to hold he continued to hold unchanged; for he believed that the Syracusans ought to be free and dwell under the best laws. Consequently, it is no matter of surprise if some Deity has made Hipparinus also come to share his views about government and be of the same mind. Now the manner in which these views originated is a story well worth hearing for young and old alike, and I shall endeavour to narrate it to you from the beginning; for at the present moment it is opportune.

In the days of my youth my experience was the same as that of many others. I thought that as soon as I should become my own master I would immediately enter into public life. But it so happened, I found, that the following changes occurred in the political situation.

In the government then existing, reviled as it was by many, a revolution took place; and the revolution was headed by fifty-one leaders, of whom eleven were in the City and ten in the Piraeus—each of these sections dealing with the market and with all municipal matters requiring management—and Thirty were established as irresponsible rulers of all. Now of these some were actually connexions and acquaintances of mine;[1] and indeed they invited me at once to join their administration, thinking it would be congenial. The feelings I then experienced, owing to my youth, were in no way surprising: for I imagined that they would administer the State by leading it out of an unjust way of life into a just way, and consequently I gave my mind to them very diligently, to see what they would do. And indeed I saw how these men within a short time caused men to look back on the former government as a golden age; and above all how they treated my aged friend Socrates, whom I would hardly scruple to call the most just of men then living, when they tried to send him, along with others, after one of the citizens, to fetch him by force that he might be put to death —their object being that Socrates, whether he wished or no, might be made to share in their political actions; he, however, refused to obey and risked the uttermost penalties rather than be a partaker in their unholy deeds.[2] So when I beheld all these actions and others of a similar grave kind,[3] I was indignant, and I withdrew myself from the evil practices then going on. But in no long time the power of the Thirty was overthrown together with the whole of the government which then existed. Then once again I was really, though less urgently, impelled with a desire to take part in public and political affairs. Many deplorable events, however, were still happening in those times, troublous as they were, and it was not surprising that in some instances, during these revolutions, men were avenging themselves on their foes too fiercely; yet, notwith-

[1] Plato's uncle Charmides and his cousin Critias were among the leaders of "The Thirty."

[2] For this episode see *Apology* 32.

[3] Possibly an allusion to the execution of Theramenes by Critias.

standing, the exiles who then returned[4] exercised no little moderation. But, as ill-luck would have it, certain men of authority[5] summoned our comrade Socrates before the law-courts, laying a charge
against him which was most unholy, and which Socrates of all men
least deserved; for it was on the charge of impiety that those men
summoned him and the rest condemned and slew him—the very
man who on the former occasion, when they themselves had the
misfortune to be in exile, had refused to take part in the unholy
arrest of one of the friends of the men then exiled.

When, therefore, I considered all this, and the type of men who
were administering the affairs of State, with their laws too and
their customs, the more I considered them and the more I advanced in years myself, the more difficult appeared to me the task
of managing affairs of State rightly. For it was impossible to take
action without friends and trusty companions; and these it was not
easy to find ready to hand; since our State was no longer managed
according to the principles and institutions of our forefathers; while
to acquire other new friends with any facility was a thing impossible. Moreover, both the written laws and the customs were being
corrupted, and that with surprising rapidity. Consequently, although at first I was filled with an ardent desire to engage in public
affairs, when I considered all this and saw how things were shifting about anyhow in all directions, I finally became dizzy; and although I continued to consider by what means some betterment
could be brought about not only in these matters but also in the
government as a whole, yet as regards political action I kept constantly waiting for an opportune moment; until, finally, looking at
all the States which now exist, I perceived that one and all they
are badly governed; for the state of their laws is such as to be almost incurable without some marvellous overhauling and good-
luck to boot. So in my praise of the right philosophy I was compelled to declare that by it one is enabled to discern all forms of
justice both political and individual. Wherefore the classes of
mankind (I said) will have no cessation from evils until either the
class of those who are right and true philosophers attains political

---

[4] *I.e.* the democrats under Thrasybulus and Thrasyllus.

[5] Meletus and Anytus, the accusers of Socrates; see the *Apology*.

supremacy, or else the class of those who hold power in the States becomes, by some dispensation of Heaven, really philosophic.[6]

[Plato's *first visit* to Sicily. His view of its evil social and political conditions. The friendship he formed with Dion, who came to share his ethical and political creed. How he was urged by Dion, after the death of Dionysius the Elder, to revisit Syracuse, and aid him in effecting a political reformation by training up the young Dionysius to become a philosopher-king.]

This was the view I held when I came to Italy and Sicily, at the time of my first arrival. And when I came I was in no wise pleased at all with "the blissful life," as it is there termed, replete as it is with Italian and Syracusan banquetings; for thus one's existence is spent in gorging food twice a day and never sleeping alone at night, and all the practices which accompany this mode of living. For not a single man of all who live beneath the heavens could ever become wise if these were his practices from his youth, since none will be found to possess a nature so admirably compounded; nor would he ever be likely to become temperate; and the same may truly be said of all other forms of virtue. And no State would remain stable under laws of any kind, if its citizens, while supposing that they ought to spend everywhere to excess, yet believed that they ought to cease from all exertion except feastings and drinkings and the vigorous pursuit of their amours. Of necessity these States never cease changing into tyrannies, oligarchies, and democracies, and the men who hold power in them cannot endure so much as the mention of the name of a just government with equal laws. Holding these views, then, as well as those previously formed, I travelled through to Syracuse—possibly as luck would have it, though it seems likely that one of the Superior Powers was contriving at that time to lay the foundation of the events which have now taken place in regard to Dion and in regard to Syracuse; and of still more events, as is to be feared, unless you now hearken to the counsel I offer you now, for the second time.[7]

What, then, do I mean by saying that my arrival in Sicily on that occasion was the foundation of everything? When I associated with Dion, who was then a youth, instructing him verbally in what

[6] This echoes the famous passage in the *Republic* v. 473; hereunder p. 322.

[7] The first occasion being at Olympia in 360 B.C.; *cf.* 350 B ff.

I believed was best for mankind and counselling him to realize it in action, it seems that I was not aware that I was, in a way, unwittingly contriving the future overthrow of the tyranny. For Dion in truth, being quick-witted, both in other respects and in grasping the arguments I then put forward, hearkened to me with a keenness and ardour that I have never yet found in any of the youth whom I have met; and he determined to live the rest of his life in a different manner from the majority of the Italians and Sicilians, counting virtue worthy of more devotion than pleasure and all other kinds of luxury. In consequence, his way of life was in ill-odour with those who were conforming to the customary practices of the tyranny, until the death of Dionysius[8] occurred.

After this event, he came to the belief that this belief, which he himself had acquired through right instruction, would not always be confined to himself; and in fact he saw it being implanted in others also—not in many, it is true, but yet implanted in some; and of these he thought that Dionysius (with Heaven's help) might become one, and that, if he did become a man of this mind, both his own life and that of all the rest of the Syracusans would, in consequence, be a life of immeasurable felicity. Moreover, Dion considered that I ought, by all means, to come to Syracuse with all speed to be his partner in this task, since he bore in mind our intercourse with one another and how happily it had wrought on him to acquire a longing for the noblest and best life; and if now, in like manner, he could effect this result in Dionysius, as he was trying to do, he had great hopes of establishing the blissful and true life throughout all the land without massacres and murders and the evils which have now come about.

Holding these right views, Dion persuaded Dionysius to summon me; and he himself also sent a request that I should by all means come with all speed, before that any others should encounter Dionysius and turn him aside to some way of life other than the best. And these were the terms—long though they are to repeat—in which his request was couched: "What opportunities (he asked) are we to wait for that could be better than those that have now been presented by a stroke of divine good fortune?" And he dwelt in detail on the extent of the empire in Italy and Sicily and his own power therein, and the youth of Dionysius, mentioning also how

[8] Dionysius the Elder died in 367 B.C.

great a desire he had for philosophy and education, and he spoke of his own nephews[9] and connexions, and how they would be not only easily converted themselves to the doctrines and the life I always taught, but also most useful in helping to influence Dionysius; so that now, if ever (he concluded), all our hopes will be fulfilled of seeing the same persons at once philosophers and rulers of mighty States.

By these and a vast number of other like arguments Dion kept exhorting me; but as regards my own opinion, I was afraid how matters would turn out so far as the young people were concerned—for the desires of such as they change quickly, and frequently in a contrary direction; although, as regards Dion's own character, I knew that it was stable by nature and already sufficiently mature. Wherefore as I pondered the matter and was in doubt whether I should make the journey and take his advice, or what, I ultimately inclined to the view that if we were ever to attempt to realize our theories concerning laws and government, now was the time to undertake it; for should I succeed in convincing one single person sufficiently I should have brought to pass all manner of good.

[Plato's *second visit* to Sicily. How he was induced to go by the fear of seeming to prove false both to his friendship for Dion and to the cause of philosophy. But his visit proved a failure. Hostile factions slandered Dion and secured his banishment by the young Dionysius, while Plato himself was treated with suspicion. None the less, he kept doing his utmost to influence Dionysius aright.] Holding this view and in this spirit of adventure it was that I set out from home,—not in the spirit which some have supposed, but dreading self-reproach most of all, lest haply I should seem to myself to be utterly and absolutely nothing more than a mere voice and never to undertake willingly any action, and now to be in danger of proving false, in the first instance, to my friendship and association with Dion, when he is actually involved in no little danger. Suppose, then, that some evil fate should befall him, or that he should be banished by Dionysius and his other foes and then come to us as an exile and question us in these words—"O Plato, I come to you as an exile not to beg for foot-soldiers, nor

---

[9] Probably sisters' sons of Dion, and not including Hipparinus (who would be too young at this date).

because I lack horse-soldiers to ward off mine enemies, but to beg for arguments and persuasion, whereby you above all, as I know, are able to convert young men to what is good and just and thereby to bring them always into a state of mutual friendliness and comradeship. And it is because you have left me destitute of these that I have now quitted Syracuse and come hither. My condition, however, casts a lesser reproach on you; but as for Philosophy, which you are always belauding, and saying that she is treated with ignominy by the rest of mankind, surely, so far as it depends on you, she too is now betrayed as well as I. Now if we had happened to be living at Megara,[10] you would no doubt have come to assist me in the cause for which I summoned you, on pain of deeming yourself of all men the most base; and now, forsooth, do you imagine that when you plead in excuse the length of the journey and the great strain of the voyage and of the labour involved you can possibly be acquitted of the charge of cowardice? Far from it, indeed."

If he had spoken thus, what plausible answer should I have had to such pleadings? There is none. Well then, I came for good and just reasons so far as it is possible for men to do so; and it was because of such motives that I left my own occupations, which were anything but ignoble, to go under a tyranny which ill became, as it seemed, both my teaching and myself. And by my coming I freed myself from guilt in the eyes of Zeus Xenios and cleared myself from reproach on the part of Philosophy, seeing that she would have been calumniated if I, through poorness of spirit and timidity, had incurred the shame of cowardice.

On my arrival—I must not be tedious—I found Dionysius's kingdom all full of civil strife and of slanderous stories brought to the court concerning Dion. So I defended him, so far as I was able, though it was little I could do; but about three months later, charging Dion with plotting against the tyranny, Dionysius set him aboard a small vessel and drove him out with ignominy. After that all of us who were Dion's friends were in alarm lest he should punish any of us on a charge of being accomplices in Dion's plot; and regarding me a report actually went abroad in Syracuse that I had been put to death by Dionysius as being responsible for all the events of that time. But when Dionysius perceived us all in

---

[10] A town close to Athens to which the disciples of Socrates retreated after his death.

this state of mind, he was alarmed lest our fears should bring about some worse result; so he was for receiving us all back in a friendly manner; and, moreover, he kept consoling me and bidding me be of good courage and begging me by all means to remain. For my fleeing away from him would have brought him no credit, but rather my remaining; and that was why he pretended to beg it of me so urgently. But the requests of tyrants are coupled, as we know, with compulsory powers. So in order to further this plan he kept hindering my departure; for he brought me into the Acropolis and housed me in a place from which no skipper would have brought me off, and that not merely if prevented by Dionysius but also if he failed to send them a messenger charging them to take me off. Nor would any trader nor any single one of the officers at the ports of the country have let me pass out by myself, without arresting me on the spot and bringing me back again to Dionysius, especially as it had already been proclaimed abroad, contrary to the former report, that "Dionysius is wonderfully devoted to Plato." But what were the facts? For the truth must be told. He became indeed more and more devoted as time advanced, according as he grew familiar with my disposition and character, but he was desirous that I should praise him more than Dion and regard him rather than Dion as my special friend, and this triumph he was marvellously anxious to achieve. But the best way to achieve this, if it was to be achieved—namely, by occupying himself in learning and in listening to discourses on philosophy and by associating with me—this he always shirked owing to his dread of the talk of slanderers, lest he might be hampered in some measure and Dion might accomplish all his designs. I, however, put up with all this, holding fast the original purpose with which I had come, in the hope that he might possibly gain a desire for the philosophic life; but he, with his resistance, won the day.

[Now Plato must turn to the main purpose of his letter, which is to give *counsel to Dion's friends*. But a counselor, like a doctor, can prescribe only for those who are willing to act on his advice. And it is a mistake to force the unwilling or to use violent means to rectify the conduct of a father or a fatherland.]

These, then, were the causes which brought about my visit to Sicily and my sojourn there, on the first occasion. After this I went away, and I returned again on receiving a most urgent summons

from Dionysius. That my motives for doing so and all my actions
were reasonable and just, all this I will try to explain later on, for
the benefit of those who ask what object I had in going the second
time. But first I must counsel you as to the course you ought to
adopt in view of the present circumstances, so as not to give the first
place to matters of secondary importance. What I have to say,
then, is this:

Ought not the doctor that is giving counsel to a sick man who
is indulging in a mode of life that is bad for his health to try first of
all to change his life, and only proceed with the rest of his advice
if the patient is willing to obey? But should he prove unwilling,
then I would esteem him both manly and a true doctor if he with-
draws from advising a patient of that description, and contrari-
wise unmanly and unskilled if he continues to advise. So too with
a State, whether it has one ruler or many, if so be that it asks for
some salutary advice when its government is duly proceeding by
the right road, then it is the act of a judicious man to give advice
to such people. But in the case of those who altogether exceed the
bounds of right government and wholly refuse to proceed in its
tracks, and who warn their counsellor to leave the government
alone and not disturb it, on pain of death if he does disturb it, while
ordering him to advise as to how all that contributes to their desires and appetites may most easily and quickly be secured for
ever and ever—then, in such a case, I should esteem unmanly the
man who continued to engage in counsels of this kind, and the man
who refused to continue, manly.

This, then, being the view I hold, whenever anyone consults me
concerning any very important affair relating to his life—the acquisition of wealth, for instance, or the care of his body or his soul,
—if I believe that he is carrying on his daily life in a proper way, or
that he will be willing to obey my advice in regard to the matters
disclosed, then I give counsel readily and do not confine myself to
some merely cursory reply. But if he does not ask my advice at all
or plainly shows that he will in no wise obey his adviser, I do not of
my own instance come forward to advise such an one, nor yet to
compel him, not even were he my own son. To a slave, however, I
would give advice, and if he refused it I would use compulsion.
But to a father or mother I deem it impious to apply compulsion,
unless they are in the grip of the disease of insanity; but if they are

living a settled life which is pleasing to them, though not to me, I would neither irritate them with vain exhortations nor yet minister to them with flatteries by providing them with means to satisfy appetites of a sort such that I, were I addicted to them, would refuse to live. So likewise it behooves the man of sense to hold, while he lives, the same view concerning his own State: if it appears to him to be ill governed he ought to speak, if so be that his speech is not likely to prove fruitless nor to cause his death; but he ought not to apply violence to his fatherland in the form of a political revolution, whenever it is impossible to establish the best kind of polity without banishing and slaughtering citizens, but rather he ought to keep quiet and pray for what is good both for himself and for his State.

[So Plato's present advice will be similar to that formerly given by him and Dion to Dionysius. They urged him to cultivate self-control and to make loyal friends, warning him by the unhappy example of his father; and they advised him as to his policy. But slander and treachery again prevailed and Dion was exiled. But he returned and by deeds instead of words taught Dionysius in severer fashion, until treachery and slander again attacked him with fatal results. He was accused of seeking to make himself a despot, and two false friends did him to death. It is true that his murderers were Athenians, but no slur should be cast on Athens on that account, for was not his best friend also an Athenian?]

This, then, is the way in which I would counsel you—even as Dion and I together used to counsel Dionysius that he should, in the first place, so order his daily life as to gain the greatest possible mastery over himself, and to win for himself trusty friends and companions; that so he might avoid the evils suffered by his father. For he, when he had recovered many great cities of Sicily which had been laid waste by the barbarians, was unable, when he settled them, to establish in each a loyal government composed of true comrades,—whether strangers from abroad or men of his own kin whom he himself had reared up in their youth and had raised from a private position to one of authority and from a state of poverty to surpassing wealth. Neither by persuasion nor instruction, neither by benefits nor by ties of kindred, was he able to make any one of them worthy of a share in his government. Thus he was

seven times more unhappy than Darius[11] who trusted men who
neither were his brothers nor reared up by himself but merely colleagues who had helped him to crush the Mede and the Eunuch;
and he divided amongst them seven provinces, each greater than
the whole of Sicily; and these colleagues he found loyal, neither did
they make any attack either on himself or on one another. And
thus he left an example of the character which should belong to
the good lawgiver and king; for by the laws he framed he has preserved the empire of the Persians even until this day. Moreover,
the Athenians also, after taking over many of the Greek cities
which had fallen into the hands of the barbarians, though they
had not colonized them themselves yet held their sway over them
securely for seventy years because they possessed citizens who were
their friends in each of those cities.[12] But Dionysius, though he
amalgamated the whole of Sicily into one City-State, because in
his wisdom he distrusted everyone, barely achieved safety; for he
was poor in men who were loyal friends, and there exists no surer
sign of a man's virtue or vice than whether he is or is not destitute
of men of that kind.

Such, then, was the counsel which Dion and I always gave to
Dionysius. Inasmuch as the result of his father's conduct was to
leave him unprovided with education and unprovided with suitable
intercourse, he should, in the first place, make it his aim to acquire
other friends for himself from among his kindred and contemporaries who were in harmony about virtue; and to acquire, above all
else, this harmony within himself, since in this he was surprisingly
deficient. Not that we expressed this openly, for it would not have
been safe; but we put it in veiled terms and maintained by argument that this is how every man will save both himself and all those
under his leadership, whereas if he does not adopt this course he
will bring about entirely opposite results. And if he pursued the
course we describe, and made himself right-minded and sober-
minded, then, if he were to re-people the devastated cities of
Sicily and bind them together by laws and constitutions so that

[11] Darius wrested the kingdom of Persia from the usurper Pseudo-Smerdis by the
aid of six other Persian nobles.

[12] The maritime empire of the Athenians lasted for some seventy years after
Salamis (480 B.C.).

they should be leagued both with himself and with one another
against barbarian reinforcements, he would thus not merely
double the empire of his father but actually multiply it many
times over; for if this came to pass, it would be an easy task to enslave the Carthaginians far more than they had been enslaved in
the time of Gelon,[13] whereas now, on the contrary, his father had
contracted to pay tribute to the barbarians.

Such was the advice and exhortation given to Dionysius by us,
who were plotting against him, as statements pouring in from
many quarters alleged; which statements in fact so prevailed with
Dionysius that they caused Dion's expulsion and threw us into
a state of alarm. Then—to cut a long story short—Dion came
from the Peloponnesus and from Athens and admonished Dionysius
by deed.[14] When, however, Dion had delivered the Syracusans and
given them back their city twice, they showed the same feeling
towards him as Dionysius had done. For when Dion was trying
to train and rear him up to be a king worthy of the throne, that so
he might share with him in all his life, Dionysius listened to the
slanderers who said that Dion was plotting against the tyranny in
all that he was then doing, his scheme being that Dionysius, with
his mind infatuated with education, should neglect his empire and
entrust it to Dion, who should then seize on it for himself and expel Dionysius from his kingship by craft. And then, for the second
time, these slanderous statements triumphed with the Syracusans,
and that with a triumph that was most monstrous and shameful
for the authors of the triumph.

Those who are urging me to address myself to the affairs of to-
day ought to hear what then took place. I, a citizen of Athens, a
companion of Dion, an ally of his own, went to the tyrant in order
that I might bring about friendship instead of war; but in my
struggle with the slanderers I was worsted. But when Dionysius
tried to persuade me by means of honours and gifts of money to
side with him so that I should bear witness, as his friend, to the
propriety of his expulsion of Dion, in this design he failed utterly.
And later on, while returning home from exile, Dion attached to

---

[13] Gelon succeeded Hippocrates as tyrant of Gela about 490 B.C. and then captured Syracuse and made it his capital. His defeat of the Carthaginians at Himera,
480 B.C., was celebrated by the poet Simonides.

[14] *I.e.* by a military campaign ("deed" as opposed to "word") in 357 B.C.

himself two brothers from Athens, men whose friendship was not derived from philosophy, but from the ordinary companionship out of which most friendships spring, and which comes from mutual entertaining and sharing in religion and mystic ceremonies. So, too, in the case of these two friends who accompanied him home; it was for these reasons and because of their assistance in his homeward voyage that they became his companions. But on their arrival in Sicily, when they perceived that Dion was slanderously charged before the Siceliots whom he had set free with plotting to become tyrant, they not only betrayed their companion and host but became themselves, so to say, the authors of his murder, since they stood beside the murderers, ready to assist, with arms in their hands. For my own part, I neither slur over the shamefulness and sinfulness of their action nor do I dwell on it, since there are many others who make it their care to recount these doings and will continue to do so in time to come. But I do take exception to what is said about the Athenians, that these men covered their city with shame; for I assert that it was also an Athenian who refused to betray the very same man when, by doing so, he might have gained wealth and many other honours. For he had become his friend not in the bonds of a venal friendship but owing to association in liberal education; since it is in this alone that the judicious man should put his trust, rather than in kinship of soul or of body. Consequently, the two murderers of Dion are not important enough to cast a reproach upon our city, as though they had ever yet shown themselves men of mark.

[This account of the advice he gave Dionysius and its sequel is intended as an admonition also to those who consult him now. The policy advised was the abolition of despotism in Sicily and the establishment of constitutional government, with just laws in all the cities. Dionysius, because he rejected this advice, now lives an ignoble life; Dion, because he followed it, has met a noble death. If only Dion had been successful, he would have secured for all Sicily the blessings which can come only from the reign of law. Let his friends, therefore, follow now in his footsteps; let them cease from party strife and reprisals; let them practice moderation and self-control in the hour of victory; and, seeing that the Ideal State under a philosopher-king is now impracticable, let them form a constitution in which law is king.]

All this has been said by way of counsel to Dion's friends and relatives. And one piece of counsel I add, as I repeat now for the third time to you in the third place the same counsel as before, and the same doctrine. Neither Sicily, nor yet any other State—such is my doctrine—should be enslaved to human despots but rather to laws; for such slavery is good neither for those who enslave nor those who are enslaved—themselves, their children and their children's children; rather is such an attempt wholly ruinous, and the dispositions that are wont to grasp gains such as these are petty and illiberal, with no knowledge of what belongs to goodness and justice, divine or human, either in the present or in the future. Of this I attempted to persuade Dion in the first place, secondly Dionysius, and now, in the third place, you. Be ye, then, persuaded for the sake of Zeus, Third Saviour,[15] and considering also the case of Dionysius and of Dion, of whom the former was unpersuaded and is living now no noble life, while the latter was persuaded and has nobly died. For whatsoever suffering a man undergoes when striving after what is noblest both for himself and for his State is always right and noble. For by nature none of us is immortal, and if any man should come to be so he would not be happy, as the vulgar believe; for no evil nor good worthy of account belongs to what is soulless, but they befall the soul whether it be united with a body or separated therefrom. But we ought always truly to believe the ancient and holy doctrines which declare to us that the soul is immortal and that it has judges and pays the greatest penalties, whensoever a man is released fom his body; wherefore also one should account it a lesser evil to suffer than to perform the great iniquities and injustices. But to these doctrines the man who is fond of riches but poor in soul listens not, or if he listens he laughs them (as he thinks) to scorn, while he shamelessly plunders from all quarters everything which he thinks likely to provide himself, like a beast, with food or drink or the satiating himself with the slavish and graceless pleasure which is miscalled by the name of the Goddess of Love; for he is blind and fails to see what a burden of sin—how grave an evil—ever accompanies each wrong-doing; which burden the wrong-doer must of necessity drag after him both while he moves about on earth and when he has

[15] An allusion to the custom of offering the third (and last) cup at banquets as a libation to Zeus.

gone beneath the earth again on a journey that is unhonoured and in all ways utterly miserable.

Of these and other like doctrines I tried to persuade Dion, and I have the best of rights to be angry with the men who slew him, very much as I have to be angry also with Dionysius; for both they and he have done the greatest of injuries both to me, and, one may say, to all the rest of mankind—they by destroying the man who purposed to practise justice, and he by utterly refusing to practise justice, when he had supreme power, throughout all his empire; although if, in that empire, philosophy and power had really been united in the same person the radiance thereof would have shone through the whole world of Greeks and barbarians, and fully imbued them with the true conviction that no State nor any individual man can ever become happy unless he passes his life in subjection to justice combined with wisdom, whether it be that he possesses these virtues within himself or as the result of being reared and trained righteously under holy rulers in their ways. Such were the injuries committed by Dionysius; and, compared to these, the rest of the injuries he did I would count but small. And the murderer of Dion is not aware that he has brought about the same result as Dionysius. For as to Dion, I know clearly—in so far as it is possible for a man to speak with assurance about men—that, if he had gained possession of the kingdom, he would never have adopted for his rule any other principle than this: when he had first brought gladness to Syracuse, his own fatherland, by delivering her from bondage, and had established her in a position of freedom, he would have endeavoured next, by every possible means, to set the citizens in order by suitable laws of the best kind; and as the next step after this, he would have done his utmost to colonize the whole of Sicily and to make it free from the barbarians, by driving out some of them and subduing others more easily than did Hiero.[16] And if all this had been done by a man who was just and courageous and temperate and wisdom-loving, the most of men would have formed the same opinion of virtue which would have prevailed, one may say, throughout the whole world, if Dionysius had been persuaded by me, and which would have saved all. But as it is, the onset of some

[16] Hiero, tyrant of Syracuse (478–466 B.C.), waged successful war against the Carthaginians.

deity or some avenging spirit, by means of lawlessness and god-lessness and, above all, by the rash acts of ignorance—that ignorance which is the root whence all evils for all men spring and which will bear hereafter most bitter fruit for those who have planted it—this it is which for the second time has wrecked and ruined all.

But now, for the third time, let us speak good words, for the omen's sake. Nevertheless, I counsel you, his friends, to imitate Dion in his devotion to his fatherland and in his temperate mode of life; and to endeavour to carry out his designs, though under better auspices; and what those designs were you have learnt from me clearly. But if any amongst you is unable to live in the Dorian fashion of his forefathers and follows after the Sicilian way of life and that of Dion's murderers, him you should neither call to your aid nor imagine that he could ever perform a loyal or sound action; but all others you should call to aid you in repeopling all Sicily and giving it equal laws, calling them both from Sicily itself and from the whole of the Peloponnese, not fearing even Athens itself; for there too there are those who surpass all men in virtue, and who detest the enormities of men who slay their hosts. But—though these results may come about later,—if for the present you are beset by the constant quarrels of every kind which spring up daily between the factions, then every single man on whom the grace of Heaven has bestowed even a small measure of right opinion must surely be aware that there is no cessation of evils for the warring factions until those who have won the mastery cease from perpetuating feuds by assaults and expulsions and executions, and cease from seeking to wreak vengeance on their foes; and, exercising mastery over themselves, lay down impartial laws which are framed to satisfy the vanquished no less than themselves; and compel the vanquished to make use of these laws by means of two compelling forces, namely, Reverence and Fear—Fear, inasmuch as they make it plain that they are superior to them in force; and Reverence, because they show themselves superior both in their attitude to pleasures and in their greater readiness and ability to subject themselves to the laws. In no other way is it possible for a city at strife within itself to cease from evils, but strife and enmity and hatred and suspicion are wont to keep for ever recurring in cities when their inner state is of this kind.

Now those who have gained the mastery, whenever they become desirous of safety, ought always to choose out among themselves such men of Greek origin as they know by inquiry to be most excellent—men who are, in the first place, old, and who have wives and children at home, and forefathers as numerous and good and famous as possible, and who are all in possession of ample property; and for a city of ten thousand citizens, fifty such men would be a sufficient number. These men they should fetch from their homes by means of entreaties and the greatest possible honours; and when they have fetched them they should entreat and enjoin them to frame laws, under oath that they will give no advantage either to conquerors or conquered, but equal rights in common to the whole city. And when the laws have been laid down, then everything depends upon the following condition. On the one hand, if the victors prove themselves subservient to the laws more than the vanquished, then all things will abound in safety and happiness, and all evils will be avoided; but should it prove otherwise, neither I nor anyone else should be called in to take part in helping the man who refuses to obey our present injunctions. For this course of action is closely akin to that which Dion and I together, in our plans for the welfare of Syracuse, attempted to carry out, although it is but the second-best;[17] for the first was that which we first attempted to carry out with the aid of Dionysius himself—a plan which would have benefited all alike, had it not been that some Chance, mightier than men, scattered it to the winds. Now, however, it is for you to endeavour to carry out our policy with happier results by the aid of Heaven's blessing and divine good-fortune.

[Plato, having thus concluded his "counsel" to Dion's friends, proceeds with the narrative of his relations with Dionysius. His second visit to Sicily had been ended by the outbreak of war, but he had promised to return after the war on condition that Dion was recalled from exile. But when the tyrant wished to defer the recall of Dion, Plato was reluctant to return. Finally, however, he yielded to the urgent entreaties of Dionysius, backed up by the advice of Dion, his Athenian friends, and his friend Archytas of Tarentum. It was reported that Dionysius had recovered

[17] Alluding to the attempt then being made by Dion's party at Leontini, under Hipparinus (his nephew), to overthrow Callippus.

his enthusiasm for philosophy; and Plato felt that, if this were true, he dare not miss the possible chance of seeing his dreams and Dion's fulfilled.]

Let this, then, suffice as my counsel and my charge, and the story of my former visit to the court of Dionysius. In the next place, he that cares to listen may hear the story of my later journey by sea, and how naturally and reasonably it came about. For (as I said) I had completed my account of the first period of my stay in Sicily before I gave my counsel to the intimates and companions of Dion. What happened next was this: I urged Dionysius by all means possible to let me go, and we both made a compact that when peace was concluded (for at that time there was war in Sicily) Dionysius, for his part, should invite Dion and me back again, as soon as he had made his own power more secure; and he asked Dion to regard the position he was now in not as a form of exile but rather as a change of abode; and I gave a promise that upon these conditions I would return. When peace was made he kept sending for me; but he asked Dion to wait still another year, although he kept demanding most insistently that I should come. Dion, then, kept urging and entreating me to make the voyage; for in truth constant accounts were pouring in from Sicily how Dionysius was now once more marvellously enamoured of philosophy; and for this reason Dion was strenuously urging me not to disobey his summons. I was of course well aware that such things often happen to the young in regard to philosophy; but none the less I deemed it safer, at least for the time, to give a wide berth both to Dion and Dionysius, and I angered them both by replying that I was an old man and that none of the steps which were now being taken were in accordance with our compact.

Now it seems that after this Archytas[18] arrived at the court of Dionysius; for when I sailed away, I had, before my departure, effected a friendly alliance between Archytas and the Tarentines and Dionysius; and there were certain others in Syracuse who had had some teaching from Dion, and others again who had been taught by these, men who were stuffed with some borrowed philosophical doctrines. These men, I believe, tried to discuss these subjects with Dionysius, on the assumption that Dionysius was thoroughly instructed in all my system of thought. Now besides

---

[18] A famous scientist and statesman of Tarentum.

being naturally gifted otherwise with a capacity for learning Dionysius has an extraordinary love of glory. Probably, then, he was pleased with what was said and was ashamed of having it known that he had no lessons while I was in the country; and in consequence of this he was seized with a desire to hear my doctrines more explicitly, while at the same time he was spurred on by his love of glory: and we have already explained, in the account we gave a moment ago, the reasons why he had not been a hearer of mine during my previous sojourn. So when I had got safely home and had refused his second summons, as I said just now, Dionysius was greatly afraid, I believe, because of his love of glory, lest any should suppose that it was owing to my contempt for his nature and disposition, together with my experience of his mode of life, that I was ungracious and was no longer willing to come to his court.

Now I am bound to tell the truth, and to put up with it should anyone, after hearing what took place, come to despise, after all, my philosophy and consider that the tyrant showed intelligence. For, in fact, Dionysius, on this third occasion, sent a trireme to fetch me, in order to secure my comfort on the voyage; and he sent Archedemus, one of the associates of Archytas, believing that I esteemed him above all others in Sicily, and other Sicilians of my acquaintance; and all these were giving me the same account, how that Dionysius had made marvellous progress in philosophy. And he sent an exceedingly long letter, since he knew how I was disposed towards Dion and also Dion's eagerness that I should make the voyage and come to Syracuse; for his letter was framed to deal with all these circumstances, having its commencement couched in some such terms as these—"Dionysius to Plato," followed by the customary greetings; after which, without further preliminary—"If you are persuaded by us and come now to Sicily, in the first place you will find Dion's affairs proceeding in whatever way you yourself may desire—and you will desire, as I know, what is reasonable, and I will consent thereto; but otherwise none of Dion's affairs, whether they concern himself or anything else, will proceed to your satisfaction." Such were his words on this subject, but the rest it were tedious and inopportune to repeat. And other letters kept coming both from Archytas and from the men in Tarentum, eulogizing the philosophy of Dionysius, and saying that unless I come now I should utterly dissolve their friendship with Dionysius which I had brought about, and which was of no small political importance. Such then being the nature of the summons which I then received,—when on the one hand the Sicilians and Italians were pulling me in and the Athenians, on the other, were literally pushing me out, so to say, by their entreaties,—once again the same argument recurred, namely, that it was my duty not to betray Dion, nor yet my hosts and comrades in Tarentum. And I felt also myself that there would be nothing surprising in a young man, who was apt at learning, attaining to a love of the best life through hearing lectures on subjects of importance. So it seemed to be my duty to determine clearly in which way the matter really stood, and in no wise to prove false to this duty, nor to leave myself open to a reproach that would be truly serious, if so be that any of these reports were true.

[On this his *third visit* to Sicily, Plato decided to begin by putting to the test the tyrant's interest in philosophy. The test was made by explaining the toil and time it involved owing to the length of the necessary propedeutic. Only those who can face the ordeal of "plain living and high thinking" survive this test.]

So having blindfolded myself with this argumentation I made the journey, although, naturally, with many fears and none too happy forebodings. However, when I arrived the third time, I certainly did find it really a case of "the Third to the Saviour": for happily I did get safely back again; and for this I ought to give thanks, after God, to Dionysius, seeing that, when many had planned to destroy me, he prevented them and paid some regard to reverence in his dealings with me. And when I arrived, I deemed that I ought first of all to gain proof of this point,—whether Dionysius was really inflamed by philosophy, as it were by fire, or all this persistent account which had come to Athens was empty rumour. Now there is a method of testing such matters which is not ignoble but really suitable in the case of tyrants, and especially such as are crammed with borrowed doctrines; and this was certainly what had happened to Dionysius, as I perceived as soon as I arrived. To such persons one must point out what the subject is as a whole, and what its character, and how many preliminary subjects it entails and how much labour. For on hearing this, if the pupil be truly philosophic, in sympathy with the subject and worthy of it, because divinely gifted, he believes that he has been shown a marvellous pathway and that he must brace himself at once to follow it, and that life will not be worth living if he does otherwise. After this he braces both himself and him who is guiding him on the path, nor does he desist until either he has reached the goal of all his studies, or else has gained such power as to be capable of directing his own steps without the aid of the instructor. It is thus, and in this mind, that such a student lives, occupied indeed in whatever occupations he may find himself, but always beyond all else cleaving fast to philosophy and to that mode of daily life which will best make him apt to learn and of retentive mind and able to reason within himself soberly; but the mode of life which is opposite to this he continually abhors. Those, on the other hand, who are in reality not philosophic, but superficially tinged by opinions,—like men whose bodies are sunburnt on the surface—when they see how many studies are required and how great labour, and how the orderly mode of daily life is that which befits the subject, they deem it difficult or impossible for themselves, and thus they become in fact incapable of pursuing it; while some of them persuade themselves that they have been sufficiently instructed in the whole subject and no longer require any further effort.

Now this test proves the clearest and most infallible in dealing with those who are luxurious and incapable of enduring labour, since it prevents any of them from ever casting the blame on his instructor instead of on himself and his own inability to pursue all the studies which are accessory to his subject.

[A long *digression* is here made, dealing with Plato's views on philosophy and its teaching. Dionysius, he says, was an unsatisfactory pupil, since he claimed to be already an expert in philosophy. Later on, it is said, he wrote a treatise on metaphysics himself which he claimed to be superior to Plato's lectures. But he and all others who make such claims are impostors. The deepest doctrines do not admit of written expression, and can only be the fruit of lifelong study; hence, says Plato, I have never written them down myself, nor would the attempt be anything but harmful.

Why the ultimate realities are thus incommunicable is shown by an analysis of philosophic apprehension and expression. *Knowledge*, and the *Real* which is its object, are approached through sense-perception and verbal description. The elements of this last are the *Name* and the *Definition;* while what the senses perceive is the phenomenon or *Image.* And we must apprehend Name, Definition, Image and Knowledge ("the first Four") before we attain to the Real ("the Fifth").

For we must be clear as to how the Real differs from the Sensible and its expression. The Name and the Definition give us *quality,* not *essence.* And Name and Definition, like the sensible Image, are never fixed but always shifting and relative. So because the nature of "the Four" is thus defective, the student who seeks to apprehend through them "the Fifth" (Ideal Reality) is filled with confusion; for in seeking the *essence* he finds the *quality* always intruding. .And it is only by searching scrutiny of the "First Four" concomitants of apprehension that the student can hope to win through to a vision of the Real—and then only if he be of his own nature akin to that Ideal Object of reason; and that vision comes, when it does come, by a sudden flash, "as it were a light from heaven."

The approach to Philosophy being thus arduous, no "serious" teacher would ever try to teach these "serious" themes in public or write them down. So that if Dionysius has written on metaphysics it only shows that he misunderstands the subject, and that his motive is to gain a cheap reputation of culture. For he received one lesson only on metaphysics from Plato. But whatever be the tyrant's views regarding philosophy and his own philosophic competence, it is monstrous that he should have shown such disrespect as he did to Plato, the acknowledged master-philosopher.]

This, then, was the purport of what I said to Dionysius on that occasion. I did not, however, expound the matter fully, nor did Dionysius ask me to do so; for he claimed that he himself knew many of the most important doctrines and was sufficiently informed owing to the versions he had heard from his other teachers. And I am even told that later on he himself wrote a treatise on the subjects in which I then instructed him, composing it as though it were something of his own invention and quite different from what he had heard; but of all this I know nothing. I know indeed that certain others have written about these same subjects; but what manner of men they are not even themselves know. But thus much I can certainly declare concerning all these writers, or prospective writers, who claim to know the subjects which I seriously study, whether as hearers of mine or of other teachers, or from their own discoveries; it is impossible, in my judgement at least, that these men should understand anything about this subject. There does not exist, nor will there ever exist, any treatise of mine dealing therewith. For it does not at all admit of verbal expression like other studies, but, as a result of continued application to the subject itself and communion therewith, it is brought to birth in the soul on a sudden, as light that is kindled by a leaping spark, and thereafter it nourishes itself. Notwithstanding, of thus much I am certain, that the best statement of these doctrines in writing or in speech would be my own statement; and further, that if they should be badly stated in writing, it is I who would be the person most deeply pained. And if I had thought that these subjects ought to be fully stated in writing or in speech to the public, what nobler action could I have performed in my life than that of writing what is of great benefit to mankind and bringing forth to the light for all men the nature of reality? But were I to undertake this task it would not, as I think, prove a good thing for men, save for some few who are able to discover the truth themselves with but little instruction; for as to the rest, some it would most unseasonably fill with a mistaken contempt, and others with an overweening and empty aspiration, as though they had learnt some sublime mysteries.

But concerning these studies I am minded to speak still more at length; since the subject with which I am dealing will perhaps be clearer when I have thus spoken. For there is a certain true argument which confronts the man who ventures to write anything at all of these matters,—an argument which, although I have frequently stated it in the past, seems to require statement also at the present time.

Every existing object has three things which are the necessary means by which knowledge of that object is acquired; and the knowledge itself is a fourth thing; and as a fifth one must postulate the object itself which is cognizable and true. First of these comes the name; secondly the definition; thirdly the image; fourthly the knowledge. If you wish, then, to understand what I am now saying, take a single example and learn from it what applies to all. There is an object called a circle, which has for its *name* the word we have just mentioned; and, secondly, it has a *definition*, com-

posed of names and verbs; for "that which is everywhere equi-
distant from the extremities to the centre" will be the definition
of that object which has for its name "round" and "spherical" and
"circle." And in the third place there is that object which is in
course of being portrayed and obliterated, or of being shaped with
a lathe, and falling into decay; but none of these affections is suffered by the circle itself, whereto all these others are related inasmuch as it is distinct therefrom. Fourth comes *knowledge* and intelligence and true opinion regarding these objects; and these we
must assume to form a single whole, which does not exist in vocal
utterance or in bodily forms but in souls; whereby it is plain that it
differs both from the nature of the circle itself and from the three
previously mentioned. And of those four intelligence approaches
most nearly in kinship and similarity to the fifth, and the rest are
further removed.

The same is true alike of the straight and of the spherical form,
and of colour, and of the good and the fair and the just, and of all
bodies whether manufactured or naturally produced (such as fire
and water and all such substances), and of all living creatures, and
of all moral actions or passions in souls. For unless a man somehow or other grasps the four of these, he will never perfectly acquire knowledge of the fifth. Moreover, these four attempt to express the quality of each object no less than its real essence, owing
to the weakness inherent in language; and for this reason, no man
of intelligence will ever venture to commit to it the concepts of his
reason, especially when it is unalterable—as is the case with what
is formulated in writing.

But here again you must learn further the meaning of this last
statement. Every one of the circles which are drawn in geometric
exercises or are turned by the lathe is full of what is opposite to the
fifth, since it is in contact with the straight everywhere; whereas the
circle itself, as we affirm, contains within itself no share greater or
less of the opposite nature. And none of the objects, we affirm, has
any fixed name, nor is there anything to prevent forms which
are now called "round" from being called "straight," and the
"straight" "round";[19] and men will find the names no less firmly
fixed when they have shifted them and apply them in an opposite

[19] *Cf. Cratyl.* 384 D, E for the view that names are not natural but conventional
fixities.

sense. Moreover, the same account holds good of the Definition also, that, inasmuch as it is compounded of names and verbs, it is in no case fixed with sufficient firmness.[20] And so with each of the Four, their inaccuracy is an endless topic; but, as we mentioned a moment ago, the main point is this, that while there are two separate things, the real essence and the quality, and the soul seeks to know not the quality but the essence, each of the Four proffers to the soul either in word or in concrete form that which is not sought; and by thus causing each object which is described or exhibited to be always easy of refutation by the senses, it fills practically all men with all manner of perplexity and uncertainty. In respect, however, of those other objects the truth of which, owing to our bad training, we usually do not so much as seek—being content with such of the images as are proffered,—those of us who answer are not made to look ridiculous by those who question, we being capable of analysing and convicting the Four. But in all cases where we compel a man to give the Fifth as his answer and to explain it, anyone who is able and willing to upset the argument gains the day, and makes the person who is expounding his view by speech or writing or answers appear to most of his hearers to be wholly ignorant of the subjects about which he is attempting to write or speak; for they are ignorant sometimes of the fact that it is not the soul of the writer or speaker that is being convicted but the nature of each of the Four, which is essentially defective. But it is the methodical study of all these stages, passing in turn from one to another, up and down, which with difficulty implants knowledge, when the man himself, like his object, is of a fine nature; but if his nature is bad—and, in fact, the condition of most men's souls in respect of learning and of what are termed "morals" is either naturally bad or else corrupted,—then not even Lynceus himself could make such folk see. In one word, neither receptivity nor memory will ever produce knowledge in him who has no affinity with the object, since it does not germinate to start with in alien states of mind; consequently neither those who have no natural connexion or affinity with things just, and all else that is fair, although they are both receptive and retentive in various ways of other things, nor yet those who possess such affinity but are unreceptive and unretentive—none, I say, of these will ever learn to the utmost possible

[20] Cf. *Theaet.* 208 B ff. for the instability of Definitions.

extent the truth of virtue nor yet of vice. For in learning these objects it is necessary to learn at the same time both what is false and what is true of the whole of Existence, and that through the most diligent and prolonged investigation, as I said at the commencement; and it is by means of the examination of each of these objects, comparing one with another—names and definitions, visions and sense-perceptions,—proving them by kindly proofs and employing questionings and answerings that are void of envy—it is by such means, and hardly so, that there bursts out the light of intelligence and reason regarding each object in the mind of him who uses every effort of which mankind is capable.

And this is the reason why every serious man in dealing with really serious subjects carefully avoids writing, lest thereby he may possibly cast them as a prey to the envy and stupidity of the public. In one word, then, our conclusion must be that whenever one sees a man's written compositions—whether they be the laws of a legislator or anything else in any other form,—these are not his most serious works, if so be that the writer himself is serious: rather those works abide in the fairest region he possesses. If, however, these really are his serious efforts, and put into writing, it is not "the gods" but mortal men who "Then of a truth themselves have utterly ruined his senses."

Whosoever, then, has accompanied me in this story and this wandering of mine will know full well that, whether it be Dionysius or any lesser or greater man who has written something about the highest and first truths of Nature, nothing of what he has written, as my argument shows, is based on sound teaching or study. Otherwise he would have reverenced these truths as I do, and would not have dared to expose them to unseemly and degrading treatment. For the writings of Dionysius were not meant as aids to memory, since there is no fear lest anyone should forget the truth if once he grasps it with his soul, seeing that it occupies the smallest possible space; rather, if he wrote at all, it was to gratify his base love of glory, either by giving out the doctrines as his own discoveries, or else by showing, forsooth, that he shared a culture which he by no means deserved because of his lust for the fame accruing from its possession. Well, then, if such was the effect produced on Dionysius by our one conversation, perhaps it was so; but how this effect was produced "God troweth," as the Theban says; for as I said, I explained my doctrine to him then on one occasion only, and never again since then.

And if anyone is concerned to discover how it was that things actually happened as they did in regard to this matter, he ought to consider next the reason why we did not explain our doctrine a second time, or a third time, or still more often. Does Dionysius fancy that he possesses knowledge, and is his knowledge adequate, as a result of hearing me once only, or as the result of his own researches, or of previous instruction from other teachers? Or does he regard my doctrines as worthless? Or, thirdly, does he believe them to be beyond and above his capacity, and that he himself would be really incapable of living a life devoted to wisdom and virtue? For if he deems them worthless he will be in conflict with many witnesses who maintain the opposite, men who should be vastly more competent judges of such matters than Dionysius. While if he claims that he has found out these truths by research or by instruction, and if he admits their value for the liberal education of the soul, how could he possibly (unless he is a most extraordinary person) have treated the leading authority[21] on this subject with such ready disrespect? And how he showed this disrespect I will now relate.

[The narrative of the *third Sicilian visit* is now *resumed*, after the philosophic digression; and it is a narrative of the insults heaped on Plato by Dionysius. To begin with, the latter broke his agreement by refusing to allow the revenues of the exiled Dion to be sent to him. In anger at this Plato said he would return home; but on the tyrant's proposing easier terms for Dion, he consented to remain until they got a reply from Dion. Presently, however, Dionysius turned round and said that he would have all Dion's property sold, keep a half of it for Dion's son, and let Plato take the balance to Dion.

As this happened when the sailing-season (summer of 361 B.C.) was already over, it was useless to expostulate further; and Plato, caged like a bird, was intent only on escaping as soon as possible. Soon after this a mutiny arose among the mercenary force at Syracuse, owing to the attempt of Dionysius to cut down their pay. For this the blame was thrown on Heracleides, the democratic leader, and his arrest was ordered. Theodotes, however, pleaded

---

[21] I.e., Plato himself.

for his life, and Dionysius agreed to let him leave the country unharmed. But this agreement he broke the next day, in spite of the renewed intervention of Theodotes and Plato, by sending out soldiers to hunt for Heracleides and seize him. Luckily, however, he made his escape.

Dionysius's next piece of disrespect was to turn Plato out of the Acropolis and give him a lodging near the soldier's quarters. And he found a new pretext for quarrelling in the visits paid by Plato to Theodotes, the friend of Dion and Heracleides, which he regarded as a slight to himself. Plato found himself threatened also with violence at the hands of the soldiers amongst whom he lived; so he appealed for help to Archytas of Tarentum, and a Tarentine vessel was dispatched with a request to Dionysius that he should allow Plato to leave Sicily; which request was granted.]

It happened next, after no long interval, that whereas Dionysius had previously allowed Dion to remain in possession of his own property and to enjoy the income, he now ceased to permit Dion's trustees to remit it to the Peloponnese, just as though he had entirely forgotten the terms of his letter, claiming that the property belonged not to Dion but to his son, his own nephew, of whom he was the legal trustee. Such were his actions during this period up to this point; and when matters had turned out thus, I perceived clearly what kind of love Dionysius had for philosophy; and, moreover, I had good reason to be annoyed, whether I wished it or not. For by then it was already summer and the season for ships to sail. Still I judged that I had no right to be more angry with Dionysius than with myself and those who had forced me to come the third time to the straits adjoining Scylla—"There yet again to traverse the length of deadly Charybdis"; rather I should inform Dionysius that it was impossible for me to remain now that Dion was so insultingly treated. He, however, tried to talk me over and entreated me to remain, as he thought it would not be to his own credit that I should hurry away in person to convey such tidings; and when he failed to persuade me he promised to provide a passage for me himself. For I was proposing to embark and sail in the trading-vessels; because I was enraged and thought that I ought to stop at nothing, in case I were hindered, seeing that I was manifestly doing no wrong but suffering wrong. But when he saw that I had no inclination to remain he devised a scheme of the following kind to secure my remaining over that sailing-season. On the following day he came and addressed me in these plausible terms: "You and I," he said, "must get Dion and Dion's affairs cleared out of the way, to stop our frequent disputes about them. And this," said he, "is what I will do for Dion for your sake. I require that he shall remove his property and reside in the Peloponnese, not, however, as an exile but possessing the right to visit this country also whenever it is mutually agreed by him and by me and by you his friends. But this is on condition that he does not conspire against me; and you and your associates and Dion's here in Sicily shall be the guarantors of these terms, and he shall furnish you with his security. And all the property he shall take shall be deposited in the Peloponnese and Athens with such persons as you shall think fit; and he shall enjoy the income from it but shall not be authorized to remove it without your consent. For I do not altogether trust him to act justly towards me if he had the use of these funds—for they will be by no means small; and I put more trust in you and your friends.   So consider whether this arrangement contents you, and remain on these terms for the present year, and when next season arrives depart and take with you these funds of Dion. And I am well assured that Dion will be most grateful to you for having effected this arrangement on his behalf."

And I, when I heard this speech, was annoyed, but none the less I replied that I would think it over and let him know next day my decision about the matter; and to this we both then agreed. So after this, when I was by myself, I was thinking it over, very much perturbed. And in my deliberation the first and foremost reflexion was this—"Come now, suppose that Dionysius has no intention of performing any of his promises, and suppose that on my departure he sends a plausible note to Dion—both writing himself and charging many of his friends also to do so—stating the proposal he is now making to me, and how in spite of his wish I had refused to do what he had invited me to do, and had taken no interest at all in Dion's affairs; and beyond all this, suppose that he is no longer willing to send me away by giving his own personal order to one of the shipmasters, but makes it plain to them all that he has no wish for me to sail away in comfort—in this case would any of them consent to convey me as a passenger, starting off from the residence of Dionysius?" For, in addition to my other misfortunes,

I was lodging in the garden adjoining his residence, and out of this not even the doorkeeper would have allowed me to pass without a permit sent him from Dionysius. "On the other hand, if I stay on for the year I shall be able to write and tell Dion the position in which I am placed and what I am doing; and if Dionysius should actually perform any of his promises, I shall have accomplished something not altogether contemptible—for Dion's property, if it is rightly valued, amounts probably to as much as a hundred talents; whereas if the events now dimly threatening come to pass in the way that seems likely, I am at a loss to know what I shall do with myself. Notwithstanding, I am obliged, it appears, to endure another year of toil and endeavour to test by actual experience the devices of Dionysius."

When I had come to this decision, I said to Dionysius on the following day—"I have decided to remain. I request you, however," I said, "not to regard me as Dion's master, but to join with me yourself in sending him a letter explaining what we have now decided, and asking him whether it satisfies him; and if not, and if he desires and claims other conditions, let him write them to us immediately; and do you refrain till then from taking any new step in regard to his affairs." This is what was said, and this is what we agreed, pretty nearly in the terms I have now stated.

After this the vessels had put to sea and it was no longer possible for me to sail; and then it was that Dionysius remembered to tell me that one half of the property ought to belong to Dion, the other half to his son; and he said that he would sell it, and when sold he would give me the one half to convey to Dion, and leave the half intended for his son where it was; for that was the most equitable arrangement. I, then, although I was dumbfounded at his statement, deemed that it would be utterly ridiculous to gainsay him any more; I replied, however, that we ought to wait for the letter from Dion, and then send him back this proposal by letter. But immediately after this he proceeded to sell the whole of Dion's property in a very high-handed fashion, where and how and to what purchasers he chose, without ever saying a single word to me about the matter; and verily I, in like manner, forbore to talk to him at all any longer about Dion's affairs; for I thought that there was no longer any profit in so doing.

Now up to this time I had been assisting in this way philosophy and my friends; but after this, the kind of life we lived, Dionysius and I, was this—I was gazing out of my cage, like a bird that is longing to fly off and away, while he was scheming how he might shoo me back without paying away any of Dion's money; nevertheless, to the whole of Sicily we appeared to be comrades.

Now Dionysius attempted, contrary to his father's practice, to reduce the pay of the older members of his mercenary force, and the soldiers, being infuriated, assembled together and refused to permit it. And when he kept trying to force them by closing the gates of the citadel,[22] they immediately rushed up to the walls shouting out a kind of barbaric war-chant; whereupon Dionysius became terribly alarmed and conceded all and even more than all to those of the peltasts that were then assembled.

Then a report quickly got abroad that Heracleides was to blame for all this trouble; and Heracleides, on hearing this, took himself off and vanished. Then Dionysius was seeking to capture him, and finding himself at a loss he summoned Theodotes to his garden; and it happened that at the time I too was walking in the garden. Now the rest of their conversation I neither know nor heard, but I both know and remember what Theodotes said to Dionysius in my presence. "Plato," he said, "I am urging this course on our friend Dionysius: if I prove able to fetch Heracleides here to answer the charges now made against him, in case it is decided that he must not reside in Sicily, I claim that he should have a passage to the Peloponnese, taking his son and his wife, and reside there without doing injury to Dionysius, and enjoying the income from his property. In fact I have already sent to fetch him, and I will now send again, in case he should obey either my former summons or the present one. And I request and beseech Dionysius that, should anyone meet with Heracleides, whether in the country or here in the city, no harm should be inflicted on him beyond his removal out of the country until Dionysius has come to some further decision." And addressing Dionysius he said, "Do you agree to this?" "I agree," he replied, "that even if he be seen at your house he shall suffer no harm beyond what has now been mentioned."

Now on the next day, at evening, Eurybius and Theodotes came to me hurriedly, in an extraordinary state of perturbation; and Theodotes said—"Plato, were you present yesterday at the agreement

[22] The mercenaries lived in the island of Ortygia, but beyond the walls of the Acropolis; so when Plato had to quit the Acropolis he was surrounded by them in his new lodgings.

which Dionysius made with us both concerning Heracleides?" "Of
course I was," I replied. "But now," he said, "peltasts[23] are running
about seeking to capture Heracleides, and he is probably somewhere
about here. But do you now by all means accompany us to Dionysius." So we set off and went in to where he was; and while they
two stood in silence, weeping, I said to him—"My friends here
are alarmed lest you should take any fresh step regarding Heracleides, contrary to our agreement of yesterday; for I believe it
is known that he has taken refuge somewhere hereabouts." On
hearing this, Dionysius fired up and went all colours, just as an
angry man would do; and Theodotes fell at his knees and grasping his hand besought him with tears to do no such thing. And I
interposed and said by way of encouragement—"Cheer up, Theodotes; for Dionysius will never dare to act otherwise contrary to
yesterday's agreement." Then Dionysius, with a highly tyrannical
glare at me, said—"With you I made no agreement, great or small."
"Heaven is witness," I replied, "that you did,—not to do what this
man is now begging you not to do." And when I had said this I
turned away and went out. After this Dionysius kept on hunting
after Heracleides, while Theodotes kept sending messengers to
Heracleides bidding him to flee. And Dionysius sent out Tisias
and his peltasts with orders to pursue him; but Heracleides, as it
was reported, forestalled them by a fraction of a day and made his
escape into the Carthaginians' province.

Now after this Dionysius decided that his previous plot of refusing to pay over Dion's money would furnish him with a plausible ground for a quarrel with me; and, as a first step, he sent me
out of the citadel, inventing the excuse that the women had to
perform a sacrifice of ten days' duration in the garden where I was
lodging; so during this period he gave orders that I should stay
outside with Archedemus. And while I was there Theodotes sent
for me and was loud in his indignation at what had then taken
place and in his blame of Dionysius; but the latter, when he heard
that I had gone to the house of Theodotes, by way of making this a
new pretext, akin to the old, for his quarrel against me, sent a man
to ask me whether I had really visited Theodotes when he invited
me. "Certainly," I replied; and he said—"Well then, he ordered
me to tell you that you are not acting at all honourably in always

[23] *I.e.* light-armed soldiers, so called from the kind of light shield they carried.

preferring Dion and Dion's friends to him." Such were his words, and after this he did not summon me again to his house, as though it was now quite clear that I was friendly towards Theodotes and Heracleides but hostile to him; and he supposed that I bore him no goodwill because of the clean sweep he was making of Dion's moneys.

Thereafter I was residing outside the citadel among the mercenaries; and amongst others some of the servants who were from Athens, fellow-citizens of my own, came to me and reported that I had been slanderously spoken of amongst the peltasts; and that some of them were threatening that if they could catch me they would make away with me. So I devised the following plan to save myself: I sent to Archytas and my other friends in Tarentum stating the position in which I found myself: and they, having found some pretext for an Embassy from the State, dispatched a thirty-oared vessel, and with it one of themselves, called Lamiscus; and he, when he came, made request to Dionysius concerning me, saying that I was desirous to depart, and begging him by all means to give his consent. To this he agreed, and he sent me forth after giving me supplies for the journey; but as to Dion's money, neither did I ask for any of it nor did anyone pay me any.

[On his return from this third Sicilian expedition Plato visited Olympia, where he met Dion. Dion was eager to begin military operations against Dionysius, but Plato refused his support on the ground that he had been the guest of the tyrant and was averse to fomenting discord, foreseeing the evils that would inevitably result from civil war. But his counsels of moderation went unheeded. Yet Dion did not seek power for his own sake but for the sake of the public good; he was not selfish or avaricious or vengeful, but strove to establish the reign of Justice in the State by just means. Prudent though he was, his fall was due to an error of judgment: he failed to gauge accurately the depth of the wickedness of the men with whom he had to deal. The dagger that slew Dion in the hour of his success plunged deep into the very heart of Sicily.]

On arriving at Olympia,[24] in the Peloponnese, I came upon Dion, who was attending the Games; and I reported what had taken place. And he, calling Zeus to witness, was invoking me and my relatives and friends to prepare at once to take vengeance on Dio-

[24] *I.e.* for the festival of 360 B.C.

nysius,—we on account of his treachery to guests (for that was what
Dion said and meant), and he himself on account of his wrongful
expulsion and banishment. And I, when I heard this, bade him
summon my friends to his aid, should they be willing—"But as
for me," I said, "it was you yourself, with the others, who by main
force, so to say, made me an associate of Dionysius at table and at
hearth and a partaker in his holy rites; and he, though he probably
believed that I, as many slanderers asserted, was conspiring with
you against himself and his throne, yet refrained from killing me,
and showed compunction. Thus, not only am I no longer, as I may
say, of an age to assist anyone in war, but I also have ties in common with you both, in case you should ever come to crave at all for
mutual friendship and wish to do one another good; but so long as
you desire to do evil, summon others." This I said because I
loathed my Sicilian wandering and its ill-success. They, however,
by their disobedience and their refusal to heed my attempts at
conciliation have themselves to blame for all the evils which have
now happened; for, in all human probability, none of these would
ever have occurred if Dionysius had paid over the money to Dion
or had even become wholly reconciled to him, for both my will and
my power were such that I could have easily restrained Dion. But,
as things are, by rushing the one against the other they have flooded
the world with woes.

And yet Dion had the same designs as I myself should have had
(for so I would maintain) or anyone else whose purpose regarding
his own power and his friends and his city was the reasonable one of
achieving the greatest height of power and privilege by conferring
the greatest benefits. But a man does not do this if he enriches
himself, his comrades, and his city by means of plotting and collecting conspirators, while in reality he himself is poor and not
his own master but the cowardly slave of pleasures; nor does he do
so if he proceeds next to slay the owners of property, dubbing them
"enemies," and to dissipate their goods, and to charge his accomplices and comrades not to blame him if any of them complains of
poverty. So likewise if a man receives honour from a city for conferring on it such benefits as distributing the goods of the few to
the many by means of decrees; or if, when he is at the head of a
large city which holds sway over many smaller ones, he distributes
the funds of the smaller cities to his own, contrary to what is just.

For neither Dion nor any other will ever voluntarily[25] aim thus at a power that would bring upon himself and his race an everlasting curse, but rather at a moderate government and the establishment of the justest and best of laws by means of the fewest possible exiles and executions.

Yet when Dion was now pursuing this course, resolved to suffer rather than to do unholy deeds—although guarding himself against so suffering[26]—none the less when he had attained the highest pitch of superiority over his foes he stumbled. And therein he suffered no surprising fate. For while, in dealing with the unrighteous, a righteous man who is sober and sound of mind will never be wholly deceived concerning the souls of such men; yet it would not, perhaps, be surprising if he were to share the fate of a good pilot, who, though he certainly would not fail to notice the oncoming of a storm, yet might fail to realize its extraordinary and unexpected violence, and in consequence of that failure might be forcibly overwhelmed. And Dion's downfall was, in fact, due to the same cause; for while he most certainly did not fail to notice that those who brought him down were evil men, yet he did fail to realize to what a pitch of folly they had come, and of depravity also and voracious greed; and thereby he was brought down and lies fallen, enveloping Sicily in immeasurable woe.

[*Conclusion:* The "counsel" based on the experiences now related has been already set forth. And the narrative of the third visit has been given at this length in order to refute distorted accounts in which Plato's acts and motives had been misrepresented. If it serves to fulfil this purpose and convince his readers that he was justified in what he said and did, he will be well content.]

What counsel I have to offer, after this narrative of events, has been given already, and so let it suffice. But I deemed it necessary to explain the reasons why I undertook my second journey to Sicily[27] because absurd and irrational stories are being told about it. If, therefore, the account I have now given appears to anyone more rational, and if anyone believes that it supplies sufficient excuses for what took place, then I shall regard that account as both reasonable and sufficient.

[25] According to the Socratic dictum, "No one sins voluntarily."

[26] For "suffering" wrong as a bar to complete happiness *cf. Laws* 829 A.

[27] *I.e.* Plato's *third* Sicilian visit (as he does not count the first), *cf.* 330 C, 337 E.

THE WORLD OF THE CHANGING

On the Flux in Notation (*Cratylus*)
On the Flux of Pleasure and Its Measurement (*Protagoras*)
On the Flux of Opinion and Its Correction (*Theaetetus*)

The most persistent contrast in Plato, as the child of his age, is between the changing and the permanent. With the former is equated opinion, with the latter knowledge. For men, born into the world of change, there is no royal road, though there is a road, to the changeless. The course of the road is the career of knowledge. However Plato arrives at the goal—a procedure we shall presently note—there is ample evidence through many dialogues that he treated seriously the realm where precariousness rules. If the yonder is ever to be discovered, it is to be found, thought he, through clues to it here and now. He is reputed to have studied early with a disciple of Heraclitus, Cratylus (in whose [dis]honor the dialogue is named from which we are now to quote first). Whether or not such studies were the cause, Plato was always greatly impressed with the mobility of temporal existence and the effect of this mobility upon knowledge and general human fortune. Opinion, which is the best one can get from the senses, is really a guide to life for most men, and a not impossible guide. But it never guides one out of change, and so it remains in method a second best. Such a level of insight becomes in the moral field hedonism, which is tentatively defended in the "Protagoras," severely qualified in the "Philebus," and transcended in the "Gorgias" and the "Republic." In the political field it becomes democracy, a social order, as he thought, where unequals are counted as equals and men are just ready to burst with liberty for all impulses alike. And in the field of logic ("Theaetetus" and "Parmenides"), knowledge is mere approximation so long as the world of change is accepted as the theater for mind's career. To discern in the changing the changeless is to see what the changing means and is to renounce the false claim that we know "with" our senses in favor of the true claim that we know "through" our senses. Plato transcended the Sophists by admitting what they claimed and then claiming more than they could admit: man, who is the measure of all things, must measure himself by true being.

. . .

ON THE FLUX IN NOTATION

Cratylus. Fowler translation ("Loeb Classical Library" series). A mere fragment from the close of the dialogue. The headings in this section are mine.—T. V. S.

Soc. If it be true that things can be learned either through names or through themselves, which would be the better and surer way of learning? To learn from the image whether it is itself a good imitation and also to learn the truth which it imitates, or to learn from the truth both the truth itself and whether the image is properly made?

Cra. I think it is certainly better to learn from the truth.

Soc. How realities are to be learned or discovered is perhaps too great a question for you or me to determine; but it is worth while to have reached even this conclusion, that they are to be learned and sought for, not from names but much better through themselves than through names.

Cra. That is clear, Socrates.

Soc. Then let us examine one further point to avoid being deceived by the fact that most of these names tend in the same direction. Suppose it should prove that although those who gave the names gave them in the belief that all things are in motion and flux—I myself think they did have that belief—still in reality that is not the case, and the name-givers themselves, having fallen into a kind of vortex, are whirled about, dragging us along with them. Consider, my worthy Cratylus, a question about which I often dream. Shall we assert that there is any absolute beauty, or good, or any other absolute existence, or not?

Cra. I think there is, Socrates.

Soc. Then let us consider the absolute, not whether a particular face, or something of that sort, is beautiful, or whether all these things are in flux. Is not, in our opinion, absolute beauty always such as it is?

Cra. That is inevitable.

THERE WOULD BE NO KNOWLEDGE IF ALL IS IN FLUX

Soc. Can we, then, if it is always passing away, correctly say that it is this, then that it is that, or must it inevitably, in the very instant while we are speaking, become something else and pass away and no longer be what it is?

Cra. That is inevitable.

Soc. How, then, can that which is never in the same state be anything? For if it is ever in the same state, then obviously at that time it is not changing; and if it is always in the same state and is always the same, how can it ever change or move without relinquishing its own form?

Cra. It cannot do so at all.

Soc. No, nor can it be known by anyone. For at the moment when he who seeks to know it approaches, it becomes something else and different, so that its nature and state can no longer be known; and surely there is no knowledge which knows that which is in no state.

Cra. It is as you say.

Soc. But we cannot even say that there is any knowledge, if all things are changing and nothing remains fixed; for if knowledge itself does not change and cease to be knowledge, then knowledge would remain, and there would be knowledge, but if the very essence of knowledge changes, at the moment of the change to another essence of knowledge there would be no knowledge, and if it is always changing, there will always be no knowledge, and by this reasoning there will be neither anyone to know nor anything to be known. But if there is always that which knows and that which is known—if the beautiful, the good, and all the other verities exist—I do not see how there is any likeness between these conditions of which I am now speaking and flux or motion. Now whether this is the nature of things, or the doctrine of Heracleitus and many others is true, is another question; but surely no man of sense can put himself and his soul under the control of names, and trust in names and their makers to the point of affirming that he knows anything; nor will he condemn himself and all things and say that there is no health in them, but that all things are flowing like leaky pots, or believe that all things are just like people afflicted with catarrh, flowing and running all the time. Perhaps, Cratylus, this theory is true, but perhaps it is not. Therefore you must consider courageously and thoroughly and not accept anything carelessly—

for you are still young and in your prime; then, if after investigation you find the truth, impart it to me.

CRA. I will do so. However, I assure you, Socrates, that I have already considered the matter, and after toilsome consideration I think the doctrine of Heracleitus is much more likely to be true.

SOC. Some other time, then, my friend, you will teach me, when you come back; but now go into the country as you have made ready to do; and Hermogenes here will go with you a bit.

CRA. Very well, Socrates, and I hope you also will continue to think of these matters.

ON THE FLUX OF PLEASURE AND ITS MEASUREMENT

Protagoras. Lamb translation ("Loeb Classical Library" series). Only a small segment from a long dialogue.—T. V. S.

Do you speak of some men, Protagoras, I [Socrates] asked, as living well, and others ill?

Yes.

Then do you consider that a man would live well if he lived in distress and anguish?

No, he said.

Well now, if he lived pleasantly and so ended his life, would you not consider he had thus contrived to live well?

I would, he said.

And, I suppose, to live pleasantly is good, and unpleasantly, bad?

Yes, he said, if one lived in the enjoyment of honourable things.

But, Protagoras, will you tell me you agree with the majority in calling some pleasant things bad and some painful ones good? I mean to say—Are not things good in so far as they are pleasant, putting aside any other result they may have; and again, are not painful things in just the same sense bad—in so far as they are painful?

I cannot tell, Socrates, he replied, whether I am to answer, in such absolute fashion as that of your question, that all pleasant things are good and painful things bad: I rather think it safer for me to reply, with a view not merely to my present answer but to all the rest of my life, that some pleasant things are not good, and also that some painful things are not bad, and some are, while a third class of them are indifferent—neither bad nor good.[28]

You call pleasant, do you not, I asked, things that partake of pleasure or cause pleasure?

Certainly, he said.

So when I put it to you, whether things are not good in so far as they are pleasant, I am asking whether pleasure itself is not a good thing.

Let us examine the matter, Socrates, he said, in the form in which you put it at each point, and if the proposition seems to be reasonable, and pleasant and good are found to be the same, we shall agree upon it; if not, we shall dispute it there and then.

And would you like, I asked, to be leader in the inquiry, or am I to lead.

You ought to lead, he replied, since you are the inaugurator of this discussion.

Well then, I proceeded, will the following example give us the light we need? Just as, in estimating a man's health or bodily efficiency by his appearance, one might look at his face and the lower part of his arms and say: Come now, uncover your chest too and your back and show them, that I may examine you thoroughly,—so the same sort of desire comes over me in regard to our inquiry. Observing your condition to be as you describe in respect of the good and the pleasant, I am fair to say something like this: Come, my good Protagoras, uncover some more of your thoughts: how are you in regard to knowledge? Do you share the view that most people take of this, or have you some other? The

---

[28] Cf. on this distinction of what is now called "intrinsic" and "extrinsic" goodness Plato's remark in the *Republic* 357 [Glaucon questioning Socrates]: "Do you agree that there is a kind of good which we would choose to possess, not from desire for its after effects, but welcoming it for its own sake? As, for example, joy and such pleasures as are harmless and nothing results from them afterwards save to have and to hold the enjoyment." "I recognize that kind," said I. "And again a kind that we love both for its own sake and for its consequences, such as understanding, sight, and health? For these I presume we welcome for both reasons." "Yes," I said. "And can you discern a third form of good under which falls exercise and being healed when sick and the art of healing and the making of money generally? For of them we would say that they are laborious and painful yet beneficial, and for their own sake we would not accept them, but only for the rewards and other benefits that accrue from them." "Why yes," I said, "I must admit this third class also."— T. V. S.

opinion generally held of knowledge is something of this sort—
that it is no strong or guiding or governing thing; it is not regarded as anything of that kind, but people think that, while a
man often has knowledge in him, he is not governed by it, but by
something else—now by passion, now by pleasure, now by pain,
at times by love, and often by fear; their feeling about knowledge
is just what they have about a slave, that it may be dragged about
by any other force. Now do you agree with this view of it, or do
you consider that knowledge is something noble and able to govern
man, and that whoever learns what is good and what is bad will
never be swayed by anything to act otherwise than as knowledge
bids, and that intelligence is a sufficient succour for mankind?

My view, Socrates, he replied, is precisely that which you express, and what is more, it would be a disgrace for me above all
men to assert that wisdom and knowledge were aught but the
highest of all human things.

Well and truly spoken, I said. Now you know that most people
will not listen to you and me, but say that many, while knowing
what is best, refuse to perform it, though they have the power, and
do other things instead. And whenever I have asked them to tell
me what can be the reason of this, they say that those who act so
are acting under the influence of pleasure or pain, or under the
control of one of the things I have just mentioned.

Yes, Socrates, he replied, I regard this as but one of the many
erroneous sayings of mankind.

Come then, and join me in the endeavour to persuade the world
and explain what is this experience of theirs, which they call "being
overcome by pleasure," and which they give as the reason why
they fail to do what is best though they have knowledge of it. For
perhaps if we said to them: What you assert, good people, is not
correct, but quite untrue—they might ask us: Protagoras and
Socrates, if this experience is not "being overcome by pleasure"
what on earth is it, and what do you call it? Tell us that.

Why, Socrates, must we consider the opinion of the mass of
mankind, who say just what occurs to them?

I fancy, I replied, that this will be a step towards discovering
how courage is related to the other parts of virtue. So if you think
fit to abide by the arrangement we made a while ago—that I
should lead in the direction which seems best for elucidating the

matter—you must now follow; but if you would rather not, to suit your wishes I will let it pass.

No, he said, your plan is quite right: go on to the end as you began.

Once more then, I proceeded, suppose they should ask us: Then what do you call this thing which we described as "being overcome by pleasures"? The answer I should give them would be this: Please attend: Protagoras and I will try to explain it to you. Do you not say that this thing occurs, good people, in the common case of a man being overpowered by the pleasantness of food or drink or sexual acts, and doing what he does though he knows it to be wicked? They would admit it. Then you and I would ask them again: In what sense do you call such deeds wicked? Is it that they produce those pleasures and are themselves pleasant at the moment, or that later on they cause diseases and poverty, and have many more such ills in store for us? Or, even though they have none of these things in store for a later day, and cause us only enjoyment, would they still be evil just because, forsooth, they cause enjoyment in some way or other? Can we suppose, Protagoras, that they will make any other answer than that these things are evil, not according to the operation of the actual pleasure of the moment, but owing to the later results in disease and those other ills?

I think, said Protagoras, that most people would answer thus.

Then in causing diseases they cause pains? And in causing poverty they cause pains. They would admit this, I imagine.

Protagoras agreed.

Then does it seem to you, my friends, as Protagoras and I assert, that the only reason why these things are evil is that they end at last in pains, and deprive us of other pleasures? Would they admit this?

We both agreed that they would.

Then again, suppose we should ask them the opposite: You, sirs, who tell us on the other hand that good things are painful;—do you not give such instances as physical training, military service, and medical treatment conducted by cautery, incision, drugs, or starvation, and say that these are good, but painful: Would they not grant it?

He agreed that they would.

Then do you call them good because they produce extreme pangs and anguish for the moment, or because later on they result in health and good bodily condition, the deliverance of cities, dominion over others, and wealth? They would assent to this, I suppose.

He agreed.

And are these things good for any other reason than that they end at last in pleasures and relief and riddance of pains? Or have you some other end to mention, with respect to which you call them good, apart from pleasures and pains? They could not find one, I fancy.

I too think they could not, said Protagoras.

Then do you pursue pleasure as being a good thing, and shun pain as being a bad one?

He agreed that we do.

So one thing you hold to be bad—pain; and pleasure you hold to be good, since the very act of enjoying you call bad as soon as it deprives us of greater pleasures than it has in itself, or leads to greater pains than the pleasures it contains. For if it is with reference to something else that you call the act of enjoyment bad, and with a view to some other end, you might be able to tell it us; but this you will be unable to do.

I too think that they cannot, said Protagoras.

Then is not the same thing repeated in regard to the state of being pained? You call being pained a good thing as soon as it either rids us of greater pains than those it comprises, or leads to greater pleasures than its pains. Now if you have in view some other end than those which I mention when you call being pained good, you can tell it us; but you never can.

Truly spoken, said Protagoras.

Once more then, I proceeded; if you were to ask me, my friends, Now why on earth do you speak at such length on this point, and in so many ways? I should reply, Forgive me: in the first place, it is not easy to conclude what it is that you mean when you say "overcome by pleasures"; and secondly, on this point hang all our conclusions. But it is still quite possible to retract, if you can somehow contrive to say that the good is different from pleasure, or the bad from pain. Is it enough for you to live out your life pleasantly, without pain? If it is, and you are unable to tell us of

any other good or evil that does not end in pleasure or pain, listen
to what I have to say next. I tell you that if this is so, the argument
becomes absurd, when you say that it is often the case that a man,
knowing the evil to be evil, nevertheless commits it, when he might
avoid it, because he is driven and dazed by his pleasures; while on
the other hand you say that a man, knowing the good, refuses to
do good because of the momentary pleasures by which he is overcome.

The absurdity of all this will be manifest if we refrain from using
a number of terms at once, such as pleasant, painful, good, and bad;
and as there appeared to be two things, let us call them by two
names—first, good and evil, and then later on, pleasant and painful. Let us then lay it down as our statement, that a man does
evil in spite of knowing the evil of it. Now if someone asks us:
Why? we shall answer: Because he is overcome. By what? the
questioner will ask us; and this time we shall be unable to reply:
By pleasure—for this has exchanged its name for "the good."
So we must answer only with the words: Because he is overcome.
By what? says the questioner. The good—must surely be our reply. Now if our questioner chance to be an arrogant person he
will laugh and exclaim: What a ridiculous statement, that a man
does evil, knowing it to be evil, and not having to do it, because
he is overcome by the good! Is this, he will ask, because the good
is not worthy of conquering the evil in you, or because it is worthy?
Clearly we must reply: Because it is not worthy; otherwise he
whom we speak of as overcome by pleasures would not have
offended. But in what sense, he might ask us, is the good unworthy of the bad, or the bad of the good? This can only be when
the one is greater and the other smaller, or when there are more on
the one side and fewer on the other. We shall not find any other
reason to give. So it is clear, he will say, that by "being overcome"
you mean getting the greater evil in exchange for the lesser good.
That must be agreed. Then let us apply the terms "pleasant"
and "painful" to these things instead, and say that a man does
what we previously called evil, but now call painful, knowing it to
be painful, because he is overcome by the pleasant, which is obviously unworthy to conquer. What unworthiness can there be in
pleasure as against pain, save an excess or defect of one compared with the other? That is, when one becomes greater and the

other smaller, or when there are more on one side and fewer on the other, or here a greater degree and there a less. For if you should say: But, Socrates, the immediately pleasant differs widely from the subsequently pleasant or painful, I should reply: Do they differ in anything but pleasure and pain? That is the only distinction. Like a practised weigher, put pleasant things and painful in the scales, and with them the nearness and the remoteness, and tell me which count for more. For if you weight pleasant things against pleasant, the greater and the more are always to be preferred: if painful against painful, then always the fewer and smaller. If you weight pleasant against painful, and find that the painful are outbalanced by the pleasant—whether the near by the remote or the remote by the near—you must take that course of action to which the pleasant are attached; but not that course if the pleasant are outweighted by the painful. Can the case be otherwise, I should ask, than thus, my friends? I am certain they could state no alternative.

To this he too assented.

Since that is the case, then, I shall say, please answer me this: Does not the same size appear larger to your sight when near, and smaller when distant? They will admit this. And it is the same with thickness and number? And sounds of equal strength are greater when near, and smaller when distant? They would agree to this. Now if our welfare consisted in doing and choosing things of large dimensions, and avoiding and not doing those of small, what would be our salvation in life? Would it be the art of measurement, or the power of appearance? Is it not the latter that leads us astray, as we saw, and many a time causes us to take things topsy-turvy and to have to change our minds both in our conduct and in our choice of great or small? Whereas the art of measurement would have made this appearance ineffective, and by showing us the truth would have brought our soul into the repose of abiding by the truth, and so would have saved our life. Would men acknowledge, in view of all this, that the art which saves our life is measurement, or some other?

It is measurement, he agreed.

Well now, if the saving our life depended on the choice of odd or even, and on knowing when to make a right choice of the greater and when of the less—taking each by itself or comparing it with

the other, and whether near or distant—what would save our life?
Would it not be knowledge; a knowledge of measurement, since
the art here is concerned with excess and defect, and of numera-
tion, as it has to do with odd and even? People would admit this,
would they not?

Protagoras agreed that they would.

Well then, my friends, since we have found that the salvation
of our life depends on making a right choice of pleasure and pain—
of the more and the fewer, the greater and the smaller, and the
nearer and the remoter—is it not evident, in the first place, that
measurement is a study of their excess and defect and equality in
relation to each other?

This must needs be so.

And being measurement, I presume it must be an art or science?

They will assent to this.

Well, the nature of this art or science we shall consider some
other time;[29] but the mere fact of its being a science will suffice for
the proof which Protagoras and I are required to give in answer to
the question you have put to us. You asked it, if you remember,
when we were agreeing that there is nothing stronger than knowledge, and that knowledge, wherever it may be found, has always the
upper hand of pleasure or anything else; and then you said that
pleasure often masters even the man of knowledge, and on our refusing to agree with you, you went on to ask us: Protagoras and
Socrates, if this experience is not "being overcome by pleasure,"
whatever can it be, and what do you call it? Tell us. If on the spur
of the moment we had replied, "Ignorance," you would have
laughed us to scorn: but now if you laugh at us you will be laughing at yourselves as well. For you have admitted that it is from
defect of knowledge that men err, when they do err, in their choice
of pleasures and pains—that is, in the choice of good and evil; and
from defect not merely of knowledge but of the knowledge which
you have now admitted also to be that of measurement. And
surely you know well enough for yourselves that the erring act

---

[29] The intellectual control of our sense-perceptions, which differ as to the size or
number of the same things when near and when distant, etc., has an important part
in the educational scheme of the *Republic*. The measuring art is further considered,
and named the "kingly art," in the *Statesman* (283 ff.).

committed without knowledge is done through ignorance. Accordingly "to be overcome by pleasure" means just this—ignorance in the highest degree, which Protagoras here and Prodicus and Hippias profess to cure. But you, through supposing it to be something else than ignorance, will neither go yourselves nor send your children to these sophists, who are the teachers of those things —you say it cannot be taught; you are chary of your money and will give them none, and so you fare badly both in private and in public life.

Such would have been our answer to the world at large. And I ask you now, Hippias and Prodicus, as well as Protagoras—for I would have you make a joint reply—whether you think what I say is true or false.

They all thought what I had said was absolutely true.

Then you agree, I continued, that the pleasant is good and the painful bad. And let me entreat my friend Prodicus to spare me his distinction of terms: for whether you say pleasant or delightful or enjoyable, my excellent Prodicus, or in whatever style or manner you may be pleased to name these things, pray reply to the sense of my question.

At this Prodicus laughed and consented, as did all the rest.

ON THE FLUX OF OPINION AND ITS CORRECTION

Theaetetus. Fowler translation ("Loeb Classical Library" series). By adding the subheadings and keeping to the main argument rather than to its rich illustrations, I have given here the gist of the dialogue in about one-seventh of its total words.— T. V. S.

WHAT IS KNOWLEDGE?

Soc. I am in doubt about one little matter, which should be investigated with your help and that of these others. Tell me, is not learning growing wiser about that which one learns?

Theaet. Of course.

Soc. And the wise, I suppose, are wise by wisdom.

Theaet. Yes.

Soc. And does this differ at all from knowledge?

Theaet. Does what differ?

Soc. Wisdom. Or are not people wise in that of which they have knowledge.

Theaet. Of course.

Soc. Then knowledge and wisdom are the same thing?

Theaet. Yes.

Soc. Well, it is just this that I am in doubt about and cannot fully grasp by my own efforts—what knowledge really is. Can we tell that? What do you say? Who of us will speak first? And he who fails, and whoever fails in turn, shall go and sit down and be donkey, as the children say when they play ball; and whoever gets through without failing shall be our king and shall order us to answer any questions he pleases. Why are you silent?

.   .   .   .

FIRST ANSWER: KNOWLEDGE IS PERCEPTION

Theaet. Well then, Socrates, since you are so urgent it would be disgraceful for anyone not to exert himself in every way to say what he can. I think, then, that he who knows anything perceives that which he knows, and, as it appears at present, knowledge is nothing else than perception.

Soc. Good! Excellent, my body! That is the way one ought to speak out. But come now, let us examine your utterance together, and see whether it is a real offspring or a mere wind-egg. Perception, you say, is knowledge?

Theaet. Yes.

Soc. And, indeed, if I may venture to say so, it is not a bad description of knowledge that you have given, but one which Protagoras also used to give. Only, he has said the same thing in a different way. For he says somewhere that man is "the measure of all things, of the existence of the things that are and the non-existence of the things that are not."

Theaet. Yes, I have read it often.

Soc. Well, is not this about what he means, that individual things are for me such as they appear to me, and for you in turn such as they appear to you—you and I being "man"?

Theaet. Yes, that is what he says.

Soc. It is likely that a wise man is not talking nonsense; so let us follow after him.

.   .   .   .

Theaet. Certainly that is what I should like.

Soc. And so should I. But since this is the case, and we have plenty of time, shall we not quietly, without any impatience, but truly examining ourselves, consider again the nature of these appearances within us? And as we consider them, I shall say, I think, first, that nothing can ever become more or less in size or number, so long as it remains equal to itself. Is it not so?

Theaet. Yes.

Soc. And secondly, that anything to which nothing is added and from which nothing is subtracted, is neither increased nor diminished, but is always equal.

Theaet. Certainly.

Soc. And should we not say thirdly, that what was not previously could not afterwards be without becoming and having become?

Theaet. Yes, I agree.

Soc. These three assumptions contend with one another in our minds when we talk about the dice, or when we say that I, who do not, at my age, either increase in size or diminish, am in the course of a year first larger than you, who are young, and afterwards smaller, when nothing has been taken from my size, but you have grown. For I am, it seems, afterwards what I was not before, and I have not become so; for it is impossible to have become without becoming, and without losing anything of my size I could not become smaller. And there are countless myriads of such contradictions, if we are to accept these that I have mentioned. You follow me, I take it, Theaetetus, for I think you are not new at such things.

Theaet. By the gods, Socrates, I am lost in wonder when I think of all these things, and sometimes when I regard them it really makes my head swim. . . . . [*Theodorus interrupting meantime.*]

Soc. In general I like his doctrine [i.e., Protagoras's] that what appears to each one is to him, but I am amazed by the beginning of his book. I don't see why he does not say in the beginning of his *Truth*[30] that a pig or a dog-faced baboon or some still stranger creature of those that have sensations is the measure of all things. Then he might have begun to speak to us very imposingly and condescendingly, showing that while we were honouring him like a god for his wisdom, he was after all no better in intellect than any other

[30] *Truth* was apparently the title, or part of the title, of Protagoras's book.

man, or, for that matter, than a tadpole. What alternative is there, Theodorus? For if that opinion is true to each person which he acquires through sensation, and no one man can discern another's condition better than he himself, and one man has no better right to investigate whether another's opinion is true or false than he himself, but, as we have said several times, each man is to form his own opinions by himself, and these opinions are always right and true, why in the world, my friend, was Protagoras wise, so that he could rightly be thought worthy to be the teacher of other men and to be well paid, and why were we ignorant creatures obliged to go to school to him, if each person is the measure of his own wisdom? Must we not believe that Protagoras was "playing to the gallery" in saying this? I say nothing of the ridicule that I and my science of midwifery deserve in that case,—and, I should say, the whole practice of dialectics, too. For would not the investigation of one another's fancies and opinions, and the attempt to refute them, when each man's must be right, be tedious and blatant folly, if the *Truth* of Protagoras is true and he was not jesting when he uttered his oracles from the shrine of his book?

THEO. Socrates, the man was my friend, as you just remarked. So I should hate to bring about the refutation of Protagoras by agreeing with you, and I should hate also to oppose you contrary to my real convictions. So take Theaetetus again; especially as he seemed just now to follow your suggestions very carefully.

Soc. If you went to Sparta, Theodorus, and visited the wrestling-schools, would you think it fair to look on at other people naked, some of whom were of poor physique, without stripping and showing your own form, too?

THEO. Why not, if I could persuade them to allow me to do so? So now I think I shall persuade you to let me be a spectator, and not drag me into the ring, since I am old and stiff, but to take the younger and nimbler man as your antagonist.

Soc. Well, Theodorus, if that please you, it does not displease me, as the saying is. So I must attack the wise Theaetetus again. Tell me, Theaetetus, referring to the doctrine we have just expounded, do you not share my amazement at being suddenly exalted to an equality with the wisest man, or even god? Or do you think Protagoras's "measure" applies any less to gods than to men?

THEAET. By no means; and I am amazed that you ask such a

question at all; for when we were discussing the meaning of the doctrine that whatever appears to each one really is to him, I thought it was good; but now it has suddenly changed to the opposite.

. . . .

Soc. Very well, now I am going to ask the most frightfully difficult question of all. It runs, I believe, something like this: Is it possible for a person, if he knows a thing, at the same time not to know that which he knows?

Theo. Now, then, what shall we answer, Theaetetus?

Theaet. It is impossible, I should think.

Soc. Not if you make seeing and knowing identical. For what will you do with a question from which there is no escape, by which you are, as the saying is, caught in a pit, when your adversary, unabashed, puts his hand over one of your eyes and asks if you see his cloak with the eye that is covered?

Theaet. I shall say, I think, "not with that eye, but with the other."

Soc. Then you see and do not see the same things at the same time?

Theaet. After a fashion.

Soc. "That," he will reply, "is not at all what I want, and I did not ask about the fashion, but whether you both know and do not know the same thing. Now manifestly you see that which you do not see. But you have agreed that seeing is knowing and not seeing is not knowing. Very well; from all this, reckon out what the result is."

Theaet. Well, I reckon out that the result is the contrary of my hypothesis. . . . . [*Theodorus bearing the brunt again.*]

Soc. Well then Protagoras, what shall we do about the doctrine? Shall we say that the opinions which men have are always true, or sometimes true and sometimes false? For the result of either statement is that their opinions are not always true, but may be either true or false. Just think, Theodorus; would any follower of Protagoras, or you yourself, care to contend that no person thinks that another is ignorant and has false opinions?

Theo. No, that is incredible, Socrates.

Soc. And yet this is the predicament to which the doctrine that man is the measure of all things inevitably leads.

Theo. How so?

Soc. When you have come to a decision in your own mind about something, and declare your opinion to me, this opinion is, according to his doctrine, true to you; let us grant that; but may not the rest of us sit in judgement on your decision, or do we always judge that your opinion is true? Do not myriads of men on each occasion oppose their opinions to yours, believing that your judgement and belief are false?

Theo. Yes, by Zeus, Socrates, countless myriads in truth, as Homer says, and they give me all the trouble in the world.

Soc. Well then, shall we say that in such a case your opinion is true to you but false to the myriads?

Theo. That seems to be the inevitable deduction.

Soc. And what of Protagoras himself? If neither he himself thought, nor people in general think, as indeed they do not, that man is the measure of all things, is it not inevitable that the "truth" which he wrote is true to no one? But if he himself thought it was true, and people in general do not agree with him, in the first place you know that it is just so much more false than true as the number of those who do not believe it is greater than the number of those who do.

Theo. Necessarily, if it is to be true or false according to each individual opinion.

Soc. Secondly, it involves this, which is a very pretty result; he concedes about his own opinion the truth of the opinion of those who disagree with him and think that his opinion is false, since he grants that the opinions of all men are true.

Theo. Certainly.

Soc. Then would he not be conceding that his own opinion is false, if he grants that the opinion of those who think he is in error is true?

Theo. Necessarily.

Soc. But the others do not concede that they are in error, do they?

Theo. No, they do not.

Soc. And he, in turn, according to his writings, grants that this opinion also is true.

Theo. Evidently.

Soc. Then all men, beginning with Protagoras, will dispute—or rather, he will grant, after he once concedes that the opinion of the man who holds the opposite view is true—even Protagoras himself, I say, will concede that neither a dog nor any casual man is a measure of anything whatsoever that he has not learned. Is not that the case?

Theo. Yes.

Soc. Then since the "truth" of Protagoras is disputed by all, it would be true to nobody, neither to anyone else nor to him. [*Theaetetus returns*.]

Soc. Consider, then, Theaetetus, this further point about what has been said. Now you answered that perception is knowledge, did you not?

Theaet. Yes.

Soc. If, then, anyone should ask you, "By what does a man see white and black colours and by what does he hear high and low tones?" you would, I fancy, say, "by his eyes and ears."

Theaet. Yes, I should.

Soc. The easy use of words and phrases and the avoidance of strict precision is in general a sign of good breeding; indeed, the opposite is hardly worthy of a gentleman, but sometimes it is necessary, as now it is necessary, to object to your answer, in so far as it is incorrect. Just consider; which answer is more correct, that our eyes are that by which we see or that through which we see, and our ears that by which or that through which we hear?

Theaet. I think, Socrates, we perceive through rather than by them, in each case.

Soc. Yes, for it would be strange indeed, my boy, if there are many senses ensconced within us, as if we were so many wooden horses of Troy, and they do not all unite in one power, whether we should call it soul or something else, by which we perceive through these as instruments the objects of perception.

Theaet. I think what you suggest is more likely than the other way.

. . . .

Soc. Then knowledge is not in the sensations, but in the process of reasoning about them; for it is possible, apparently, to apprehend being and truth by reasoning, but not by sensation.

THEAET. So it seems.

Soc. Then, Theaetetus, perception and knowledge could never be the same.

THEAET. Evidently not, Socrates; and indeed now at last it has been made perfectly clear that knowledge is something different from perception.

SECOND ANSWER: KNOWLEDGE IS (TRUE) OPINION

Soc. But surely we did not begin our conversation in order to find out what knowledge is not, but what it is. However, we have progressed so far, at least as not to seek for knowledge in perception at all, but in some function of the soul, whatever name is given to it when it alone and by itself is engaged directly with realities.

THEAET. That, Socrates, is, I suppose, called having opinion.

Soc. You suppose rightly, my friend. Now begin again at the beginning. Wipe out all we said before, and see if you have any clearer vision, now that you have advanced to this point. Say once more what knowledge is.

THEAET. To say that all opinion is knowledge is impossible, Socrates, for there is also false opinion; but true opinion probably is knowledge. Let that be my answer. . . . .

[Here follows a long and diverting disquisition on how one can have false opinion. We can do hardly more here than indicate the positive conclusion.]

Soc. . . . . But really, Theaetetus, our talk has been badly tainted with unclearness all along; for we have said over and over again "we know" and "we do not know" and "we have knowledge" and "we have no knowledge," as if we could understand each other, while we were still ignorant of knowledge. . . . .

THEAET. But how will you converse, Socrates, if you refrain from these words?

Soc. Not at all, being the man I am; but I might if I were a real reasoner; if such a man were present at this moment he would tell us to refrain from these terms, and would criticize my talk scathingly. But since we are poor creatures, shall I venture to say what the nature of knowing is? For it seems to me that would be of some advantage.

THEAET. Venture it then, by Zeus. You shall have full pardon for not refraining from those terms.

Soc. Have you heard what they say nowadays that knowing is?

Theaet. Perhaps; however, I don't remember just at this moment.

Soc. They say it is having knowledge.

Theaet. True.

Soc. Let us make a slight change and say possessing knowledge.

Theaet. Why, how will you claim that the one differs from the other?

Soc. Perhaps it doesn't; but first hear how it seems to me to differ, and then help me to test my view.

Theaet. I will if I can.

Soc. Well, then, having does not seem to me the same as possessing. For instance, if a man bought a cloak and had it under his control, but did not wear it, we should certainly say, not that he had it, but that he possessed it.

Theaet. And rightly.

Soc. Now see whether it is possible in the same way for one who possesses knowledge not to have it, as, for instance, if a man should catch wild birds—pigeons or the like—and should arrange an aviary at home and keep them in it, we might in a way assert that he always has them because he possesses them, might we not?

Theaet. Yes.

Soc. And yet in another way that he has none of them, but that he has acquired power over them, since he has brought them under his control in his own enclosure, to take them and hold them whenever he likes, by catching whichever bird he pleased, and to let them go again; and he can do this as often as he sees fit.

Theaet. That is true.

.   .   .   .

Soc. Continuing, then, our comparison with the acquisition and hunting of the pigeons, we shall say that the hunting is of two kinds, one before the acquisition for the sake of possession, the other carried on by the possessor for the sake of taking and holding in his hands what he had acquired long before. And just so when a man long since by learning came to possess knowledge of certain things, and knew them, he may have these very things afresh by taking up again the knowledge of each of them separate and holding it—the knowledge which he had acquired long before, but had not at hand in his mind?

. . . .

THEAET. Perhaps, Socrates, we were not right in making the birds represent kinds of knowledge only, but we ought to have imagined kinds of ignorance also flying about in the soul with the others; then the hunter would catch sometimes knowledge and sometimes ignorance of the same thing, and through the ignorance he would have false, but through the knowledge true opinion.

Soc. It is not easy, Theaetetus, to refrain from praising you. However, examine your suggestion once more. Let it be as you say: the man who catches the ignorance will, you say, have false opinion. Is that it?

THEAET. Yes.

Soc. But surely he will not also think that he has false opinion.

THEAET. Certainly not.

Soc. No, but true opinion, and will have the attitude of knowing that about which he is deceived.

THEAET. Of course.

Soc. Hence he will fancy that he has caught, and has, knowledge, not ignorance.

THEAET. Evidently.

Soc. Then, after our long wanderings, we have come round again to our first difficulty. For the real reasoner will laugh and say, "Most excellent Sir, does a man who knows both knowledge and ignorance think that one of them, which he knows, is another thing which he knows; or, knowing neither of them, is he of opinion that one, which he does not know, is another thing which he does not know; or, knowing one and not the other, does he think that the one he does not know is the one he knows; or that the one he knows is the one he does not know? Or will you go on and tell me that there are kinds of knowledge of the kinds of knowledge and of ignorance, and that he who possesses these kinds of knowledge and has enclosed them in some sort of other ridiculous aviaries or waxen figments, knows them, so long as he possesses them, even if he has them not at hand in his soul? And in this fashion are you going to be compelled to trot about endlessly in the same circle without making any progress?" What shall we reply to this, Theaetetus?

THEAET. By Zeus, Socrates, I don't know what to say.

Soc. Then, my boy, is the argument right in rebuking us and in pointing out that we were wrong to abandon knowledge and seek first for false opinion? It is impossible to know the latter until we have adequately comprehended the nature of knowledge.

THEAET. As the case now stands, Socrates, we cannot help thinking as you say.

THIRD ANSWER: KNOWLEDGE IS TRUE OPINION ACCOMPANIED BY REASON

Soc. To begin, then, at the beginning once more, what shall we say knowledge is? For surely we are not going to give it up yet, are we?

THEAET. Not by any means, unless, that is, you give it up.

Soc. Tell us, then, what definition will make us contradict ourselves least?

THEAET. The one we tried before, Socrates; at any rate, I have nothing else to offer.

Soc. What one?

THEAET. That knowledge is true opinion; for true opinion is surely free from error and all its results are fine and good.

.   .   .   .

Soc. But, my friend, if true opinion and knowledge were the same thing in law courts, the best of judges could never have true opinion without knowledge; in fact, however, it appears that the two are different.

THEAET. Oh yes, I remember now, Socrates, having heard someone make the distinction, but I had forgotten it. He said that knowledge was true opinion accompanied by reason, but that unreasoning true opinion was outside of the sphere of knowledge; and matters of which there is not a rational explanation are unknowable—yes, that is what he called them—and those of which there is are knowable.

Soc. I am glad you mentioned that. But tell us how he distinguished between the knowable and the unknowable, that we may see whether the accounts that you and I have heard agree.

THEAET. But I do not know whether I can think it out; but if someone else were to make the statement of it, I think I could follow.

Soc. Listen then, while I relate it to you—"a dream for a dream." I in turn used to imagine that I heard certain persons say that the primary elements of which we and all else are composed admit of no rational explanation; for each alone by itself can only be named, and no qualification can be added, neither that it is nor that it is not, for that would at once be adding to it existence or non-existence, whereas we must add nothing to it, if we are to speak of that itself alone. Indeed, not even "itself" or "that" or "each" or "alone" or "this" or anything else of the sort, of which there are many, must be added; for these are prevalent terms which are added to all things indiscriminately and are different from the things to which they are added; but if it were possible to explain an element, and it admitted of a rational explanation of its own, it would have to be explained apart from everything else. But in fact none of the primal elements can be expressed by reason; they can only be named, for they have only a name; but the things composed of these are themselves complex, and so their names are complex and form a rational explanation; for the combination of names is the essence of reasoning. Thus the elements are not objects of reason or of knowledge, but only of perception, whereas the combinations of them are objects of knowledge and expression and true opinion. When therefore a man acquires without reasoning the true opinion about anything, his mind has the truth about it, but has no knowledge; for he who cannot give and receive a rational explanation of a thing is without knowledge of it; but when he has acquired also a rational explanation he may possibly have become all that I have said and may now be perfect in knowledge. Is that the version of the dream you have heard, or is it different?

THEAET. That was it exactly.

Soc. Are you satisfied, then, and do you state it in this way, that true opinion accompanied by reason is knowledge.

THEAET. Precisely.

Soc. Can it be, Theaetetus, that we now, in this casual manner, have found out on this day what many wise men have long been seeking and have grown grey in the search?

THEAET. I, at any rate, Socrates, think our present statement is good.

. . . .

Soc. . . . . But let us not . . . . lose sight of the question before us, which is: What is meant by the doctrine that the most perfect knowledge arises from the addition of rational explanation to true opinion?

THEAET. No, we must not.

. . . .

Soc. [This is the explanation] which most people would give, that knowledge is the ability to tell some characteristic by which the object in question differs from all others.

THEAET. As an example of the method, what explanation can you give me, and of what thing?

Soc. As an example, if you like, take the sun: I think it is enough for you to be told that it is the brightest of the heavenly bodies that revolve about the earth.

THEAET. Certainly.

Soc. Understand why I say this. It is because, as we were just saying, if you get hold of the distinguishing characteristic by which a given thing differs from the rest, you will, as some say, get hold of the definition or explanation of it; but so long as you cling to some common quality, your explanation will pertain to all those objects to which the common quality belongs.

THEAET. I understand; and it seems to me that it is quite right to call that kind a rational explanation or definition.

Soc. Then he who possesses right opinion about anything and adds thereto a comprehension of the difference which distinguishes it from other things will have acquired knowledge of that thing of which he previously had only opinion.

THEAET. That is what we affirm.

Soc. Theaetetus, now that I have come closer to our statement, I do not understand it at all. It is like coming close to a scene-painting.[31] While I stood off at a distance, I thought there was something in it.

THEAET. What do you mean?

[31] In which perspective is the main thing.

Soc. I will tell you if I can. Assume that I have right opinion about you; if I add the explanation or definition of you, then I have knowledge of you, otherwise I have merely opinion.

Theaet. Yes.

Soc. But explanation was, we agreed, the interpretation of the difference.

Theaet. It was.

Soc. Then so long as I had merely opinion, I did not grasp in my thought any of the points in which you differ from others?

Theaet. Apparently not.

Soc. Therefore I was thinking of some one of the common traits which you possess no more than other men.

Theaet. You must have been.

Soc. For heaven's sake! How in the world could I in that case have any opinion about you more than about anyone else? Suppose that I thought "That is Theaetetus which is a man and has nose and eyes and mouth" and so forth, mentioning all the parts. Can this thought make me think of Theaetetus any more than of Theodorus or of the meanest of the Mysians,[32] as the saying is?

Theaet. Of course not.

Soc. But if I think not only of a man with nose and eyes, but of one with snub nose and protruding eyes, shall I then have an opinion of you any more than of myself and all others like me?

Theaet. Not at all.

Soc. No; I fancy Theaetetus will not be the object of opinion in me until this snubnosedness of yours has stamped and deposited in my mind a memorial different from those of the other examples of snubnosedness that I have seen, and the other traits that make up your personality have done the like. Then that memorial, if I meet you again tomorrow, will awaken my memory and make me have right opinion about you.

Theaet. Very true.

Soc. Then right opinion also would have to do with difference in any given instance?

Theaet. At any rate, it seems so.

Soc. Then what becomes of the addition of reason or explanation to right opinion? For if it is defined as the addition of an opinion of

---

[32] The Mysians were despised as especially effeminate and worthless.

the way in which a given thing differs from the rest, it is an utterly absurd injunction.

THEAET. How so?

Soc. When we have a right opinion of the way in which certain things differ from other things, we are told to acquire a right opinion of the way in which those same things differ from other things! On this plan the twirling of a scytale[33] or a pestle or anything of the sort would be as nothing compared with this injunction. It might more justly be called a blind man's giving directions; for to command us to acquire that which we already have, in order to learn that of which we already have opinion, is very like a man whose sight is mightily darkened.

. . . .

THEAET. So it seems.

Soc. And it is utterly silly, when we are looking for a definition of knowledge, to say that it is right opinion with knowledge, whether of difference or of anything else whatsoever. So neither perception, Theaetetus, nor true opinion, nor reason or explanation combined with true opinion could be knowledge.

THEAET. Apparently not.

Soc. Are we then, my friend, still pregnant and in travail with knowledge? or have we brought forth everything?

THEAET. Yes, we have, and, by Zeus, Socrates, with your help I have already said more than there was in me.

Soc. Then does our art of midwifery declare to us that all the offspring that have been born are mere wind-eggs and not worth rearing?

THEAET. It does, decidedly.

Soc. If after this you ever undertake to conceive other thoughts, Theaetetus, and do conceive, you will be pregnant with better thoughts than these by reason of the present search, and if you remain barren, you will be less harsh and gentler to your associates, for you will have the wisdom not to think you know that which you do not know. So much and no more my art can accomplish; nor do I know aught of the things that are known by others, the

---

[33] A σκυτάλη was a staff, especially a staff about which a strip of leather was rolled, on which dispatches were so written that when unrolled they were illegible until rolled again upon another staff of the same size and shape.

great and wonderful men who are to-day and have been in the past. This art, however, both my mother and I received from God, she for women and I for young and noble men and for all who are fair.

And now I must go to the Porch of the King, to answer to the suit which Meletus[34] has brought against me. But in the morning, Theodorus, let us meet here again.

[34] Meletus was one of those who brought the suit which led to the condemnation and death of Socrates.

THE WORLD OF THE CHANGELESS

PARMENIDES PRESSES SOCRATES ON THE IDEAS (*Parmenides*)
MAKING THE CHANGELESS AVAILABLE FOR LIFE (*Philebus*)
THE UNCHANGEABLE WORLD AND THE FORM OF GOOD (*Republic*)

*If the world of the changing can yield only opinion (as empha-
sized in the "Cratylus" and the "Theaetetus") and if there is to
be such a thing as dependable knowledge, there must be discovered
an unchanging world. Unlike moderns, who evaluate objects by
the knowledge process that leads to them, Plato sought primarily
to validate the process by the objects to which it led. As Plato had
been influenced by Heraclitus to take change seriously, so he is
influenced by Parmenides to demand permanence of true being.
True being alone makes real knowledge possible. Plato's reflection on true being matured as his doctrine of ideas. These formal
patterns of things shine through the things themselves, and become
the intelligible stuff from which particular things arise and on
which they depend for their veritable being. More pluralistic than
Parmenides, Plato nevertheless attributes the unique Par-
menidean quality, permanency or unchangeability, to whatever
is truly real. But the realm of ideas is also ideal. Morally and
aesthetically positive ideas are granted full reality with gusto;
neutral realities exist with little doubt; but dishonorific ones have
more than doubt thrown upon their reality; at least so it appears
in the "Parmenides." Since bad things on earth have nothing to
guarantee their reality, they achieve at best a doubtful metaphysical status. If reasons are raised to the dignity of causes,
then surely good reasons will prevail, as Plato's Socrates has
made clear to us in his criticism of Anaxagoras. And so the final
cause becomes in the "Phaedo" that very good reason why anything is, and is as it is, namely, that it is better for it to be than
not to be, and to be as it is rather than to be otherwise. In the "Republic" the Idea of the Good is supreme—not only "author of
knowledge to all things known, but of their being and essence." In
the "Symposium" clairvoyance of goodness is made to culminate
in a single and higher knowledge, "the very essence of beauty."*

Unchanging ideas make knowledge possible, and true knowledge is knowledge of these ideas. True knowledge, moreover, is virtue, as Socrates taught. The knowledge which virtue is, is thus knowledge of Good. The formal good, though perfect, is not enough for mundane life. There must be a mixture, according to right principles; and in this mixture pleasure itself has a place, though a low one, as the "Philebus" concludes.

. . .

PARMENIDES PRESSES SOCRATES ON THE IDEAS

Parmenides 128–35. Fowler translation ("Loeb Classical Library" series). Only a fragment from near the beginning of one of Plato's most abstruse dialogues. Heading mine.—T. V. S.

"I see, Parmenides," said Socrates, "that Zeno here wishes to be very close to you not only in his friendship, but also in his writing. For he has written much the same thing as you, but by reversing the process he tries to cheat us into the belief that he is saying something new. For you, in your poems, say that the all is one, and you furnish proofs of this in fine and excellent fashion; and he, on the other hand, says it is not many, and he also furnishes very numerous and weighty proofs. That one of you says it is one, and the other that it is not many, and that each of you expresses himself so that although you say much the same you seem not to have said the same things at all, appears to the rest of us a feat of expression quite beyond our power."

"Yes, Socrates," said Zeno, "but you have not perceived all aspects of the truth about my writings. You follow the arguments with a scent as keen as a Laconian hound's, but you do not observe that my treatise is not by any means so pretentious that it could have been written with the intention you ascribe to it, of disguising itself as a great performance in the eyes of men. What you mentioned is a mere accident, but in truth these writings are meant to support the argument of Parmenides against those who attempt to jeer at him and assert that if the all is one many absurd results follow which contradict his theory. Now this treatise opposes the advocates of the many and gives them back their ridicule with interest, for its purpose is to show that their hypothesis that existences are many, if properly followed up, leads to still more absurd results than the hypothesis that they are one. It was in such a spirit of controversy that I wrote it when I was young, and when it was written some one stole it, so that I could not even consider whether it should be published or not. So, Socrates, you are not aware of this and you think that the cause of its composition was not the controversial spirit of a young man, but the ambition of an old one. In other respects, as I said, you guessed its meaning pretty well."

"I see," said Socrates, "and I accept your explanation. But tell me, do you not believe there is an idea of likeness in the abstract, and another idea of unlikeness, the opposite of the first, and that you and I and all things which we call many partake of these two? And that those which partake of likeness become like, and those which partake of unlikeness become unlike, and those which partake of both become both like and unlike, all in the manner and degree of their participation? And even if all things partake of both opposites, and are enabled by their participation to be both like and unlike themselves, what is there wonderful about that? For if anyone showed that the absolute like becomes unlike, or the unlike like, that would, in my opinion, be a wonder; but if he shows that things which partake of both become both like and unlike, that seems to me, Zeno, not at all strange, not even if he shows that all things are one by participation in unity and that the same are also many by participation in multitude; but if he shows that absolute unity is also many and the absolute many again are one, then I shall be amazed. The same applies to all other things. If he shows that the kinds and ideas in and by themselves possess these opposite qualities, it is marvellous; but if he shows that I am both one and many, what marvel is there in that? He will say, when he wishes to show that I am many, that there are my right parts and my left parts, my front parts and my back parts, likewise upper and lower, all different; for I do, I suppose, partake of multitude; and when he wishes to show that I am one, he will say that we here are seven persons, of whom I am one, a man, partaking also of unity; and so he shows that both assertions are true. If anyone then undertakes to show that the same things are both many and one—I mean such things as stones, sticks, and the like—we shall say that he shows that they are many and one, but not that the one is many or the many one; he says nothing wonderful, but only what we should all accept. If, how-ever, as I was saying just now, he first distinguishes the abstract ideas, such as likeness and unlikeness, multitude and unity, rest and motion, and the like, and then shows that they can be mingled and separated, I should," said he, "be filled with amazement, Zeno. Now I think this has been very manfully discussed by you; but I should, as I say, be more amazed if anyone could show in the abstract ideas, which are intellectual conceptions, this same multifarious and perplexing entanglement which you described in visible objects."

Pythodorus said that he thought at every word, while Socrates was saying this, Parmenides and Zeno would be angry, but they paid close attention to him and frequently looked at each other and smiled, as if in admiration of Socrates, and when he stopped speak-ing Parmenides expressed their approval. "Socrates," he said, "what an admirable talent for argument you have! Tell me, did you invent this distinction yourself, which separates abstract ideas from the things which partake of them? And do you think there is such a thing as abstract likeness apart from the likeness which we possess, and abstract one and many, and the other ab-stractions of which you heard Zenospeaking just now?"

"Yes, I do," said Socrates.

"And also," said Parmenides, "abstract ideas of the just, the beautiful, the good, and all such conceptions?"

"Yes," he replied.

"And is there an abstract idea of man, apart from us and all others such as we are, or of fire or water?"

"I have often," he replied, "been very much troubled, Par-menides, to decide whether there are ideas of such things or, not."

"And are you undecided about certain other things, which you might think rather ridiculous, such as hair, mud, dirt, or anything else particularly vile and worthless? Would you say that there is an idea of each of these distinct and different from the things with which we have to do, or not?"

"By no means," said Socrates. "No, I think these things are such as they appear to us, and it would be quite absurd to believe that there is an idea of them; and yet I am sometimes disturbed by the thought that perhaps what is true of one thing is true of all. Then when I have taken up this position, I run away for fear of falling into some abyss of nonsense and perishing; so when I come to those things which we were just saying do have ideas, I stay and busy myself with them."

"Yes, for you are still young," said Parmenides, "and philosophy has not yet taken hold upon you, Socrates, as I think it will later. Then you will not despise them; but now you still consider people's opinions, on account of your youth. Well, tell me; do you think that, as you say, there are ideas, and that these other things which partake of them are named from them, as, for instance, those that partake of likeness become like, those that partake of greatness great, those that partake of beauty and justice just and beautiful?"

"Certainly," said Socrates.

"Well then, does each participant object partake of the whole idea, or of a part of it? Or could there be some other third kind of participation?

"How could there be?" said he.

"Do you think the whole idea, being one, is in each of the many participants, or what?"

"Yes, for what prevents it from being in them, Parmenides?" said Socrates.

"Then while it is one and the same, the whole of it would be in many separate individuals at once, and thus it would itself be separate from itself."

"No," he replied, "for it might be like day, which is one and the same, is in many places at once, and yet is not separated from itself; so each idea, though one and the same, might be in all its participants at once."

"That," said he, "is very neat, Socrates; you make one to be in many places at once, just as if you should spread a sail over many persons and then should say it was one and all of it was over many. Is not that about what you mean?"

"Perhaps it is," said Socrates.

"Would the whole sail be over each person, or a particular part over each?"

"A part over each."

"Then," said he, "the ideas themselves, Socrates, are divisible into parts, and the objects which partake of them would partake of a part, and in each of them there would be not the whole, but only a part of each idea."

"So it appears."

"Are you, then, Socrates, willing to assert that the one idea is really divided and will still be one?"

"By no means," he replied.

"No," said Parmenides, "for if you divide absolute greatness, and each of the many great things is great by a part of greatness smaller than absolute greatness, is not that unreasonable?"

"Certainly," he said.

"Or again, will anything by taking away a particular small part of equality possess something by means of which, when it is less than absolute equality, its possessor will be equal to anything else?"

"That is impossible."

"Or let one of us have a part of the small; the small will be greater than this, since this is a part of it, and therefore the absolute small will be greater; but that to which the part of the small is added will be smaller, not greater, than before."

"That," said he, "is impossible."

"How, then, Socrates, will other things partake of those ideas of yours, if they cannot partake of them either as parts or as wholes?"

"By Zeus," he replied, "I think that is a very hard question to determine."

"Well, what do you think of this?"

"Of what?"

"I fancy your reason for believing that each idea is one is something like this; when there is a number of things which seem to you to be great, you may think, as you look at them all, that there is one and the same idea in them, and hence you think the great is one."

"That is true," he said.

"But if with your mind's eye you regard the absolute great and these many great things in the same way, will not another great appear beyond, by which all these must appear to be great?"

"So it seems."

"That is, another idea of greatness will appear, in addition to absolute greatness and the objects which partake of it; and another again in addition to these, by reason of which they are all great; and each of your ideas will no longer be one, but their number will be infinite."

"But, Parmenides," said Socrates, "each of these ideas may be only a thought, which can exist only in our minds; then each might be one, without being exposed to the consequences you have just mentioned."

"But," he said, "is each thought one, but a thought of nothing?"

"That is impossible," he replied.

"But of something?"

"Yes."

"Of something that is, or that is not?"

"Of something that is."

"A thought of some single element which that thought thinks of as appertaining to all and as being one idea?"

"Yes,"

"Then will not this single element, which is thought of as one and as always the same in all, be an idea?"

"That, again, seems inevitable."

"Well then," said Parmenides, "does not the necessity which compels you to say that all other things partake of ideas, oblige you also to believe either that everything is made of thoughts, and all things think, or that, being thoughts, they are without thought?"

"That is quite unreasonable, too," he said, "but Parmenides, I think the most likely view is, that these ideas exist in nature as patterns, and the other things resemble them and are imitations of them; their participation in ideas is assimilation to them, that and nothing else."

"Then if anything," he said, "resembles the idea, can that idea avoid being like the thing which resembles it, in so far as the thing has been made to resemble it; or is there any possibility that the like be unlike its like?"

"No, there is none."

"And must not necessarily the like partake of the same idea as its like?"

"It must."

"That by participation in which like things are made like, will be the absolute idea, will it not?"

"Certainly."

"Then it is impossible that anything be like the idea, or the idea like anything; for if they are alike, some further idea, in addition to the first, will always appear, and if that is like anything, still another, and a new idea will always be arising, if the idea is like that which partakes of it."

"Very true."

"Then it is not by likeness that other things partake of ideas; we must seek some other method of participation."

"So it seems."

"Do you see, then, Socrates, how great the difficulty is, if we maintain that ideas are separate, independent entities?"

"Yes, certainly."

"You may be sure," he said, "that you do not yet, if I may say so, grasp the greatness of the difficulty involved in your assumption that each idea is one and is something distinct from concrete things."

"How is that?" said he.

"There are many reasons," he said, "but the greatest is this: if anyone should say that the ideas cannot even be known if they are such as we say they must be, no one could prove to him that he was wrong, unless he who argued that they could be known were a man of wide education and ability and were willing to follow the proof through many long and elaborate details; he who maintains that they cannot be known would be unconvinced."

"Why is that, Parmenides?" said Socrates.

"Because, Socrates, I think that you or anyone else who claims that there is an absolute idea of each thing would agree in the first place that none of them exists in us."

"No, for if it did, it would no longer be absolute," said Socrates.

"You are right," he said. "Then those absolute ideas which are relative to one another have their own nature in relation to themselves, and not in relation to the likenesses, or whatever we choose to call them, which are amongst us, and from which we receive certain names as we participate in them. And these concrete things, which have the same names with the ideas, are likewise relative only to themselves, not to the ideas, and belong to themselves, not to the like-named ideas."

"What do you mean?" said Socrates.

"For instance," said Parmenides, "if one of us is master or slave of anyone, he is not the slave of master in the abstract, nor is the master the master of slave in the abstract; each is a man and is master or slave of a man; but mastership in the abstract is mastership of slavery in the abstract, and likewise slavery in the abstract is slavery to mastership in the abstract, but our slaves and masters are not relative to them, nor they to us; they, as I say, belong to themselves and are relative to themselves and likewise our slaves and masters are relative to themselves. You understand what I mean, do you not?"

"Certainly," said Socrates, "'I understand."

"Then knowledge also, if abstract or absolute, would be knowledge of abstract or absolute truth?"

"Certainly."

"And likewise each kind of absolute knowledge would be knowledge of each kind of absolute being, would it not?"

"Yes."

"And would not the knowledge that exists among us be the knowledge of the truth that exists among us, and each kind of our knowledge be the knowledge of each kind of truth that exists among us?"

"Yes, that is inevitable."

"But the ideas themselves, as you agree, we have not, neither can they be among us."

"No, they cannot."

"And the various classes of ideas are known by the absolute idea of knowledge?"

"Yes."

"Which we do not possess."

"No, we do not."

"Then none of the ideas is known by us, since we do not partake of absolute knowledge."

"Apparently not."

"Then the absolute good and the beautiful and all which we conceive to be absolute ideas are unknown to us."

"I am afraid they are."

"Now we come to a still more fearful consequence."

"What is it?"

"You would say, no doubt, that if there is an absolute kind of knowledge, it is far more accurate than our knowledge, and the same of beauty and all the rest?"

"Yes."

"And if anything partakes of absolute knowledge, you would say that there is no one more likely than God to possess this most accurate knowledge?"

"Of course."

"Then will it be possible for God to know human things, if he has absolute knowledge?"

"Why not?"

"Because," said Parmenides, "we have agreed that those ideas are not relative to our world, nor our world to them, but each only to themselves."

"Yes, we have agreed to that."

"Then if this most perfect mastership and this most accurate knowledge are with God, his mastership can never rule us, nor his knowledge know us or anything of our world; we do not rule the gods with our authority, nor do we know anything of the divine with our knowledge, and by the same reasoning, they likewise, being gods, are not our masters and have no knowledge of human affairs."

"But surely this," said he, "is a most amazing argument, if it makes us deprive God of knowledge."

"And yet, Socrates," said Parmenides, "these difficulties and many more besides are inseparable from the ideas, if these ideas of things exist and we declare that each of them is an absolute idea. Therefore he who hears such assertions is confused in his mind and argues that the ideas do not exist, and even if they do exist cannot by any possibility be known by man; and he thinks that what he says is reasonable, and, as I was saying just now, he is amazingly hard to convince. Only a man of very great natural gifts will be able to understand that everything has a class and absolute essence, and only a still more wonderful man can find out all these facts and teach anyone else to analyse them properly and understand them."

"I agree with you, Parmenides," said Socrates, "for what you say is very much to my mind."

"But on the other hand," said Parmenides, "if anyone, with his mind fixed on all these objections and others like them, denies the existence of ideas of things, and does not assume an idea under which each individual thing is classed, he will be quite at a loss, since he denies that the idea of each thing is always the same, and in this way he will utterly destroy the power of carrying on discussion. You seem to have been well aware of this."

"Quite true," he said.

"Then what will become of philosophy? To what can you turn, if these things are unknown?"

"I do not see at all, at least not at present."

"No, Socrates," he said, "for you try too soon, before you are properly trained, to define the beautiful, the just, the good, and all the other ideas. You see I noticed it when I heard you talking yesterday with Aristoteles here. Your impulse towards dialectic is noble and divine, you may be assured of that; but exercise and train yourself while you are still young in an art which seems to be useless and is called by most people mere loquacity; otherwise the truth will escape you."

MAKING THE CHANGELESS AVAILABLE FOR LIFE

Philebus. [Fowler translation and introduction, "Loeb Classical Library" series —T. V. S.]. The object of the *Philebus* is the determination of "the good." Philebus, a totally unknown person whose name serves as the title of the dialogue, is represented as a thinker of the hedonistic school. He has, apparently, been lecturing or taking part in a discussion, but has withdrawn on account of weariness. He speaks only a few short sentences in the whole dialogue. Protarchus, son of the wealthy Callias, serves to give the form of dialogue to the discourse, but his personality is not even outlined, and his remarks are as colourless as are those of the younger Socrates in *The Statesman.* Even Socrates himself, as in *The Sophist, The Statesman,* and other dialogues of approximately the same date, shows little personality: he is merely the mouthpiece of the doctrine.

This dialogue, like *The Sophist* and *The Statesman,* contains a preliminary illustration of method; for the discussion of sounds in speech (17 ff.) serves the same purpose as the "angler" in *The Sophist* and the "art of weaving" in *The Statesman.* The *Philebus* seems to be slightly later in date than the other two dialogues.

In opposition to the assertion ascribed to Philebus, that pleasure is the good, Socrates seems at first prepared to maintain (with Eucleides and the Cynics) that knowledge is the good, but presently announces his suspicion that some third competitor will be awarded the first place, and that even the second place will not be held by pleasure. It is soon agreed that a mixture of knowledge and pleasure is necessary for the most desirable life. The discussion is carried on in great measure by means of classification or division, which is here founded on the principles (derived from Pythagorean sources) of the Limited and the Unlimited. Pleasure and pain, and everything which is capable of degrees of intensity, belong to the class of the Unlimited, whereas number, measure, and knowledge belong to that of the Limited, which is regarded as essentially superior.

The composition of the mixture which is necessary for the most perfect life is discussed in detail. This involves a description and condemnation of excess in the most intense pleasures and an interesting analysis of the mixture of pain and pleasure in anger, pity, revenge, and other emotions as they affect us in theatrical representations or in real life. The pleasures of scientific knowledge are said to be absolutely pure and unmixed, therefore truer than all mixed pleasures and preferable to them. Again, pleasure being, according to certain hedonists, a process or Becoming, is found to be on that account inferior to knowledge, which is a state or Being. The discussion of kinds of knowledge (55 c ff.) includes (55 E) the distinction between scientific knowledge, based on arithmetic, measuring, and weighing, and such knowledge as rests upon the mere schooling of the senses.

In the end the order in which possessions may be called good is established as follows: (1) measure, moderation, fitness, and the like; (2) proportion, beauty, perfection, and their kin; (3) mind and wisdom; (4) sciences, arts, and true opinions; (5) pure pleasures.

This dialogue, though it lacks the dramatic qualities which make many of Plato's works take rank among the most charming products of all literature, and in spite of certain inconsistencies and even defects of reasoning—for instance, the confusion between goodness and a good thing (55 B) or the insistence upon the existence of false pleasures, though the epithet "false" belongs really to opinion, not to the pleasures themselves—is an interesting and instructive presentation of an important subject. It also exhibits clearly one side, at least, of Plato's development at a time which must be somewhat after the middle of his career.

CHARACTERS
SOCRATES, PROTARCHUS, PHILEBUS

Soc. Observe, then, Protarchus, what the doctrine is which you are now to accept from Philebus, and what our doctrine is, against which you are to argue, if you do not agree with it. Shall we make a brief statement of each of them?

Pro. By all means.

Soc. Very well: Philebus says that to all living beings enjoyment and pleasure and gaiety and whatever accords with that sort of thing are a good; whereas our contention is that not these, but wisdom and thought and memory and their kindred, right opinion and true reasonings, are better and more excellent than pleasure for all who are capable of taking part in them, and that for all those now existing or to come who can partake of them they are the most advantageous of all things. Those are pretty nearly the two doctrines we maintain, are they not, Philebus?

Phi. Yes, Socrates, exactly.

Soc. And do you, Protarchus, accept this doctrine which is now committed to you?

Pro. I must accept it; for our handsome Philebus has withdrawn.

Soc. And must the truth about these doctrines be attained by every possible means?

Pro. Yes, it must.

Soc. Then let us further agree to this:

Pro. To what?

Soc. That each of us will next try to prove clearly that it is a condition and disposition of the soul which can make life happy for all human beings. Is not that what we are going to do?

Pro. It is..

Soc. Then you will show that it is the condition of pleasure, and I that it is that of wisdom?

Pro. True.

Soc. What if some other life be found superior to these two? Then if that life is found to be more akin to pleasure, both of us are defeated, are we not, by the life which has firm possession of this superiority, but the life of pleasure is victor over the life of wisdom.

Pro. Yes.

Soc. But if it is more akin to wisdom, then wisdom is victorious and pleasure is vanquished? Do you agree to that? Or what do you say?

Pro. Yes, I at least am satisfied with that.

Soc. But how about you, Philebus? What do you say?

Phi. I think and always shall think that pleasure is the victor. But you, Protarchus, will make your own decision.

Pro. Since you entrusted the argument to me, Philebus, you can no longer dictate whether to make the agreement with Socrates or not.

Phi. True; and for that reason I wash my hands of it and now call upon the goddess[35] herself to witness that I do so.

Pro. And we also will bear witness to these words of yours. But all the same, Socrates, Philebus may agree or do as he likes, let us try to finish our argument in due order.

Soc. We must try, and let us begin with the very goddess who Philebus says is spoken of as Aphrodite but is most truly named Pleasure.

Pro. Quite right.

[35] The goddess of Pleasure, Ἡδονή personified.

Soc. My awe, Protarchus, in respect to the names of the gods is always beyond the greatest human fear. And now I call Aphrodite by that name which is agreeable to her; but pleasure I know has various aspects, and since, as I said, we are to begin with her, we must consider and examine what her nature is. For, when you just simply hear her name, she is only one thing, but surely she takes on all sorts of shapes which are even, in a way, unlike each other. For instance, we say that the man who lives without restraint has pleasure, and that the self-restrained man takes pleasure in his very self-restraint; and again that the fool who is full of foolish opinions and hopes is pleased, and also that the wise man takes pleasure in his very wisdom. And would not any person who said these two kinds of pleasure were like each other be rightly regarded as a fool?

Pro. No, Socrates, for though they spring from opposite sources, they are not in themselves opposed to one another; for how can pleasure help being of all things most like pleasure, that is, like itself?

Soc. Yes, my friend, and colour is like colour; in so far as every one of them is a colour they will all be the same, yet we all recognize that black is not only different from white, but is its exact opposite. And so, too, figure is like figure; they are all one in kind; but the parts of the kind are in some instances absolutely opposed to each other, and in other cases there is endless variety of difference; and we can find many other examples of such relations. Do not, therefore, rely upon this argument, which makes all the most absolute opposites identical. I am afraid we shall find some pleasures the opposites of other pleasures.

Pro. Perhaps; but why will that injure my contention?

Soc. Because I shall say that, although they are unlike, you apply to them a different designation. For you say that all pleasant things are good. Now no argument contends that pleasant things are not pleasant; but whereas most of them are bad and only some are good, as we assert, nevertheless you call them all good, though you confess, if forced to it by argument, that they are unlike. Now what is the identical element which exists in the good and bad pleasures alike and makes you call them all a good?

Pro. What do you mean, Socrates? Do you suppose anyone

who asserts that the good is pleasure will concede, or will endure to hear you say, that some pleasures are good and others bad?

Soc. But you will concede that they are unlike and in some instances opposed to each other.

Pro. Not in so far as they are pleasures.

Soc. Here we are again at the same old argument, Protarchus, and we shall presently assert that one pleasure is not different from another, but all pleasures are alike, and the examples just cited do not affect us at all, but we shall behave and talk just like the most worthless and inexperienced reasoners.

Pro. In what way do you mean?

Soc. Why, if I have the face to imitate you and to defend myself by saying that the utterly unlike is most completely like that which is most utterly unlike it, I can say the same things you said, and we shall prove ourselves to be excessively inexperienced, and our argument will be shipwrecked and lost. Let us, then, back her out, and perhaps if we start fair again we may come to an agreement.

Pro. How? Tell me.

Soc. Assume, Protarchus, that I am questioned in turn by you.

Pro. What question do I ask?

Soc. Whether wisdom and knowledge and intellect and all the things which I said at first were good, when you asked me what is good, will not have the same fate as this argument of yours.

Pro. How is that?

Soc. It will appear that the forms of knowledge collectively are many and some of them are unlike each other; but if some of them turn out to be actually opposites, should I be fit to engage in dialectics now if, through fear of just that, I should say that no form of knowledge is unlike any other, and then, as a consequence, our argument should vanish and be lost, like a tale that is told, and we ourselves should be saved by clinging to some irrational notion?

Pro. No, that must never be, except the part about our being saved. However, I like the equal treatment of your doctrine and mine. Let us grant that pleasures are many and unlike and that the forms of knowledge are many and different.

Soc. With no concealment, then, Protarchus, of the difference between my good and yours, but with fair and open acknowledgement of it, let us be bold and see if perchance on examination they will tell us whether we should say that pleasure is the good, or wisdom, or some other third principle. For surely the object of our present controversy is not to gain the victory for my assertions or yours, but both of us must fight for the most perfect truth.

Pro. Yes, we must.

Soc. Then let us establish this principle still more firmly by means of an agreement.

Pro. What principle?

Soc. The principle which gives trouble to all men, to some of them sometimes against their will.

Pro. Speak more plainly.

Soc. I mean the principle which came in our way just now; its nature is quite marvellous. For the assertions that one is many and many are one are marvellous, and it is easy to dispute with anyone who makes either of them.

Pro. You mean when a person says that I, Protarchus, am by nature one and that there are also many of me which are opposites of each other, asserting that I, the same Protarchus, am great and small and heavy and light and countless other things?

Soc. Those wonders concerning the one and the many which you have mentioned, Protarchus, are common property, and almost everybody is agreed that they ought to be disregarded because they are childish and easy and great hindrances to speculation; and this sort of thing also should be disregarded, when a man in his discussion divides the members and likewise the parts of anything, acknowledges that they all collectively are that one thing, and then mockingly refutes himself because he has been compelled to declare miracles—that the one is many and infinite and the many only one.

Pro. But what other wonders do you mean, Socrates, in relation to this same principle, which are not yet common property and generally acknowledged?

Soc. I mean, my boy, when a person postulates unity which is not the unity of one of the things which come into being and perish, as in the examples we had just now. For in cases of a unity of that sort, as I just said, it is agreed that refutation is needless. But when the assertion is made that man is one, or ox is one, or beauty is one, or the good is one, the intense interest in these and similar unities becomes disagreement and controversy.

PRO. How is that?

SOC. The first question is whether we should believe that such unities really exist; the second, how these unities, each of which is one, always the same, and admitting neither generation nor destruction, can nevertheless be permanently this one unity; and the third, how in the infinite number of things which come into being this unity, whether we are to assume that it is dispersed and has become many, or that it is entirely separated from itself—which would seem to be the most impossible notion of all—being the same and one, is to be at the same time in one and in many. These are the questions, Protarchus, about this kind of one and many, not those others, which cause the utmost perplexity, if ill solved, and are, if well solved, of the greatest assistance.

PRO. Then is it now, Socrates, our first duty to thresh this matter out?

SOC. Yes, that is what I should say.

PRO. You may assume, then, that we are all willing to agree with you about that; and perhaps it is best not to ask Philebus any questions; let sleeping dogs lie.

SOC. Very well; then where shall we begin this great and vastly complicated battle about the matters at issue? Shall we start at this point?

PRO. At what point?

SOC. We say that one and many are identified by reason, and always, both now and in the past, circulate everywhere in every thought that is uttered. This is no new thing and will never cease; it is, in my opinion, a quality within us which will never die or grow old, and which belongs to reason itself as such. And any young man, when he first has an inkling of this, is delighted, thinking he has found a treasure of wisdom; his joy fills him with enthusiasm; he joyously sets every possible argument in motion, sometimes in one direction, rolling things up and kneading them into one, and sometimes again unrolling and dividing them; he gets himself into a muddle first and foremost, then anyone who happens to be near him, whether he be younger or older or of his own age; he spares neither father nor mother nor any other human being who can hear, and hardly even the lower animals, for he would certainly not spare a foreigner,[36] if he could get an interpreter anywhere.

[36] Apparently foreigners are considered among the lower animals.

PRO. Socrates, do you not see how many we are and that we are all young men? Are you not afraid that we shall join with Philebus and attack you, if you revile us? However—for we understand your meaning—if there is any way or means of removing this confusion gently from our discussion and finding some better road than this to bring us towards the goal of our argument, kindly lead on, and we will do our best to follow; for our present discussion, Socrates, is no trifling matter.

SOC. No, it is not, boys, as Philebus calls you; and there certainly is no better road, nor can there ever be, than that which I have always loved, though it has often deserted me, leaving me lonely and forlorn.

PRO. What is the road? Only tell us.

SOC. One which is easy to point out, but very difficult to follow; for through it all the inventions of art have been brought to light. See; this is the road I mean.

PRO. Go on; what is it?

SOC. A gift of gods to men, as I believe, was tossed down from some divine source through the agency of a Prometheus together with a gleaming fire; and the ancients, who were better than we and lived nearer the gods, handed down the tradition that all the things which are ever said to exist are sprung from one and many and have inherent in them the finite and the infinite. This being the way in which these things are arranged, we must always assume that there is in every case one idea of everything and must look for it—for we shall find that it is there—and if we get a grasp of this, we must look next for two, if there be two, and if not, for three or some other number; and again we must treat each of those units in the same way, until we can see not only that the original unit is one and many and infinite, but just how many it is. And we must not apply the idea of infinite to plurality until we have a view of its whole number between infinity and one; then, and not before, we may let each unit of everything pass on unhindered into infinity. The gods, then, as I said, handed down to us this mode of investigating, learning, and teaching one another; but the wise men of the present day make the one and the many too quickly or too slowly, in haphazard fashion, and they put infinity immediately after unity; they disregard all that lies between them, and this it is which distinguishes between the dialectic and the disputatious methods of discussion.

PRO. I think I understand you in part, Socrates, but I need a clearer statement of some things.

SOC. Surely my meaning, Protarchus, is made clear in the letters of the alphabet, which you were taught as a child; so learn it from them.

PRO. How?

SOC. Sound, which passes out through the mouth of each and all of us, is one, and yet again it is infinite in number.

PRO. Yes, to be sure.

SOC. And one of us is no wiser than the other merely for knowing that it is infinite or that it is one; but that which makes each of us a grammarian is the knowledge of the number and nature of sounds.

PRO. Very true.

SOC. And it is this same knowledge which makes the musician.

PRO. How is that?

SOC. Sound is one in the art of music also, so far as that art is concerned.

PRO. Of course.

SOC. And we may say that there are two sounds, low and high, and a third, which is the intermediate, may we not?

PRO. Yes.

SOC. But knowledge of these facts would not suffice to make you a musician, although ignorance of them would make you, if I may say so, quite worthless in respect to music.

PRO. Certainly.

SOC. But, my friend, when you have grasped the number and quality of the intervals of the voice in respect to high and low pitch, and the limits of the intervals, and all the combinations derived from them, which the men of former times discovered and handed down to us, their successors, with the traditional name of harmonies, and also the corresponding effects in the movements of the body, which they say are measured by numbers and must be called rhythms and measures—and they say that we must also understand that every one and many should be considered in this way—when you have thus grasped the facts, you have become a musician, and when by considering it in this way you have obtained a grasp of any other unity of all those which exist, you have become wise in respect to that unity. But the infinite number of individuals and the infinite number in each of them makes you in every instance indefinite in thought and of no account and not to be considered among the wise, so long as you have never fixed your eye upon any definite number in anything.

Pro. I think, Philebus, that what Socrates has said is excellent.

Phi. So do I; it is excellent in itself, but why has he said it now to us, and what purpose is there in it?

Soc. Protarchus, that is a very proper question which Philebus has asked us.

Pro. Certainly it is, so please answer it.

Soc. I will, when I have said a little more on just this subject. For if a person begins with some unity or other, he must, as I was saying, not turn immediately to infinity, but to some definite number; now just so, conversely, when he has to take the infinite first, he must not turn immediately to the one, but must think of some number which possesses in each case some plurality, and must end by passing from all to one. Let us revert to the letters of the alphabet to illustrate this.

Pro. How?

Soc. When some one, whether god or godlike man,—there is an Egyptian story that his name was Theuth—observed that sound was infinite, he was the first to notice that the vowel sounds in that infinity were not one, but many, and again that there were other elements which were not vowels but did have a sonant quality, and that these also had a definite number; and he distinguished a third kind of letters which we now call mutes. Then he divided the mutes until he distinguished each individual one, and he treated the vowels and semi-vowels in the same way, until he knew the number of them and gave to each and all the name of letters. Perceiving, however, that none of us could learn any one of them alone by itself without learning them all, and considering that this was a common bond which made them in a way all one, he assigned to them all a single science and called it grammar.

Phi. I understand that more clearly than the earlier statement, Protarchus, so far as the reciprocal relations of the one and the many are concerned, but I still feel the same lack as a little while ago.

Soc. Do you mean, Philebus, that you do not see what this has to do with the question?

Phi. Yes; that is what Protarchus and I have been trying to discover for a long time.

Soc. Really, have you been trying, as you say, for a long time to discover it, when it was close to you all the while?

Phi. How is that?

Soc. Was not our discussion from the beginning about wisdom and pleasure and which of them is preferable?

Phi. Yes, of course.

Soc. And surely we say that each of them is one.

Phi. Certainly.

Soc. This, then, is precisely the question which the previous discussion puts to us: How is each of them one and many, and how is it that they are not immediately infinite, but each possesses a definite number, before the individual phenomena become infinite?

Pro. Philebus, somehow or other Socrates has led us round and plunged us into a serious question. Consider which of us shall answer it. Perhaps it is ridiculous that I, after taking your place in entire charge of the argument, should ask you to come back and answer this question because I cannot do so, but I think it would be still more ridiculous if neither of us could answer. Consider, then, what we are to do. For I think Socrates is asking us whether there are or are not kinds of pleasure, how many kinds there are, and what their nature is, and the same of wisdom.

Soc. You are quite right, son of Callias; for, as our previous discussion showed, unless we can do this in the case of every unity, every like, every same, and their opposites, none of us can ever be of any use in anything.

Pro. That, Socrates, seems pretty likely to be true. However, it is splendid for the wise man to know everything, but the next best thing, it seems, is not to be ignorant of himself. I will tell you why I say that at this moment. You, Socrates, have granted to all of us this conversation and your co-operation for the purpose of determining what is the best of human possessions. For when Philebus said it was pleasure and gaiety and enjoyment and all that sort of thing, you objected and said it was not those things, but another sort, and we very properly keep reminding ourselves voluntarily of this, in order that both claims may be present in our memory for examination. You, as it appears, assert that the good which is rightly to be called better than pleasure is mind, knowledge, intelligence, art, and all their kin; you say we ought to acquire these, not that other sort. When those two claims were made and an argument arose, we playfully threatened that we would not let you go home until the discussion was brought to some satisfactory conclusion. You agreed and put yourself at our disposal for that purpose. Now, we say that, as children put it, you cannot take back a gift once fairly given. So cease this way of meeting all that we say.

Soc. What way do you mean?

Pro. I mean puzzling us and asking questions to which we cannot at the moment give a satisfactory answer. Let us not imagine that the end of our present discussion is a mere puzzling of us all, but if we cannot answer, you must do so; for you gave us a promise. Consider, therefore, whether you yourself must distinguish the kinds of pleasure and knowledge or will let that go, in case you are able and willing to make clear in some other way the matters now at issue among us.

Soc. I need no longer anticipate anything terrible, since you put it in that way; for the words "in case you are willing" relieve me of all fear. And besides, I think some god has given me a vague recollection.

Pro. How is that, and what is the recollection about?

Soc. I remember now having heard long ago in a dream, or perhaps when I was awake, some talk about pleasure and wisdom to the effect that neither of the two is the good, but some third thing, different from them and better than both. However, if this be now clearly proved to us, pleasure is deprived of victory; for the good would no longer be identical with it. Is not that true?

Pro. It is.

Soc. And we shall have, in my opinion, no longer any need of distinguishing the kinds of pleasure. But the progress of the discussion will make that still clearer.

Pro. Excellent! Just go on as you have begun.

Soc. First, then, let us agree on some further small points.

Pro. What are they?

Soc. Is the nature of the good necessarily perfect or imperfect?

Pro. The most perfect of all things, surely, Socrates.

Soc. Well, and is the good sufficient?

Pro. Of course; so that it surpasses all other things in sufficiency.

Soc. And nothing, I should say, is more certain about it than that every intelligent being pursues it, desires it, wishes to catch and get possession of it, and has no interest in anything in which the good is not included.

Pro. There is no denying that.

Soc. Let us, then, look at the life of pleasure and the life of wisdom separately and consider and judge them.

Pro. How do you mean?

Soc. Let there be no wisdom in the life of pleasure and no pleasure in the life of wisdom. For if either of them is the good, it cannot have need of anything else, and if either be found to need anything, we can no longer regard it as our true good.

Pro. No, of course not.

Soc. Shall we then undertake to test them through you?

Pro. By all means.

Soc. Then answer.

Pro. Ask.

Soc. Would you, Protarchus, be willing to live your whole life in the enjoyment of the greatest pleasures?

Pro. Of course I should.

Soc. Would you think you needed anything further, if you were in complete possession of that enjoyment?

Pro. Certainly not.

Soc. But consider whether you would not have some need of wisdom and intelligence and power of calculating your wants and the like.

Pro. Why should I? If I have enjoyment, I have everything.

Soc. Then living thus you would enjoy the greatest pleasures all your life?

Pro. Yes; why not?

Soc. But if you did not possess mind or memory or knowledge or true opinion, in the first place, you would not know whether you were enjoying your pleasures or not. That must be true, since you are utterly devoid of intellect, must it not?

Pro. Yes, it must.

Soc. And likewise, if you had no memory you could not even remember that you ever did enjoy pleasure, and no recollection whatever of present pleasure could remain with you; if you had no true opinion you could not think you were enjoying pleasure at the time when you were enjoying it, and if you were without power of calculation you would not be able to calculate that you would enjoy it in the future; your life would not be that of a man, but of a mollusc or some other shell-fish like the oyster. Is that true, or can we imagine any other result?

PRO. We certainly cannot.

Soc. And can we choose such a life?

PRO. This argument, Socrates, has made me utterly speechless for the present.

Soc. Well, let us not give in yet. Let us take up the life of mind and scrutinize that in turn.

PRO. What sort of life do you mean?

Soc. I ask whether anyone would be willing to live possessing wisdom and mind and knowledge and perfect memory of all things, but having no share, great or small, in pleasure, or in pain, for that matter, but being utterly unaffected by everything of that sort.

PRO. Neither of the two lives can ever appear desirable to me, Socrates, or, I think, to anyone else.

Soc. How about the combined life, Protarchus, made up by a union of the two?

PRO. You mean a union of pleasure with mind or wisdom?

Soc. Yes, I mean a union of such elements.

PRO. Every one will prefer this life to either of the two others— yes, every single person without exception.

Soc. Then do we understand the consequences of what we are now saying?

PRO. Certainly. Three lives have been proposed, and of two of them neither is sufficient or desirable for man or any other living being.

Soc. Then is it not already clear that neither of these two contained the good? For if it did contain the good, it would be sufficient and perfect, and such as to be chosen by all living creatures which would be able to live thus all their lives; and if any of us chose anything else, he would be choosing contrary to the nature of the truly desirable, not of his own free will, but from ignorance or some unfortunate necessity.

PRO. That seems at any rate to be true.

Soc. And so I think we have sufficiently proved that Philebus's divinity is not to be considered identical with the good.

Phi. But neither is your "mind" the good, Socrates; it will be open to the same objections.

Soc. My mind, perhaps, Philebus; but not so, I believe, the true mind, which is also divine; that is different. I do not as yet claim for mind the victory over the combined life, but we must look and see what is to be done about the second place; for each of us might perhaps put forward a claim, one that mind is the cause of this combined life, the other that pleasure is the cause; and thus neither of these two would be the good, but one or the other of them might be regarded as the cause of the good. On this point I might keep up the fight all the more against Philebus and contend that in this mixed life it is mind that is more akin and more similar than pleasure to that, whatever it may be, which makes it both desirable and good; and from this point of view pleasure could advance no true claim to the first or even the second place. It is farther behind than the third place, if my mind is at all to be trusted at present.

Pro. Certainly, Socrates, it seems to me that pleasure has fought for the victory and has fallen in this bout, knocked down by your words. And we can only say, as it seems, that mind was wise in not laying claim to the victory; for it would have met with the same fate. Now pleasure, if she were to lose the second prize, would be deeply humiliated in the eyes of her lovers; for she would no longer appear even to them so lovely as before.

Soc. Well, then, is it not better to leave her now and not to pain her by testing her to the utmost and proving her in the wrong?

Pro. Nonsense, Socrates!

Soc. Nonsense because I spoke of paining pleasure, and that is impossible?

Pro. Not only that, but because you do not understand that not one of us will let you go yet until you have finished the argument about these matters.

Soc. Whew, Protarchus! Then we have a long discussion before us, and not an easy one, either, this time. For in going ahead to fight mind's battle for the second place, I think I need a new contrivance—other weapons, as it were, than those of our previous discussion, though perhaps some of the old ones will serve. Must I then go on?

Pro. Of course you must.

Soc. Then let us try to be careful in making our beginning.

Pro. What kind of a beginning do you mean?

Soc. Let us divide all things that now exist in the universe into two, or rather, if you please, three classes.

Pro. Please tell us on what principle you would divide them.

Soc. Let us take some of the subjects of our present discussion.

Pro. What subjects?

Soc. We said that God revealed in the universe two elements, the infinite and the finite, did we not?

Pro. Certainly.

Soc. Let us, then, assume these as two of our classes, and a third, made by combining these two. But I cut a ridiculous figure, it seems, when I attempt a division into classes and an enumeration.

Pro. What do you mean, my friend?

Soc. I think we need a fourth class besides.

Pro. Tell us what it is.

Soc. Note the cause of the combination of those two and assume that as the fourth in addition to the previous three.

Pro. And then will you not need a fifth, which has the power of separation?

Soc. Perhaps; but not at present, I think. However, if we do need a fifth, you will pardon me for going after it.

Pro. Of course.

Soc. First, then, let us take three of the four and, as we see that two of these are split up and scattered each one into many, let us try, by collecting each of them again into one, to learn how each of them was both one and many.

Pro. If you could tell me more clearly about them, I might be able to follow you.

Soc. I mean, then, that the two which I select are the same which I mentioned before, the infinite and the finite. I will try to show that the infinite is, in a certain sense, many; the finite can wait.

Pro. Yes.

Soc. Consider then. What I ask you to consider is difficult and debatable; but consider it all the same. In the first place, take hotter and colder and see whether you can conceive any limit of them, or whether the more and less which dwell in their very nature do not, so long as they continue to dwell therein, preclude the possibility of any end; for if there were any end of them, the more and less would themselves be ended.

PRO. Very true.

SOC. But always, we affirm, in the hotter and colder there is the more and less.

PRO. Certainly.

SOC. Always, then, the argument shows that these two have no end; and being endless, they are of course infinite.

PRO. Most emphatically, Socrates.

SOC. I am glad you responded, my dear Protarchus, and reminded me that the word "emphatically" which you have just used, and the word "gently" have the same force as "more" and "less." For wherever they are present, they do not allow any definite quantity to exist; they always introduce in every instance a comparison—more emphatic than that which is quieter, or *vice versa*—and thus they create the relation of more and less, thereby doing away with fixed quantity. For, as I said just now, if they did not abolish quantity, but allowed it and measure to make their appearance in the abode of the more and less, the emphatically and gently, those latter would be banished from their own proper place. When once they had accepted definite quantity, they would no longer be hotter or colder; for hotter and colder are always progressing and never stationary; but quantity is at rest and does not progress. By this reasoning hotter and its opposite are shown to be infinite.

PRO. That appears to be the case, Socrates; but, as you said, these subjects are not easy to follow. Perhaps, however, continued repetition might lead to a satisfactory agreement between the questioner and him who is questioned.

SOC. That is a good suggestion, and I must try to carry it out. However, to avoid waste of time in discussing all the individual examples, see if we can accept this as a designation of the infinite.

PRO. Accept what?

SOC. All things which appear to us to become more or less, or to admit of emphatic and gentle and excessive and the like, are to be put in the class of the infinite as their unity, in accordance with what we said a while ago, if you remember, that we ought to collect all things that are scattered and split up and impress upon them to the best of our ability the seal of some single nature.

Pro. I remember.

Soc. And the things which do not admit of more and less and the like, but do admit of all that is opposed to them—first equality and the equal, then the double, and anything which is a definite number or measure in relation to such a number or measure—all these might properly be assigned to the class of the finite. What do you say to that?

Pro. Excellent, Socrates.

Soc. Well, what shall we say is the nature of the third class, made by combining these two?

Pro. You will tell me, I fancy, by answering your own question.

Soc. Nay, a god will do so, if any god will give ear to my prayers.

Pro. Pray, then, and watch.

Soc. I am watching; and I think, Protarchus, one of the gods has this moment been gracious unto me.

Pro. What do you mean, and what evidence have you?

Soc. I will tell you, of course. Just follow what I say.

Pro. Say on.

Soc. We spoke just now of hotter and colder, did we not?

Pro. Yes.

Soc. Add to them drier and wetter, more and less, quicker and slower, greater and smaller, and all that we assigned before to the class which unites more and less.

Pro. You mean the class of the infinite?

Soc. Yes. Mix with that the second class, the offspring of the limit.

Pro. What class do you mean?

Soc. The class of the finite, which we ought just now to have reduced to unity, as we did that of the infinite. We have not done that, but perhaps we shall even now accomplish the same end, if these two are both unified and then the third class is revealed.

Pro. What third class, and what do you mean?

Soc. The class of the equal and double and everything which puts an end to the differences between opposites and makes them commensurable and harmonious by the introduction of number.

Pro. I understand. I think you mean that by mixture of these elements certain results are produced in each instance.

Soc. Yes, you are right.

Pro. Go on.

Soc. In cases of illness, does not the proper combination of these elements produce health?

Pro. Certainly.

Soc. And in the acute and the grave, the quick and the slow, which are unlimited, the addition of these same elements creates a limit and establishes the whole art of music in all its perfection, does it not?

Pro. Excellent.

Soc. And again in the case of cold and hot weather, the introduction of these elements removes the excess and indefiniteness and creates moderation and harmony.

Pro. Assuredly.

Soc. And thence arise the seasons and all the beauties of our world, by mixture of the infinite with the finite?

Pro. Of course.

Soc. There are countless other things which I pass over, such as health, beauty, and strength of the body and the many glorious beauties of the soul. For this goddess, my fair Philebus, beholding the violence and universal wickedness which prevailed, since there was no limit of pleasures or of indulgence in them, established law and order, which contain a limit. You say she did harm; I say, on the contrary, she brought salvation. What do you think, Protarchus?

Pro. What you say, Socrates, pleases me greatly.

Soc. I have spoken of these three classes, you observe.

Pro. Yes, I believe I understand; I think you mean that the infinite is one class and the finite is another class among existing things; but what you wish to designate as the third class, I do not comprehend very well.

Soc. No, because the multitude which springs up in the third class overpowers you; and yet the infinite also comprised many classes, nevertheless, since they were sealed with the seal of the more and less, they were seen to be of one class.

Pro. True.

Soc. And the finite, again, did not contain many classes, nor were we disturbed about its natural unity.

Pro. Of course not.

Soc. No, not at all. And as to the third class, understand that

I mean every offspring of these two which comes into being as a result of the measures created by the co-operation of the finite.

Pro. I understand.

Soc. But we said there was, in addition to three classes, a fourth to be investigated. Let us do that together. See whether you think that everything which comes into being must necessarily come into being through a cause.

Pro. Yes, I do; for how could it come into being apart from a cause?

Soc. Does not the nature of that which makes or creates differ only in name from the cause, and may not the creative agent and the cause be properly considered one?

Pro. Yes.

Soc. And, again, we shall find that, on the same principle, that which is made or created differs in name only from that which comes into being, shall we not?

Pro. We shall.

Soc. And the creative agent always naturally leads, and that which is created follows after it as it comes into being?

Pro. Certainly.

Soc. Then the cause and that which is the servant of the cause for the purpose of generation are not the same.

Pro. Of course not.

Soc. Did not the things which come into being and the things out of which they come into being furnish us all the three classes?

Pro. Certainly.

Soc. And that which produces all these, the cause, we call the fourth, as it has been satisfactorily shown to be distinct from the others?

Pro. Yes, it is distinct.

Soc. It is, then, proper, now that we have distinguished the four, to make sure that we remember them separately by enumerating them in order.

Pro. Yes, certainly.

Soc. The first, then, I call infinite, the second limit or finite, and the third; something generated by a mixture of these two. And should I be making a mistake if I called the cause of this mixture and creation the fourth?

Pro. Certainly not.

Soc. Now what is the next step in our argument, and what was our purpose in coming to the point we have reached? Was it not this? We were trying to find out whether the second place belonged to pleasure or to wisdom, were we not?

Pro. Yes, we were.

Soc. And may we not, perhaps, now that we have finished with these points, be better able to come to a decision about the first and second places, which was the original subject of our discussion?

Pro. Perhaps.

Soc. Well then; we decided that the mixed life of pleasure and wisdom was the victor, did we not?

Pro. Yes.

Soc. And do we not see what kind of life this is, and to what class it belongs?

Pro. Of course we do.

Soc. We shall say that it belongs to the third class; for that class is not formed by mixture of any two things, but of all the things which belong to the infinite, bound by the finite; and therefore this victorious life would rightly be considered a part of this class.

Pro. Quite rightly.

Soc. Well then, what of your life, Philebus, of unmixed pleasure? In which of the aforesaid classes may it properly be said to belong? But before you tell me, please answer this question.

Phi. Ask your question.

Soc. Have pleasure and pain a limit, or are they among the things which admit of more and less?

Phi. Yes, they are among those which admit of the more, Socrates; for pleasure would not be absolute good if it were not infinite in number and degree.

Soc. Nor would pain, Philebus, be absolute evil; so it is not the infinite which supplies any element of good in pleasure; we must look for something else. Well, I grant you that pleasure and pain are in the class of the infinite; but to which of the aforesaid classes, Protarchus and Philebus, can we now without irreverence assign wisdom, knowledge, and mind? I think we must find the right answer to this question, for our danger is great if we fail.

Phi. Oh Socrates, you exalt your own god.

Soc. And you your goddess, my friend. But the question calls for an answer, all the same.

Pro. Socrates is right, Philebus; you ought to do as he asks.

Phi. Did you not, Protarchus, elect to reply in my place?

Pro. Yes; but now I am somewhat at a loss, and I ask you, Socrates, to be our spokesman yourself, that we may not select the wrong representative and so say something improper.

Soc. I must do as you ask, Protarchus; and it is not difficult. But did I really, as Philebus said, embarrass you by playfully exalting my god, when I asked to what class mind and knowledge should be assigned?

Pro. You certainly did, Socrates.

Soc. Yet the answer is easy; for all philosophers agree—whereby they really exalt themselves—that mind is king of heaven and earth. Perhaps they are right. But let us, if you please, investigate the question of its class more at length.

Pro. Speak just as you like, Socrates. Do not consider length, so far as we are concerned; you cannot bore us.

Soc. Good. Then let us begin by asking a question.

Pro. What is the question?

Soc. Shall we say, Protarchus, that all things and this which is called the universe are governed by an irrational and fortuitous power and mere chance, or, on the contrary, as our forefathers said, are ordered and directed by mind and a marvellous wisdom?

Pro. The two points of view have nothing in common, my wonderful Socrates. For what you are now saying seems to me actually impious. But the assertion that mind orders all things is worthy of the aspect of the world, of sun, moon, stars, and the whole revolving universe; I can never say or think anything else about it.

Soc. Do you, then, think we should assent to this and agree in the doctrine of our predecessors, not merely intending to repeat the words of others, with no risk to ourselves, but ready to share with them in the risk and the blame, if any clever man declares that this world is not thus ordered, but is without order?

Pro. Yes, of course I do.

Soc. Then observe the argument that now comes against us.

Pro. Go on.

Soc. We see the elements which belong to the natures of all living beings, fire, water, air, and earth—or, as the storm-tossed mariners say, land in sight—in the constitution of the universe.

PRO. Certainly; and we are truly storm-tossed in the puzzling cross-currents of this discussion.

SOC. Well, here is a point for you to consider in relation to each of these elements as it exists in us.

PRO. What is the point?

SOC. Each element in us is small and poor and in no way pure at all or endowed with the power which is worthy of its nature. Take one example and apply it to all. Fire, for instance, exists in us and also in the universe.

PRO. Of course.

SOC. And that which is in us is small, weak, and poor, but that which is in the universe is marvellous in quantity, beauty, and every power which belongs to fire.

PRO. What you say is very true.

SOC. Well, is the fire of the universe nourished, originated, and ruled by the fire within us, or, on the contrary, does my fire, and yours, and that of all living beings derive nourishment and all that from the universal fire?

PRO. That question does not even deserve an answer.

SOC. True; and you will, I fancy, say the same of the earth which is in us living creatures and that which is in the universe, and concerning all the other elements about which I asked a moment ago your answer will be the same.

PRO. Yes. Who could answer otherwise without being called a lunatic?

SOC. Nobody, I fancy. Now follow the next step. When we see that all the aforesaid elements are gathered together into a unit, do we not call them a body?

PRO. Of course.

SOC. Apply the same line of thought to that which we call the universe. It would likewise be a body, being composed of the same elements.

PRO. Quite right.

SOC. Does our body derive, obtain, and possess from that body, or that body from ours, nourishment and everything else that we mentioned just now?

PRO. That, Socrates, is another question not worth asking.

Soc. Well, is this next one worth asking? What will you say to it?

Pro. What is it?

Soc. Shall we not say that our body has a soul?

Pro. Clearly we shall.

Soc. Where did it get it, Protarchus, unless the body of the universe had a soul, since that body has the same elements as ours, only in every way superior?

Pro. Clearly it could get it from no other source.

Soc. No; for we surely do not believe, Protarchus, that of those four elements, the finite, the infinite, the combination, and the element of cause which exists in all things, this last, which gives to our bodies souls and the art of physical exercise and medical treatment when the body is ill, and which is in general a composing and healing power, is called the sum of all wisdom, and yet, while these same elements exist in the entire heaven and in great parts thereof, and are, moreover, fair and pure, there is no means of including among them that nature which is the fairest and most precious of all.

Pro. Certainly there would be no sense in that.

Soc. Then if that is not the case, it would be better to follow the other line of thought and say, as we have often said, that there is in the universe a plentiful infinite and a sufficient limit, and in addition a by no means feeble cause which orders and arranges years and seasons and months, and may most justly be called wisdom and mind.

Pro. Yes, most justly.

Soc. Surely reason and mind could never come into being without soul.

Pro. No, never. ·

Soc. Then in the nature of Zeus you would say that a kingly soul and a kingly mind were implanted through the power of the cause, and in other deities other noble qualities from which they derive their favourite epithets.

Pro. Certainly.

Soc. Now do not imagine, Protarchus, that this is mere idle talk of mine; it confirms the utterances of those who declared of old[37] that mind always rules the universe.

[37] Anaxagoras and probably some now unknown precursors.

PRO. Yes, certainly.

SOC. And to my question it has furnished the reply that mind belongs to that one of our four classes which was called the cause of all. Now, you see, you have at last my answer.

PRO. Yes, and a very sufficient one; and yet you answered without my knowing it.

SOC. Yes, Protarchus, for sometimes a joke is a restful change from serious talk.

PRO. You are right.

SOC. We have now, then, my friend, pretty clearly shown to what class mind belongs and what power it possesses.

PRO. Certainly.

SOC. And likewise the class of pleasure was made clear some time ago.

PRO. Yes, it was.

SOC. Let us, then, remember concerning both of them that mind was akin to cause and belonged more or less to that class, and that pleasure was itself infinite, and belonged to the class which, in and by itself, has not and never will have either beginning or middle or end.

PRO. We will remember that, of course.

SOC. Our next task is to see in what and by means of what feeling each of them comes into being whenever they do come into being. We will take pleasure first and discuss these questions in relation to pleasure, as we examined its class first. But we cannot examine pleasure successfully apart from pain.

PRO. If that is our proper path, let us follow it.

SOC. Do you agree with us about the origin of pleasure?

PRO. What do you think it is?

SOC. I think pain and pleasure naturally originate in the combined class.

PRO. Please, my dear Socrates, remind us which of the aforesaid classes you mean by the combined class.

SOC. I will do so, as well as I can, my brilliant friend.

PRO. Thank you.

SOC. By combined class, then, let us understand that which we said was the third of the four.

PRO. The one you mentioned after the infinite and the finite, and in which you put health and also, I believe, harmony?

Soc. You are quite right. Now please pay very close attention.

Pro. I will. Say on.

Soc. I say, then, that when, in us living beings, harmony is broken up, a disruption of nature and a generation of pain also take place at the same moment.

Pro. What you say is very likely.

Soc. But if harmony is recomposed and returns to its own nature, then I say that pleasure is generated, if I may speak in the fewest and briefest words about matters of the highest import.

Pro. I think you are right, Socrates; but let us try to be more explicit.

Soc. It is easiest to understand common and obvious examples, is it not?

Pro. What examples?

Soc. Is hunger a kind of breaking up and a pain?

Pro. Yes.

Soc. And eating, which is a filling up again, is a pleasure?

Pro. Yes.

Soc. Thirst again is a destruction and a pain, but the filling with moisture of that which was dried up is a pleasure. Then, too, the unnatural dissolution and disintegration we experience through heat are a pain, but the natural restoration and cooling are a pleasure.

Pro. Certainly.

Soc. And the unnatural hardening of the moisture in an animal through cold is pain; but the natural course of the elements returning to their place and separating is a pleasure. See, in short, if you think it is a reasonable statement that whenever in the class of living beings, which, as I said before, arises out of the natural union of the infinite and the finite, that union is destroyed, the destruction is pain, and the passage and return of all things to their own nature is pleasure.

Pro. Let us accept that; for it seems to me to be true in its general lines.

Soc. Then we may assume this as one kind of pain and pleasure arising severally under the conditions I have described?

Pro. Let that be assumed.

Soc. Now assume within the soul itself the anticipation of these conditions, the sweet and cheering hope of pleasant things to come, the fearful and woeful expectation of painful things to come.

Pro. Yes, indeed, this is another kind of pleasure and pain, which belongs to the soul itself, apart from the body, and arises through expectation.

Soc. You are right. I think that in these two kinds, both of which are, in my opinion, pure, and not formed by mixture of pain and pleasure, the truth about pleasure will be made manifest, whether the entire class is to be desired or such desirability is rather to be attributed to some other class among those we have mentioned, whereas pleasure and pain, like heat, cold, and other such things, are sometimes desirable and sometimes undesirable, because they are not good in themselves, though some of them sometimes admit on occasion the nature of the good.

Pro. You are quite right in saying that we must track our quarry on this trail.

Soc. First, then, let us agree on this point: If it is true, as we said, that destruction is pain and restoration is pleasure, let us consider the case of living beings in which neither destruction nor restoration is going on, and what their state is under such conditions. Fix your mind on my question: Must not every living being under those conditions necessarily be devoid of any feeling of pain or pleasure, great or small?

Pro. Yes, necessarily.

Soc. Have we, then, a third condition, besides those of feeling pleasure and pain?

Pro. Certainly.

Soc. Well then, do your best to bear it in mind; for remembering or forgetting it will make a great difference in our judgement of pleasure. And I should like, if you do not object, to speak briefly about it.

Pro. Pray do so.

Soc. You know that there is nothing to hinder a man from living the life of wisdom in this manner.

Pro. You mean without feeling pleasure or pain?

Soc. Yes, for it was said, you know, in our comparison of the lives that he who chose the life of mind and wisdom was to have no feeling of pleasure, great or small.

Pro. Yes, surely, that was said.

Soc. Such a man, then, would have such a life; and perhaps it is not unreasonable, if that is the most divine of lives.

Pro. Certainly it is not likely that gods feel either joy or its opposite.

Soc. No, it is very unlikely; for either is unseemly for them. But let us reserve the discussion of that point for another time, if it is appropriate, and we will give mind credit for it in contending for the second place, if we cannot count it for the first.

Pro. Quite right.

Soc. Now the other class of pleasure, which we said was an affair of the soul alone, originates entirely in memory.

Pro. How is that?

Soc. We must, apparently, first take up memory, and perception even before memory, if these matters are to be made clear to us properly.

Pro. What do you mean?

Soc. Assume that some of the affections of our body are extinguished in the body before they reach the soul, leaving the soul unaffected, and that other affections permeate both body and soul and cause a vibration in both conjointly and in each individually.

Pro. Let us assume that.

Soc. Shall be we right in saying that the soul forgets those which do not permeate both, and does not forget those which do?

Pro. Yes, certainly.

Soc. Do not in the least imagine that when I speak of forgetting I mean that forgetfulness arises in this case; for forgetfulness is the departure of memory, and in the case under consideration memory has not yet come into being; now it is absurd to speak of the loss of that which does not exist and has not yet come into being, is it not?

Pro. Certainly.

Soc. Then just change the terms.

Pro. How?

Soc. Instead of saying that the soul forgets, when it is unaffected by the vibrations of the body, apply the term want of perception to that which you are now calling forgetfulness.

Pro. I understand.

Soc. And the union of soul and body in one common affection and one common motion you may properly call perception.

Pro. Very true.

Soc. Then do we now understand what we mean by perception?

Pro. Certainly.

Soc. I think, then, that memory may rightly be defined as the preservation of perception.

Pro. Quite rightly.

Soc. But do we not say that memory differs from recollection?

Pro. Perhaps.

Soc. And is this the difference?

Pro. What?

Soc. When the soul alone by itself, apart from the body, recalls completely any experience it has had in company with the body, we say that it recollects, do we not?

Pro. Certainly.

Soc. And again when the soul has lost the memory of a perception or of something it has learned and then alone by itself regains this, we call everything of that kind recollection.

Pro. You are right.

Soc. Now my reason for saying all this is—

Pro. What?

Soc. That henceforth we may comprehend as completely and clearly as possible the pleasure of the soul, and likewise its desire, apart from the body; for both of these appear to be made plain by what has been said about memory and recollection.

Pro. Let us, then, Socrates, discuss the next point.

Soc. We must, it seems, consider many things in relation to the origin and general aspect of pleasure; but now I think our first task is to take up the nature and origin of desire.

Pro. Then let us examine that; for we shall not lose anything.

Soc. Oh yes, Protarchus, we shall lose a great deal! When we find what we are seeking we shall lose our perplexity about these very questions.

Pro. That is a fair counter; but let us try to take up the next point.

Soc. Did we not say just now that hunger, thirst, and the like were desires?

Pro. They are, decidedly.

Soc. What sort of identity have we in view when we call these, which are so different, by one name?

Pro. By Zeus, Socrates, that question may not be easy to answer, yet it must be answered.

Soc. Let us, then, begin again at that point with the same examples.

Pro. At what point?

Soc. We say of a thing on any particular occasion, "it's thirsty," do we not?

Pro. Of course.

Soc. And that means being empty?

Pro. Certainly.

Soc. And is thirst, then, a desire?

Pro. Yes, of drink.

Soc. Of drink, or of being filled with drink?

Pro. Of being filled, I suppose.

Soc. The man, then, who is empty desires, as it appears, the opposite of what he feels; for, being empty, he longs to be filled.

Pro. That is very plain.

Soc. Well then, is there any source from which a man who is empty at first can gain a comprehension, whether by perception or by memory, of fulness, a thing which he does not feel at the time and has never felt before?

Pro. It cannot be done.

Soc. And yet he who desires, desires something, we say.

Pro. Of course.

Soc. And he does not desire that which he feels; for he is thirsty, and that is emptiness, but he desires fulness.

Pro. Yes.

Soc. Then somehow some part of him who is thirsty can apprehend fulness.

Pro. Yes, obviously.

Soc. But it cannot be the body, for that is empty.

Pro. True.

Soc. The only remaining possibility is that the soul apprehends it, which it must do by means of memory; for what other means could it employ?

Pro. No other, I should say.

Soc. And do we understand the consequences of this argument?

Pro. What are the consequences?

Soc. This argument declares that we have no bodily desire.

Pro. How so?

Soc. Because it shows that the endeavour of every living being is always towards the opposite of the actual conditions of the body.

Pro. Yes, certainly.

Soc. And the impulse which leads towards the opposite of those conditions shows that there is a memory of the opposite of the conditions.

Pro. Certainly.

Soc. And the argument, by showing that memory is that which leads us towards the objects of desire, has proved that all the impulse, the desire, and the ruling principle in every living being are of the soul.

Pro. Quite right.

Soc. So the argument denies utterly that the body hungers or thirsts or has any such affection.

Pro. Very true.

Soc. Let us consider a further point in connexion with those very affections. For I think the purpose of the argument is to point out to us a state of life existing in them.

Pro. Of what sort of life are you speaking, and in what affections does it exist?

Soc. In the affections of fulness and emptiness and all which pertain to the preservation and destruction of living beings, and I am thinking that if we fall into one of these we feel pain, which is followed by joy when we change to the other.

Pro. That is true.

Soc. And what if a man is between the two?

Pro. How between them?

Soc. Because of his condition, he is suffering, but he remembers the pleasures the coming of which would bring him an end of his pain; as yet, however, he does not possess them. Well then, shall we say that he is between the affections, or not?

Pro. Let us say so.

Soc. Shall we say that he is wholly pained or wholly pleased?

Pro. No, by Zeus, but he is afflicted with a twofold pain; he suffers in body from his sensation, and in soul from expectation and longing.

Soc. How could you, Protarchus, speak of twofold pain? Is not an empty man sometimes possessed of a sure hope of being filled, and sometimes, on the contrary, quite hopeless?

Pro. Certainly.

Soc. And do you not think that when he has a hope of being filled he takes pleasure in his memory, and yet at the same time, since he is at the moment empty, suffers pain?

Pro. It cannot be otherwise.

Soc. At such a time, then, a man, or any other animal, has both pain and pleasure at once.

Pro. Yes, I suppose so.

Soc. And when an empty man is without hope of being filled, what then? Is not that the time when the twofold feeling of pain would arise, which you just now observed and thought the pain simply was twofold?

Pro. Very true, Socrates.

Soc. Let us make use of our examination of those affections for a particular purpose.

Pro. For what purpose?

Soc. Shall we say that those pleasures and pains are true or false, or that some are true and others not so?

Pro. But, Socrates, how can there be false pleasures or pains?

Soc. But, Protarchus, how can there be true and false fears, or true and false expectations, or true and false opinions?

Pro. Opinions I would grant you, but not the rest.

Soc. What? I am afraid we are starting a very considerable discussion.

Pro. You are right.

Soc. And yet we must consider, thou son of that man,[38] whether the discussion is relevant to what has gone before.

Pro. Yes, no doubt.

Soc. We must dismiss everything else, tedious or otherwise, that is irrelevant.

Pro. Right.

Soc. Now tell me; for I am always utterly amazed by the same questions we were just proposing.

---

[38] "Son of that man" may mean "son of Philebus," in so far as Protarchus is a pupil of Philebus, or (so Bury) "son of Gorgias," the orator and teacher (cf. 58 b), or the father of Protarchus may be referred to by the pronoun, possibly because Socrates does not at the moment recall his name or because he wishes to imply that he was a man of mark.

Pro. What do you mean?

Soc. Are not some pleasures false and others true?

Pro. How could that be?

Soc. Then, as you maintain, nobody, either sleeping or waking or insane or deranged, ever thinks he feels pleasure when he does not feel it, and never, on the other hand, thinks he suffers pain when he does not suffer it?

Pro. We have, Socrates, always believed that all this is as you suggest.

Soc. But is the belief correct? Shall we consider whether it is so or not?

Pro. I should say we ought to consider that.

Soc. Then let us analyse still more clearly what we were just now saying about pleasure and opinion. There is a faculty of having an opinion, is there not?

Pro. Yes.

Soc. And of feeling pleasure?

Pro. Yes.

Soc. And there is an object of opinion?

Pro. Of course.

Soc. And something by which that which feels pleasure is pleased?

Pro. Certainly.

Soc. And that which has opinion, whether right or wrong, never loses its function of really having opinion?

Pro. Of course not.

Soc. And that which feels pleasure, whether rightly or wrongly, will clearly never lose its function of really feeling pleasure?

Pro. Yes, that is true, too.

Soc. Then we must consider how it is that opinion is both true and false and pleasure only true, though the holding of opinion and the feeling of pleasure are equally real.

Pro. Yes, so we must.

Soc. You mean that we must consider this question because falsehood and truth are added as attributes to opinion, and thereby it becomes not merely opinion, but opinion of a certain quality in each instance?

Pro. Yes.

Soc. And furthermore, we must reach an agreement on the

question whether, even if some things have qualities, pleasure and pain are not merely what they are, without qualities or attributes.

Pro. Evidently we must.

Soc. But it is easy enough to see that they have qualities. For we said a long time ago that both pains and pleasures are great and small and intense.

Pro. Yes, certainly.

Soc. And if badness becomes an attribute of any of these, Protarchus, shall we say that the opinion or the pleasure thereby becomes bad?

Pro. Why certainly, Socrates.

Soc. And what if rightness or its opposite becomes an attribute of one of them? Shall we not say that the opinion is right, if it has rightness, and the pleasure likewise?

Pro. Obviously.

Soc. And if that which is opined is mistaken, must we not agree that the opinion, since it is at the moment making a mistake, is not right or rightly opining?

Pro. Of course.

Soc. And what if we see a pain or a pleasure making a mistake in respect of that by which the pain or pleasure is caused? Shall we give it the attribute of right or good or any of the words which denote excellence?

Pro. That is impossible if the pleasure is mistaken.

Soc. And certainly pleasure often seems to come to us in connexion with false, not true, opinion.

Pro. Of course it does; and in such a case, Socrates, we call the opinion false; but nobody would ever call the actual pleasure false.

Soc. You are an eager advocate of the case of pleasure just now, Protarchus.

Pro. Oh no, I merely say what I hear.

Soc. Is there no difference, my friend, between the pleasure which is connected with right opinion and knowledge and that which often comes to each of us with falsehood and ignorance?

Pro. There is likely to be a great difference.

Soc. Then let us proceed to the contemplation of the difference between them.

Pro. Lead on as you think best.

Soc. Then this is the way I lead.

PRO. What way?

SOC. Do we agree that there is such a thing as false opinion and also as true opinion?

PRO. There is.

SOC. And, as we were saying just now, pleasure and pain often follow them—I mean true and false opinion.

PRO. Certainly.

SOC. And do not opinion and the power of forming an opinion always come to us from memory and perception?

PRO. Certainly.

SOC. Do we, then, believe that our relation to these faculties is somewhat as follows?

PRO. How?

SOC. Would you say that often when a man sees things at a distance and not very clearly, he wishes to distinguish between the things which he sees?

PRO. Yes, I should say so.

SOC. Next, then, would he not ask himself—

PRO. What?

SOC. "What is that which is visible standing beside the rock under a tree?" Do you not think a man might ask himself such a question if he saw such objects presented to his view?

PRO. To be sure.

SOC. And after that our gazer might reply to himself correctly "It is a man"?

PRO. Certainly.

SOC. Or, again, perhaps he might be misled into the belief that it was a work of some shepherds, and then he would call the thing which he saw an image.

PRO. Yes, indeed.

SOC. And if some one is with him, he might repeat aloud to his companion what he had said to himself, and thus that which we called an opinion now becomes a statement?

PRO. Certainly.

SOC. But if he is alone when he has this thought, he sometimes carries it about in his mind for a long time.

PRO. Undoubtedly.

SOC. Well, is your view about what takes place in such cases the same as mine?

Pro. What is yours?

Soc. I think the soul at such a time is like a book.

Pro. How is that?

Soc. Memory unites with the senses, and they and the feelings which are connected with them seem to me almost to write words in our souls; and when the feeling in question writes the truth, true opinions and true statements are produced in us, but when the writer within us writes falsehoods, the resulting opinions and statements are the opposite of true.

Pro. That is my view completely, and I accept it as stated.

Soc. Then accept also the presence of another workman in our souls at such a time.

Pro. What workman?

Soc. A painter, who paints in our souls pictures to illustrate the words which the writer has written.

Pro. But how do we say he does this, and when?

Soc. When a man receives from sight or some other sense the opinions and utterances of the moment and afterwards beholds in his own mind the images of those opinions and utterances. That happens to us often enough, does it not?

Pro. It certainly does.

Soc. And the images of the true opinions are true, and those of the false are false?

Pro. Assuredly.

Soc. Then if we are right about that, let us consider a further question.

Pro. What is it?

Soc. Whether this is an inevitable experience in relation to the present and the past, but not in relation to the future.

Pro. It is in the same relation to all kinds of time.

Soc. Was it not said a while ago that the pleasures and pains which belong to the soul alone might come before the pleasures and pains of the body, so that we have the pleasure and pain of anticipation, which relate to the future?

Pro. Very true.

Soc. Do the writings and pictures, then, which we imagined a little while ago to exist within us, relate to the past and present, but not to the future?

Pro. To the future especially.

Soc. Do you say "to the future especially" because they are

all hopes relating to the future and we are always filled with hopes all our lives?

Pro. Precisely.

Soc. Well, here is a further question for you to answer.

Pro. What is it?

Soc. A just, pious, and good man is surely a friend of the gods, is he not?

Pro. Certainly.

Soc. And an unjust and thoroughly bad man is the reverse?

Pro. Of course.

Soc. But, as we were just now saying, every man is full of many hopes?

Pro. Yes, to be sure.

Soc. And there are in all of us written words which we call hopes?

Pro. Yes.

Soc. And also the images painted there; and often a man sees an abundance of gold coming into his possession, and in its train many pleasures; and he even sees a picture of himself enjoying himself immensely.

Pro. Yes, certainly.

Soc. Shall we or shall we not say that of these pictures those are for the most part true which are presented to the good, because they are friends of the gods, whereas those presented to the bad are for the most part false?

Pro. Surely we must say that.

Soc. Then the bad also, no less than the good, have pleasures painted in their souls, but they are false pleasures.

Pro. Yes, surely.

Soc. Then the bad rejoice for the most part in the false, and the good in true pleasures.

Pro. That is inevitably true.

Soc. According to our present view, then, there are false pleasures in the souls of men, imitations or caricatures of the true pleasures; and pains likewise.

Pro. There are.

Soc. We saw, you remember, that he who had an opinion at all always really had an opinion, but it was sometimes not based upon realities, whether present, past, or future.

Pro. Certainly.

Soc. And this it was, I believe, which created false opinion and the holding of false opinions, was it not?

Pro. Yes.

Soc. Very well, must we not also grant that pleasure and pain stand in the same relation to realities?

Pro. What do you mean?

Soc. I mean that he who feels pleasure at all in any way or manner always really feels pleasure, but it is sometimes not based upon realities, whether present or past, and often, perhaps most frequently, upon things which will never even be realities in the future.

Pro. This also, Socrates, must inevitably be the case.

Soc. And the same may be said of fear and anger and all that sort of thing—that they are all sometimes false?

Pro. Certainly.

Soc. Well, can we say that opinions become bad or good except as they become false?

Pro. No.

Soc. And we understand, I believe, that pleasures also are not bad except by being false.

Pro. No; you have said quite the reverse of the truth, Socrates; for no one would be at all likely to call pains and pleasures bad because they are false, but because they are involved in another great and manifold evil.

Soc. Then of the evil pleasures which are such because of evil we will speak a little later, if we still care to do so; but of the false pleasures we must prove in another way that they exist and come into existence in us often and in great numbers; for this may help us to reach our decisions.

Pro. Yes, of course; that is, if such pleasures exist.

Soc. But they do exist, Protarchus, in my opinion; however, until we have established the truth of this opinion, it cannot be unquestioned.

Pro. Good.

Soc. Then let us, like athletes, approach and grapple with this new argument.

Pro. Let us do so.

Soc. We said, you may remember, a little while ago, that when desires, as they are called, exist in us, the soul is apart from the body and separate from it in feelings.

Pro. I remember; that was said.

Soc. And was not the soul that which desired the opposites of the conditions of the body and the body that which caused pleasure or pain because of feeling?

Pro. Yes, that was the case.

Soc. Then draw the conclusion as to what takes place in these circumstances.

Pro. Go on.

Soc. What takes place is this: in these circumstances pleasures and pains exist at the same time and the sensations of opposite pleasures and pains are present side by side simultaneously, as was made clear just now.

Pro. Yes, that is clear.

Soc. And have we not also said and agreed and settled something further?

Pro. What?

Soc. That both pleasure and pain admit of the more and less and are of the class of the infinite.

Pro. Yes, we have said that, certainly.

Soc. Then what means is there of judging rightly of this?

Pro. How and in what way do you mean?

Soc. I mean to ask whether the purpose of our judgement of these matters in such circumstances is to recognize in each instance which of these elements is greater or smaller or more intense, comparing pain with pleasure, pain with pain, and pleasure with pleasure.

Pro. Certainly there are such differences, and that is the purpose of our judgement.

Soc. Well then, in the case of sight, seeing things from too near at hand or from too great a distance obscures their real sizes and causes us to have false opinions; and does not this same thing happen in the case of pains and pleasures?

Pro. Yes, Socrates, even much more than in the case of sight.

Soc. Then our present conclusion is the opposite of what we said a little while ago.

Pro. To what do you refer?

Soc. A while ago these opinions, being false or true, imbued the pains and pleasures with their own condition of truth or falsehood.

Pro. Very true.

Soc. But now, because they are seen at various and changing distances and are compared with one another, the pleasures themselves appear greater and more intense by comparison with the pains, and the pains in turn, through comparison with the pleasures, vary inversely as they.

Pro. That is inevitable for the reasons you have given.

Soc. They both, then, appear greater and less than the reality. Now if you abstract from both of them this apparent, but unreal, excess or inferiority, you cannot say that its appearance is true, nor again can you have the face to affirm that the part of pleasure or pain which corresponds to this is true or real.

Pro. No, I cannot.

Soc. Next, then, we will see whether we may not in another direction come upon pleasures and pains still more false than these appearing and existing in living beings.

Pro. What pleasures and what method do you mean?

Soc. It has been said many times that pains and woes and aches and everything that is called by names of that sort are caused when nature in any instance is corrupted through combinations and dissolutions, fillings and emptyings, increases and diminutions.

Pro. Yes, that has been said many times.

Soc. And we agreed that when things are restored to their natural condition, that restoration is pleasure.

Pro. Right.

Soc. But when neither of these changes takes place in the body, what then?

Pro. When could that be the case, Socrates?

Soc. That question of yours is not to the point, Protarchus.

Pro. Why not?

Soc. Because you do not prevent my asking my own question again.

Pro. What question?

Soc. Why, Protarchus, I may say, granting that such a condition does not arise, what would be the necessary result if it did?

Pro. You mean if the body is not changed in either direction?

Soc. Yes.

Pro. It is clear, Socrates, that in that case there would never be either pleasure or pain.

Soc. Excellent. But you believe, I fancy, that some such change must always be taking place in us, as the philosophers[39] say; for all things are always flowing and shifting.

PRO. Yes, that is what they say, and I think their theory is important.

SOC. Of course it is, in view of their own importance. But I should like to avoid this argument which is rushing at us. I am going to run away; come along and escape with me.

PRO. What is your way of escape?

SOC. "We grant you all this" let us say to them. But answer me this, Protarchus, are we and all other living beings always conscious of everything that happens to us—of our growth and all that sort of thing—or is the truth quite the reverse of that?

PRO. Quite the reverse, surely; for we are almost entirely unconscious of everything of that sort.

SOC. Then we were not right in saying just now that the fluctuations and changes cause pains and pleasures.

PRO. No, certainly not.

SOC. A better and more unassailable statement would be this.

PRO. What?

SOC. That the great changes cause pains and pleasures in us, but the moderate and small ones cause no pains or pleasures at all.

PRO. That is more correct than the other statement, Socrates.

SOC. But if that is the case, the life of which we spoke just now would come back again.

PRO. What life?

SOC. The life which we said was painless and without joys.

PRO. Very true.

SOC. Let us, therefore, assume three lives, one pleasant, one painful, and one neither of the two; or do you disagree?

PRO. No, I agree to this, that there are the three lives.

SOC. Then freedom from pain would not be identical with pleasure?

PRO. Certainly not.

SOC. When you hear anyone say that the pleasantest of all things is to live all one's life without pain, what do you understand him to mean?

PRO. I think he means that freedom from pain is pleasure.

SOC. Now let us assume that we have three things; no matter

[39] Heraclitus and his followers.

what they are, but let us use fine names and call one gold, another silver, and the third neither of the two.

PRO. Agreed.

SOC. Now can that which is neither become either gold or silver?

PRO. Certainly not.

SOC. Neither can that middle life of which we spoke ever be rightly considered in opinion or called in speech pleasant or painful, at any rate by those who reason correctly.

PRO. No, certainly not.

SOC. But surely, my friend, we are aware of persons who call it and consider it so.

PRO. Certainly.

SOC. Do they, then, think they feel pleasure whenever they are not in pain?

PRO. That is what they say.

SOC. Then they do think they feel pleasure at such times; for otherwise they would not say so.

PRO. Most likely.

SOC. Certainly, then, they have a false opinion about pleasure, if there is an essential difference between feeling pleasure and not feeling pain.

PRO. And we certainly found that difference.

SOC. Then shall we adopt the view that there are, as we said just now, three states, or that there are only two—pain, which is an evil to mankind, and freedom from pain, which is of itself a good and is called pleasure?

PRO. Why do we ask ourselves that question now, Socrates? I do not understand.

SOC. No, Protarchus, for you certainly do not understand about the enemies of our friend Philebus.

PRO. Whom do you mean?

SOC. Certain men who are said to be master thinkers about nature, and who deny the existence of pleasures altogether.

PRO. Is it possible?

SOC. They say that what Philebus and his school call pleasures are all merely refuges from pain.

PRO. Do you recommend that we adopt their view, Socrates?

SOC. No, but that we make use of them as seers who divine the truth, not by acquired skill, but by some innate and not ignoble repugnance which makes them hate the power of pleasure and think it so utterly unsound that its very attractiveness is mere trickery, not pleasure. You may make use of them in this way, considering also their other expressions of dislike; and after that you shall learn of the pleasures which seem to me to be true, in order that we may consider the power of pleasure from both points of view and form our judgement by comparing them.

Pro. You are right.

Soc. Let us, then, consider these men as allies and follow them in the track of their dislike. I fancy their method would be to begin somewhere further back and ask whether, if we wished to discover the nature of any class—take the hard, for instance—we should be more likely to learn it by looking at the hardest things or at the least hard. Now you, Protarchus, must reply to them as you have been replying to me.

Pro. By all means, and I say to them that we should look at the greatest things.

Soc. Then if we wished to discover what the nature of pleasure is, we should look, not at the smallest pleasures, but at those which are considered most extreme and intense.

Pro. Every one would agree to that now.

Soc. And the commonest and greatest pleasures are, as we have often said, those connected with the body, are they not?

Pro. Certainly.

Soc. Are they greater, then, and do they become greater in those who are ill or in those who are in health? Let us take care not to answer hastily and fall into error. Perhaps we might say they are greater in those who are in health.

Pro. That is reasonable.

Soc. Yes, but are not those pleasures the greatest which gratify the greatest desires?

Pro. That is true.

Soc. But do not people who are in a fever, or in similar diseases, feel more intensely thirst and cold and other bodily sufferings which they usually have; and do they not feel greater want, followed by greater pleasure when their want is satisfied? Is this true, or not?

Pro. Now that you have said it, it certainly appears to be true.

Soc. Then should we appear to be right in saying that if we wished to discover the greatest pleasures we should have to look, not at health, but at disease? Now do not imagine that I mean to ask you whether those who are very ill have more pleasures than those who are well, but assume that I am asking about the greatness of pleasure, and where the greatest intensity of such feeling normally occurs. For we say that it is our task to discover the nature of pleasure and what those who deny its existence altogether say that it is.[40]

Pro. I think I understand you.

Soc. Presently, Protarchus, you will show that more clearly, for I want you to answer a question. Do you see greater pleasures—I do not mean greater in number, but greater in intensity and degree—in riotous living or in a life of self-restraint? Be careful about your reply.

Pro. I understand you, and I see that there is a great difference. For the self-restrained are always held in check by the advice of the proverbial expression "nothing too much," which guides their actions; but intense pleasure holds sway over the foolish and dissolute even to the point of madness and makes them notorious.

Soc. Good; and if that is true, it is clear that the greatest pleasures and the greatest pains originate in some depravity of soul and body, not in virtue.

Pro. Certainly.

Soc. Then we must select some of these pleasures and see what there is about them which made us say that they are the greatest.

Pro. Yes, we must.

Soc. Now see what there is about the pleasures which are related to certain diseases.

Pro. What diseases?

Soc. Repulsive diseases which the philosophers of dislike whom we mentioned utterly abominate.

Pro. What are the pleasures?

Soc. For instance, the relief of the itch and the like by scratching, no other treatment being required. For in Heaven's name what shall we say the feeling is which we have in this case? Is it pleasure or pain?

Pro. I think, Socrates, it is a mixed evil.

Soc. I did not introduce this question on Philebus' account;

[40] This paradox means "what those say it is who deny that it is really pleasure."

but unless we consider these pleasures and those that follow in their train, Protarchus, we can probably never settle the point at issue.

Pro. Then we must attack this family of pleasures.

Soc. You mean those which are mixed?

Pro. Certainly.

Soc. Some mixtures are concerned with the body and are in the body only, and some belong only to the soul and are in the soul; and we shall also find some mingled pains and pleasures belonging both to the soul and to the body, and these are sometimes called pleasures, sometimes pains.

Pro. How so?

Soc. Whenever, in the process of restoration or destruction, anyone has two opposite feelings, as we sometimes are cold, but are growing warm, or are hot, but are growing cold, the desire of having the one and being free from the other, the mixture of bitter and sweet, as they say, joined with the difficulty in getting rid of the bitter, produces impatience and, later, wild excitement.

Pro. What you say is perfectly true.

Soc. And such mixtures sometimes consist of equal pains and pleasures and sometimes contain more of one or the other, do they not?

Pro. Of course.

Soc. In the case of the mixtures in which the pains are more than the pleasures—say the itch, which we mentioned just now, or tickling—when the burning inflammation is within and is not reached by the rubbing and scratching, which separate only such mixtures as are on the surface, sometimes by bringing the affected parts to the fire or to something cold we change from wretchedness to inexpressible pleasures, and sometimes the opposition between the internal and the external produces a mixture of pains and pleasures, whichever happens to preponderate; this is the result of the forcible separation of combined elements, or the combination of those that were separate, and the concomitant juxtaposition of pains and pleasures.

Pro. Very true.

Soc. And when the pleasure is the predominant element in the mixture, the slight tincture of pain tickles a man and makes him mildly impatient, or again an excessive proportion of pleasure ex-

cites him and sometimes even makes him leap for joy; it produces
in him all sorts of colours, attitudes, and pantings, and even causes
great amazement and foolish shouting, does it not?

Pro. Certainly.

Soc. And it makes him say of himself, and others say of him,
that he is pleased to death with these delights, and the more unrestrained and foolish he is, the more he always gives himself up
to the pursuit of these pleasures; he calls them the greatest of all
things and counts that man the happiest who lives most entirely in
the enjoyment of them.

Pro. Socrates, you have described admirably what happens
in the case of most people.

Soc. That may be, Protarchus, so far as concerns purely bodily
pleasures in which internal and external sensations unite; but concerning the pleasures in which the soul and the body contribute
opposite elements, each adding pain or pleasure to the other's pleasure or pain, so that both unite in a single mixture—concerning
these I said before that when a man is empty he desires to be filled,
and rejoices in his expectation, but is pained by his emptiness, and
now I add, what I did not say at that time, that in all these cases,
which are innumerable, of opposition between soul and body, there
is one single mixture of pain and pleasure.

Pro. I believe you are quite right.

Soc. One further mixture of pain and pleasure is left.

Pro. What is it?

Soc. That mixture of its own feelings which we said the soul
often experiences.

Pro. And what do we call this?

Soc. Do you not regard anger, fear, yearning, mourning, love,
jealousy, envy, and the like as pains of the soul and the soul only?

Pro. I do.

Soc. And shall we not find them full of ineffable pleasures? Or
must I remind you of the anger

> Which stirs a man, though very wise, to wrath,
> And sweeter is than honey from the comb,

and of the pleasures mixed with pains, which we find in mournings
and longings?

PRO. No, you need not remind me; those things occur just as you suggest.

SOC. And you remember, too, how people enjoy weeping at tragedies?

PRO. Yes, certainly.

SOC. And are you aware of the condition of the soul at comedies, how there also we have a mixture of pain and pleasure?

PRO. I do not quite understand.

SOC. Indeed it is by no means easy, Protarchus, to understand such a condition under those circumstances.

PRO. No; at least I do not find it so.

SOC. Well, then, let us take this under consideration, all the more because of its obscurity; then we can more readily understand the mixture of pain and pleasure in other cases.

PRO. Please go on.

SOC. Would you say that envy, which was mentioned just now, was a pain of the soul, or not?

PRO. I say it is.

SOC. But certainly we see the envious man rejoicing in the misfortunes of his neighbours.

PRO. Yes, very much so.

SOC. Surely ignorance is an evil, as is also what we call stupidity.

PRO. Surely.

SOC. Next, then, consider the nature of the ridiculous.

PRO. Please proceed.

SOC. The ridiculous is in its main aspect a kind of vice which gives its name to a condition; and it is that part of vice in general which involves the opposite of the condition mentioned in the inscription at Delphi.

PRO. You mean "Know thyself," Socrates?

SOC. Yes; and the opposite of that, in the language of the inscription, would evidently be not to know oneself at all.

PRO. Of course.

SOC. Protarchus, try to divide this into three.

PRO. How do you mean? I am afraid I can never do it.

SOC. Then you say that I must now make the division?

PRO. Yes, I say so, and I beg you to do so, besides.

SOC. Must not all those who do not know themselves be affected by their condition in one of three ways?

Pro. How is that?

Soc. First in regard to wealth; such a man thinks he is richer than he is.

Pro. Certainly a good many are affected in that way.

Soc. And there are still more who think they are taller and handsomer than they are and that they possess better physical qualities in general than is the case.

Pro. Certainly.

Soc. But by far the greatest number, I fancy, err in the third way, about the qualities of the soul, thinking that they excel in virtue when they do not.

Pro. Yes, most decidedly.

Soc. And of all the virtues, is not wisdom the one to which people in general lay claim, thereby filling themselves with strife and false conceit of wisdom?

Pro. Yes, to be sure.

Soc. And we should surely be right in calling all that an evil condition.

Pro. Very much so.

Soc. Then this must further be divided into two parts, if we are to gain insight into childish envy with its absurd mixture of pleasure and pain. "How shall we divide it," do you say? All who have this false and foolish conceit of themselves fall, like the rest of mankind, into two classes: some necessarily have strength and power, others, as I believe, the reverse.

Pro. Yes, necessarily.

Soc. Make the division, then, on that principle; those of them who have this false conceit and are weak and unable to revenge themselves when they are laughed at you may truly call ridiculous, but those who are strong and able to revenge themselves you will define most correctly to yourself by calling them powerful, terrible, and hateful, for ignorance in the powerful is hateful and infamous —since whether real or feigned it injures their neighbours—but ignorance in the weak appears to us as naturally ridiculous.

Pro. Quite right. But the mixture of pleasure and pain in all this is not yet clear to me.

Soc. First, then, take up the nature of envy.

Pro. Go on.

Soc. Is envy a kind of unrighteous pain and also a pleasure?

Pro. Undoubtedly.

Soc. But it is neither wrong nor envious to rejoice in the misfortunes of our enemies, is it?

Pro. No, of course not.

Soc. But when people sometimes see the misfortunes of their friends and rejoice instead of grieving, is not that wrong?

Pro. Of course it is.

Soc. And we said that ignorance was an evil to every one, did we not?

Pro. True.

Soc. Then the false conceits of our friends concerning their wisdom, their beauty, and their other qualities which we mentioned just now, saying that they belong to three classes, are ridiculous when they are weak, but hateful when they are powerful. Shall we, or shall we not, affirm that, as I said just now, this state of mind when possessed in its harmless form by any of our friends, is ridiculous in the eyes of others?

Pro. Certainly it is ridiculous.

Soc. And do we not agree that ignorance is in itself a misfortune?

Pro. Yes, a great one.

Soc. And do we feel pleasure or pain when we laugh at it?

Pro. Pleasure, evidently.

Soc. Did we not say that pleasure in the misfortunes of friends was caused by envy?

Pro. There can be no other cause.

Soc. Then our argument declares that when we laugh at the ridiculous qualities of our friends, we mix pleasure with pain, since we mix it with envy; for we have agreed all along that envy is a pain of the soul, and that laughter is a pleasure, yet these two are present at the same time on such occasions.

Pro. True.

Soc. So now our argument shows that in mournings and tragedies and comedies, not merely on the stage, but in all the tragedy and comedy of life, and in countless other ways, pain is mixed with pleasure.

Pro. It is impossible not to agree with that, Socrates, even though one be most eager to maintain the opposite opinion.

Soc. Again we mentioned anger, yearning, mourning, love, jealousy, envy, and the like, as conditions in which we should find a mixture of the two elements we have now often named, did we not?

Pro. Yes.

Soc. And we understand that all the details I have been describing just now are concerned only with sorrow and envy and anger?

Pro. Of course we understand that.

Soc. Then there are still many others of those conditions left for us to discuss.

Pro. Yes, very many.

Soc. Now why do you particularly suppose I pointed out to you the mixture of pain and pleasure in comedy? Was it not for the sake of convincing you, because it is easy to show the mixture in love and fear and the rest, and because I thought that when you had made this example your own, you would relieve me from the necessity of discussing those other conditions in detail, and would simply accept the fact that in the affections of the body apart from the soul, of the soul apart from the body, and of the two in common, there are plentiful mixtures of pain and pleasure? So tell me; will you let me off, or will you keep on till midnight? But I think I need say only a few words to induce you to let me off. I will agree to give you an account of all these matters to-morrow, but now I wish to steer my bark towards the remaining points that are needful for the judgement which Philebus demands.

Pro. Good, Socrates; just finish what remains in any way you please.

Soc. Then after the mixed pleasures we should naturally and almost of necessity proceed in turn to the unmixed.

Pro. Very good.

Soc. So I will turn to them and try to explain them; for I do not in the least agree with those who say that all pleasures are merely surcease from pain, but, as I said, I use them as witnesses to prove that some pleasures are apparent, but not in any way real, and that there are others which appear to be both great and numerous, but are really mixed up with pains and with cessations of the greatest pains and distresses of body and soul.

Pro. But what pleasures, Socrates, may rightly be considered true?

Soc. Those arising from what are called beautiful colours, or from forms, most of those that arise from odours and sounds, in short all those the want of which is unfelt and painless, whereas the satisfaction furnished by them is felt by the senses, pleasant, and unmixed with pain.

PRO. Once more, Socrates, what do you mean by this?

SOC. My meaning is certainly not clear at the first glance, and I must try to make it so. For when I say beauty of form, I am trying to express, not what most people would understand by the words, such as the beauty of animals or of paintings, but I mean, says the argument, the straight line and the circle and the plane and solid figures formed from these by turning-lathes and rulers and patterns of angles; perhaps you understand. For I assert that the beauty of these is not relative, like that of other things, but they are always absolutely beautiful by nature and have peculiar pleasures in no way subject to comparison with the pleasures of scratching; and there are colours which possess beauty and pleasures of this character. Do you understand?

PRO. I am trying to do so, Socrates; and I hope you also will try to make your meaning still clearer.

SOC. I mean that those sounds which are smooth and clear and send forth a single pure note are beautiful, not relatively, but absolutely, and that there are pleasures which pertain to these by nature and result from them.

PRO. Yes, that also is true.

SOC. The pleasures of smell are a less divine class; but they have no necessary pains mixed with them, and wherever and in whatever we find this freedom from pain, I regard it always as a mark of similarity to those other pleasures. These, then, are two classes of the pleasures of which I am speaking. Do you understand me?

PRO. I understand.

SOC. And further let us add to these the pleasures of knowledge, if they appear to us not to have hunger for knowledge or pangs of such hunger as their source.

PRO. I agree to that.

SOC. Well, if men are full of knowledge and then lose it through forgetfulness, do you see any pains in the losses?

PRO. Not by their inherent nature, but sometimes there is pain in reflecting on the event, when a man who has lost knowledge is pained by the lack of it.

Soc. True, my dear fellow, but just at present we are recounting natural feelings only, not reflection.

Pro. Then you are right in saying that we feel no pain in the loss of knowledge.

Soc. Then we may say that these pleasures of knowledge are unmixed with pain and are felt not by the many but only by very few.

Pro. Yes, certainly.

Soc. And now that we have fairly well separated the pure pleasures and those which may be pretty correctly called impure, let us add the further statement that the intense pleasures are without measure and those of the opposite sort have measure; those which admit of greatness and intensity and are often or seldom great or intense we shall assign to the class of the infinite, which circulates more or less freely through the body and soul alike, and the others we shall assign to the class of the limited.

Pro. Quite right, Socrates.

Soc. There is still another question about them to be considered.

Pro. What is it?

Soc. What kind of thing is most closely related to truth? The pure and unadulterated, or the violent, the widespread, the great, and the sufficient?

Pro. What is your object, Socrates, in asking that question?

Soc. My object, Protarchus, is to leave no gap in my test of pleasure and knowledge, if some part of each of them is pure and some part impure, in order that each of them may offer itself for judgement in a condition of purity, and thus make the judgement easier for you and me and all our audience.

Pro. Quite right.

Soc. Very well, let us adopt that point of view towards all the classes which we call pure. First let us select one of them and examine it.

Pro. Which shall we select?

Soc. Let us first, if agreeable to you, consider whiteness.

Pro. By all means.

Soc. How can we have purity in whiteness, and what purity? Is it the greatest and most widespread, or the most unmixed, that in which there is no trace of any other colour?

Pro. Clearly it is the most unadulterated.

Soc. Right. Shall we not, then, Protarchus, declare that this, and not the most numerous or the greatest, is both the truest and the most beautiful of all whitenesses?

Pro. Quite right.

Soc. Then we shall be perfectly right in saying that a little pure white is whiter and more beautiful and truer than a great deal of mixed white.

Pro. Perfectly right.

Soc. Well then, we shall have no need of many such examples in our discussion of pleasure; we see well enough from this one that any pleasure, however small or infrequent, if uncontaminated with pain, is pleasanter and more beautiful than a great or often repeated pleasure without purity.

Pro. Most certainly; and the example is sufficient.

Soc. Here is another point. Have we not often heard it said of pleasure that it is always a process or generation and that there is no state or existence of pleasure? There are some clever people who try to prove this theory to us, and we ought to be grateful to them.

Pro. Well, what then?

Soc. I will explain this whole matter, Protarchus, by asking questions.

Pro. Go on; ask your questions.

Soc. There are two parts of existence, the one self-existent, the other always desiring something else.

Pro. What do you mean? What are these two?

Soc. The one is by nature more imposing, the other inferior.

Pro. Speak still more plainly.

Soc. We have seen beloved boys who are fair and good, and brave lovers of them.

Pro. Yes, no doubt of it.

Soc. Try to find another pair like these in all the relations we are speaking of.

Pro. Must I say it a third time? Please tell your meaning more plainly, Socrates.

Soc. It is no riddle, Protarchus; the talk is merely jesting with us and means that one part of existences always exists for the sake of something, and the other part is that for the sake of which the former is always coming into being.

Pro. I can hardly understand after all your repetition.

Soc. Perhaps, my boy, you will understand better as the discussion proceeds.

Pro. I hope so.

Soc. Let us take another pair.

Pro. What are they?

Soc. One is the generation of all things (the process of coming into being) the other is existence or being.

Pro. I accept your two, generation and being.

Soc. Quite right. Now which of these shall we say is for the sake of the other, generation for the sake of being, or being for the sake of generation?

Pro. You are now asking whether that which is called being is what it is for the sake of generation?

Soc. Yes, plainly.

Pro. For Heaven's sake, is this the kind of question you keep asking me, "Tell me, Protarchus, whether you think shipbuilding is for the sake of ships, or ships for the sake of shipbuilding," and all that sort of thing?

Soc. Yes, that is just what I mean, Protarchus.

Pro. Then why did you not answer it yourself, Socrates?

Soc. There is no reason why I should not; but I want you to take part in the discussion.

Pro. Certainly.

Soc. I say that drugs and all sorts of instruments and materials are always employed for the sake of production or generation, but that every instance of generation is for the sake of some being or other, and generation in general is for the sake of being in general.

Pro. That is very clear.

Soc. Then pleasure, if it is a form of generation, would be generated for the sake of some form of being.

Pro. Of course.

Soc. Now surely that for the sake of which anything is generated is in the class of the good, and that which is generated for the sake of something else, my friend, must be placed in another class.

Pro. Most undeniably.

Soc. Then if pleasure is a form of generation, we shall be right in placing it in a class other than that of the good, shall we not?

Pro. Quite right.

Soc. Then, as I said when we began to discuss this point, we ought to be grateful to him who pointed out that there is only a generation, but no existence, of pleasure; for he is clearly making a laughing-stock of those who assert that pleasure is a good.

Pro. Yes, most emphatically.

Soc. And he will also surely make a laughing-stock of all those who find their highest end in forms of generation.

Pro. How is that, and to whom do you refer?

Soc. To those who, when cured of hunger or thirst or any of the troubles which are cured by generation, are pleased because of the generation, as if it were pleasure, and say that they would not wish to live without thirst and hunger and the like, if they could not experience the feelings which follow after them.

Pro. That seems to be their view.

Soc. We should all agree that the opposite of generation is destruction, should we not?

Pro. Inevitably.

Soc. And he who chooses as they do would be choosing destruction and generation, not that third life in which there was neither pleasure nor pain, but only the purest possible thought.

Pro. It is a great absurdity, as it appears, Socrates, to tell us that pleasure is a good.

Soc. Yes, a great absurdity, and let us go still further.

Pro. How?

Soc. Is it not absurd to say that there is nothing good in the body or many other things, but only in the soul, and that in the soul the only good is pleasure, and that courage and self-restraint and understanding and all the other good things of the soul are nothing of the sort; and beyond all this to be obliged to say that he who is not feeling pleasure, and is feeling pain, is bad when he feels pain, though he be the best of men, and that he who feels pleasure is, when he feels pleasure, the more excellent in virtue the greater the pleasure he feels?

Pro. All that, Socrates, is the height of absurdity.

Soc. Now let us not undertake to subject pleasure to every possible test and then be found to give mind and knowledge very gentle treatment. Let us rather strike them boldly everywhere to see if their metal rings unsound at any point; so we shall find out what is by nature purest in them, and then we can make use of the truest elements of these and of pleasure to form our judgement of both.

PRO. Right.

Soc. Well, then, one part of knowledge is productive, the other has to do with education and support. Is that true?

PRO. It is.

Soc. Let us first consider whether in the manual arts one part is more allied to knowledge, and the other less, and the one should be regarded as purest, the other as less pure.

PRO. Yes, we ought to consider that.

Soc. And should the ruling elements of each of them be separated and distinguished from the rest?

PRO. What are they, and how can they be separated?

Soc. For example, if arithmetic and the sciences of measurement and weighing were taken away from all arts, what was left of any of them would be, so to speak, pretty worthless.

PRO. Yes, pretty worthless.

Soc. All that would be left for us would be to conjecture and to drill the perceptions by practice and experience, with the additional use of the powers of guessing, which are commonly called arts and acquire their efficacy by practice and toil.

PRO. That is undeniable.

Soc. Take music first; it is full of this; it attains harmony by guesswork based on practice, not by measurement; and flute music throughout tries to find the pitch of each note as it is produced by guess, so that the amount of uncertainty mixed up in it is great, and the amount of certainty small.

PRO. Very true.

Soc. And we shall find that medicine and agriculture and piloting and generalship are all in the same case.

PRO. Certainly.

Soc. But the art of building, I believe, employs the greatest number of measures and instruments which give it great accuracy and make it more scientific than most arts.

PRO. In what way?

Soc. In shipbuilding and house-building, and many other branches of wood-working. For the artisan uses a rule, I imagine, a lathe, compasses, a chalk-line, and an ingenious instrument called a vice.

Pro. Certainly, Socrates; you are right.

Soc. Let us, then, divide the arts, as they are called, into two kinds, those which resemble music, and have less accuracy in their works, and those which, like building, are more exact.

Pro. Agreed.

Soc. And of these the most exact are the arts which I just now mentioned first.

Pro. I think you mean arithmetic and the other arts you mentioned with it just now.

Soc. Certainly. But, Protarchus, ought not these to be divided into two kinds? What do you say?

Pro. What kinds?

Soc. Are there not two kinds of arithmetic, that of the people and that of philosophers?

Pro. How can one kind of arithmetic be distinguished from the other?

Soc. The distinction is no small one, Protarchus. For some arithmeticians reckon unequal units, for instance, two armies and two oxen and two very small or incomparably large units; whereas others refuse to agree with them unless each of countless units is declared to differ not at all from each and every other unit.

Pro. You are certainly quite right in saying that there is a great difference between the devotees of arithmetic, so it is reasonable to assume that it is of two kinds.

Soc. And how about the arts of reckoning and measuring as they are used in building and in trade when compared with philosophical geometry and elaborate computations—shall we speak of each of these as one or as two?

Pro. On the analogy of the previous example, I should say that each of them was two.

Soc. Right. But do you understand why I introduced this subject?

Pro. Perhaps; but I wish you would give the answer to your question.

Soc. This discussion of ours is now, I think, no less than when we began it, seeking a counterpart of pleasure, and therefore it has introduced the present subject and is considering whether there is one kind of knowledge purer than another, as one pleasure is purer than another.

Pro. That is very clear; it was evidently introduced with that object.

Soc. Well, had not the discussion already found in what preceded that the various arts had various purposes and various degrees of exactness?

Pro. Certainly.

Soc. And after having given an art a single name in what has preceded, thereby making us think that it was a single art, does not the discussion now assume that the same art is two and ask whether the art of the philosophers or that of the non-philosophers possesses the higher degree of clearness and purity?

Pro. Yes, I think that is just the question it asks.

Soc. Then what reply shall we make, Protarchus?

Pro. Socrates, we have found a marvellously great difference in the clearness of different kinds of knowledge.

Soc. That will make the reply easier, will it not?

Pro. Yes, to be sure; and let our reply be this, that the arithmetical and metrical arts far surpass the others and that of these the arts which are stirred by the impulse of the true philosophers are immeasurably superior in accuracy and truth about measures and numbers.

Soc. We accept that as our judgement, and relying upon you we make this confident reply to those who are clever in straining arguments—

Pro. What reply?

Soc. That there are two arts of arithmetic and two of measuring, and many other arts which, like these, are twofold in this way, but possess a single name in common.

Pro. Let us give this answer, Socrates, to those who you say are clever; I hope we shall have luck with it.

Soc. These, then, we say, are the most exact arts or sciences?

Pro. Certainly.

Soc. But the art of dialectic would spurn us, Protarchus, if we should judge that any other art is preferable to her.

Pro. But what is the art to which this name belongs?

Soc. Clearly anybody can recognize the art I mean; for I am confident that all men who have any intellect whatsoever believe that the knowledge which has to do with being, reality, and eternal immutability is the truest kind of knowledge. What do you think, Protarchus?

Pro. I have often heard Gorgias constantly maintain that the art of persuasion surpasses all others; for this, he said, makes all things subject to itself, not by force, but by their free will, and is by far the best of all arts; so now I hardly like to oppose either him or you.

Soc. It seems to me that you wanted to speak and threw down your arms out of modesty.

Pro. Very well; have it as you like.

Soc. Is it my fault that you have misunderstood?

Pro. Misunderstood what?

Soc. My question, dear Protarchus, was not as yet what art or science surpasses all others by being the greatest and best and most useful to us: what I am trying to find out at present is which art, however little and of little use, has the greatest regard for clearness, exactness, and truth. See; you will not make Gorgias angry if you grant that his art is superior for the practical needs of men, but say that the study of which I spoke is superior in the matter of the most perfect truth, just as I said in speaking about the white that if it was small and pure it was superior to that which was great but impure. Now, therefore, with careful thought and due consideration, paying attention neither to the usefulness nor to the reputation of any arts or sciences, but to that faculty of our souls, if such there be, which by its nature loves the truth and does all things for the sake of the truth, let us examine this faculty and say whether it is most likely to possess mind and intelligence in the greatest purity, or we must look for some other faculty which has more valid claims.

Pro. I am considering, and I think it is difficult to concede that any other science or art cleaves more closely to truth than this.

Soc. In saying that, did you bear in mind that the arts in general, and the men who devote themselves to them, make use of opinion and persistently investigate things which have to do with opinion? And even if they think they are studying nature, they are spending their lives in the study of the things of this world, the manner of their production, their action, and the forces to which they are subjected. Is not that true?

Pro. Yes, it is.

Soc. Such thinkers, then, toil to discover, not eternal verities, but transient productions of the present, the future, or the past?

Pro. Perfectly true.

Soc. And can we say that any of these things becomes certain, if tested by the touchstone of strictest truth, since none of them ever was, will be, or is in the same state?

Pro. Of course not.

Soc. How can we gain anything fixed whatsoever about things which have no fixedness whatsoever?

Pro. In no way, as it seems to me.

Soc. Then no mind or science which is occupied with them possesses the most perfect truth.

Pro. No, it naturally does not.

Soc. Then we must dismiss the thought of you and me and Gorgias and Philebus, and make this solemn declaration on the part of our argument.

Pro. What is the solemn declaration?

Soc. That fixed and pure and true and what we call unalloyed knowledge has to do with the things which are eternally the same without change or mixture, or with that which is most akin to them; and all other things are to be regarded as secondary and inferior.

Pro. Very true.

Soc. And of the names applied to such matters, it would be fairest to give the finest names to the finest things, would it not?

Pro. That is reasonable.

Soc. Are not mind, then, and wisdom the names which we should honour most?

Pro. Yes.

Soc. Then these names are applied most accurately and correctly to cases of contemplation of true being.

Pro. Certainly.

Soc. And these are precisely the names which I brought forward in the first place as parties to our suit.

Pro. Yes, of course they are, Socrates.

Soc. Very well. As to the mixture of wisdom and pleasure, if anyone were to say that we are like artisans, with the materials before us from which to create our work, the simile would be a good one.

Pro. Certainly.

Soc. And is it, then, our next task to try to make the mixture?

Pro. Surely.

Soc. Would it not be better first to repeat certain things and recall them to our minds?

Pro. What things?

Soc. Those which we mentioned before. I think the proverb "we ought to repeat twice and even three times that which is good" is an excellent one.

Pro. Surely.

Soc. Well then, in God's name; I think this is the gist of our discussion.

Pro. What is it?

Soc. Philebus says that pleasure is the true goal of every living being and that all ought to aim at it, and that therefore this is also the good for all, and the two designations "good" and "pleasant" are properly and essentially one; Socrates, however, says that they are not one, but two in fact as in name, that the good and the pleasant differ from one another in nature, and that wisdom's share in the good is greater than pleasure's. Is not and was not that what was said, Protarchus?

Pro. Yes, certainly.

Soc. And furthermore, is not and was not this a point of agreement among us?

Pro. What?

Soc. That the nature of the good differs from all else in this respect?

Pro. In what respect?

Soc. That whatever living being possesses the good always, altogether, and in all ways, has no further need of anything, but is perfectly sufficient. We agreed to that?

Pro. We did.

Soc. And then we tried in thought to separate each from the other and apply them to individual lives, pleasure unmixed with wisdom and likewise wisdom which had not the slightest alloy of pleasure?

Pro. Yes.

Soc. And did we think then that either of them would be sufficient for any one?

Pro. By no means.

Soc. And if we made any mistake at that time, let any one now take up the question again. Assuming that memory, wisdom, knowledge, and true opinion belong to the same class, let him ask whether anyone would wish to have or acquire anything whatsoever without these not to speak of pleasure, be it never so abundant. or intense, if he could have no true opinion that he is pleased, no knowledge whatsoever of what he has felt, and not even the slightest memory of the feeling. And let him ask in the same way about wisdom, whether anyone would wish to have wisdom without any, even the slightest, pleasure rather than with some pleasures, or all pleasures without wisdom rather than with some wisdom.

Pro. That is impossible, Socrates; it is useless to ask the same question over and over again.

Soc. Then the perfect, that which is to be desired by all and is altogether good, is neither of these?

Pro. Certainly not.

Soc. We must, then, gain a clear conception of the good, or at least an outline of it, that we may, as we said, know to what the second place is to be assigned.

Pro. Quite right.

Soc. And have we not found a road which leads to the good?

Pro. What road?

Soc. If you were looking for a particular man and first found out correctly where he lived, you would have made great progress towards finding him whom you sought.

Pro. Yes, certainly.

Soc. And just now we received an indication, as we did in the beginning, that we must seek the good, not in the unmixed, but in the mixed life.

Pro. Certainly.

Soc. Surely there is greater hope that the object of our search will be clearly present in the well mixed life than in the life which is not well mixed?

Pro. Far greater.

Soc. Let us make the mixture, Protarchus, with a prayer to the gods, to Dionysus or Hephaestus, or whoever he be who presides over the mixing.

PRO. By all means.

SOC. We are like wine-pourers, and beside us are fountains—that of pleasure may be likened to a fount of honey, and the sober, wineless fount of wisdom to one of pure, health-giving water—of which we must do our best to mix as well as possible.

PRO. Certainly we must.

SOC. Before we make the mixture, tell me: should we be most likely to succeed by mixing all pleasure with all wisdom?

PRO. Perhaps.

SOC. But that is not safe; and I think I can offer a plan by which we can make our mixture with less risk.

PRO. What is it?

SOC. We found, I believe, that one pleasure was greater than another and one art more exact than another?

PRO. Certainly.

SOC. And knowledge was of two kinds, one turning its eyes towards transitory things, the other towards things which neither come into being nor pass away, but are the same and immutable for ever. Considering them with a view to truth, we judged that the latter was truer than the former.

PRO. That is quite right.

SOC. Then what if we first mix the truest sections of each and see whether, when mixed together, they are capable of giving us the most adorable life, or whether we still need something more and different?

PRO. I think that is what we should do.

SOC. Let us assume, then, a man who possesses wisdom about the nature of justice itself, and reason in accordance with his wisdom, and has the same kind of knowledge of all other things.

PRO. Agreed.

SOC. Now will this man have sufficient knowledge, if he is master of the theory of the divine circle and sphere, but is ignorant of our human sphere and human circles, even when he uses these and other kinds of rules or patterns in building houses?

PRO. We call that a ridiculous state of intellect in a man, Socrates, which is concerned only with divine knowledge.

SOC. What? Do you mean to say that the uncertain and impure art of the false rule and circle is to be put into our mixture?

PRO. Yes, that is inevitable, if any man is ever to find his own way home.

SOC. And must we add music, which we said a little while ago was full of guesswork and imitation and lacked purity?

PRO. Yes, I think we must, if our life is to be life at all.

SOC. Shall I, then, like a doorkeeper who is pushed and hustled by a mob, give up, open the door, and let all the kinds of knowledge stream in, the impure mingling with the pure?

PRO. I do not know, Socrates, what harm it can do a man to take in all the other kinds of knowledge if he has the first.

SOC. Shall I, then, let them all flow into what Homer very poetically calls the mingling of the vales?

PRO. Certainly.

SOC. They are let in; and now we must turn again to the spring of pleasure. For our original plan for making the mixture, by taking first the true parts, did not succeed; because of our love of knowledge, we let all kinds of knowledge in together before pleasure.

PRO. Very true.

SOC. So now it is time for us to consider about pleasures also, whether these, too, shall be all let loose together, or we shall let only the true ones loose at first.

PRO. It is much safer to let loose the true first.

SOC. We will let them loose, then. But what next? If there are any necessary pleasures, as there were kinds of knowledge, must we not mix them with the true?

PRO. Of course; the necessary pleasures must certainly be added.

SOC. And as we said it was harmless and useful to know all the arts throughout our life, if we now say the same of pleasures—that is, if it is advantageous and harmless for us to enjoy all pleasures throughout life—they must all form part of the mixture.

PRO. What shall we say about these pleasures, and what shall we do?

SOC. There is no use in asking us, Protarchus; we must ask the pleasures and the arts and sciences themselves about one another.

PRO. What shall we ask them?

SOC. "Dear ones—whether you should be called pleasures or by any other name—would you choose to dwell with all wisdom, or with none at all?" I think only one reply is possible.

Pro. What is it?

Soc. What we said before: "For any class to be alone, solitary, and unalloyed is neither altogether possible nor is it profitable; but of all classes, comparing them one with another, we think the best to live with is the knowledge of all other things and, so far as is possible, the perfect knowledge of our individual selves."

Pro. "Your reply is excellent," we shall tell them.

Soc. Right. And next we must turn to wisdom and mind, and question them. We shall ask them, "Do you want any further pleasures in the mixture?" And they might reply, "What pleasures?"

Pro. Quite likely.

Soc. Then we should go on to say: "In addition to those true pleasures, do you want the greatest and most intense pleasures also to dwell with you?" "How can we want them, Socrates," they might perhaps say, "since they contain countless hindrances for us, inasmuch as they disturb with maddening pleasures the souls of men in which we dwell, thereby preventing us from being born at all, and utterly destroying for the most part, through the carelessness and forgetfulness which they engender, those of our children which are born? But the true and pure pleasures, of which you spoke, you must consider almost our own by nature, and also those which are united with health and self-restraint, and furthermore all those which are handmaids of virtue in general and follow everywhere in its train as if it were a god,—add these to the mixture; but as for the pleasures which follow after folly and all baseness, it would be very senseless for anyone who desires to discover the most beautiful and most restful mixture or compound, and to try to learn which of its elements is good in man and the universe, and what we should divine its nature to be, to mix these with mind." Shall we not say that this reply which mind has now made for itself and memory and right opinion is wise and reasonable?

Pro. Certainly.

Soc. But another addition is surely necessary, without which nothing whatsoever can ever come into being.

Pro. What is it?

Soc. That in which there is no admixture of truth can never truly come into being or exist.

Pro. No, of course not.

Soc. No. But if anything is still wanting in our mixture, you and Philebus must speak of it. For to me it seems that our argument is now completed, as it were an incorporeal order which shall rule nobly a living body.

Pro. And you may say, Socrates, that I am of the same opinion.

Soc. And if we were to say that we are now in the vestibule of the good and of the dwelling of the good, should we not be speaking the truth after a fashion?

Pro. I certainly think so.

Soc. What element, then, of the mixture would appear to us to be the most precious and also the chief cause why such a state is beloved of all? When we have discovered this, we will then consider whether it is more closely attached and more akin to pleasure or to mind in the universe.

Pro. Right; for that is most serviceable to us in forming our judgement.

Soc. And it is quite easy to see the cause which makes any mixture whatsoever either of the highest value or of none at all.

Pro. What do you mean?

Soc. Why, everybody knows that.

Pro. Knows what?

Soc. That any compound, however made, which lacks measure and proportion, must necessarily destroy its components and first of all itself; for it is in truth no compound, but an uncompounded jumble, and is always a misfortune to those who possess it.

Pro. Perfectly true.

Soc. So now the power of the good has taken refuge in the nature of the beautiful; for measure and proportion are everywhere identified with beauty and virtue.

Pro. Certainly.

Soc. We said that truth also was mingled with them in the compound.

Pro. Certainly.

Soc. Then if we cannot catch the good with the aid of one idea, let us run it down with three—beauty, proportion, and truth, and let us say that these, considered as one, may more properly than all other components of the mixture be regarded as the cause, and that through the goodness of these the mixture itself has been made good.

Pro. Quite right.

Soc. So now, Protarchus, any one would be able to judge about pleasure and wisdom, and to decide which of them is more akin to the highest good and of greater value among men and gods.

Pro. That is clear; but still it is better to carry on the discussion to the end.

Soc. Let us, then, judge each of the three separately in its relation to pleasure and mind; for it is our duty to see to which of the two we shall assign each of them as more akin.

Pro. You refer to beauty, truth, and measure?

Soc. Yes. Take truth first, Protarchus; take it and look at the three—mind, truth, and pleasure; take plenty of time, and answer to yourself whether pleasure or mind is more akin to truth.

Pro. Why take time? For the difference, to my mind, is great. For pleasure is the greatest of impostors, and the story goes that in the pleasures of love, which are said to be the greatest, perjury is even pardoned by the gods, as if the pleasures were like children, utterly devoid of all sense. But mind is either identical with truth or of all things most like it and truest.

Soc. Next, then, consider measure in the same way, and see whether pleasure possesses more of it than wisdom, or wisdom than pleasure.

Pro. That also is an easy thing to consider. For I think nothing in the world could be found more immoderate than pleasure and its transports, and nothing more in harmony with measure than mind and knowledge.

Soc. However, go on and tell about the third. Has mind or pleasure the greater share in beauty?

Pro. But Socrates, no one, either asleep or awake, ever saw or knew wisdom or mind to be or become unseemly at any time or in any way whatsoever.

Soc. Right.

Pro. But pleasures, and the greatest pleasures at that, when we see anyone enjoying them and observe the ridiculous or utterly disgraceful element which accompanies them, fill us with a sense of shame; we put them out of sight and hide them, so far as possible; we confine everything of that sort to the night time, as unfit for the sight of day.

Soc. Then you will proclaim everywhere, Protarchus, by messengers to the absent and by speech to those present, that pleasure is not the first of possessions, nor even the second, but first the eternal nature has chosen measure, moderation, fitness, and all which is to be considered similar to these.

Pro. That appears to result from what has now been said.

Soc. Second, then, comes proportion, beauty, perfection, sufficiency, and all that belongs to that class.

Pro. Yes, so it appears.

Soc. And if you count mind and wisdom as the third, you will, I prophesy, not wander far from the truth.

Pro. That may be.

Soc. And will you not put those properties fourth which we said belonged especially to the soul—sciences, arts, and true opinions they are called—and say that these come after the first three, and are fourth, since they are more akin than pleasure to the good?

Pro. Perhaps.

Soc. And fifth, those pleasures which we separated and classed as painless, which we called pure pleasures of the soul itself, those which accompany knowledge and, sometimes, perceptions?

Pro. May be.

Soc. "But with the sixth generation," says Orpheus, "cease the rhythmic song." It seems that our discussion, too, is likely to cease with the sixth decision. So after this nothing remains for us but to give our discussion a sort of head.

Pro. Yes, that should be done.

Soc. Come then, let us for the third time call the same argument to witness before Zeus the saviour, and proceed.

Pro. What argument?

Soc. Philebus declared that pleasure was entirely and in all respects the good.

Pro. Apparently, Socrates, when you said "the third time" just now, you meant that we must take up our argument again from the beginning.

Soc. Yes; but let us hear what follows. For I, perceiving the truths which I have now been detailing, and annoyed by the theory held not only by Philebus but by many thousands of others, said that mind was a far better and more excellent thing for human life than pleasure.

Pro. True.

Soc. But suspecting that there were many other things to be considered, I said that if anything should be found better than these two, I should support mind against pleasure in the struggle for the second place, and even the second place would be lost by pleasure.

Pro. Yes, that is what you said.

Soc. And next it was most sufficiently proved that each of these two was insufficient.

Pro. Very true.

Soc. In this argument, then, both mind and pleasure were set aside; neither of them is the absolute good, since they are devoid of self-sufficiency, adequacy, and perfection?

Pro. Quite right.

Soc. And on the appearance of a third competitor, better than either of these, mind is now found to be ten thousand times more akin than pleasure to the victor.

Pro. Certainly.

Soc. Then, according to the judgement which has now been given by our discussion, the power of pleasure would be fifth.

Pro. So it seems.

Soc. But not first, even if all the cattle and horses and other beasts in the world, in their pursuit of enjoyment, so assert. Trusting in them, as augurs trust in birds, the many judge that pleasures are the greatest blessings in life, and they imagine that the lusts of beasts are better witnesses than are the aspirations and thoughts inspired by the philosophic muse.

Pro. Socrates, we all now declare that what you have said is perfectly true.

Soc. Then you will let me go?

Pro. There is still a little left, Socrates. I am sure you will not give up before we do, and I will remind you of what remains.

THE UNCHANGEABLE WORLD AND THE FORM OF GOOD

Republic (Davies and Vaughan trans.) 508E–509B.

Understand the condition of the soul to be as follows. Whenever it has fastened upon an object, over which truth and real existence are shining, it seizes that object by an act of reason, and knows it, and thus proves itself to be possessed of reason; but whenever it has fixed upon objects that are blent with darkness,—the world of birth and death,—then it rests in *opinion*, and its sight grows dim as its opinions shift backwards and forwards, and it has the appearance of being destitute of reason.

True, it has.

Now, this power, which supplies the objects of real knowledge with the truth that is in them, and which renders to him who knows them the faculty of knowing them, you must consider to be the essential Form of Good, and you must regard it as the origin of science, and of truth, so far as the latter comes within the range of knowledge; and though knowledge and truth are both very beautiful things, you will be right in looking upon good as something distinct from them, and even more beautiful. And just as, in the analogous case, it is right to regard light and vision as resembling the sun, but wrong to identify them with the sun; so, in the case of science and truth, it is right to regard both of them as resembling good, but wrong to identify either of them with good; because, on the contrary, the quality of the good ought to have a still higher value set upon it.

That implies an inexpressible beauty, if it not only is the source of science and truth, but also surpasses them in beauty; for, I presume, you do not mean by it pleasure.

Hush! I exclaimed, not a word of that. But you had better examine the illustration further, as follows.

Show me how.

I think you will admit that the sun ministers to visible objects, not only the faculty of being seen, but also their vitality, growth, and nutriment, though it is not itself equivalent to vitality.

Of course it is not.

Then admit that, in like manner, the objects of knowledge not only derive from the good the gift of being known, but are further endowed by it with a real and essential existence; though the good, far from being identical with real existence, actually transcends it in dignity and power.

THE BRIDGE FROM THE CHANGING TO THE PERMANENT

THE BRIDGE FROM OPINION TO KNOWLEDGE (*Republic*)
ON LOVE AS WINGS FOR THE ASPIRING (*Symposium*)

Since the world of change, with which we start, yields only opinion, and yet there is a realm of unchanging objects to make true knowledge possible, the method becomes of supreme importance whereby the eternal is realized in the temporal or beyond the temporal. This problem of method, in logic as well as in life, grew upon Plato. He is equally clear that we must start with, and yet not end with, what the senses can give us. The bridge, or ladder, which his concern with this problem builds from the world of sense to the realm of ideas is called dialectics—"the coping-stone" of all knowledge, as he puts it in the "Republic." This dialectical process becomes for him the content of logic, the technique of education, and the major preoccupation of his philosopher-kings. The education so elaborately provided for in the "Republic" is the curriculum for the climb. Even Meno's slave can, through reminiscence, with some prompting, be made to see the eternal breaking through the perceptual; but only the most gifted, and they after half a lifetime of rigorous mathematical discipline, can follow the gleam from the confusion of sensuous chaos straight through to what in the "Phaedrus" he calls "the colorless, formless, and intangible truly existing essence, ... visible only to the mind, the pilot of the soul." The famous "knowledge line" in the "Republic," to which we pass below, represents the logical layout of Plato's dialectics. Doubts cast on his logic, however, by the "Parmenides" seems not to affect his final goal; for the course of Platonic insight is more than logical. It is a quest for beauty, beginning with infatuation with particulars and finding fulfilment in complete universality. In the acquisition of final knowledge, the dialectic of the "Republic" is no more important than the "Platonic love" of the "Symposium." In the climb of the soul, such is the deep wisdom of Diotima, "the best helper that our human nature can hope to find is Love."

The aesthetic motif thus catches up the logical when logic falters, and the dizzy soul rises on wings of beauty to visions of reality not vouchsafed to mere prosaic-seekers after truth. Hints of mystic rapture, not to say of divine madness, recur in descriptions of the soul's final lap, as it, blinded by "beauty shining in brightness," stumbles across the threshold of understanding to claim its glowing guerdon, described in the "Phaedrus" myth below as "knowledge absolute in existence absolute."

. . .

THE BRIDGE FROM OPINION TO KNOWLEDGE

Republic (Davies and Vaughan trans.) 509E–511.

Now understand that, according to us, there are two powers reigning, one over an intellectual, and the other over a visible region and class of objects;—if I were to use the term 'firmament' you might think I was playing on the word. Well then, are you in possession of these as two kinds,—one visible, the other intellectual?

Yes, I am.

Suppose you take a line divided into two unequal parts,—one to represent the visible class of objects, the other the intellectual,—divide each part again into two segments on the same scale. Then, if you make the lengths of the segments represent degrees of distinctness or indistinctness, one of the two segments of the part which stands for the visible world will represent all images:—meaning by images, first of all, shadows; and, in the next place, reflections in water, and in close-grained, smooth, bright substances, and everything of the kind, if you understand me.

Yes, I do understand.

Let the other segment stand for the real objects corresponding to these images,—namely, the animals about us, and the whole world of nature and of art.

Very good.

Would you also consent to say that, with reference to this class, there is, in point of truth and untruthfulness, the same distinction between the copy and the original, that there is between what is matter of opinion and what is matter of knowledge?

Certainly I should.

Then let us proceed to consider how we must divide that part of the whole line which represents the intellectual world.

How must we do it?

Thus: one segment of it will represent what the soul is compelled to investigate by the aid of the segments of the other part, which it employs as images, starting from hypotheses, and travelling not to a first principle, but to a conclusion. The other segment will represent the objects of the soul, as it makes its way from an hypothesis to a first principle which is not hypothetical, unaided by those images which the former division employs, and shaping its journey by the sole help of real essential forms.

I have not understood your description so well as I could wish.

Then we will try again. You will understand me more easily when I have made some previous observations. I think you know that the students of subjects like geometry and calculation, assume by way of materials, in each investigation, all odd and even numbers, figures, three kinds of angles, and other similar data. These things they are supposed to know, and having adopted them as hypotheses, they decline to give any account of them, either to themselves or to others, on the assumption that they are self-evident; and, making these their starting point, they proceed to travel through the remainder of the subject, and arrive at last, with perfect unanimity, at that which they have proposed as the object of investigation.

I am perfectly aware of the fact, he replied.

Then you also know that they summon to their aid visible forms, and discourse about them, though their thoughts are busy not with these forms, but with their originals, and though they discourse not with a view to the particular square and diameter which they draw, but with a view to the absolute square and the absolute diameter, and so on. For while they employ by way of images those figures and diagrams aforesaid, which again have their shadows and images in water, they are really endeavouring to behold those abstractions which a person can only see with the eye of thought.

True.

This, then, was the class of things which I called intellectual; but I said that the soul is constrained to employ hypotheses while engaged in the investigation of them,—not travelling to a first principle (because it is unable to step out of, and mount above, its hypotheses) but using, as images, just the copies that are presented by things below,—which copies, as compared with the originals, are vulgarly esteemed distinct and valued accordingly.

I understand you to be speaking of the subject-matter of the various branches of geometry and the kindred arts.

Again, by the second segment of the intellectual world understand me to mean all that the mere reasoning process apprehends by the force of dialectic, when it avails itself of hypotheses not as first principles, but as genuine hypotheses, that is to say, as stepping-stones and impulses, whereby it may force its way up to something that is not hypothetical, and arrive at the first principle of every thing, and seize it in its grasp; which done, it turns round, and takes hold of that which takes hold of this first principle, till at last it comes down to a conclusion, calling in the aid of no sensible object whatever, but simply employing abstract, self-subsisting forms, and terminating in the same.

I do not understand you so well as I could wish, for I believe you to be describing an arduous task; but at any rate I understand that you wish to declare distinctly, that the field of real existence and pure intellect, as contemplated by the science of dialectic, is more certain than the field investigated by what are called the arts, in which hypotheses constitute first principles, which the students are compelled, it is true, to contemplate with the mind and not with the senses; but, at the same time, as they do not come back, in the course of inquiry, to a first principle, but push on from hypothetical premises, you think that they do not exercise pure reason on the questions that engage them, although taken in connexion with a first principle these questions come within the domain of the pure reason. And I believe you apply the term understanding, not pure reason, to the mental habit of such people as geometricians,—regarding understanding as something intermediate between opinion and pure reason.

You have taken in my meaning most satisfactorily; and I beg you will accept these four segments,—namely pure reason corresponding to the highest, understanding to the second, belief to the third, and conjecture to the last; and pray arrange them in gradation, and believe them to partake of distinctness in a degree corresponding to the truth of their respective objects.

I understand you, said he. I quite agree with you, and will arrange them as you desire.

ON LOVE AS WINGS FOR THE ASPIRING

Symposium. (Lamb translation and introduction, "Loeb Classical Library" series. The dialogue is complete.—T. V. S.). The *Symposium* of Plato holds an acknowledged place among those few masterpieces of human art which unveil and interpret something of the central mystery of life. It has been a source of light and inspiration to successive ages since the revival of learning, and is revisited by the same reader at different times of life with fresh wonder and praise. Like other great works of art, it provides its own introduction; so perfectly is the scene set and presented that even at the distance of twenty-three centuries we are able to catch the various tones of the speakers, first in the ripple of their casual talk, and then in the flow of their competitive eloquence. But while the modern reader can hardly miss the main effect of the simple narrative, as it develops the lively drama in which the sparkle of satiric wit is made to enhance the glow of high poetic rapture, there are one or two points to which attention may be usefully directed, in order that the work may convey the fullest possible measure of its meaning and value.

Its theme is the passion of personal love, so often the subject or occasion of literary art, but rarely examined in its moral aspect with any true perception or profit. Love is here treated with a sense of its universal importance and with a reach and certainty of insight which do not appear in any other of the great religious or moral teachers. This confident mastery was one of the extraordinary powers of Socrates which Plato at this stage of his writing was intent on portraying; it was one of the strangely memorable impressions which the elder man left on his associates, in spite of his simple, inquisitive manner and his constant avowals of ignorance. In some of his more positive moods he described himself as an inveterate "lover," in the sense of a declared and devout worshipper of the great energy of Nature which in its various workings amongst men was called by the general name of "Eros." Often he would feign, in his playful, paradoxical way, to put himself on a level with ordinary sensual men, and by discussing their views—if they had any, and consented to state them—would endeavour to lead the talk on to his own conception of love, where it was to be approached on the loftiest and most serious plane of thought. For the very purpose of a telling contrast with the common attitude to the matter, he would make a humorous use of the terms of ordinary love-passion to produce a sudden surprise in his hearers, when they found that his own pursuit of intellectual refinement through friendly or affectionate intercourse was independent of the outward attractions of sense. So much of explanation may perhaps be necessary, and may just suffice, for a right understanding of his banter with Alcibiades in this dialogue.

It is one of the great dramatic excellences of Plato that he shows us how Socrates adapted his tone and language to the characters of his hearers and to the several stages of his argument or exposition. This ready sense of the daily lives and thoughts of his companions, no less than the half-logical, half-mystical bent of his energetic mind, led him to the knowledge that, however easily or completely he might have freed his own faculties from the confusing trammels of carnal appetite, the mass of mankind was subject to the sway of bodily beauty; and that no theory of love could be satisfactory which did not take due account of this elemental fact of human nature. So he seizes this favourable moment in the talk at Agathon's party to suggest that visible beauty is the most obvious and distinct reflection in our terrene life of an eternal, immutable Beauty, perceived not with the eye but with the mind. He preaches no avoidance of the contest with appetite, but rather the achievement of a definite victory over the lower elements of love-passion, and the pursuit of beauty on higher and higher levels until, as in a sudden flash, its ultimate and all-rewarding essence is revealed. His modest attribution of the theory to his instructress, the wise woman of Mantinea, is probably meant to indicate that we are passing beyond the bounds of Socratic thought and listening really to Plato; but it is quite possible and reasonable to suppose that Socrates is relating the actual results of his own cogitation after a discussion with some revered and impressive counsellor.

In this dialogue the theory is only adumbrated for an exalted moment in convivial talk: its far-reaching developments in psychology and metaphysics are set forth in the *Republic*, *Phaedrus*, *Phaedo*, and elsewhere. Here, through the glow of poetic speculation, we get a glimpse, not merely of a logical theory, but of a whole philosophy or way of life—a progress towards complete enlightenment which is commended to all who have opened their eyes enough to see that they walk in the shades of ignorance. The final stages, it seems, may be too difficult even for Socrates himself to comprehend: thus with many hesitations and apologies the great master of inquiry seeks to communicate a thrilling adventure of his thought—a wondering recognition of the general "idea" or immaterial form which presides over all similar appearances in the material world. An absorbing thought, we are told, kept him standing in the street for some time before he joined the dinner-party: so here he shows us something of his endeavours to reach the summit of wisdom, and to move in a realm of absolute being which perhaps is beyond the utmost flight of philosophy. But the main thesis seeks to show how through the slavish trance of sensual charm we may pass with ever wakening and widening powers to the best and freest activity of our faculties, the contemplation of invisible, eternal verity. The lowest is linked with the highest; and it is noteworthy that Alcibiades' eulogy of Socrates serves to fix attention on the practical beginnings of the progress, by demonstrating that a rare intellectual communion may be built on the defeat of mere sensual aims.

In the proportions of its design and the texture of its style the *Symposium* stands out from even the best writings of Plato as a marvel of artistic ease and grace. Translations have frequently succeeded in presenting his vivid picture of the social manners of the place and time, and much of the beauty of his eloquence; but they have failed to transmit his brilliant characterization of the individual speakers in the style of their addresses. An attempt has been made here to indicate in different sorts and degrees the "euphuistic" influence of Sicilian rhetoric in the speeches of Phaedrus, Pausanias, and Agathon; the "medical college" manner of Eryximachus; the racy, extravagant humour of Aristophanes; the lofty solemnity of Diotima; and the frank, unbosoming tone of Alcibiades.

The date of the opening conversation is about 400 B.C.; the banquet itself was in 416 B.C. Apollodorus, whom we meet also in the *Phaedrus* (59), was noted for his enthusiastic attachment to Socrates in his last years; Aristodemus, who related to him the story of the banquet, was the Master's intimate of an earlier time. Agathon, the brilliant and courteous host, has just won the prize with the first part of a "tetralogy" or group of four plays at a dramatic festival: he was born about 447 B.C., and studied rhetoric under Gorgias and Prodicus. Phaedrus, who makes the first speech at the party, was a disciple of Hippias (*Protag.* 315 c), and a friend of Plato, who gave his name to the other dialogue (the *Phaedrus*) which especially deals with the subject of love. Pausanias, the next speaker, was a disciple of Prodicus (*Protag.* 315 D) and a passionate admirer of Agathon; his speech is a typical exhibition of the plausible, ornamental rhetoric of the literary sophists. Eryximachus, son of the physician Acumenus, followed his father's profession and belonged to the great medical guild of the Asclepiadae. He has the unbending gravity and cold, dogmatic utterance of the student and upholder of science. Aristophanes, the great comic poet and close contemporary of Agathon, had seized on the originality which distinguished Socrates from the ordinary sophists, and also on his scientific learning and argumentative subtlety, to make him the central figure of fun in the *Clouds* (423 B.C.). Here he makes the theme of love the occasion for a satirical sketch, in his own fantastic spirit and brilliant style, of physiological theories of the day. Alcibiades (*c.* 450-404 B.C.) is shown at the height of his popularity, a year before he sailed with the Sicilian Expedition. The tipsy immodesty of his mood throws into noble relief the passionate warmth of his admiration for the character of Socrates.

APOLLODORUS TELLS HIS COMPANIONS HOW HE HEARD
ABOUT THE BANQUET

AP. I believe I have got the story you inquire of pretty well by heart. The day before yesterday I chanced to be going up to town from my house in Phalerum, when one of my acquaintance caught sight of me from behind, some way off, and called in a bantering tone—"Hullo, Phalerian! I say, Apollodorus, wait a moment." So I stopped and waited. Then, "Apollodorus," he said, "do you know, I have just been looking for you, as I want to hear all about the banquet that brought together Agathon and Socrates and Alcibiades and the rest of that party, and what were the speeches they delivered upon love. For somebody else was relating to me the account he had from Phoenix, son of Philip, and he mentioned that you knew it too. But he could not tell it at all clearly; so you must give me the whole story, for you are the most proper reporter of your dear friend's discourses. But first tell me this," he went on; "were you at that party yourself, or not?" To which my answer was: "You have had anything but a clear account from your informant, if you suppose the party you are asking about to have been such a recent affair that I could be included." "So I did suppose," he said. "How so, Glaucon?" said I. "You must know it is many a year that Agathon has been away from home and country, and not yet three years that I have been consorting with Socrates and making it my daily care to know whatever he says or does. Before that time, what with running about at random and thinking I did things, I was the wretchedest man alive; just as you are at present, thinking philosophy is none of your business." "Instead of jeering at me," he said, "tell me when it was that this party took place." "When you and I were only children," I told him; "on the occasion of Agathon's victory with his first tragedy: the day after that of the dedicatory feast which he and his players held for its celebration." "Ah, quite a long while ago, it would seem," said he; "but who gave you the account of it? Socrates himself?" "Goodness, no!" I answered. "It was the person who told Phoenix— Aristodemus of Cydathenaeum, a little man, who went always barefoot. He was of the company there, being one of the chief among Socrates' lovers at that time, I believe. But all the same, I have since questioned Socrates on some details of the story I had from his friend, and he acknowledged them to be in accordance with his account." "Come then," he said, "let me have it now; and in fact the road up to town is well suited for telling and hearing as we go along."

So on we went, discoursing the while of this affair; and hence, as I began by saying, I have it pretty well by heart. So, friends, if you too must hear the whole story, I had better tell it. For my own part, indeed, I commonly find that, setting aside the benefit I conceive they do me, I take an immense delight in philosophic discourses, whether I speak them myself or hear them from others: whereas in the case of other sorts of talk—especially that of your wealthy, money-bag friends—I am not only annoyed myself but sorry for dear intimates like you, who think you are doing a great deal when you really do nothing at all. From your point of view, I daresay, I seem a hapless creature, and I think your thought is true. I, however, do not think it of you: I know it for sure.

COMP. You are the same as ever, Apollodorus,—always defaming your self and every one else! Your view, I take it, is that all men alike are miserable, save Socrates, and that your own plight is the worst. How you may have come by your title of "crazy," I do not know: though, of course, you are always like that in your way of speech—raging against yourself and everybody except Socrates.

Ap. My dear sir, obviously it must be a mere crazy aberration in me, to hold this opinion of myself and of you all!

Comp. It is waste of time, Apollodorus, to wrangle about such matters now. Come, without more ado, comply with our request and relate how the speeches went.

Ap. Well then, they were somewhat as follows,—but stay, I must try and tell you all in order from the beginning, just as my friend told it to me.

HOW ARISTODEMUS FELL IN WITH SOCRATES AND CAME TO THE BANQUET

He said that he met with Socrates fresh from the bath and wearing his best pair of slippers—quite rare events with him—and asked him whither he was bound in such fine trim.

"To dinner at Agathon's," he answered. "I evaded him and his celebrations yesterday, fearing the crowd; but I agreed to be present to-day. So I got myself up in this handsome style in order to be a match for my handsome host. Now tell me," said he, "do you feel in the mood for going unasked to dinner?"

"For anything," he said he replied, "that you may bid me do."

"Come along then," he said; "let us corrupt the proverb with a new version:

> What if they go of their own accord,
> The good men to our Goodman's board?

Though indeed Homer may be said to have not merely corrupted the adage, but debauched it: for after setting forth Agamemnon as a man eminently good at warfare, and Menelaus as only 'a spearman spiritless,' he makes the latter come unbidden to the banquet of the former, who was offering sacrifice and holding a feast; so the worse man was the guest of the better."

To this my friend's answer, as he told me, was: "I am afraid mine, most likely, is a case that fits not your version, Socrates, but Homer's—a dolt coming unbidden to the banquet of a scholar. Be sure, then, to have your excuse quite ready when you bring me; for I shall not own to coming unasked, but only on your invitation."

" 'If two go along together,' " he remarked, " 'there's one before another,' in devising what we are to say. Well, off we go."

After some such conversation, he told me, they started off. Then Socrates, becoming absorbed in his own thoughts by the way, fell behind him as they went; and when my friend began to wait for him he bade him go on ahead. So he came to Agathon's house, and found the door open; where he found himself in a rather ridiculous position. For he was met immediately by a servant from within, who took him where the company was reclining, and he found them just about to dine. However, as soon as Agathon saw him—"Ha, Aristodemus," he cried, "right welcome to a place at table with us! If you came on some other errand, put it off to another time: only yesterday I went round to invite you, but failed to see you. But how is it you do not bring us Socrates?"

At that I turned back for Socrates, he said, but saw no sign of him coming after me: so I told them how I myself had come along with Socrates, since he had asked me to dine with them.

"Very good of you to come," he said, "but where is the man?"

"He was coming in just now behind me: I am wondering myself where he can be."

"Go at once," said Agathon to the servant, "and see if you can fetch in Socrates. You, Aristodemus, take a place by Eryximachus."

So the attendant washed him and made him ready for reclining, when another of the servants came in with the news that our good Socrates had retreated into their neighbours' porch; there he was standing, and when bidden to come in, he refused.

"How strange!" said Agathon, "you must go on bidding him, and by no means let him go."

But this Aristodemus forbade: "No," said he, "let him alone; it is a habit he has. Occasionally he turns aside, anywhere at random, and there he stands. He will be here presently, I expect. So do not disturb him; let him be."

"Very well then," said Agathon, "as you judge best. Come, boys," he called to the servants, "serve the feast for the rest of us. You are to set on just whatever you please, now that you have no one to direct you (a method I have never tried before).[41] To-day

---

[41] This clause is probably an "aside" to his guests.

you are to imagine that I and all the company here have come on your invitation: so look after us, and earn our compliments."

Thereupon, he said, they all began dinner, but Socrates did not arrive; and though Agathon ever and anon gave orders that they should go and fetch him, my friend would not allow it. When he did come, it was after what, for him, was no great delay, as they were only about half-way through dinner. Then Agathon, who happened to be sitting alone in the lowest place, said: "Here, Socrates, come sit by me, so that by contact with you I may have some benefit from that piece of wisdom that occurred to you there in the porch. Clearly you have made the discovery and got hold of it; for you would not have come away before."

Then Socrates sat down, and—"How fine it would be, Agathon," he said, "if wisdom were a sort of thing that could flow out of the one of us who is fuller into him who is emptier, by our mere contact with each other, as water will flow through wool from the fuller cup into the emptier. If such is indeed the case with wisdom, I set a great value on my sitting next to you: I look to be filled with excellent wisdom drawn in abundance out of you. My own is but meagre, as disputable as a dream; but yours is bright and expansive, as the other day we saw it shining forth from your youth, strong and splendid, in the eyes of more than thirty thousand Greeks."

"You rude mocker, Socrates!" said Agathon. "A little later on you and I shall go to law on this matter of our wisdom, and Dionysus shall be our judge. For the present, let the dinner be your first concern."

After this, it seems, when Socrates had taken his place and had dined with the rest, they made libation and sang a chant to the god and so forth, as custom bids, till they betook them to drinking. Then Pausanias opened a conversation after this manner: "Well, gentlemen, what mode of drinking will suit us best? For my part, to tell the truth, I am in very poor form as a result of yesterday's bout, and I claim a little relief; it is so, I believe, with most of you, for you were at yesterday's party: so consider what method of drinking would suit us best."

On this Aristophanes observed: "Now that, Pausanias, is a good suggestion of yours, that we make a point of consulting our comfort in our cups: for I myself am one of those who got such a soaking yesterday."

When Eryximachus, son of Acumenus, heard this; "You are quite right, sirs," he said; "and there is yet one other question on which I request your opinion, as to what sort of condition Agathon finds himself in for drinking."

"No, no," said Agathon, "I am not in good condition for it either."

"It would be a piece of luck for us, I take it," the other went on, "that is, for me, Aristodemus, Phaedrus, and our friends here, if you who are the stoutest drinkers are now feeling exhausted. We, of course, are known weaklings. Socrates I do not count in the matter: he is fit either way, and will be content with whichever choice we make. Now as it appears that nobody here present is eager for copious draughts, perhaps it will be the less irksome to you if I speak of intoxication, and tell you truly what it is. The practice of medicine, I find, has made this clear to me—that drunkenness is harmful to mankind; and neither would I myself agree, if I could help it, to an excess of drinking, nor would I recommend it to another, especially when his head is still heavy from a bout of the day before."

Here Phaedrus of Myrrhinus interrupted him, saying: "Why, you know I always obey you, above all in medical matters; and so now will the rest of us, if they are well advised." Then all of them, on hearing this, consented not to make their present meeting a tipsy affair, but to drink just as it might serve their pleasure.

"Since it has been resolved then," said Eryximachus, "that we are to drink only so much as each desires, with no constraint on any, I next propose that the flute-girl who came in just now be dismissed: let her pipe to herself or, if she likes, to the women-folk within, but let us seek our entertainment to-day in conversation. I am ready, if you so desire, to suggest what sort of discussion it should be."

ERYXIMACHUS PROPOSES THE THEME OF LOVE

They all said they did so desire, and bade him make his proposal. So Eryximachus proceeded: "The beginning of what I have to say is in the words of Euripides' Melanippe, for 'not mine the tale' that I intend to tell; it comes from Phaedrus here. He is constantly complaining to me and saying,—Is it not a curious thing, Eryximachus, that while other gods have hymns and psalms indited in their honour by the poets, the god of Love, so ancient and so great, has had no song of praise composed for him by a single one of all the many poets that ever have been? And again, pray consider our worthy professors, and the eulogies they frame of Hercules and others in prose,—for example, the excellent Prodicus. This indeed is not so surprising; but I recollect coming across a book by somebody, in which I found Salt superbly lauded for its usefulness, and many more such matters I could show you celebrated there. To think of all this bustle about such trifles, and not a single man ever essaying till this day to make a fitting hymn to Love! So great a god, and so neglected! Now I think Phaedrus's protest a very proper one. Accordingly I am not only desirous of obliging him with a contribution of my own, but I also pronounce the present to be a fitting occasion for us here assembled to honour the god. So if you on your part approve, we might pass the time well enough in discourses; for my opinion is that we ought each of us to make a speech in turn, from left to right, praising Love as beautifully as he can. Phaedrus shall open first; for he has the topmost place at table, and besides is father of our debate."

"No one, Eryximachus," said Socrates, "will vote against you: I do not see how I could myself decline, when I set up to understand nothing but love-matters; nor could Agathon and Pausanias either, nor yet Aristophanes, who divides his time between Dionysus and Aphrodite; nor could any other of the persons I see before me. To be sure, we who sit at the bottom do not get a fair chance: but if the earlier speakers rise nobly to the occasion, we shall be quite content. So now let Phaedrus, with our best wishes, make a beginning and give us a eulogy of Love."

To this they assented one and all, bidding him do as Socrates said. Now the entire speech in each case was beyond Aristodemus's recollection, and so too the whole of what he told me is beyond mine: but those parts which, on account also of the speakers, I deemed most memorable, I will tell you successively as they were delivered.

THE SPEECH OF PHAEDRUS

First then, as I said, he told me that the speech of Phaedrus began with points of this sort—that Love was a great god, among men and gods a marvel; and this appeared in many ways, but notably in his birth. "Of the most venerable are the honours of this god, and the proof of it is this: parents of Love there are none, nor are any recorded in either prose or verse. Hesiod says that Chaos came first into being—

> and thereafter rose
> Broad-breasted Earth, sure seat of all for aye,
> And Love.

Acusilaus[42] also agrees with Hesiod, saying that after Chaos were born these two, Earth and Love. Parmenides says of Birth that she 'invented Love before all other gods.'

"Thus Love is by various authorities allowed to be of most venerable standing; and as most venerable, he is the cause of all our highest blessings. I for my part am at a loss to say what greater blessing a man can have in earliest youth than an honourable lover, or a lover than an honourable favourite. For the guiding principle we should choose for all our days, if we are minded to live a comely life, cannot be acquired either by kinship or office or wealth or anything so well as by Love. What shall I call this power? The shame that we feel for shameful things, and ambition for what is noble; without which it is impossible for city or person to perform any high and noble deeds. Let me then say that a man in love, should he be detected in some shameful act or in a cowardly submission to shameful treatment at another's hands, would not feel half so much distress at anyone observing it, whether father or comrade or anyone in the world, as when his favourite did; and in the selfsame way we see how the beloved is especially ashamed before his lovers when he is observed to be about some shameful business. So that if we could somewise contrive to have a city or an army composed of lovers and their favourites,[43] they could not be better citizens of their country than by thus refraining from all that is base in a mutual rivalry for honour; and such men as these, when fighting side by side, one might almost consider able to make even a little band victorious over all the world. For a man in love would surely choose to have all the rest of the host rather than his favou-

---

[42] An Argive compiler of genealogies in the first part of the fifth century B.C.

[43] There was such a "sacred band" at Thebes, which distinguished itself at Leuctra (371 B.C.).

rite see him forsaking his station or flinging away his arms; sooner
than this, he would prefer to die many deaths: While, as for leaving
his favourite in the lurch, or not succouring him in his peril, no man
is such a craven that Love's own influence cannot inspire him with a
valour that makes him equal to the bravest born; and without
doubt what Homer calls a 'fury inspired' by a god in certain heroes
is the effect produced on lovers by Love's peculiar power.

"Furthermore, only such as are in love will consent to die for
others; not merely men will do it, but women too. Sufficient witness is borne to this statement before the people of Greece by
Alcestis, daughter of Pelias, who alone was willing to die for her
husband, though he had both father and mother. So high did her
love exalt her over them in kindness, that they were proved alien to
their son and but nominal relations; and when she achieved this
deed, it was judged so noble by gods as well as men that, although
among all the many doers of noble deeds they are few and soon
counted to whom the gods have granted the privilege of having
their souls sent up again from Hades, hers they thus restored in admiration of her act. In this manner even the gods give special honour to zeal and courage in concerns of love. But Orpheus, son of
Oeagrus, they sent back with failure from Hades, showing him only
a wraith of the woman for whom he came; her real self they would
not bestow, for he was accounted to have gone upon a coward's
quest, too like the minstrel that he was, and to have lacked the
spirit to die as Alcestis did for the sake of love, when he contrived
the means of entering Hades alive. Wherefore they laid upon him
the penalty he deserved, and caused him to meet his death at the
hands of women: whereas Achilles, son of Thetis, they honoured
and sent to his place in the Isles of the Blest, because having learnt
from his mother that he would die as surely as he slew Hector, but
if he slew him not, would return home and end his days an aged
man, he bravely chose to go and rescue his lover Patroclus, avenged
him, and sought death not merely in his behalf but in haste to be
joined with him whom death had taken. For this the gods so highly
admired him that they gave him distinguished honour, since he set
so great a value on his lover. And Aeschylus talks nonsense when he
says that it was Achilles who was in love with Patroclus; for he
excelled in beauty not Patroclus alone but assuredly all the other
heroes, being still beardless and, moreover, much the younger, by

Homer's account. For in truth there is no sort of valour more respected by the gods than this which comes of love; yet they are even more admiring and delighted and beneficent when the beloved is fond of his lover than when the lover is fond of his favourite; since a lover, filled as he is with a god, surpasses his favourite in divinity. This is the reason why they honoured Achilles above Alcestis, giving him his abode in the Isles of the Blest.

"So there is my description of Love—that he is the most venerable and valuable of the gods, and that he has sovereign power to provide all virtue and happiness for men whether living or departed."

THE SPEECH OF PAUSANIAS

Such in the main was Phaedrus' speech as reported to me. It was followed by several others, which my friend could not recollect at all clearly; so he passed them over and related that of Pausanias, which ran as follows: "I do not consider, Phaedrus, our plan of speaking a good one, if the rule is simply that we are to make eulogies of Love. If Love were only one, it would be right; but, you see, he is not one, and this being the case, it would be more correct to have it previously announced what sort we ought to praise. Now this defect I will endeavour to amend, and will first decide on a Love who deserves our praise, and then will praise him in terms worthy of his godhead. We are all aware that there is no Aphrodite or Love-passion without a Love. True, if that goddess were one, then Love would be one: but since there are two of her, there must needs be two Loves also. Does anyone doubt that she is double? Surely there is the elder, of no mother born, but daughter of Heaven, whence we name her Heavenly; while the younger was the child of Zeus and Dione, and her we call Popular. It follows then that of the two Loves also the one ought to be called Popular, as fellow-worker with the one of those goddesses, and the other Heavenly. All gods, of course, ought to be praised: but none the less I must try to describe the faculties of each of these two. For of every action it may be observed that as acted by itself it is neither noble nor base. For instance, in our conduct at this moment, whether we drink or sing or converse, none of these things is noble in itself; each only turns out to be such in the doing, as the manner of doing it may be. For when the doing of it is noble and right, the thing itself becomes noble; when wrong, it becomes base. So also it is with loving, and Love is not in every case noble or worthy of celebration, but only when he impels us to love in a noble manner.

"Now the Love that belongs to the Popular Aphrodite is in very truth popular and does his work at haphazard: this is the Love we see in the meaner sort of men; who, in the first place, love women as well as boys; secondly, where they love, they are set on the body more than the soul; and thirdly, they choose the most witless people they can find, since they look merely to the accomplishment and care not if the manner be noble or no. Hence they find themselves doing everything at haphazard, good or its opposite, without distinction: for this Love proceeds from the goddess who is far the younger of the two, and who in her origin partakes of both female and male. But the other Love springs from the Heavenly goddess who, firstly, partakes not of the female but only of the male; and secondly, is the elder, untinged with wantonness: wherefore those who are inspired by this Love betake them to the male, in fondness for what has the robuster nature and a larger share of mind. Even in the passion for boys you may note the way of those who are under the single incitement of this Love: they love boys only when they begin to acquire some mind—a growth associated with that of down on their chins. For I conceive that those who begin to love them at this age are prepared to be always with them and share all with them as long as life shall last: they will not take advantage of a boy's green thoughtlessness to deceive him and make a mock of him by running straight off to another. Against this love of boys a law should have been enacted, to prevent the sad waste of attentions paid to an object so uncertain: for who can tell where a boy will end at last, vicious or virtuous in body and soul? Good men, however, voluntarily make this law for themselves, and it is a rule which those 'popular' lovers ought to be forced to obey, just as we force them, so far as we can, to refrain from loving our freeborn women. These are the persons responsible for the scandal which prompts some to say it is a shame to gratify one's lover: such are the cases they have in view, for they observe all their reckless and wrongful doings; and surely, whatsoever is done in an orderly and lawful manner can never justly bring reproach.

"Further, it is easy to note the rule with regard to love in other cities: there it is laid down in simple terms, while ours here is complicated. For in Elis and Boeotia and where there is no skill in speech they have simply an ordinance that it is seemly to gratify lovers, and no one whether young or old will call it shameful, in order, I suppose, to save themselves the trouble of trying what speech can do to persuade the youths; for they have no ability for speaking. But in Ionia and many other regions where they live under foreign sway, it is counted a disgrace. Foreigners hold this thing, and all training in philosophy and sports, to be disgraceful, because of their despotic government; since, I presume, it is not to the interest of their princes to have lofty notions engendered in their subjects, or any strong friendships and communions; all of which Love is pre-eminently apt to create. It is a lesson that our despots learnt by experience; for Aristogeiton's love and Harmodius's friendship grew to be so steadfast that it wrecked their power. Thus where it was held a disgrace to gratify one's lover, the tradition is due to the evil ways of those who made such a law— that is, to the encroachments of the rulers and to the cowardice of the ruled. But where it was accepted as honourable without any reserve, this was due to a sluggishness of mind in the law-makers. In our city we have far better regulations, which, as I said, are not so easily grasped.

"Consider, for instance, our saying that it is more honourable to love openly than in secret, especially when the beloved excels not so much in beauty as in nobility and virtue; and again, what a wonderful encouragement a lover gets from us all: we have no thought of his doing anything unseemly, and success in his pursuit is counted honourable and failure disgraceful; and how in his endeavours for success our law leaves him a free hand for performing such admirable acts as may win him praise; while the same acts, if attempted for any other purpose or effect to which one might be inclined, would bring one nothing in return but the sharpest reproach. For suppose that with the view of gaining money from another, or some office, or any sort of influence, a man should allow himself to behave as lovers commonly do to their favourites—pressing their suit with supplications and entreaties, binding themselves with vows, sleeping on doorsteps, and submitting to such slavery as no slave would ever endure—both the friends and the enemies of such a man would hinder his behaving in such fashion; for while the latter would reproach him with adulation and ill-breeding, the former would admonish him and feel ashamed of his conduct. But in a lover all such doings only win him favour: by free grant of our law he may behave thus without reproach, as compassing a most honourable end. Strangest of all, he alone in the vulgar opinion has indulgence from the gods when he forsakes the vow he has sworn; for the vow of love-passion, they say, is no vow. So true it is that both gods and men have given absolute licence to the lover, as our Athenian law provides. Thus far, then, we have ground for supposing that here in our city both loving some one and showing affection to one's lover are held in highest honour. But it happens that fathers put tutors in charge of their boys when they are beloved, to prevent them from conversing with their lovers: the tutor has strict injunctions on the matter, and when they observe a boy to be guilty of such a thing his playmates and fellows reproach him, while his reproachers are not in their turn withheld or upbraided by their elders as speaking amiss; and from this it might rather be inferred that his behaviour is held to be a great disgrace in Athens. Yet the truth of it, I think, is this: the affair is no simple thing; you remember we said that by itself it was neither noble nor base, but that it was noble if nobly conducted, and base if basely. To do the thing basely is to gratify a wicked man in a wicked manner: 'nobly' means having to do with a good man in a noble manner. By 'wicked' we mean that popular lover, who craves the body rather than the soul: as he is not in love with what abides, he himself is not abiding. As soon as the bloom of the body he so loved begins to fade he 'flutters off and is gone,' leaving all his speeches and promises dishonoured: whereas the lover of a nature that is worthy abides throughout life, as being fused into one with the abiding.

"Now our law has a sure and excellent test for the trial of these persons, showing which are to be favoured and which to be shunned. In the one case, accordingly, it encourages pursuit, but flight in the other, applying ordeals and tests in each case, whereby we are able to rank the lover and the beloved on this side or on that. And so it is for this reason that our convention regards a quick capitulation as a disgrace: for there ought, first, to be a certain interval—the generally approved touchstone—of time; and, second, it is disgraceful if the surrender is due to gold or public preferment, or is a mere cowering away from the endurance of ill-treatment, or shows the youth not properly contemptuous of such benefits as he may re-

ceive in pelf or political success. For in these there appears nothing
steadfast or abiding, unless it be the impossibility of their producing
a noble friendship. One way remains in our custom whereby a favourite may rightly gratify his lover: it is our rule that, just as in
the case of the lovers it was counted no flattery or scandal for them
to be willingly and utterly enslaved to their favourites, so there is
left one sort of voluntary thraldom which is not scandalous; I mean,
in the cause of virtue.

"It is our settled tradition that when a man freely devotes his
service to another in the belief that his friend will make him better
in point of wisdom, it may be, or in any of the other parts of virtue,
this willing bondage also is no sort of baseness or flattery. Let us
compare the two rules—one dealing with the passion for boys, and
the other with the love of wisdom and all virtuous ways: by this we
shall see if we are to conclude it a good thing that a favourite should
gratify his lover. For when lover and favourite come together, each
guided by his own rule—on the one side, of being justified in doing
any service to the favourite who has obliged him, and on the other,
of being justified in showing any attentions to the friend who
makes him wise and good; the elder of his plenty contributing to
intellectual and all other excellence, the younger in his paucity
acquiring education and all learned arts: only then, at the meeting
of these two principles in one place, only then and there, and in no
other case, can it befall that a favourite may honourably indulge his
lover. To have such hopes deceived is no disgrace; while those of
any other sort must be disgraceful, whether deceived or not. For
suppose that a youth had a lover he deemed to be wealthy and, after
obliging him for the sake of his wealth, were to find himself deceived and no money to be got, since the lover proved to be poor;
this would be disgraceful all the same; since the youth may be said
to have revealed his character, and shown himself ready to do anyone any service for pelf, and this is not honourable. By the same
token, when a youth gratifies a friend, supposing him to be a good
man and expecting to be made better himself as a result of his
lover's affection, and then finds he is deceived, since his friend
proves to be vile and destitute of virtue; even so the deception is
honourable. For this youth is also held to have discovered his
nature, by showing that he would make anyone the object of his
utmost ardour for the sake of virtuous improvement; and this by

contrast is supremely honourable. Thus by all means it is right to bestow this favour for the sake of virtue.

"This is the Love that belongs to the Heavenly Goddess, heavenly itself and precious to both public and private life: for this compels lover and beloved alike to feel a zealous concern for their own virtue. But lovers of the other sort belong all to the other Goddess, the Popular. Such, Phaedrus, is the contribution I am able to offer you, on the spur of the moment, towards the discussion of Love."

Pausanias' praise made a pause with this phrase—you see what jingles the schoolmen are teaching me! The next speaker, so Aristodemus told me, was to have been Aristophanes: but a surfeit or some other cause had chanced to afflict him with a hiccough, which prevented him from speaking; and he could only just say to Eryximachus the doctor, whose place was next below him, "I look to you Eryximachus, either to stop my hiccough, or to speak in my stead until I can stop it." "Why, I will do both," replied Eryximachus "for I will take your turn for speaking, and when you have stopped it, you shall take mine. But during my speech, if on your holding your breath a good while the hiccough chooses to stop, well and good; otherwise, you must gargle with some water. If, however, it is a very stubborn one, take something that will tickle your nostrils, and sneeze: do this once or twice, and though it be of the stubbornest, it will stop." "Start away with your speech," said Aristophanes, "and I will do as you advise."

THE SPEECH OF ERYXIMACHUS

Then Eryximachus spoke as follows: "Well then, since Pausanias did not properly finish off the speech he began so well, I must do my best to append a conclusion thereto. His division of Love into two sorts appears to me a good one: but medicine, our great mystery, has taught me to observe that Love is not merely an impulse of human souls towards beautiful men but the attraction of all creatures to a great variety of things, which works in the bodies of all animals and all growths upon the earth, and practically in everything that is; and I have learnt how mighty and wonderful and universal is the sway of this god over all affairs both human and divine.[44] Reverence for my profession prompts me to begin with the

[44] This cosmic theory was derived from Empedocles, who spoke of Love as the combining, and Strife as the disruptive, force pervading the universe.

witness of medicine. This double Love belongs to the nature of all
bodies: for between bodily health and sickness there is an admitted difference or dissimilarity, and what is dissimilar craves and
loves dissimilar things. Hence the desire felt by a sound body is
quite other than that of a sickly one. Now I agree with what
Pausanias was just saying, that it is right to gratify good men, base
to gratify the dissolute: similarly, in treating actual bodies it is
right and necessary to gratify the good and healthy elements of
each, and this is what we term the physician's skill; but it is a disgrace to do aught but disappoint the bad and sickly parts, if one
aims at being an adept. For the art of medicine may be summarily
described as a knowledge of the love-matters of the body in regard
to repletion and evacuation; and the master-physician is he who can
distinguish there between the nobler and baser Loves, and can effect
such alteration that the one passion is replaced by the other; and he
will be deemed a good practitioner who is expert in producing Love
where it ought to flourish but exists not, and in removing it from
where it should not be. Indeed he must be able to make friends and
happy lovers of the keenest opponents in the body. Now the most
contrary qualities are most hostile to each other—cold and hot,
bitter and sweet, dry and moist, and the rest of them. It was by
knowing how to foster love and unanimity in these that, as our two
poets[45] here relate, and as I myself believe, our forefather Asclepius
composed this science of ours. And so not merely is all medicine
governed, as I propound it, through the influence of this god, but
likewise athletics and agriculture. Music also, as is plain to any the
least curious observer, is in the same sort of case: perhaps Heraclitus intends as much by those perplexing words, 'The One at variance with itself is drawn together, like harmony of bow or lyre.'[46]
Now it is perfectly absurd to speak of a harmony at variance, or
as formed from things still varying. Perhaps he meant, however,
that from the grave and acute which were varying before, but
which afterwards came to agreement, the harmony was by musical
art created. For surely there can be no harmony of acute and grave
while still at variance: harmony is consonance, and consonance is
a kind of agreement; and agreement of things varying, so long as

---

[45] Aristophanes and Agathon.

[46] Heraclitus fr. 45 (Bywater). The universe is held together by the strain of
opposing forces, just as the right use of bow or lyre depends on opposite tension.

they are at variance, is impossible. On the other hand, when a thing varies with no disability of agreement, then it may be harmonized; just as rhythm is produced by fast and slow, which in the beginning were at variance but later came to agree. In all these cases the agreement is brought about by music which, like medicine in the former instance, introduces a mutual love and unanimity. Hence in its turn music is found to be a knowledge of love-matters relating to harmony and rhythm. In the actual system of harmony or rhythm we can easily distinguish these love-matters; as yet the double Love is absent: but when we come to the application of rhythm and harmony to social life, whether we construct what are called 'melodies' or render correctly, by what is known as 'training,' tunes and measures already constructed, we find here a certain difficulty and require a good craftsman. Round comes the same conclusion: well-ordered men, and the less regular only so as to bring them to better order, should be indulged in this Love, and this is the sort we should preserve; this is the noble, the Heavenly Love, sprung from the Heavenly Muse. But the Popular Love comes from the Queen of Various Song; in applying him we must proceed with all caution, that no debauchery be implanted with the reaping of his pleasure, just as in our craft we set high importance on a right use of the appetite for dainties of the table, that we may cull the pleasure without disease. Thus in music and medicine and every other affair whether human or divine, we must be on the watch as far as may be for either sort of Love; for both are there.

"Note how even the system of the yearly seasons is full of these two forces; how the qualities I mentioned just now, heat and cold, drought and moisture, when brought together by the orderly Love, and taking on a temperate harmony as they mingle, become bearers of ripe fertility and health to men and animals and plants, and are guilty of no wrong. But when the wanton-spirited Love gains the ascendant in the seasons of the year, great destruction and wrong does he wreak. For at these junctures are wont to arise pestilences and many other varieties of disease in beasts and herbs; likewise hoar-frosts, hails, and mildews, which spring from mutual encroachments and disturbances in such love-connexions as are studied in relation to the motions of the stars and the yearly seasons by what we term astronomy. So further, all sacrifices and ceremonies controlled by divination, namely, all means of communion between gods and men, are only concerned with either the preservation or the cure of Love. For impiety is usually in each case the result of refusing to gratify the orderly Love or to honour and prefer him in all our affairs, and of yielding to the other in questions of duty towards one's parents whether alive or dead, and also towards the gods. To divination is appointed the task of supervising and treating the health of these Loves; wherefore that art, as knowing what human love-affairs will lead to seemliness and pious observance, is indeed a purveyor of friendship betwixt gods and men.

"Thus Love, conceived as a single whole, exerts a wide, a strong, nay, in short, a complete power: but that which is consummated for a good purpose, temperately and justly, both here on earth and in heaven above, wields the mightiest power of all and provides us with a perfect bliss; so that we are able to consort with one another and have friendship with the gods who are above us. It may well be that with the best will in the world I have omitted many points in the praise I owe to Love; but any gaps which I may have left it is your business, Aristophanes, to fill: or if you intend some different manner of glorifying the god, let us hear your eulogy, for you have stopped your hiccough now."

Then, as my friend related, Aristophanes took up the word and said: "Yes, it has stopped, though not until it was treated with a course of sneezing, such as leaves me wondering that the orderly principle of the body should call for the noises and titillations involved in sneezing; you see, it stopped the very moment I applied the sneeze to it."

"My good Aristophanes," replied Eryximachus, "take heed what you are about. Here are you buffooning before ever you begin, and compelling me to be on the watch for the first absurdity in your speech, when you might deliver it in peace."

At this Aristophanes laughed, and—"Quite right, Eryximachus," he said; "I unsay all that I have said. Do not keep a watch on me; for as to what is going to be said, my fear is not so much of saying something absurd—since that would be all to the good and native to my Muse—as something utterly ridiculous."

"You think you can just let fly, Aristophanes, and get off unscathed! Have a good care to speak only what you can defend; though perhaps I may be pleased to let you off altogether."

THE SPEECH OF ARISTOPHANES

"It is indeed my intention, Eryximachus," said Aristophanes, "to speak in somewhat different strain from you and Pausanias. For in my opinion humanity has entirely failed to perceive the power of Love: if men did perceive it, they would have provided him with splendid temples and altars, and would splendidly honour him with sacrifice; whereas we see none of these things done for him, though they are especially his due. He of all gods is most friendly to men; he succours mankind and heals those ills whose cure must be the highest happiness of the human race. Hence I shall try and introduce you to his power, that you may transmit this teaching to the world at large. You must begin your lesson with the nature of man and its development. For our original nature was by no means the same as it is now. In the first place, there were three kinds of human beings, not merely the two sexes, male and female, as at present: there was a third kind as well, which had equal shares of the other two, and whose name survives though the thing itself has vanished. For 'man-woman'[47] was then a unity in form no less than name, composed of both sexes, and sharing equally in male and female; whereas now it has come to be merely a name of reproach. Secondly, the form of each person was round all over, with back and sides encompassing it every way; each had four arms, and legs to match these, and two faces perfectly alike on a cylindrical neck. There was one head to the two faces, which looked opposite ways; there were four ears, two privy members, and all the other parts, as may be imagined, in proportion. The creature walked upright as now, in either direction as it pleased; and whenever it started running fast, it went like our acrobats, whirling over and over with legs stuck out straight; only then they had eight limbs to support and speed them swiftly round and round. The number and features of these three sexes were owing to the fact that the male was originally the offspring of the sun, and the female of the earth; while that which partook of both sexes was born of the moon, for the moon also partakes of both.[48] They were globular in their shape as in their progress, since they took after their parents. Now, they were of surprising strength and vigour, and so lofty in their notions that

[47] *I.e.* "hermaphrodite."

[48] The double sex of the moon is mentioned in an Orphic hymn.

they even conspired against the gods; and the same story is told of them as Homer relates of Ephialtes and Otus, that scheming to assault the gods in fight they essayed to mount high heaven.

"Thereat Zeus and the other gods debated what they should do, and were perplexed: for they felt they could not slay them like the Giants, whom they had abolished root and branch with strokes of thunder—it would be only abolishing the honours and observances they had from men; nor yet could they endure such sinful rioting. Then Zeus, putting all his wits together, spake at length and said: 'Methinks I can contrive that men, without ceasing to exist, shall give over their iniquity through a lessening of their strength. I propose now to slice every one of them in two, so that while making them weaker we shall find them more useful by reason of their multiplication; and they shall walk erect upon two legs. If they continue turbulent and do not choose to keep quiet, I will do it again,' said he; 'I will slice every person in two, and then they must go their ways on one leg, hopping.' So saying, he sliced each human being in two, just as they slice sorb-apples to make a dry preserve, or eggs with hairs; and at the cleaving of each he bade Apollo turn its face and half-neck to the section side, in order that every one might be made more orderly by the sight of the knife's work upon him; this done, the god was to heal them up. Then Apollo turned their faces about, and pulled their skin together from the edges over what is now called the belly, just like purses which you draw close with a string; the little opening he tied up in the middle of the belly, so making what we know as the navel. For the rest, he smoothed away most of the puckers and figured out the breast with some such instrument as shoemakers use in smoothing the wrinkles of leather on the last; though he left there a few which we have just about the belly and navel, to remind us of our early fall. Now when our first form had been cut in two, each half in longing for its fellow would come to it again; and then would they fling their arms about each other and in mutual embraces yearn to be grafted together, till they began to perish of hunger and general indolence, through refusing to do anything apart. And whenever on the death of one half the other was left alone, it went searching and embracing to see if it might happen on that half of the whole woman which now we call a woman, or perchance the half of the whole man. In this plight they were perishing away, when Zeus in his pity provided a fresh device. He moved their privy parts to the front—for until then they had these, like all else, on the outside, and did their begetting and bringing forth not on each other but on the earth, like the crickets. These parts he now shifted to the front, to be used for propagating on each other—in the female member by means of the male; so that if in their embracements a man should happen on a woman there might be conception and continuation of their kind; and also, if male met with male they might have satiety of their union and a relief, and so might turn their hands to their labours and their interest to ordinary life. Thus anciently is mutual love in-grained in mankind, reassembling our early estate and endeavour-ing to combine two in one and heal the human sore.

"Each of us, then, is but a tally[49] of a man, since every one shows like a flat-fish the traces of having been sliced in two; and each is ever searching for the tally that will fit him. All the men who are sections of that composite sex that at first was called man-woman are woman-courters; our adulterers are mostly descended from that sex, whence likewise are derived our man-courting women and adulteresses. All the women who are sections of the woman have no great fancy for men: they are inclined rather to women, and of this stock are the she-minions. Men who are sections of the male pursue the masculine, and so long as their boyhood lasts they show themselves to be slices of the male by making friends with men and delighting to lie with them and to be clasped in men's embraces; these are the finest boys and striplings, for they have the most man-ly nature. Some say they are shameless creatures, but falsely: for their behaviour is due not to shamelessness but to daring, manliness, and virility, since they are quick to welcome their like. Sure evi-dence of this is the fact that on reaching maturity these alone prove in a public career to be men. So when they come to man's estate they are boy-lovers, and have no natural interest in wiving and getting children, but only do these things under stress of custom; they are quite contented to live together unwedded all their days. A man of this sort is at any rate born to be a lover of boys or the willing mate of a man, eagerly greeting his own kind. Well, when one of them—whether he be a boy-lover or a lover of any other sort—

---

[49] A tally, or notched stick matching another, is the nearest English equivalent for σύμβολον, which was a half of a broken die given and kept as a token of friendship; see below, 193 A (λίσπαι).

happens on his own particular half, the two of them are wondrously thrilled with affection and intimacy and love, and are hardly to be induced to leave each other's side for a single moment. These are they who continue together throughout life, though they could not even say what they would have of one another. No one could imagine this to be the mere amorous connexion, or that such alone could be the reason why each rejoices in the other's company with so eager a zest: obviously the soul of each is wishing for something else that it cannot express, only divining and darkly hinting what it wishes. Suppose that, as they lay together, Hephaestus should come and stand over them, and showing his implements[50] should ask: 'What is it, good mortals, that you would have of one another?'—and suppose that in their perplexity he asked them again: 'Do you desire to be joined in the closest possible union, so that you shall not be divided by night or by day? If that is your craving, I am ready to fuse and weld you together in a single piece, that from being two you may be made one; that so long as you live, the pair of you, being as one, may share a single life; and that when you die you may also in Hades yonder be one instead of two, having shared a single death. Bethink yourselves if this is your heart's desire, and if you will be quite contented with this lot.' No one on hearing this, we are sure, would demur to it or would be found wishing for anything else: each would unreservedly deem that he had been offered just what he was yearning for all the time, namely, to be so joined and fused with his beloved that the two might be made one.

"The cause of it all is this, that our original form was as I have described, and we were entire; and the craving and pursuit of that entirety is called Love. Formerly, as I have said, we were one; but now for our sins we are all dispersed by God, as the Arcadians were by the Lacedaemonians;[51] and we may well be afraid that if we are disorderly towards Heaven we may once more be cloven asunder and may go about in the shape of those outline-carvings on the tombs, with our noses sawn down the middle, and may thus become like tokens of split dice. Wherefore we ought all to exhort our neighbours to a pious observance of the gods, in order that we may

---

[50] *I.e.* his anvil, bellows, tongs, and hammer.

[51] Probably referring to the dispersal of Mantinea into villages in 358 B.C.

escape harm and attain to bliss under the gallant leadership of Love. Let none in act oppose him—and it is opposing him to incur the hate of Heaven: if we make friends with the god and are reconciled, we shall have the fortune that falls to few in our day, of discovering our proper favourites. And let not Eryximachus interrupt my speech with a comic mock, and say I refer to Pausanias and Agathon; it may be they do belong to the fortunate few, and are both of them males by nature; what I mean is—and this applies to the whole world of men and women—that the way to bring happiness to our race is to give our love its true fulfilment: let every one find his own favourite, and so revert to his primal estate. If this be the best thing of all, the nearest approach to it among all acts open to us now must accordingly be the best to choose; and that is, to find a favourite whose nature is exactly to our mind. Love is the god who brings this about; he fully deserves our hymns. For not only in the present does he bestow the priceless boon of bringing us to our very own, but he also supplies this excellent hope for the future, that if we will supply the gods with reverent duty he will restore us to our ancient life and heal and help us into the happiness of the blest.

"There, Eryximachus, is my discourse on Love, of a different sort from yours. As I besought you, make no comic sport of it, for we want to hear what the others will say in their turn—I rather mean the other two, since only Agathon and Socrates are left."

"Well, I will obey you," said Eryximachus, "for in fact I enjoyed your speech. Had I not reason to know the prowess of Socrates and Agathon in love-matters, I should have great fears of their being at a loss for eloquence after we have heard it in such copious variety: but you see, my confidence is unshaken."

Whereon Socrates remarked: "Your own performance, Eryximachus, made a fine hit: but if you could be where I am now—or rather, I should say, where I shall be when Agathon has spoken—you would be fitly and sorely afraid, and would be as hard put to it as I am."

"You want to throw a spell over me, Socrates," said Agathon, "so that I may be flustered with the consciousness of the high expectations the audience has formed of my discourse."

"Nay, Agathon, how forgetful I should be," replied Socrates, "if after noticing your high and manly spirit as you stepped upon the platform with your troupe—how you sent a straight glance at that vast assembly to show that you meant to do yourself credit with your production, and how you were not dismayed in the slightest—if I should now suppose you could be flustered on account of a few fellows like us."

"Why, Socrates," said Agathon, "I hope you do not always fancy me so puffed up with the playhouse as to forget that an intelligent speaker is more alarmed at a few men of wit than at a host of fools."

"No, Agathon, it would be wrong of me indeed," said Socrates, "to associate you with any such clownish notion: I am quite sure that on finding yourself with a few persons whom you considered clever you would make more account of them than of the multitude. Yet we, perhaps, are the latter; for we were there, and among the crowd: but suppose you found yourself with other folk who were clever, you would probably feel ashamed that they should witness any shameful act you might feel yourself to be doing. Will you agree to that?"

"Quite true," he said.

"Whereas before the multitude you would not be ashamed if you felt you were doing anything shameful?"

Here Phaedrus interposed: "My dear Agathon, if you go on answering Socrates he will be utterly indifferent to the fate of our present business, so long as he has some one to argue with, especially some one handsome. For my part, I enjoy listening to Socrates' arguments; but I am responsible for our eulogy of Love, and must levy a speech from every one of you in turn. Let each of you two, then, give the god his meed before you have your argument."

"You are quite right, Phaedrus," said Agathon, "and there is nothing to hinder my speaking; for I shall find many other occasions for arguing with Socrates."

THE SPEECH OF AGATHON

"I propose first to speak of the plan most proper for my speaking, and after that to speak. Every one of the previous speakers, instead of eulogizing the god, has merely, as it seems to me, felicitated humanity on the benefits he bestows: not one of them has told us what is the nature of the benefactor himself. There is but one correct method of giving anyone any kind of praise, namely to make the words unfold the character of him, and of the blessings brought by him, who is to be our theme. Hence it is meet that we praise him first for what he is and then for what he gives.

"So I say that, while all gods are blissful, Love—with no irreverence or offence be it spoken—is the most blissful, as being the most beautiful and the best. How most beautiful, I will explain. First of all, Phaedrus, he is youngest of the gods. He himself supplies clear evidence of this; for he flies and flees from old age—a swift thing obviously, since it gains on us too quickly for our liking. Love hates it by nature, and refuses to come within any distance of it. He is ever consorting with the young, and such also is he: well says the old saw, 'Like and like together strike.'[52] And though in much else I agree with Phaedrus, in this I agree not, that Love by his account is more ancient than Cronos and Iapetus:[53] I say he is youngest of the gods and ever young, while those early dealings with the gods which Hesiod[54] and Parmenides relate, I take to have been the work of Necessity, not of Love, if there is any truth in those stories. For there would have been no gelding or fettering of each other, nor any of those various violences, if Love had been amongst them; rather only amity and peace, such as now subsist ever since Love has reigned over the gods. So then he is young, and delicate withal: he requires a poet such as Homer to set forth his delicacy divine. Homer it is who tells of Ate as both divine and delicate; you recollect those delicate feet of hers, where he says—

> Yet delicate are her feet, for on the ground
> She speeds not, only on the heads of men.[55]

So I hold it convincing proof of her delicacy that she goes not on hard things but on soft. The same method will serve us to prove the delicacy of Love. Not upon earth goes he, nor on our crowns, which are not very soft;[56] but takes his way and abode in the softest things that exist. The tempers and souls of gods and men are his chosen habitation: not indeed any soul as much as another; when

---

[52] So Homer, *Od.* xvii. 218: "Heaven ever bringeth like and like together."

[53] These two Titans, the sons of Heaven and Earth, were proverbially the original inhabitants of the world.

[54] Hesiod, *Theog.* 176 foll., 746 foll. There are no such stories in the remaining fragments of Parmenides.

[55] Homer, *Il.* xix. 92–93.

[56] Perhaps here he smiles at or touches the bald head of Socrates.

he comes upon one whose temper is hard, away he goes, but if it be soft, he makes his dwelling there. So if with feet and every way he is wont ever to get hold of the softest parts of the softest creatures, he needs must be most delicate. Youngest, then, and most delicate is he, and withal pliant of form: for he would never contrive to fold himself about us every way, nor begin by stealing in and out of every soul so secretly, if he were hard. Clear evidence of his fit proportion and pliancy of form is found in his shapely grace, a quality wherein Love is in every quarter allowed to excel: unshapeliness and Love are ever at war with one another. Beauty of hue in this god is evinced by his seeking his food among flowers: for Love will not settle on body or soul or aught else that is flowerless or whose flower has faded away; while he has only to light on a plot of sweet blossoms and scents to settle there and stay.

"Enough has now been said, though much remains unsaid, of the beauty of our god; next shall Love's goodness be my theme. The strongest plea for this is that neither to a god he gives nor from a god receives any injury, nor from men receives it nor to men gives it. For neither is the usage he himself gets a violent usage, since violence takes not hold of Love; nor is there violence in his dealings, since Love wins all men's willing service; and agreements on both sides willingly made are held to be just by 'our city's sovereign, the law.' Then, over and above his justice, he is richly endowed with temperance. We all agree that temperance is a control of pleasures and desires, while no pleasure is stronger than Love: if they are the weaker, they must be under Love's control, and he is their controller; so that Love, by controlling pleasures and desires, must be eminently temperate. And observe how in valour 'not even the God of War withstands'[57] him; for we hear, not of Love caught by Ares, but of Ares caught by Love—of Aphrodite. The captor is stronger than the caught; and as he controls what is braver than any other, he must be bravest of all. So much for justice and temperance and valour in the god: it remains to speak of skill; and here I must try my best to be adequate. First, if I in turn may dignify our craft as Eryximachus did his, the god is a composer so accomplished that he is a cause of composing in others: every one, you know, becomes a poet, 'though alien to the Muse before,' when Love gets hold of him. This we may fitly take for a testimony that Love is a

[57] Sophocl. *Thyest.* fr. 235 "Necessity, whom not the God of War withstands."

poet well skilled—I speak summarily—in all composing that has to do with music; for whatever we have not or know not we can neither give to another nor teach our neighbour. And who, let me ask, will gainsay that the composing of all forms of life is Love's own craft, whereby all creatures are begotten and produced? Again, in artificial manufacture, do we not know that a man who has this god for teacher turns out a brilliant success, whereas he on whom Love has laid no hold is obscure? If Apollo invented archery and medicine and divination, it was under the guidance of Desire and Love; so that he too may be deemed a disciple of Love as likewise may the Muses in music, Hephaestus in metal-work, Athene in weaving and Zeus 'in pilotage of gods and men.' Hence also those dealings of the gods were contrived by Love—clearly of beauty—astir in them, for Love has no concern with ugliness; though aforetime, as I began by saying, there were many strange doings among the gods, as legend tells, because of the dominion of Necessity. But since this god arose, the loving of beautiful things has brought all kinds of benefits both to gods and to men.

"Thus I conceive, Phaedrus, that Love was originally of surpassing beauty and goodness, and is latterly the cause of similar excellences in others. And now I am moved to summon the aid of verse, and tell how it is he who makes—

> Peace among men, and a windless waveless main;
> Repose for winds, and slumber in our pain.[58]

He it is who casts alienation out, draws intimacy in; he brings us together in such friendly gatherings as the present; at feasts and dances and oblations he makes himself our leader; politeness contriving, moroseness outdriving; kind giver of amity, giving no enmity; gracious, superb; a marvel to the wise, a delight to the gods; coveted of such as share him not, treasured of such as good share have got; father of luxury, tenderness, elegance, graces and longing and yearning; careful of the good, careless of the bad; in toil and fear, in drink and discourse, our trustiest helmsman, boatswain, champion, deliverer; ornament of all gods and men; leader fairest and best, whom every one should follow, joining tunefully in the burthen of his song, wherewith he enchants the thought of every god and man.

[58] Cf. Od. v. 391: "Then ceased the wind, and came a windless calm." Agathon is here displaying his own poetic skill, not quoting.

"There, Phaedrus," he said, "is the speech I would offer at his shrine: I have done my best to mingle amusement with a decent gravity."

At the end of Agathon's speech, as Aristodemus told me, there was tumultuous applause from all present, at hearing the youngster speak in terms so appropriate to himself and to the god. Then Socrates, with a glance at Eryximachus, said: "Son of Acumenus, do you really call it an unfearful fear that has all this while affrighted me, and myself no prophet in saying just now that Agathon would make a marvellous speech, and I be hard put to it?"

"In one part of your statement, that he would speak finely," replied Eryximachus, "I think you were a true prophet; but as to your being hard put to it, I do not agree."

"But surely, my good sir," said Socrates, "I am bound to be hard put, I or anyone else in the world who should have to speak after such a fine assortment of eloquence. The greater part of it was not so very astounding; but when we drew towards the close, the beauty of the words and phrases could not but take one's breath away. For myself, indeed, I was so conscious that I should fail to say anything half as fine, that for very shame I was on the point of slinking away, had I had any chance. For his speech so reminded me of Gorgias that I was exactly in the plight described by Homer:[59] I feared that Agathon in his final phrases would confront me with the eloquent Gorgias' head, and by opposing his speech to mine would turn me thus dumbfounded into stone. And so in that moment I realized what a ridiculous fool I was to fall in with your proposal that I should take my turn in your eulogies of Love, and to call myself an expert in love-matters, when really I was ignorant of the method in which eulogies ought to be made at all. For I was such a silly wretch as to think that one ought in each case to speak the truth about the person eulogized; on this assumption I hoped we might pick out the fairest of the facts and set these forth in their comeliest guise. I was quite elated with the notion of what a fine speech I should make, for I felt that I knew the truth. But now, it appears that this is not what is meant by a good speech of praise; which is rather an ascription of all the highest and fairest

---

[59] *Od.* xi. 632, where Odysseus is sore afraid that Persephone will send up the Gorgon's head among the crowd of ghosts from Hades. Agathon has just displayed his addiction to the elegant rhetoric of Gorgias.

qualities, whether the case be so or not; it is really no matter if they are untrue. Our arrangement, it seems, was that each should appear to eulogize Love, not that he should make a real eulogy. Hence it is, sirs, I suppose, that you muster every kind of phrase for your tribute to Love, declaring such and such to be his character and influence, in order to present him in the best and fairest light; successfully, of course, before those who do not know him, though it must be otherwise before those who do; your praise has such a fine impressive air! No, I find I was quite mistaken as to the method required; it was in ignorance that I agreed to take my turn in the round of praising. 'The tongue,' you see, undertook, 'the mind' did not;[60] so good-bye to my bond. I am not to be called upon now as an eulogist in your sense; for such I cannot be. Nevertheless I am ready, if you like, to speak the mere truth in my own way; not to rival your discourses, and so be your laughing-stock. Decide then, Phaedrus, whether you have any need of such a speech besides, and would like to hear the truth told about Love in whatsoever style of terms and phrases may chance to occur by the way."

So Phaedrus and the others bade him speak, just in any manner he himself should think fit.

"Then allow me further, Phaedrus, to put some little questions to Agathon, so as to secure his agreement before I begin my speech."

"You have my leave," said Phaedrus; "so ask him." After that, my friend told me, Socrates started off in this sort of way:

"I must say, my dear Agathon, you gave your speech an excellent introduction, by stating that your duty was first to display the character of Love, and then to treat of his acts. Those opening words I thoroughly admire. So come now, complete your beautiful and magnificent description of Love, and tell me this: Are we so to view his character as to take Love to be love of some object, or of none? My question is not whether he is love of a mother or a father—how absurd it would be to ask whether Love is love of mother or father!—but as though I were asking about our notion of 'father,' whether one's father is a father of somebody or not. Surely you would say, if you cared to give the proper answer, that the father is father of son or of daughter, would you not?"

"Yes, of course," said Agathon.

[60] Eurip. *Hippol.* 612 "The tongue hath sworn; the mind is yet unsworn."

"And you would say the same of the mother?" He agreed to this too.

"Then will you give me just a few more answers," said Socrates, "so that you may the better grasp my meaning? Suppose I were to ask you, 'Well now, a brother, viewed in the abstract, is he brother of somebody or not?' "

"He is," said Agathon.

"That is, of brother or of sister?" He agreed.

"Now try and tell me about Love: is he a love of nothing or of something?"

"Of something, to be sure."

"Now then," said Socrates, "keep carefully in mind what is the object of Love, and only tell me whether he desires the particular thing that is his object."

"Yes, to be sure," he replied.

"Has he or has he not the object of his desire and love when he desires and loves it?"

"He does not have it, most likely," he said.

"Not as a likelihood," said Socrates, "but as a necessity, consider if the desiring subject must have desire for something it lacks, and again, no desire if it has no lack. I at least, Agathon, am perfectly sure it is a necessity. How does it strike you?"

"I am sure of it also," said he.

"Very good. Now could a tall man wish to be tall, or a strong man to be strong?"

"By what has been admitted, this is impossible."

"Since, I suppose, the man in each case would not be lacking the quality mentioned."

"True."

"For if, being strong, he should wish to be strong," said Socrates, or being swift, to be swift, or being healthy, to be healthy,—since we are apt to *suppose* in these and all such cases that men of this or that sort, possessing these qualities, do also desire what they have already: I put this in, to prevent any misconception; these men, Agathon, if you consider, are bound to have at the very moment each thing that they have whether they wish it or not; and how, I ask, is a man going to desire that? No, when a person says, 'I being healthy, want to be healthy; being rich, I want to be rich; I desire the very things that I have'—we shall tell him, 'My good sir, riches you possess, and health and strength, which you would like to possess in the future also: for the time now present you have them whether you would or no. When you say—*I desire these present things*—we suggest you are merely saying—*I wish these things now present to be present also in the future.* Would he not admit our point?" To this Agathon assented.

"And so," continued Socrates, "a man may be said to love a thing not yet provided or possessed, when he would have the presence of certain things secured to him for ever in the future."

"Certainly," he said.

"Then such a person, and in general all who feel desire, feel it for what is not provided or present; for something they have not or are not or lack; and that sort of thing is the object of desire and love?"

"Assuredly," he said.

"Now then," said Socrates, "let us agree to what we have so far concluded. First, is not Love directed to certain things; of which, in the second place, he has a want?"

"Yes," he said.

"Then, granting this, recollect what things you named in our discussion as the objects of Love: if you like, I will remind you. What you said, I believe, was to the effect that the gods contrived the world from a love of beautiful things, for of ugly there was no love. Did you not say something of the sort?"

"Yes, I did," said Agathon.

"And quite properly, my friend," said Socrates; "then, such being the case, must not Love be only love of beauty, and not of ugliness?" He assented.

"Well then, we have agreed that he loves what he lacks and has not?"

"Yes," he replied.

"And what Love lacks and has not is beauty?"

"That needs must be," he said.

"Well now, will you say that what lacks beauty, and in no wise possesses it, is beautiful?

"Surely not."

"So can you still allow Love to be beautiful, if this is the case?"

Whereupon Agathon said, "I greatly fear, Socrates, I knew nothing of what I was talking about."

"Ah, your words were beautiful enough, Agathon; but pray give me one or two more: you hold, do you not, that good things are beautiful?"

"I do."

"Then if Love lacks beautiful things, and good things are beautiful, he must lack good things too."

"I see no means, Socrates, of contradicting you," he replied; "let it be as you say."

"No, it is Truth, my lovable Agathon, whom you cannot contradict: Socrates you easily may."

THE SPEECH OF SOCRATES

"And now I shall let you alone, and proceed with the discourse upon Love which I heard one day from a Mantinean woman named Diotima:[61] in this subject she was skilled, and in many others too; for once, by bidding the Athenians offer sacrifices ten years before the plague, she procured them so much delay in the advent of the sickness. Well, I also had my lesson from her in love-matters; so now I will try and follow up the points on which Agathon and I have just agreed by narrating to you all on my own account, as well as I am able, the speech she delivered to me. So first, Agathon, I must unfold, in your manner of exposition, who and what sort of being is Love, and then I shall tell of his works. The readiest way, I think, will be to give my description that form of question and answer which the stranger woman used for hers that day. For I spoke to her in much the same terms as Agathon addressed just now to me, saying Love was a great god, and was of beautiful things; and she refuted me with the very arguments I have brought against our young friend, showing that by my account that god was neither beautiful nor good.

" 'How do you mean, Diotima?' said I; 'is Love then ugly and bad?'

" 'Peace for shame!' she replied: 'or do you imagine that whatever is not beautiful must needs be ugly?'

" 'To be sure I do.'

" 'And what is not skilled, ignorant? Have you not observed that there is something halfway between skill and ignorance?'

[61] These names suggest a connexion respectively with prophecy and with the favour of Heaven.

" 'What is that?'

" 'You know, of course, that to have correct opinion, if you can give no reason for it, is neither full knowledge—how can an unreasoned thing be knowledge?—nor yet ignorance; for what hits on the truth cannot be ignorance. So correct opinion, I take it, is just in that position, between understanding and ignorance.'

" 'Quite true,' I said.

" 'Then do not compel what is not beautiful to be ugly,' she said, 'or what is not good to be bad. Likewise of Love, when you find yourself admitting that he is not good nor beautiful, do not therefore suppose he must be ugly and bad, but something betwixt the two.'

" 'And what of the notion,' I asked, 'to which every one agrees, that he is a great god?'

" 'Every one? People who do not know,' she rejoined, 'or those who know also?'

" 'I mean everybody in the world.'

"At this she laughed and said, 'But how, Socrates, can those agree that he is a great god who say he is no god at all?'

" 'What persons are they?' I asked.

" 'You are one,' she replied, 'and I am another.'

" 'How do you make that out?' I said.

" 'Easily,' said she; 'tell me, do you not say that all gods are happy and beautiful? Or will you dare to deny that any god is beautiful and happy?'

" 'Bless me!' I exclaimed, 'not I.'

" 'And do you not call those happy who possess good and beautiful things?'

" 'Certainly I do.'

" 'But you have admitted that Love, from lack of good and beautiful things, desires these very things that he lacks.'

" 'Yes, I have.'

" 'How then can he be a god, if he is devoid of things beautiful and good?'

" 'By no means, it appears.'

" 'So you see,' she said, 'you are a person who does not consider Love to be a god.'

" 'What then,' I asked, 'can Love be? A mortal?'

" 'Anything but that.'

" 'Well what?'

" 'As I previously suggested, between a mortal and an immortal.'

" 'And what is that, Diotima?'

" 'A great spirit, Socrates: for the whole of the spiritual[62] is between divine and mortal.'

" 'Possessing what power?' I asked.

" 'Interpreting and transporting human things to the gods and divine things to men; entreaties and sacrifices from below, and ordinances and requitals from above: being midway between, it makes each to supplement the other, so that the whole is combined in one. Through it are conveyed all divination and priestcraft concerning sacrifice and ritual and incantations, and all soothsaying and sorcery. God with man does not mingle: but the spiritual is the means of all society and converse of men with gods and of gods with men, whether waking or asleep. Whosoever has skill in these affairs is a spiritual man; to have it in other matters, as in common arts and crafts, is for the mechanical. Many and multifarious are these spirits, and one of them is Love.'

" 'From what father and mother sprung?' I asked.

" 'That is rather a long story,' she replied; 'but still, I will tell it you. When Aphrodite was born, the gods made a great feast, and among the company was Resource the son of Cunning. And when they had banqueted there came Poverty abegging, as well she might in an hour of good cheer, and hung about the door. Now Resource, grown tipsy with nectar—for wine as yet there was none—went into the garden of Zeus, and there, overcome with heaviness, slept. Then Poverty, being of herself so resourceless, devised the scheme of having a child by Resource, and lying down by his side she conceived Love. Hence it is that Love from the beginning has been attendant and minister to Aphrodite, since he was begotten on the day of her birth, and is, moreover, by nature a lover bent on beauty since Aphrodite is beautiful. Now, as the son of Resource and Poverty, Love is in a peculiar case. First, he is ever poor, and far from tender or beautiful as most suppose him: rather is he hard and parched, shoeless and homeless; on the bare ground always he lies with no bedding, and takes his rest on doorsteps and waysides in the open air; true to his mother's nature, he ever dwells with want.

---

[62] Δαίμονες and τὸ δαιμόνιον represent the mysterious agencies and influences by which the gods communicate with mortals.

But he takes after his father in scheming for all that is beautiful and good; for he is brave, strenuous and high-strung, a famous hunter, always weaving some stratagem; desirous and competent of wisdom, throughout life ensuing the truth; a master of jugglery, witchcraft, and artful speech. By birth neither immortal nor mortal, in the selfsame day he is flourishing and alive at the hour when he is abounding in resource; at another he is dying, and then reviving again by force of his father's nature: yet the resources that he gets will ever be ebbing away; so that Love is at no time either resourceless or wealthy, and furthermore, he stands midway betwixt wisdom and ignorance. The position is this: no gods ensue wisdom or desire to be made wise; such they are already; nor does anyone else that is wise ensue it. Neither do the ignorant ensue wisdom, nor desire to be made wise: in this very point is ignorance distressing, when a person who is not comely or worthy or intelligent is satisfied with himself. The man who does not feel himself defective has no desire for that whereof he feels no defect.'

" 'Who then, Diotima,' I asked, 'are the followers of wisdom, if they are neither the wise nor the ignorant?'

" 'Why, a child could tell by this time,' she answered, 'that they are the intermediate sort, and amongst these also is Love. For wisdom has to do with the fairest things, and Love is a love directed to what is fair; so that Love must needs be a friend of wisdom, and, as such, must be between wise and ignorant. This again is a result for which he has to thank his origin: for while he comes of a wise and resourceful father, his mother is unwise and resourceless. Such, my good Socrates, is the nature of this spirit. That you should have formed your other notion of Love is no surprising accident. You supposed, if I am to take your own words as evidence, that the beloved and not the lover was Love. This led you, I fancy, to hold that Love is all-beautiful. The lovable, indeed, is the truly beautiful, tender, perfect, and heaven-blest; but the lover is of a different type, in accordance with the account I have given.'

"Upon this I observed: 'Very well then, madam, you are right; but if Love is such as you describe him, of what use is he to mankind?'

" 'That is the next question, Socrates,' she replied, 'on which I will try to enlighten you. While Love is of such nature and origin as I have related, he is also set on beautiful things, as you say.

Now, suppose some one were to ask us: In what respect is he Love of beautiful things, Socrates and Diotima? But let me put the question more clearly thus: What is the love of the lover of beautiful things?'

" 'That they may be his,' I replied.

" 'But your answer craves a further query,' she said, 'such as this: What will he have who gets beautiful things?'

"This question I declared I was quite unable now to answer off-hand.

" 'Well,' she proceeded, 'imagine that the object is changed, and the inquiry is made about the good instead of the beautiful. Come, Socrates (I shall say), what is the love of the lover of good things?'

" 'That they may be his,' I replied.

" 'And what will he have who gets good things?'

" 'I can make more shift to answer this,' I said; 'he will be happy.'

" 'Yes,' she said, 'the happy are happy by acquisition of good things, and we have no more need to ask for what end a man wishes to be happy, when such is his wish: the answer seems to be ultimate.'

" 'Quite true,' I said.

" 'Now do you suppose this wish or this love to be common to all mankind, and that every one always wishes to have good things? Or what do you say?'

" 'Even so,' I said; 'it is common to all.'

" 'Well then, Socrates,' she said, 'we do not mean that all men love, when we say that all men love the same things always; we mean that some people love and others do not?'

" 'I am wondering myself,' I replied.

" 'But you should not wonder,' she said, 'for we have singled out a certain form of love, and applying thereto the name of the whole, we call it love; and there are other names that we commonly abuse.'

" 'As, for example —?' I asked.

" 'Take the following: you know that *poetry*[63] is more than a single thing. For of anything whatever that passes from not being into being the whole cause is composing or poetry; so that the productions of all arts are kinds of poetry, and their craftsmen are all poets.'

[63] *Cf.* above, 197 A.

" 'That is true.'

" 'But still, as you are aware,' said she, 'they are not called poets: they have other names, while a single section disparted from the whole of poetry—merely the business of music and metres—is entitled with the name of the whole. This and no more is called poetry; those only who possess this branch of the art are poets.'

" 'Quite true,' I said.

" 'Well, it is just the same with love. Generically, indeed, it is all that desire of good things and of being happy[64]—Love most mighty and all-beguiling. Yet, whereas those who resort to him in various other ways—in money-making, an inclination to sports, or philosophy—are not described either as loving or as lovers, all those who pursue him seriously in one of his several forms obtain, as loving and as lovers, the name of the whole.'

" 'I fancy you are right,' I said.

" 'And certainly there runs a story,' she continued, 'that all who go seeking their other half[65] are in love; though by my account love is neither for half nor for whole, unless, of course, my dear sir, this happens to be something good. For men are prepared to have their own feet and hands cut off if they feel these belongings to be harmful. The fact is, I suppose, that each person does not cherish his belongings except where a man calls the good his own property and the bad another's; since what men love is simply and solely the good. Or is your view otherwise?'

" 'Faith, no,' I said.

" 'Then we may state unreservedly that men love the good?'

" 'Yes,' I said.

" 'Well now, must we not extend it to this, that they love the good to be theirs?'

" 'We must.'

" 'And do they love it to be not merely theirs but theirs always?'

" 'Include that also.'

" 'Briefly then,' said she, 'love loves the good to be one's own for ever.'

" 'That is the very truth,' I said.

" 'Now if love is always for this,' she proceeded, 'what is the

[64] Cf. above, 204 E–205 A.   [65] A "prophetic" allusion to Aristophanes' speech, 192 foll.

method of those who pursue it, and what is the behaviour whose eagerness and straining are to be termed love? What actually is this effort? Can you tell me?'

" 'Ah, Diotima,' I said; 'in that case I should hardly be admiring you and your wisdom, and sitting at your feet to be enlightened on just these questions.'

" 'Well, I will tell you,' said she; 'it is begetting on a beautiful thing by means of both the body and the soul.'

" 'It wants some divination to make out what you mean,' I said; 'I do not understand.'

" 'Let me put it more clearly,' she said. 'All men are pregnant, Socrates, both in body and in soul: on reaching a certain age our nature yearns to beget. This it cannot do upon an ugly person, but only on the beautiful: the conjunction of man and woman is a begetting for both.[66] It is a divine affair, this engendering and bringing to birth, an immortal element in the creature that is mortal; and it cannot occur in the discordant. The ugly is discordant with whatever is divine, whereas the beautiful is accordant. Thus Beauty presides over birth as Fate and Lady of Travail; and hence it is that when the pregnant approaches the beautiful it becomes not only gracious but so exhilarate, that it flows over with begetting and bringing forth; though when it meets the ugly it coils itself close in a sullen dismay: rebuffed and repressed, it brings not forth, but goes in labour with the burden of its young. Therefore when a person is big and teeming-ripe he feels himself in a sore flutter for the beautiful, because its possessor can relieve him of his heavy pangs. For you are wrong, Socrates, in supposing that love is of the beautiful.'

" 'What then is it?'

" 'It is of engendering and begetting upon the beautiful.'

" 'Be it so,' I said.

" 'To be sure it is,' she went on; 'and how of engendering? Because this is something ever-existent and immortal in our mortal life. From what has been admitted, we needs must yearn for immortality no less than for good, since love loves good to be one's own for ever. And hence it necessarily follows that love is of immortality.'

---

[66] The argument requires the application of "begetting" and other such terms indifferently to either sex.

"All this instruction did I get from her at various times when she discoursed of love-matters; and one time she asked me, 'What do you suppose, Socrates, to be the cause of this love and desire? For you must have observed the strange state into which all the animals are thrown, whether going on earth or winging the air, when they desire to beget: they are all sick and amorously disposed, first to have union one with another, and next to find food for the new-born; in whose behalf they are ready to fight hard battles, even the weakest against the strongest, and to sacrifice their lives; to be racked with starvation themselves if they can but nurture their young, and be put to any sort of shift. As for men,' said she, 'one might suppose they do these things on the promptings of reason; but what is the cause of this amorous condition in the animals? Can you tell me?'

"Once more I replied that I did not know; so she proceeded: 'How do you design ever to become a master of love-matters, if you can form no notion of this?'

" 'Why, it is just for this, I tell you, Diotima—as I stated a moment ago—that I have come to see you, because I noted my need of an instructor. Come, tell me the cause of these effects as well as of the others that have relation to love.'

" 'Well then,' she said, 'if you believe that love is by nature bent on what we have repeatedly admitted, you may cease to wonder. For here, too, on the same principle as before, the mortal nature ever seeks, as best it can, to be immortal. In one way only can it succeed, and that is by generation; since so it can always leave behind it a new creature in place of the old. It is only for a while that each live thing can be described as alive and the same, as a man is said to be the same person from childhood until he is advanced in years: yet though he is called the same he does not at any time possess the same properties; he is continually becoming a new person, and there are things also which he loses, as appears by his hair, his flesh, his bones, and his blood and body altogether. And observe that not only in his body but in his soul besides we find none of his manners or habits, his opinions, desires, pleasures, pains or fears, ever abiding the same in his particular self; some things grow in him, while others perish. And here is a yet stranger fact: with regard to the possessions of knowledge, not merely do some of them grow and others perish in us, so that neither in what we know are we ever the same persons; but a like fate attends each single sort of knowledge. What we call *conning* implies that our knowledge is departing; since forgetfulness is an egress of knowledge, while conning substitutes a fresh one in place of that which departs, and so preserves our knowledge enough to make it seem the same. Every mortal thing is preserved in this way; not by keeping it exactly the same for ever, like the divine, but by replacing what goes off or is antiquated with something fresh, in the semblance of the original. Through this device, Socrates, a mortal thing partakes of immortality, both in its body and in all other respects; by no other means can it be done. So do not wonder if everything naturally values its own offshoot; since all are beset by this eagerness and this love with a view to immortality.'

"On hearing this argument I wondered, and said: 'Really, can this in truth be so, most wise Diotima?'

"Whereat she, like the professors in their glory: 'Be certain of it, Socrates; only glance at the ambition of the men around you, and you will have to wonder at the unreasonableness of what I have told you, unless you are careful to consider how singularly they are affected with the love of winning a name, "and laying up fame immortal for all time to come."[67] For this, even more than for their children, they are ready to run all risks, to expend money, perform any kind of task, and sacrifice their lives. Do you suppose,' she asked, 'that Alcestis would have died for Admetus, or Achilles have sought death on the corpse of Patroclus, or your own Codrus[68] have welcomed it to save the children of his queen, if they had not expected to win "a deathless memory for valour," which now we keep? Of course not. I hold it is for immortal distinction and for such illustrious renown as this that they all do all they can, and so much the more in proportion to their excellence. They are in love with what is immortal. Now those who are teeming in body betake them rather to women, and are amorous on this wise: by getting children they acquire an immortality, a memorial, and a state of bliss, which in their imagining they "for all succeeding time procure." But pregnancy of soul—for there are persons,' she declared, 'who in their souls still more than in their bodies conceive those

[67] Diotima, like Agathon, breaks into verse of her own composing.

[68] A legendary king of Athens who exposed his life because an oracle had said that the Dorian invaders would conquer if they did not slay the Athenian king.

things which are proper for soul to conceive and bring forth; and what are those things? Prudence, and virtue in general; and of these the begetters are all the poets and those craftsmen who are styled *inventors*. Now by far the highest and fairest part of prudence is that which concerns the regulation of cities and habitations; it is called sobriety and justice. So when a man's soul is so far divine that it is made pregnant with these from his youth, and on attaining manhood immediately desires to bring forth and beget, he too, I imagine, goes about seeking the beautiful object whereon he may do his begetting, since he will never beget upon the ugly. Hence it is the beautiful rather than the ugly bodies that he welcomes in his pregnancy, and if he chances also on a soul that is fair and noble and well-endowed, he gladly cherishes the two combined in one; and straightway in addressing such a person he is resourceful in discoursing of virtue and of what should be the good man's character and what his pursuits; and so he takes in hand the other's education. For I hold that by contact with the fair one and by consorting with him he bears and brings forth his long-felt conception, because in presence or absence he remembers his fair. Equally too with him he shares the nurturing of what is begotten, so that men in this condition enjoy a far fuller community with each other than that which comes with children, and a far surer friendship, since the children of their union are fairer and more deathless. Every one would choose to have got children such as these rather than the human sort—merely from turning a glance upon Homer and Hesiod and all the other good poets, and envying the fine offspring they leave behind to procure them a glory immortally renewed in the memory of men. Or only look,' she said, 'at the fine children whom Lycurgus[69] left behind him in Lacedaemon to deliver his country and—I may almost say—the whole of Greece; while Solon is highly esteemed among you for begetting his laws; and so are divers men in divers other regions, whether among the Greeks or among foreign peoples, for the number of goodly deeds shown forth in them, the manifold virtues they begot. In their name has many a shrine been reared because of their fine children; whereas for the human sort never any man obtained this honour.

" 'Into these love-matters even you, Socrates, might haply be initiated; but I doubt if you could approach the rites and revela-

[69] The legendary creator of Spartan laws and customs.

tions to which these, for the properly instructed, are merely the avenue. However I will speak of them,' she said, 'and will not stint my best endeavours; only you on your part must try your best to follow. He who would proceed rightly in this business must not merely begin from his youth to encounter beautiful bodies. In the first place, indeed, if his conductor guides him aright, he must be in love with one particular body, and engender beautiful converse therein; but next he must remark how the beauty attached to this or that body is cognate to that which is attached to any other, and that if he means to ensue beauty in form, it is gross folly not to regard as one and the same the beauty belonging to all; and so, having grasped this truth, he must make himself a lover of all beautiful bodies, and slacken the stress of his feeling for one by contemning it and counting it a trifle. But his next advance will be to set a higher value on the beauty of souls than on that of the body, so that however little the grace that may bloom in any likely soul it shall suffice him for loving and caring, and for bringing forth and soliciting such converse as will tend to the betterment of the young; and that finally he may be constrained to contemplate the beautiful as appearing in our observances and our laws, and to behold it all bound together in kinship and so estimate the body's beauty as a slight affair. From observances he should be led on to the branches of knowledge, that there also he may behold a province of beauty, and by looking thus on beauty in the mass may escape from the mean, meticulous slavery of a single instance, where he must centre all his care, like a lackey, upon the beauty of a particular child or man or single observance; and turning rather towards the main ocean of the beautiful may by contemplation of this bring forth in all their splendour many fair fruits of discourse and meditation in a plenteous crop of philosophy; until with the strength and increase there acquired he descries a certain single knowledge connected with a beauty which has yet to be told. And here, I pray you,' said she, 'give me the very best of your attention.

" 'When a man has been thus far tutored in the lore of love, passing from view to view of beautiful things, in the right and regular ascent, suddenly he will have revealed to him, as he draws to the close of his dealings in love, a wondrous vision, beautiful in its nature; and this, Socrates, is the final object of all those previous toils. First of all, it is ever-existent and neither comes to be nor perishes, neither waxes nor wanes; next, it is not beautiful in part and in part ugly, nor is it such at such a time and other at another, nor in one respect beautiful and in another ugly, nor so affected by position as to seem beautiful to some and ugly to others. Nor again will our initiate find the beautiful presented to him in the guise of a face or of hands or any other portion of the body, nor as a particular description or piece of knowledge, nor as existing somewhere in another substance, such as an animal or the earth or sky or any other thing; but existing ever in singularity of form independent by itself, while all the multitude of beautiful things partake of it in such wise that, though all of them are coming to be and perishing, it grows neither greater nor less, and is affected by nothing. So when a man by the right method of boy-loving ascends from these particulars and begins to descry that beauty, he is almost able to lay hold of the final secret. Such is the right approach or induction to love-matters. Beginning from obvious beauties he must for the sake of that highest beauty be ever climbing aloft, as on the rungs of a ladder, from one to two, and from two to all beautiful bodies; from personal beauty he proceeds to beautiful observances, from observance to beautiful learning, and from learning at last to that particular study which is concerned with the beautiful itself and that alone; so that in the end he comes to know the very essence of beauty. In that state of life above all others, my dear Socrates,' said the Mantinean woman, 'a man finds it truly worth while to live, as he contemplates essential beauty. This, when once beheld, will outshine your gold and your vesture, your beautiful boys and striplings, whose aspect now so astounds you and makes you and many another, at the sight and constant society of your darlings, ready to do without either food or drink if that were any way possible, and only gaze upon them and have their company. But tell me, what would happen if one of you had the fortune to look upon essential beauty entire, pure and unalloyed; not infected with the flesh and colour of humanity, and ever so much more of mortal trash? What if he could behold the divine beauty itself, in its unique form? Do you call it a pitiful life for a man to lead—looking that way, observing that vision by the proper means, and having it ever with him? Do but consider,' she said, 'that there only will it befall him, as he sees the beautiful through that which makes it visible, to breed not illusions but true examples of virtue, since his contact is not

with illusion but with truth. So when he has begotten a true virtue
and has reared it up he is destined to win the friendship of Heaven;
he, above all men, is immortal.'

"This, Phaedrus and you others, is what Diotima told me, and I
am persuaded of it; in which persuasion I pursue my neighbours, to
persuade them in turn that towards this acquisition the best helper
that our human nature can hope to find is Love. Wherefore I tell
you now that every man should honour Love, as I myself do honour
all love-matters with especial devotion, and exhort all other men to
do the same; both now and always do I glorify Love's power and
valour as far as I am able. So I ask you, Phaedrus, to be so good as
to consider this account as a eulogy bestowed on Love, or else to
call it by any name that pleases your fancy."

After Socrates had thus spoken, there was applause from all the
company except Aristophanes, who was beginning to remark on the
allusion which Socrates' speech had made to his own;[70] when suddenly there was a knocking at the outer door, which had a noisy
sound like that of revellers, and they heard notes of a flute-girl.
"Go and see to it," said Agathon to the servants; "and if it be one
of our intimates, invite him in: otherwise, say we are not drinking,
but just about to retire."

A few moments after, they heard the voice of Alcibiades in the
forecourt, very drunken and bawling loud, to know where Agathon
was, and bidding them bring him to Agathon. So he was brought
into the company by the flute-girl and some others of his people
supporting him: he stood at the door, crowned with a bushy
wreath of ivy and violets, and wearing a great array of ribands on
his head. "Good evening, sirs," he said; "will you admit to your
drinking a fellow very far gone in liquor, or shall we simply set a
wreath on Agathon—which indeed is what we came for—and so
away? I tell you, sir, I was hindered from getting to you yesterday;
but now I am here with these ribands on my head, so that I can pull
them off mine and twine them about the head of the cleverest, the
handsomest, if I may speak the—see, like this![71] Ah, you would
laugh at me because I am drunk? Well, for my part, laugh as you
may, I am sure I am speaking the truth. Come, tell me straight out,

---

[70] See 205 E.

[71] His drunken gesture interrupts what he means to say and resumes later,—"If
I may speak the truth."

am I to enter on the terms stated or not? Will you take a cup with me or no?"

At this they all boisterously acclaimed him, bidding him enter and take a seat, and Agathon also invited him. So he came along with the assistance of his people; and while unwinding the ribands for his purpose of wreathing his friend he so held them before his eyes that he failed to notice Socrates, and actually took a seat next to Agathon, between Socrates and him: for Socrates had moved up when he caught sight of Alcibiades. So there he sat, and he saluted Agathon and began to twine his head.

Then Agathon said to the servants, "Take off Alcibiades' shoes, so that he can recline here with us two."

"By all means," said Alcibiades; "but who is our third at table?" With that he turned about and saw Socrates, and the same moment leapt up and cried, "Save us, what a surprise! Socrates here! So it was to lie in wait for me again that you were sitting there— your old trick of turning up on a sudden where least I expected you! Well, what are you after now? Tell me, I say, why you took a seat here and not by Aristophanes or some one else who is absurd and means to be? Why did you intrigue to get a seat beside the handsomest person in the room?"

Then Socrates said, "Agathon, do your best to protect me, for I have found my love for this fellow no trifling affair. From the time when I fell in love with him I have not had a moment's liberty either to look upon or converse with a single handsome person, but the fellow flies into a spiteful jealousy which makes him treat me in a monstrous fashion, girding at me and hardly keeping his hands to himself. So take care that he does no mischief now: pray reconcile us; or if he sets about using force, protect me, for I shudder with alarm at his amorous frenzy."

"No," said Alcibiades; "no reconcilement for you and me. I will have my revenge on you for this another time: for the present, Agathon, give me some of your ribands, that I may also deck this person's head, this astonishing head. He shall not reproach me with having made a garland for you and then, though he conquers every one in discourse—not once in a while, like you the other day, but always—bestowing none upon him." So saying he took some of the ribands and, after decking the head of Socrates, resumed his seat.

Reclining there, he proceeded: "Now then, gentlemen, you

look sober: I cannot allow this; you must drink, and fulfil our agreement. So I appoint as president of this bout, till you have had a reasonable drink—myself. Agathon, let the boy bring me as large a goblet as you have. Ah well, do not trouble," he said: "boy, bring me that cooler there,"—for he saw it would hold a good half-gallon and more. This he got filled to the brim, and after quaffing it off himself bade them fill up for Socrates, saying, "Against Socrates, sirs, my crafty plan is as nought. However large the bumper you order him, he will quaff it all off and never get tipsy with it."

Socrates drank as soon as the boy had filled: but—"What procedure is this, Alcibiades?" asked Eryximachus. "Are we to have nothing to say or sing over the cup? Are we going to drink just like any thirsty folk?"

To this Alcibiades answered: "Ha, Eryximachus, 'of noblest, soberest sire most noble son'; all hail!"

"And the same to you," said Eryximachus: "but what are we to do?"

"Whatever you command, for we are bound to obey you:

> One learned leech is worth the multitude.[72]

So prescribe what you please."

"Then listen," said Eryximachus. "We resolved, before your arrival, that each in order from left to right should make the finest speech he could upon Love, and glorify his name. Now all of us here have spoken; so you, since you have made no speech and have drained the cup, must do your duty and speak. This done, you shall prescribe what you like for Socrates, and he for his neighbour on the right, and so on with the rest."

"Very good, Eryximachus," said Alcibiades; "but to pit a drunken man against sober tongues is hardly fair. Besides, my gifted friend, you are surely not convinced by anything that Socrates has just told you? You must know the case is quite the contrary of what he was saying. It is he who, if I praise any god in his presence or any person other than himself, will not keep his hands off me."

"Come, enough of this," said Socrates.

"On the honour of a gentleman," said Alcibiades, "it is no use

[72] Homer, *Il.* xi. 514.

your protesting, for I could not praise anyone else in your presence."

"Well, do that if you like," said Eryximachus; "praise Socrates."

"You mean it?" said Alcibiades; "you think I had better, Eryximachus? Am I to set upon the fellow and have my revenge before you all?"

"Here," said Socrates; "what are you about,—to make fun of me with your praises, or what?"

"I shall speak the truth; now, will you permit me?"

"Ah well, so long as it is the truth, I permit you and command you to speak."

"You shall hear it this moment," said Alcibiades; "but there is something you must do. If I say anything that is false, have the goodness to take me up short and say that there I am lying; for I will not lie if I can help it. Still, you are not to be surprised if I tell my reminiscences at haphazard; it is anything but easy for a man in my condition to give a fluent and regular enumeration of your oddities."

ALCIBIADES' PRAISE OF SOCRATES

"The way I shall take, gentlemen, in my praise of Socrates, is by similitudes. Probably he will think I do this for derision; but I choose my similitude for the sake of truth, not of ridicule. For I say he is likest to the Silenus-figures that sit in the statuaries' shops; those, I mean, which our craftsmen make with pipes or flutes in their hands: when their two halves are pulled open, they are found to contain images of gods. And I further suggest that he resembles the satyr Marsyas. Now, as to your likeness, Socrates, to these in figure, I do not suppose even you yourself will dispute it; but I have next to tell you that you are like them in every other respect. You are a fleering fellow, eh? If you will not confess it, I have witnesses at hand. Are you not a piper? Why, yes, and a far more marvellous one than the satyr. His lips indeed had power to entrance mankind by means of instruments; a thing still possible today for anyone who can pipe his tunes: for the music of Olympus's flute belonged, I may tell you, to Marsyas his teacher. So that if anyone, whether a fine flute-player or paltry flute-girl, can but flute his tunes, they have no equal for exciting a ravishment, and will indicate by the divinity that is in them who are apt recipients of the deities and their sanctifications. You differ from him in one point only—that you produce the same effect with simple prose unaided by instruments. For example, when we hear any other person—quite an excellent orator, perhaps—pronouncing one of the usual discourses, no one, I venture to say, cares a jot; but so soon as we hear you, or your discourses in the mouth of another,—though such person be ever so poor a speaker, and whether the hearer be a woman or a man or a youngster—we are all astounded and entranced. As for myself, gentlemen, were it not that I might appear to be absolutely tipsy, I would have affirmed on oath all the strange effects I personally have felt from his words, and still feel even now. For when I hear him I am worse than any wild fanatic; I find my heart leaping and my tears gushing forth at the sound of his speech, and I see great numbers of other people having the same experience. When I listened to Pericles and other skilled orators I thought them eloquent, but I never felt anything like this; my spirit was not left in a tumult and had not to complain of my being in the condition of a common slave: whereas the influence of our Marsyas here has often thrown me into such a state that I thought my life not worth living on these terms. In all this, Socrates, there is nothing that you can call untrue. Even now I am still conscious that if I consented to lend him my ear, I could not resist him, but would have the same feeling again. For he compels me to admit that, sorely deficient as I am, I neglect myself while I attend to the affairs of Athens. So I withhold my ears perforce as from the Sirens, and make off as fast as I can, for fear I should go on sitting beside him till old age was upon me. And there is one experience I have in presence of this man alone, such as nobody would expect in me; and that is, to be made to feel ashamed; he alone can make me feel it. For he brings home to me that I cannot disown the duty of doing what he bids me, but that as soon as I turn from his company I fall a victim to the favours of the crowd. So I take a runaway's leave of him and flee away; when I see him again I think of those former admissions, and am ashamed. Often I could wish he had vanished from this world; yet again, should this befall, I am sure I should be more distressed than ever; so I cannot tell what to do with the fellow at all.

"Such then is the effect that our satyr can work upon me and many another with his piping; but let me tell you how like he is in other respects to the figures of my comparison, and what a wondrous power he wields. I assure you, not one of you knows him; well, I shall reveal him, now that I have begun. Observe how Socrates is amorously inclined to handsome persons; with these he is always busy and enraptured. Again, he is utterly stupid and ignorant, as he affects. Is not this like a Silenus? Exactly. It is an outward casing he wears, similarly to the sculptured Silenus. But if you opened his inside, you cannot imagine how full he is, good cup-companions, of sobriety. I tell you, all the beauty a man may have is nothing to him; he despises it more than any of you can believe; nor does wealth attract him, nor any sort of honour that is the envied prize of the crowd. All these possessions he counts as nothing worth, and all of us as nothing, I assure you; he spends his whole life in chaffing and making game of his fellow-men. Whether anyone else has caught him in a serious moment and opened him, and seen the images inside, I know not; but I saw them one day, and thought them so divine and golden, so perfectly fair and wondrous, that I simply had to do as Socrates bade me. And believing he had a serious affection for my youthful bloom, I supposed I had here a godsend and a rare stroke of luck, thinking myself free at any time by gratifying his desires to hear all that our Socrates knew; for I was enormously proud of my youthful charms. So with this design I dismissed the attendant whom till then I invariably brought to my meetings with Socrates, and I would go and meet him alone: I am to tell you the whole truth; you must all mark my words, and, Socrates, you shall refute me if I lie. Yes, gentlemen, I went and met him, and the two of us would be alone; and I thought he would seize the chance of talking to me as a lover does to his dear one in private, and I was glad. But nothing of the sort occurred at all: he would merely converse with me in his usual manner, and when he had spent the day with me he would leave me and go his way. After that I proposed he should go with me to the trainer's, and I trained with him, expecting to gain my point there. So he trained and wrestled with me many a time when no one was there. The same story! I got no further with the affair. Then, as I made no progress that way, I resolved to charge full tilt at the man, and not to throw up the contest once I had entered upon it: I felt I must clear up the situation. Accordingly I invited him to dine with me, for all the world like a lover scheming to ensnare his favourite.

Even this he was backward to accept; however, he was eventually persuaded. The first time he came, he wanted to leave as soon as he had dined. On that occasion I was ashamed and let him go. The second time I devised a scheme: when we had dined I went on talking with him far into the night, and when he wanted to go I made a pretext of the lateness of the hour and constrained him to stay. So he sought repose on the couch next to me, on which he had been sitting at dinner, and no one was sleeping in the room but ourselves.

"Now up to this point my tale could fairly be told to anybody; but from here onwards I would not have continued in your hearing were it not, in the first place, that wine, as the saying goes, whether you couple 'children' with it or no, is 'truthful'; and in the second, I consider it dishonest, when I have started on the praise of Socrates, to hide his deed of lofty disdain. Besides, I share the plight of the man who was bitten by the snake: you know it is related of one in such a plight that he refused to describe his sensations to any but persons who had been bitten themselves, since they alone would understand him and stand up for him if he should give way to wild words and actions in his agony. Now I have been bitten by a more painful creature, in the most painful way that one can be bitten: in my heart, or my soul, or whatever one is to call it, I am stricken and stung by his philosophic discourses, which adhere more fiercely than any adder when once they lay hold of a young and not ungifted soul, and force it to do or say whatever they will; I have only to look around me, and there is a Phaedrus, an Agathon, an Eryximachus, a Pausanias, an Aristodemus, and an Aristophanes— I need not mention Socrates himself—and all the rest of them; every one of you has had his share of philosophic frenzy and transport, so all of you shall hear. You shall stand up alike for what then was done and for what now is spoken. But the domestics, and all else profane and clownish, must clap the heaviest of doors upon their ears.

"Well, gentlemen, when the lamp had been put out and the servants had withdrawn, I determined not to mince matters with him, but to speak out freely what I intended. So I shook him and said, 'Socrates, are you asleep?'

" 'Why, no,' he replied.

" 'Let me tell you what I have decided.'

" 'What is the matter?' he asked.

" 'I consider,' I replied, 'that you are the only worthy lover I
have had, and it looks to me as if you were shy of mentioning it to
me. My position is this: I count it sheer folly not to gratify you in
this as in any other need you may have of either my property or
that of my friends. To me nothing is more important than the at-
tainment of the highest possible excellence, and in this aim I believe I can find no abler ally than you. So I should feel a far worse
shame before sensible people for not gratifying such a friend than I
should before the senseless multitude for gratifying him.'

"When he heard this, he put on that innocent air which habit has
made so characteristic of him, and remarked: 'My dear Alcibiades,
I daresay you are not really a dolt, if what you say of me is the
actual truth, and there is a certain power in me that could help you
to be better; for then what a stupendous beauty you must see in
me, vastly superior to your comeliness! And if on espying this you
are trying for a mutual exchange of beauty for beauty, it is no
slight advantage you are counting on—you are trying to get genuine
in return for reputed beauties, and in fact are designing to fetch off
the old bargain of *gold for bronze*.[73] But be more wary, my gifted
friend: you may be deceived and I may be worthless. Remember,
the intellectual sight begins to be keen when the visual is entering
on its wane; but you are a long way yet from that time.'

"To this I answered: 'You have heard what I had to say; not
a word differed from the feeling in my mind: it is for you now to
consider what you judge to be best for you and me.'

"Ah, there you speak to some purpose,' he said: 'for in the days
that are to come we shall consider and do what appears to be best
for the two of us in this and our other affairs.'

"Well, after I had exchanged these words with him and, as it
were, let fly my shafts, I fancied he felt the wound: so up I got, and
without suffering the man to say a word more I wrapped my own
coat about him—it was winter-time; drew myself under his cloak,
so; wound my arms about this truly spiritual and miraculous creature; and lay thus all the night long. Here too, Socrates, you are
unable to give me the lie. When I had done all this, he showed such
superiority and contempt, laughing my youthful charms to scorn,
and flouting the very thing on which I prided myself, gentlemen of

---

[73] Homer, *Il.* vi. 236—Glaucus foolishly exchanging his golden armour for the
bronze armour of Diomedes.

the jury—for you are here to try Socrates for his lofty disdain: you may be sure, by gods—and goddesses—that when I arose I had in no more particular sense slept a night with Socrates than if it had been with my father or my elder brother.

"After that, you can imagine what a state of mind I was in, feeling myself affronted, yet marvelling at the sobriety and integrity of his nature: for I had lighted on a man such as I never would have dreamt of meeting—so sensible and so resolute. Hence I could find neither a reason for being angry and depriving myself of his society nor a ready means of enticing him. For I was well aware that he was far more proof against money on every side than Ajax against a spear; and in what I thought was my sole means of catching him he had eluded me. So I was at a loss, and wandered about in the most abject thraldom to this man that ever was known. Now all this, you know, had already happened to me when we later went on a campaign together to Potidaea;[74] and there we were messmates. Well, first of all, he surpassed not me only but every one else in bearing hardships; whenever we were cut off in some place and were compelled, as often in campaigns, to go without food, the rest of us were nowhere in point of endurance. Then again, when we had plenty of good cheer, he alone could enjoy it to the full, and though unwilling to drink, when once overruled he used to beat us all; and, most surprising of all, no man has ever yet seen Socrates drunk. Of this power I expect we shall have a good test in a moment. But it was in his endurance of winter—in those parts the winters are awful—that I remember, among his many marvellous feats, how once there came a frost about as awful as can be; we all preferred not to stir abroad, or if any of us did, we wrapped ourselves up with prodigious care, and after putting on our shoes we muffled up our feet with felt and little fleeces. But he walked out in that weather, clad in just such a coat as he was always wont to wear, and he made his way more easily over the ice unshod than the rest of us did in our shoes. The soldiers looked askance at him, thinking that he despised them.

"So much for that: 'but next, the valiant deed our strong-souled hero dared'[75] on service there one day, is well worth hearing. Immersed in some problem at dawn, he stood in the same spot con-

[74] 432 B.C.   [75] Homer, *Od.* iv. 242.

sidering it; and when he found it a tough one, he would not give it up but stood there trying. The time drew on to midday, and the men began to notice him, and said to one another in wonder: 'Socrates has been standing there in a study ever since dawn!' The end of it was that in the evening some of the Ionians after they had supped—this time it was summer—brought out their mattresses and rugs and took their sleep in the cool; thus they waited to see if he would go on standing all night too. He stood till dawn came and the sun rose; then walked away, after offering a prayer to the Sun.

"Then, if you care to hear of him in battle—for there also he must have his due—on the day of the fight in which I gained my prize for valour from our commanders, it was he, out of the whole army, who saved my life: I was wounded, and he would not forsake me, but helped me to save both my armour and myself. I lost no time, Socrates, in urging the generals to award the prize for valour to you; and here I think you will neither rebuke me nor give me the lie. For when the generals, out of regard for my consequence, were inclined to award the prize to me, you outdid them in urging that I should have it rather than you. And further let me tell you, gentlemen, what a notable figure he made when the army was retiring in flight from Delium:[76] I happened to be there on horseback, while he marched under arms. The troops were in utter disorder, and he was retreating along with Laches, when I chanced to come up with them and, as soon as I saw them, passed them the word to have no fear, saying I would not abandon them. Here, indeed, I had an even finer view of Socrates than at Potidaea—for personally I had less reason for alarm, as I was mounted; and I noticed, first, how far he outdid Laches in collectedness, and next I felt—to use a phrase of yours, Aristophanes—how there he stepped along, as his wont is in our streets, 'strutting like a proud marshgoose, with ever a sidelong glance,'[77] turning a calm sidelong look on friend and foe alike, and convincing anyone even from afar that whoever cares to touch this person will find he can put up a stout enough defence. The result was that both he and his comrade got

[76] The Athenians were defeated by the Thebans, 424 B.C.

[77] Aristoph., *Clouds* 362.

away unscathed: for, as a rule, people will not lay a finger on those who show this disposition in war; it is men flying in headlong rout that they pursue.

"There are many more quite wonderful things that one could find to praise in Socrates: but although there would probably be as much to say about any other one of his habits, I select his unlikeness to anybody else, whether in the ancient or in the modern world, as calling for our greatest wonder. You may take the character of Achilles and see his parallel in Brasidas or others; you may couple Nestor, Antenor, or others I might mention, with Pericles; and in the same order you may liken most great men; but with the odd qualities of this person, both in himself and in his conversation, you would not come anywhere near finding a comparison if you searched either among men of our day or among those of the past, unless perhaps you borrowed my words and matched him, not with any human being, but with the Silenuses and satyrs, in his person and his speech.

"For there is a point I omitted when I began—how his talk most of all resembles the Silenuses that are made to open. If you chose to listen to Socrates' discourses you would feel them at first to be quite ridiculous; on the outside they are clothed with such absurd words and phrases—all, of course, the gift of a mocking satyr. His talk is of pack-asses, smiths, cobblers, and tanners, and he seems always to be using the same terms for the same things; so that anyone inexpert and thoughtless might laugh his speeches to scorn. But when these are opened, and you obtain a fresh view of them by getting inside, first of all you will discover that they are the only speeches which have any sense in them; and secondly, that none are so divine, so rich in images of virtue, so largely—nay, so completely—intent on all things proper for the study of such as would attain both grace and worth.

"This, gentlemen, is the praise I give to Socrates: at the same time, I have seasoned it with a little fault-finding, and have told you his rude behaviour towards me. However, I am not the only person he has treated thus: there are Charmides, son of Glaucon, Euthydemus, son of Diocles, and any number of others who have found his way of loving so deceitful that he might rather be their favourite than their lover. I tell you this, Agathon, to save you from his deceit, that by laying our sad experiences to heart you may be on your guard and escape learning by your own pain, like the loon in the adage."[78]

When Alcibiades had thus spoken, there was some laughter at his frankness, which showed him still amorously inclined to Socrates; who then remarked: "I believe you are sober, Alcibiades; else you would never have enfolded yourself so charmingly all about, trying to screen from sight your object in all this talk, nor would have put it in as a mere incident at the end. The true object of all you have said was to stir up a quarrel between me and Agathon: for you think you must keep me as your undivided lover, and Agathon as the undivided object of your love. But now you are detected: your *Satyric* or *Silenic* play-scene is all shown up. Dear Agathon, do not let the plot succeed, but take measures to prevent anyone from setting you and me at odds."

To which Agathon replied: "Do you know, Socrates, I fancy you have hit on the truth. Besides, I take his sitting down between us two as an obvious attempt to draw us apart. See, he shall not gain his point: I will come and sit by your side."

"By all means," said Socrates; "here is a place for you beyond me."

"Good God!" said Alcibiades, "here's the fellow at me again. He has set his heart on having the better of me every way. But at least, you surprising person, do allow Agathon to sit between us."

"That cannot be," said Socrates: "you have praised me, and so it behoves me to praise my neighbour on the right.[79] Thus if Agathon sits beyond you, he must surely be praising me again, before receiving his due praises from me. So let him be, my good soul, and do not grudge the lad those praises of mine: for I am most eager to pronounce his eulogy."

"Ha, ha! Alcibiades," said Agathon; "there can be no question of my staying here: I shall jump up and change at once, if that will make Socrates praise me."

"There you are," said Alcibiades; "just as usual: when Socrates is present, nobody else has a chance with the handsome ones. You see how resourceful he was in devising a plausible reason why our young friend should sit beside him."

[78] Homer, *Il.* xvii. 33: "Fools get their lesson from the deed done."

[79] At § 214 c it was only agreed that each should impose *what topic he pleased* upon his neighbour.

So Agathon was getting up in order to seat himself by Socrates, when suddenly a great crowd of revellers arrived at the door, which they found just opened for some one who was going out. They marched straight into the party and seated themselves: the whole place was in a uproar and, losing all order, they were forced to drink a vast amount of wine. Then, as Aristodemus related, Eryximachus, Phaedrus, and some others took their leave and departed; while he himself fell asleep, and slumbered a great while, for the nights were long. He awoke towards dawn, as the cocks were crowing; and immediately he saw that all the company were either sleeping or gone, except Agathon, Aristophanes, and Socrates, who alone remained awake and were drinking out of a large vessel, from left to right; and Socrates was arguing with them. As to most of the talk, Aristodemus had no recollection, for he had missed the beginning and was also rather drowsy; but the substance of it was, he said, that Socrates was driving them to the admission that the same man could have the knowledge required for writing comedy and tragedy—that the fully skilled tragedian could be a comedian as well. While they were being driven to this, and were but feebly following it, they began to nod; first Aristophanes dropped into a slumber, and then, as day began to dawn, Agathon also. When Socrates had seen them comfortable, he rose and went away,—followed in the usual manner by my friend; on arriving at the Lyceum, he washed himself, and then spent the rest of the day in his ordinary fashion; and so, when the day was done, he went home for the evening and reposed.

INTELLIGENCE AND THE SOCIAL ORDER
On Philosopher-Kings (*Republic*)
On the Kingly Art (*Statesman*)
Against Atheists and on Religion in the State (*Laws*)

Man appears in Plato as the culmination of the world of change and the connecting link with the realms of the changeless. While the properest study of mankind is not man, yet the fullest fruit of ultimate understanding is human amelioration and improvement. Those who seek power over men must be counted as moral impostors, but those who have achieved, through dialectics and love of beauty, the vision of the good must take their turn at service among the prisoners in the Cave. Population is basic to social improvement; specialization of labor is elementary wisdom for both efficiency and happiness. Education must provide a new type of leadership; and this leadership, once found, isolated, and trained, must by rights become supreme. No power is too great, no means too drastic, no "lie" too "divine," no experimentation too novel, if only a race of men can be produced who by calling the same things "mine" and "thine" can thus transcend a dualism in human society based upon acquisitiveness of both affection and property and thwarting, regardless of its basis, the precious human value of solidarity. Sex lines are leveled, the small loyalties of family derided, and the claim of individual happiness renounced in order to drive with all power against disunion in man's spiritual community. Not "power over" but "power for"—this is to be the motto of the ruling élite. A line of development in Plato's social thinking seems to pass from complete ideality in the "Republic," with self-conscious but glad sacrifice by all wise men for the general good, to a less heroic rôle of rulers in the "Statesman," weaving together eugenically and euthenically as their "kingly art" the diverse classes of the state, on to an acceptance in the "Laws" of an order that frankly is only "second best." This is an order of laws rather than of all wise men, and laws that are more the precipitates of custom than the distillates of pure thought. Traditional religion becomes a more important sanction for social order than is individually derived truth. For, as Plato says, "it is no easy task to found temples and gods." Plato never wavers from the belief that intelligence can and must count socially and politically; but the perspective required for its maturation lengthens with the shadows of his years. The moral impetuosity against poets which in the "Republic" is tempered by aesthetic magnanimity passes in the "Laws" into the easy way against religious dissenters, an eventuation made no more palatable by his rationalizing it—as still it is done today—in terms of the safety of the state.

. . .

ON PHILOSOPHER-KINGS

Republic (Shorey translation) 473 ("Loeb Classical Library" series).

". . . . We must try to discover and point out what it is that is now badly managed in our cities, and that prevents them from being so governed, and what is the smallest change that would bring a state to this manner of government, preferably a change in one thing, if not, then in two, and, failing that, the fewest possible in number and the slightest in potency." "By all means," he said. "There is one change, then," said I, "which I think that we can show would bring about the desired transformation. It is not a slight or an easy thing but it is possible." "What is that?" said he. "I am on the verge," said I, "of what we likened to the greatest wave of paradox. But say it I will, even if, to keep the figure, it is likely to wash us away on billows of laughter and scorn. Listen." "I am all attention," he said. "Unless," said I, "either philosophers become kings[80] in our states or those whom we now call our kings and rulers take to the pursuit of philosophy seriously and adequately, and there is a conjunction of these two things, political power and philosophic intelligence, while the motley horde of the natures who at present pursue either apart from the other are compulsorily excluded, there can be no cessation of troubles, dear Glaucon, for our states, nor, I fancy, for the human race either.

[80] "This," says Shorey, "is perhaps the most famous sentence in Plato." Cf. it with the foregoing declaration in *Epistle VII* 326.—T. V. S.

ON THE KINGLY ART

Statesman 305–11. Fowler translation ("Loeb Classical Library" series). This selection includes only about the last tenth of the dialogues.—T. V. S.

The art that is truly kingly ought not to act itself, but should rule over the arts that have the power of action; it should decide upon the right or wrong time for the initiation of the most important measures in the state, and the other arts should perform its behests.

Y. Soc. Right.

Str. Therefore those arts which we have just described, as they control neither one another nor themselves, but have each its own peculiar sphere of action, are quite properly called by special names corresponding to those special actions.

Y. Soc. That appears, at least, to be the case.

Str. But the art which holds sway over them all and watches over the laws and all things in the state, weaving them all most perfectly together, we may, I think, by giving to its function a designation which indicates its power over the community, with full propriety call "statecraft."

Y. Soc. Most assuredly.

Str. Shall we then proceed to discuss it after the model supplied by weaving, now that all the classes in the state have been made plain to us?

Y. Soc. By all means.

Str. Then the kingly process of weaving must be described, its nature, the manner in which it combines the threads, and the kind of web it produces.

Y. Soc. Evidently.

Str. It has, apparently, become necessary, after all, to explain a difficult matter.

Y. Soc. But certainly the explanation must be made.

Str. It is difficult, for the assertion that one part of virtue is in a way at variance with another sort of virtue may very easily be assailed by those who appeal to popular opinion in contentious arguments.

Y. Soc. I do not understand.

Str. I will say it again in another way. I suppose you believe that courage is one part of virtue.

Y. Soc. Certainly.

Str. And, of course, that self-restraint is different from courage, but is also a part of virtue of which courage is a part.

Y. Soc. Yes.

Str. Now I must venture to utter a strange doctrine about them.

Y. Soc. What is it?

Str. That, in a way, they are in a condition of great hostility and opposition to each other in many beings.

Y. Soc. What do you mean?

Str. Something quite unusual; for, you know, all the parts of virtue are usually said to be friendly to one another.

Y. Soc. Yes.

Str. Now shall we pay careful attention and see whether this is so simple, or, quite the contrary, there is in some respects a variance between them and their kin?

Y. Soc. Yes; please tell how we shall investigate the question.

Str. Among all the parts we must look for those which we call excellent but place in two opposite classes.

Y. Soc. Say more clearly what you mean.

Str. Acuteness and quickness, whether in body or soul or vocal utterance, whether they are real or exist in such likenesses as music and graphic art produce in imitation of them—have you never yourself praised one of them or heard them praised by others?

Y. Soc. Yes, of course.

Str. And do you remember in what way they praise them as occasion offers?

Y. Soc. Not in the least.

Str. I wonder if I can express to you in words what I have in mind.

Y. Soc. Why not?

Str. You seem to think that is an easy thing to do. However, let us consider the matter as it appears in the opposite classes. For example, when we admire, as we frequently do in many actions, quickness and energy and acuteness of mind or body or even of voice, we express our praise of them by one word, courage.

Y. Soc. How so?

Str. We say acute and courageous in the first instance, also quick and courageous, and energetic and courageous; and when we apply this word as a common term applicable to all persons and actions of this class, we praise them.

Y. Soc. Yes, we do.

Str. But do we not also praise the gentle type of movement in many actions?

Y. Soc. We do, decidedly.

Str. And in doing so, do we not say the opposite of what we said about the other class?

Y. Soc. How is that?

Str. We are always saying "How quiet!" and "How restrained!" when we are admiring the workings of the mind, and again we speak of actions as slow and gentle, of the voice as smooth and deep, and of every rhythmic motion and of music in general as having appropriate slowness; and we apply to them all the term which signifies, not courage, but decorum.

Y. Soc. Very true.

Str. And again, on the other hand, when these two classes seem to us out of place, we change our attitude and blame them each in turn; then we use the terms in the opposite sense.

Y. Soc. How is that?

Str. Why, whatsoever is sharper than the occasion warrants, or seems to be too quick or too hard, is called violent or mad, and whatever is too heavy or slow or gentle, is called cowardly and sluggish; and almost always we find that the restraint of one class of qualities and the courage of the opposite class, like two parties arrayed in hostility to each other, do not mix with each other in the actions that are concerned with such qualities. Moreover, if we pursue the inquiry, we shall see that the men who have these qualities in their souls are at variance with one another.

Y. Soc. In what do you mean that they are at variance?

Str. In all those points which we just mentioned, and probably in many others. For men who are akin to each class, I imagine, praise some qualities as their own and find fault with those of their opposites as alien to themselves, and thus great enmity arises between them on many grounds.

Y. Soc. Yes, that is likely to be the case.

Str. Now this opposition of these two classes is mere child's-play; but when it affects the most important matters it becomes a most detestable disease in the state.

Y. Soc. What matters does it affect?

Str. The whole course of life, in all probability. For those who are especially decorous are ready to live always a quiet and retired life and to mind their own business; this is the manner of their intercourse with every one at home, and they are equally ready at all times to keep peace in some way or other with foreign states. And because of this desire of theirs, which is often inopportune and excessive, when they have their own way they quite unconsciously become unwarlike, and they make the young men unwarlike also; they are at the mercy of aggressors; and thus in a few years they and their children and the whole state often pass by imperceptible degrees from freedom to slavery.

Y. Soc. That is a hard and terrible experience.

Str. But how about those who incline towards courage? Do they not constantly urge their countries to war, because of their excessive desire for a warlike life? Do they not involve them in hostilities with many powerful opponents and either utterly destroy their native lands or enslave and subject them to their foes?

Y. Soc. Yes, that is true, too.

Str. Then in these examples how can we deny that these two classes are always filled with the greatest hostility and opposition to one another?

Y. Soc. We certainly cannot deny it.

Str. Have we not, then, found just what we had in view in the beginning, that important parts of virtue are by nature at variance with one another and also that the persons who possess them exhibit the same opposition?

Y. Soc. Yes, I suppose that is true.

Str. Let us then take up another question.

Y. Soc. What question?

Str. Whether any constructive science voluntarily composes any, even the most worthless, of its works out of good and bad materials, or every science invariably rejects the bad, so far as possible, taking only the materials which are good and fitting, out of which, whether they be like or unlike, it gathers all elements together and produces one form or value.

Y. Soc. The latter, of course.

Str. Then neither will the true natural art of statecraft ever voluntarily compose a state of good and bad men; but obviously it will first test them in play, and after the test will entrust them in turn to those who are able to teach and help them to attain the end in view; it will itself give orders and exercise supervision, just as the art of weaving constantly commands and supervises the carders and others who prepare the materials for its web, directing each person to do the tasks which it thinks are requisite for its fabric.

Y. Soc. Certainly.

Str. In the same way I think the kingly art, keeping for itself the function of supervision, will not allow the duly appointed teachers and foster fathers to give any training, unless they can thereby produce characters suitable to the constitution it is creating, but in these things only it exhorts them to give instruction. And those men who have no capacity for courage and self-restraint and the other qualities which tend towards virtue, but by the force of an evil nature are carried away into godlessness, violence, and injustice, it removes by inflicting upon them the punishments of death and exile and deprivation of the most important civic rights.

Y. Soc. That is about what people say, at any rate.

Str. And those in turn who wallow in ignorance and craven humility it places under the yoke of slavery.

Y. Soc. Quite right.

Str. As for the rest of the people, those whose natures are capable, if they get education, of being made into something fine and noble and of uniting with each other as art requires, the kingly art takes those natures which tend more towards courage, considering that their character is sturdier, like the warp in weaving, and those which incline towards decorum, for these, to continue the simile, are spun thick and soft like the threads of the woof, and tries to combine these natures of opposite tendencies and weave them together in the following manner.

Y. Soc. In what manner?

Str. First it binds the eternal part of their souls with a divine bond, to which that part is akin, and after the divine it binds the animal part of them with human bonds.

Y. Soc. Again I ask What do you mean?

Str. I mean that really true and assured opinion about honour, justice, goodness and their opposites is divine, and when it arises in men's souls, it arises in a godlike race.

Y. Soc. That would be fitting, at any rate.

STR. Do we not know, then, that the statesman and good law-giver is the only one to whom the power properly belongs, by the inspiration of the kingly art, to implant this true opinion in those who have rightly received education, those of whom we were just now speaking?

Y. Soc. Well, probably.

STR. And let us never, Socrates, call him who has not such power by the names we are now examining.

Y. Soc. Quite right.

STR. Now is not a courageous soul, when it lays hold upon such truth, made gentle, and would it not then be most ready to partake of justice? And without it, does it not incline more towards brutality?

Y. Soc. Yes, of course.

STR. And again if the decorous nature partakes of these opinions, does it not become truly self-restrained and wise, so far as the state is concerned, and if it lacks participation in such qualities, does it not very justly receive the shameful epithet of simpleton?

Y. Soc. Certainly.

STR. Then can we say that such interweaving and binding together of the bad with the bad or of the good with the bad ever becomes enduring, or that any science would ever seriously make use of it in uniting such persons?

Y. Soc. Of course not.

STR. But we may say that in those only who were of noble nature from their birth and have been nurtured as befits such natures it is implanted by the laws, and for them this is the medicine prescribed by science, and, as we said before, this bond which unites unlike and divergent parts of virtue is more divine.

Y. Soc. Very true.

STR. The remaining bonds, moreover, being human, are not very difficult to devise or, after one has devised them, to create, when once this divine bond exists.

Y. Soc. How so? And what are the bonds?

STR. Those made between states concerning intermarriages and the sharing of children by adoption, and those relating to portionings and marriages within the state. For most people make such bonds without proper regard to the procreation of children.

Y. Soc. How is that?

STR. The pursuit of wealth or power in connexion with matrimony—but why should anyone ever take the trouble to blame it, as though it were worth arguing about?

Y. Soc. There is no reason for doing so.

STR. We have better cause, however, to speak our minds about those whose chief care is the family, in case their conduct is not what it should be.

Y. Soc. Yes; very likely.

STR. The fact is, they act on no right theory at all; they seek their ease for the moment; welcoming gladly those who are like themselves, and finding those who are unlike them unendurable, they give the greatest weight to their feeling of dislike.

Y. Soc. How so?

STR. The decorous people seek for characters like their own; so far as they can they marry wives of that sort and in turn give their daughters in marriage to men of that sort; and the courageous do the same, eagerly seeking natures of their own kind, whereas both classes ought to do quite the opposite.

Y. Soc. How so, and why?

STR. Because in the nature of things courage, if propagated through many generations with no admixture of a self-restrained nature, though at first it is strong and flourishing, in the end blossoms forth in utter madness.

Y. Soc. That is likely.

STR. But the soul, on the other hand, that is too full of modesty and contains no alloy of courage or boldness, after many generations of the same kind becomes too sluggish and finally is utterly crippled.

Y. Soc. That also is likely to happen.

STR. It was these bonds, then, that I said there was no difficulty in creating, provided that both classes have one and the same opinion about the honourable and the good. For indeed the whole business of the kingly weaving is comprised in this and this alone,—in never allowing the self-restrained characters to be separated from the courageous, but in weaving them together by common beliefs and honours and dishonours and opinions and interchanges of pledges, thus making of them a smooth and, as we say, well-woven fabric, and then entrusting to them in common for ever the offices of the state.

Y. Soc. How is that to be done?

Str. When one official is needed, by choosing a president who possesses both qualities; and when a board is desired, by combining men of each class. For the characters of self-restrained officials are exceedingly careful and just and conservative, but they lack keenness and a certain quick and active boldness.

Y. Soc. That also seems, at least, to be true.

Str. The courageous natures, on the other hand, are deficient in justice and caution in comparison with the former, but excel in boldness of action; and unless both these qualities are present it is impossible for a state to be entirely prosperous in public and private matters.

Y. Soc. Yes, certainly.

Str. This, then, is the end, let us declare, of the web of the statesman's activity, the direct interweaving of the characters of restrained and courageous men, when the kingly science has drawn them together by friendship and community of sentiment into a common life, and having perfected the most glorious and the best of all textures, clothes with it all the inhabitants of the state, both slaves and freemen, holds them together by this fabric, and omitting nothing which ought to belong to a happy state, rules and watches over them.

Y. Soc. You have given us, Stranger, a most complete and admirable treatment of the king and the statesman.

AGAINST ATHEISTS AND ON RELIGION IN THE STATE

Laws, Book x. Bury translation ("Loeb Classical Library" series). But for an opening passage, irrelevant to the subject here discussed, this is the entire (in)famous book x of the *Laws*, constituting somewhat less than one-tenth of that richly prolix work.—T. V. S.

AN ATHENIAN STRANGER AND CLINIAS OF CRETE

Ath. No one who believes, as the laws prescribe, in the existence of the gods has ever yet done an impious deed voluntarily, or uttered a lawless word: he that acts so is in one or other of these three conditions of mind—either he does not believe in what I have said; or, secondly, he believes that the gods exist, but have no care for men; or, thirdly, he believes that they are easy to win over when bribed by offerings and prayers.

CLIN. What, then, shall we do or say to such people?

ATH. Let us listen first, my good sir, to what they, as I imagine, say mockingly, in their contempt for us.

CLIN. What is it?

ATH. In derision they would probably say this: "O Strangers of Athens, Lacedaemon and Crete, what you say is true. Some of us do not believe in gods at all; others of us believe in gods of the kinds you mention. So we claim now, as you claimed in the matter of laws, that before threatening us harshly, you should first try to convince and teach us, by producing adequate proofs, that gods exist, and that they are too good to be wheedled by gifts and turned aside from justice. For as it is, this and such as this is the account of them we hear from those who are reputed the best of poets, orators, seers, priests, and thousands upon thousands of others; and consequently most of us, instead of seeking to avoid wrong-doing, do the wrong and then try to make it good. Now from lawgivers like you, who assert that you are gentle rather than severe, we claim that you should deal with us first by way of persuasion; and if what you say about the existence of the gods is superior to the arguments of others in point of truth, even though it be but little superior in eloquence, then probably you would succeed in convincing us. Try then, if you think this reasonable, to meet our challenge."

CLIN. Surely it seems easy, Stranger, to assert with truth that gods exist?

ATH. How so?

CLIN. First, there is the evidence of the earth, the sun, the stars, and all the universe, and the beautiful ordering of the seasons, marked out by years and months; and then there is the further fact that all Greeks and barbarians believe in the existence of gods.

ATH. My dear sir, these bad men cause me alarm—for I will never call it "awe"—lest haply they scoff at us. For the cause of the corruption in their case is one you are not aware of; since you imagine that it is solely by their incontinence in regard to pleasures and desires that their souls are impelled to that impious life of theirs.

CLIN. What other cause can there be, Stranger, besides this?

ATH. One which you, who live elsewhere, could hardly have any knowledge of or notice at all.

CLIN. What is this cause you are now speaking of?

ATH. A very grievous unwisdom which is reputed to be the height of wisdom.

CLIN. What do you mean?

ATH. We at Athens have accounts preserved in writing (though, I am told, such do not exist in your country, owing to the excellence of your polity), some of them being in a kind of metre, others without metre, telling about the gods: the oldest of these accounts relate how the first substance of Heaven and all else came into being, and shortly after the beginning they go on to give a detailed theogony, and to tell how, after they were born, the gods associated with one another. These accounts, whether good or bad for the hearers in other respects, it is hard for us to censure because of their antiquity; but as regards the tendance and respect due to parents, I certainly would never praise them or say that they are either helpful or wholly true accounts. Such ancient accounts, however, we may pass over and dismiss: let them be told in the way best pleasing to the gods. It is rather the novel views of our modern scientists[81] that we must hold responsible as the cause of mischief. For the result of the arguments of such people is this,—that when you and I try to prove the existence of the gods by pointing to these very objects—sun, moon, stars, and earth—as instances of deity and divinity, people who have been converted by these scientists will assert that these things are simply earth and stone, incapable of paying any heed to human affairs, and that these beliefs of ours are speciously tricked out with arguments to make them plausible.

CLIN. The assertion you mention, Stranger, is indeed a dangerous one, even if it stood alone; but now that such assertions are legion, the danger is still greater.

ATH. What then? What shall we say? What must we do? Are we to make our defence as it were before a court of impious men, where someone had accused us of doing something dreadful by assuming in our legislation the existence of gods? Or shall we rather dismiss the whole subject and revert again to our laws, lest our prelude prove actually more lengthy than the laws? For indeed our discourse would be extended in no small degree if we were to furnish

81 Materialists such as Democritus.

those men who desire to be impious with an adequate demonstration by means of argument concerning those subjects which ought, as they claimed, to be discussed, and so to convert them to fear of the gods, and then finally, when we had caused them to shrink from irreligion, to proceed to enact the appropriate laws.

CLIN. Still, Stranger, we have frequently (considering the shortness of the time) made[82] this very statement,—that we have no need on the present occasion to prefer brevity of speech to lengthiness (for, as the saying goes, "no one is chasing on our heels"); and to show ourselves choosing the briefest in preference to the best would be mean and ridiculous. And it is of the highest importance that our arguments, showing that the gods exist and that they are good and honour justice more than do men, should by all means possess some degree of persuasiveness; for such a prelude is the best we could have in defence, as one may say, of all our laws. So without any repugnance or undue haste, and with all the capacity we have for endowing such arguments with persuasiveness, let us expound them as fully as we can, and without any reservation.

ATH. This speech of yours seems to me to call for a prefatory prayer, seeing that you are so eager and ready; nor is it possible any longer to defer our statement. Come, then; how is one to argue on behalf of the existence of the gods without passion? For we needs must be vexed and indignant with the men who have been, and now are, responsible for laying on us this burden of argument, through their disbelief in those stories which they used to hear, while infants and sucklings, from the lips of their nurses and mothers—stories chanted to them, as it were, in lullabies, whether in jest or in earnest; and the same stories they heard repeated also in prayers at sacrifices, and they saw spectacles which illustrated them, of the kind which the young delight to see and hear when performed at sacrifices; and their own parents they saw showing the utmost zeal on behalf of themselves and their children in addressing the gods in prayers and supplications, as though they most certainly existed; and at the rising and setting of the sun and moon they heard and saw the prostrations and devotions of all the Greeks and barbarians, under all conditions of adversity and prosperity, directed to these luminaries, not as though they were not gods, but as though they

---

[82] All this discussion is supposed to have taken place on one and the same day,— hence the reference to "shortness of time."

most certainly were gods beyond the shadow of a doubt—all this evidence is contemned by these people, and that for no sufficient reason, as everyone endowed with a grain of sense would affirm; and so they are now forcing us to enter on our present argument. How, I ask, can one possibly use mild terms in admonishing such men, and at the same time teach them, to begin with, that the gods do exist? Yet one must bravely attempt the task; for it would never do for both parties to be enraged at once,—the one owing to greed for pleasure, the other with indignation at men like them.

So let our prefatory address to the men thus corrupted in mind be dispassionate in tone, and, quenching our passion, let us speak mildly, as though we were conversing with one particular person of the kind described, in the following terms: "My child, you are still young, and time as it advances will cause you to reverse many of the opinions you now hold: so wait till then before pronouncing judgment on matters of most grave importance; and of these the gravest of all—though at present you regard it as naught—is the question of holding a right view about the gods and so living well, or the opposite. Now in the first place, I should be saying what is irrefutably true if I pointed out to you this signal fact, that neither you by yourself nor yet your friends are the first and foremost to adopt this opinion about the gods; rather is it true that people who suffer from this disease are always springing up, in greater or less numbers. But I, who have met with many of these people, would declare this to you, that not a single man who from his youth has adopted this opinion, that the gods have no existence, has ever yet continued till old age constant in the same view; but the other two false notions about the gods do remain—not, indeed, with many, but still with some,—the notion, namely, that the gods exist, but pay no heed to human affairs, and the other notion that they do pay heed, but are easily won over by prayers and offerings. For a doctrine about them that is to prove the truest you can possibly form you will, if you take my advice, wait, considering the while whether the truth stands thus or otherwise, and making enquiries not only from all other men, but especially from the lawgiver; and in the meantime do not dare to be guilty of any impiety in respect of the gods. For it must be the endeavour of him who is legislating for you both now and hereafter to instruct you in the truth of these matters.

CLIN. Our statement thus far, Stranger, is most excellent.

ATH. Very true, O Megillus and Clinias; but we have plunged unawares into a wondrous argument.

CLIN. What is it you mean?

ATH. That which most people account to be the most scientific of all arguments.

CLIN. Explain more clearly.

ATH. It is stated by some that all things which are coming into existence, or have or will come into existence, do so partly by nature, partly by art, and partly owing to chance.

CLIN. Is it not a right statement?

ATH. It is likely, to be sure, that what men of science say is true. Anyhow, let us follow them up, and consider what it is that the people in their camp really intend.

CLIN. By all means let us do so.

ATH. It is evident, they assert, that the greatest and most beautiful things are the work of nature and of chance, and the lesser things that of art,—for art receives from nature the great and primary products as existing, and itself moulds and shapes all the smaller ones, which we commonly call "artificial."

CLIN. How do you mean?

ATH. I will explain it more clearly. Fire and water and earth and air, they say, all exist by nature and chance, and none of them by art; and by means of these, which are wholly inanimate, the bodies which come next—those, namely, of the earth, sun, moon and stars—have been brought into existence. It is by chance all these elements move, by the interplay of their respective forces, and according as they meet together and combine fittingly,—hot with cold, dry with moist, soft with hard, and all such necessary mixtures as result from the chance combination of these opposites,—in this way and by these means they have brought into being the whole Heaven and all that is in the Heaven, and all animals, too, and plants—after that all the seasons had arisen from these elements; and all this, as they assert, not owing to reason, nor to any god or art, but owing, as we have said, to nature and chance.[83] As a later product of these, art comes later; and it, being mortal

[83] This is a summary of the doctrines of the Atomists (Leucippus and Democritus) who denied the creative agency of Reason. Similar views were taught, later, by Epicurus and Lucretius.

itself and of mortal birth, begets later playthings which share but little in truth, being images of a sort akin to the arts themselves—images such as painting begets, and music, and the arts which accompany these. Those arts which really produce something serious are such as share their effect with nature,—like medicine, agriculture, and gymnastic. Politics too, as they say, shares to a small extent in nature, but mostly in art; and in like manner all legislation which is based on untrue assumptions is due, not to nature, but to art.

CLIN. What do you mean?

ATH. The first statement, my dear sir, which these people make about the gods is that they exist by art and not by nature,—by certain legal conventions which differ from place to place, according as each tribe agreed when forming their laws. They assert, moreover, that there is one class of things beautiful by nature, and another class beautiful by convention; while as to things just, they do not exist at all by nature, but men are constantly in dispute about them and continually altering them, and whatever alteration they make at any time is at that time authoritative, though it owes its existence to art and the laws, and not in any way to nature. All these, my friends, are views which young people imbibe from men of science, both prose-writers and poets, who maintain that the height of justice is to succeed by force; whence it comes that the young people are afflicted with a plague of impiety, as though the gods were not such as the law commands us to conceive them; and, because of this, factions also arise, when these teachers attract them towards the life that is right "according to nature," which consists in being master over the rest in reality, instead of being a slave to others according to legal convention.[84]

CLIN. What a horrible statement you have described, Stranger! And what widespread corruption of the young in private families as well as publicly in the States!

ATH. That is indeed true, Clinias. What, then, do you think the lawgiver ought to do, seeing that these people have been armed in this way for a long time past? Should he merely stand up in the

---

[84] The antithesis between "Nature" and "Conventions" was a familiar one in ethical and political discussions from the time of the Sophists. The supremacy of "Nature," as an ethical principle, was maintained (it is said) by Hippias and Prodicus; that of "Convention," by Protagoras and Gorgias: Plato goes behind both to the higher principle of Reason (νοῦς).

city and threaten all the people that unless they affirm that the
gods exist and conceive them in their minds to be such as the law
maintains; and so likewise with regard to the beautiful and the
just and all the greatest things, as many as relate to virtue and
vice, that they must regard and perform these in the way prescribed
by the lawgiver in his writings; and that whosoever fails to show
himself obedient to the laws must either be put to death or else be
punished, in one case by stripes and imprisonment, in another by
degradation, in others by poverty and exile? But as to persuasion,
should the lawgiver, while enacting the people's laws, refuse to
blend any persuasion with his statements, and thus tame them so
far as possible?

CLIN. Certainly not, Stranger; on the contrary, if persuasion
can be applied in such matters in even the smallest degree, no lawgiver who is of the slightest account must ever grow weary, but must
(as they say) "leave no stone unturned"[85] to reinforce the ancient
saying that gods exist, and all else that you recounted just now;
and law itself he must also defend and art, as things which exist by
nature or by a cause not inferior to nature, since according to right
reason they are the offspring of mind, even as you are now, as I
think, asserting; and I agree with you.

ATH. What now, my most ardent Clinias? Are not statements
thus made to the masses difficult for us to keep up with in argument, and do they not also involve us in arguments portentously
long?

CLIN. Well now, Stranger, if we had patience with ourselves
when we discoursed at such length on the subjects of drinking and
music, shall we not exercise patience in dealing with the gods and
similar subjects? Moreover, such a discourse is of the greatest help
for intelligent legislation, since legal ordinances when put in writing remain wholly unchanged, as though ready to submit to examination for all time, so that one need have no fear even if they are
hard to listen to at first, seeing that even the veriest dullard can
come back frequently to examine them, nor yet if they are lengthy,
provided that they are beneficial. Consequently, in my opinion,
it could not possibly be either reasonable or pious for any man to
refrain from lending his aid to such arguments to the best of his
power.

[85] Literally, "utter every voice" (leave nothing unsaid).

MEG. What Clinias says, Stranger, is, I think, most excellent.

ATH. Most certainly it is, Megillus; and we must do as he says. For if the assertions mentioned had not been sown broadcast well-nigh over the whole world of men, there would have been no need of counter-arguments to defend the existence of the gods; but as it is, they are necessary. For when the greatest laws are being destroyed by wicked men, who is more bound to come to their rescue than the lawgiver?

MEG. No one.

ATH. Come now, Clinias, do you also answer me again, for you too must take a hand in the argument: it appears that the person who makes these statements holds fire, water, earth and air to be the first of all things, and that it is precisely to these things that he gives the name of "nature," while soul he asserts to be a later product therefrom. Probably, indeed, he does not merely "appear" to do this, but actually makes it clear to us in his account.

CLIN. Certainly.

ATH. Can it be then, in Heaven's name, that now we have discovered, as it were, a very fountain-head of irrational opinion in all the men who have ever yet handled physical investigations? Consider, and examine each statement. For it is a matter of no small importance if it can be shown that those who handle impious arguments, and lead others after them, employ their arguments not only ill, but erroneously. And this seems to me to be the state of affairs.

CLIN. Well said; but try to explain wherein the error lies.

ATH. We shall probably have to handle rather an unusual argument.

CLIN. We must not shrink, Stranger. You think, I perceive, that we shall be traversing alien ground, outside legislation, if we handle such arguments. But if there is no other way in which it is possible for us to speak in concert with the truth, as now legally declared, except this way, then in this way, my good sir, we must speak.

ATH. It appears, then, that I may at once proceed with an argument that is somewhat unusual; it is this. That which is the first cause of becoming and perishing in all things, this is declared by the arguments which have produced the soul of the impious to be not first, but generated later, and that which is the later to be the earlier; and because of this they have fallen into error regarding the real nature of divine existence.

Clin. I do not yet understand.

Ath. As regards the soul, my comrade, nearly all men appear to be ignorant of its real nature and its potency, and ignorant not only of other facts about it, but of its origin especially,—how that it is one of the first existences, and prior to all bodies, and that it more than anything else is what governs all the changes and modifications of bodies. And if this is really the state of the case, must not things which are akin to soul be necessarily prior in origin to things which belong to body, seeing that soul is older than body?[86]

Clin. Necessarily.

Ath. Then opinion and reflection and thought and art and law will be prior to things hard and soft and heavy and light; and further, the works and actions that are great and primary will be those of art, while those that are natural, and nature itself,—which they wrongly call by this name—will be secondary, and will derive their origin from art and reason.

Clin. How are they wrong?

Ath. By "nature" they intend to indicate production of things primary; but if soul shall be shown to have been produced first (not fire or air), but soul first and foremost,—it would most truly be described as a superlatively "natural" existence. Such is the state of the case, provided that one can prove that soul is older than body, but not otherwise.

Clin. Most true.

Ath. Shall we then, in the next place, address ourselves to the task of proving this?

Clin. Certainly.

Ath. Let us guard against a wholly deceitful argument, lest haply it seduce us who are old with its specious youthfulness, and then elude us and make us a laughing-stock, and so we get the reputation of missing even little things while aiming at big things. Consider then. Suppose that we three had to cross a river that was in violent flood, and that I, being the youngest of the party and having often had experience of currents, were to suggest that the proper course is for me to make an attempt first by myself—leaving you two in safety—to see whether it is possible for you older men also to cross, or how the matter stands, and then, if the river proved to be clearly fordable, I were to call you, and, by my experience, help

[86] Cp. *Timaeus* 34 D.

you across, while if it proved impassable for such as you, in that case the risk should be wholly mine,—such a suggestion on my part would have sounded reasonable. So too in the present instance; the argument now in front of us is too violent, and probably impassable, for such strength as you possess; so, lest it make you faint and dizzy as it rushes past and poses you with questions you are unused to answering, and thus causes an unpleasing lack of shapeliness and seemliness, I think that I ought now to act in the way described—question myself first, while you remain listening in safety, and then return answer to myself, and in this way proceed through the whole argument until it has discussed in full the subject of soul, and demonstrated that soul is prior to body.

CLIN. Your suggestion, Stranger, we think excellent; so do as you suggest.

ATH. Come then,—if ever we ought to invoke God's aid, now is the time it ought to be done. Let the gods be invoked with all zeal to aid in the demonstration of their own existence. And let us hold fast, so to speak, to a safe cable as we embark on the present discussion. And it is safest, as it seems to me, to adopt the following method of reply when questions such as this are put on these subjects; for instance, when a man asks me—"Do all things stand still, Stranger, and nothing move? Or is the exact opposite the truth? Or do some things move and some remain at rest?" My answer will be, "Some things move, others remain at rest." "Then do not the standing things stand, and the moving things move, in a certain place?" "Of course." "And some will do this in one location, and others in several." "You mean," we will say, "that those which have the quality of being at rest at the centre move in one location, as when the circumference of circles that are said to stand still revolves?" "Yes. And we perceive that motion of this kind, which simultaneously turns in this revolution both the largest circle and the smallest, distributes itself to small and great proportionally, altering in proportion its own quantity; whereby it functions as the source of all such marvels as result from its supplying great and small circles simultaneously with harmonizing rates of slow and fast speeds—a condition of things that one might suppose to be impossible." "Quite true." "And by things moving in several places you seem to me to mean all things that move by locomotion, continually passing from one spot to another, and sometimes rest-ing on one axis and sometimes, by revolving, on several axes. And whenever one such object meets another, if the other is at rest, the moving object is split up; but if they collide with others moving to meet them from an opposite direction, they form a combination which is midway between the two." "Yes, I affirm that these things are so, just as you describe." "Further, things increase when combined and decrease when separated in all cases where the regular constitution of each persists; but if this does not remain, then both these conditions cause them to perish. And what is the condition which must occur in everything to bring about generation? Obviously whenever a starting-principle receiving increase comes to the second change, and from this to the next, and on coming to the third admits of perception by percipients. Everything comes into being by this process of change and alteration; and a thing is really existent whenever it remains fixed, but when it changes into another constitution it is utterly destroyed." Have we now, my friends, mentioned all the forms of motion, capable of numerical classification,[87] save only two?

CLIN. What two?

ATH. Those, my good sir, for the sake of which, one may say, the whole of our present enquiry was undertaken.

CLIN. Explain more clearly.

ATH. It was undertaken, was it not, for the sake of soul?

CLIN. Certainly.

ATH. As one of the two let us count that motion which is always able to move other things, but unable to move itself; and that motion which always is able to move both itself and other things,—by way of combination and separation, of increase and decrease, of generation and corruption,—let us count as another separate unit in the total number of motions.

CLIN. Be it so.

ATH. Thus we shall reckon as ninth on the list that motion which always moves another object and is moved by another; while that motion which moves both itself and another, and which is harmoniously adapted to all forms of action and passion, and is termed

---

[87] The eight kinds of motion here indicated are—(1) circular motion round a fixed centre; (2) locomotion (gliding or rolling); (3) combination; (4) separation; (5) increase; (6) decrease; (7) becoming; (8) perishing. The remaining two kinds (as described below) are—(9) other-affecting motion (or secondary causation); and (10) self-and-other-affecting motion (or primary causation).

the real change and motion of all that really exists,—it, I presume, we shall call the tenth.

CLIN. Most certainly.

ATH. Of our total of ten motions, which shall we most correctly adjudge to be the most powerful of all and excelling in effectiveness?

CLIN. We are bound to affirm that the motion which is able to move itself excels infinitely, and that all the rest come after it.

ATH. Well said. Must we, then, alter one or two of the wrong statements we have now made?

CLIN. Which do you mean?

ATH. Our statement about the tenth seems wrong.

CLIN. How?

ATH. Logically it is first in point of origin and power; and the next one is second to it, although we absurdly called it ninth a moment ago.

CLIN. What do you mean?

ATH. This: when we find one thing changing another, and this in turn another, and so on,—of these things shall we ever find one that is the prime cause of change? How will a thing that is moved by another ever be itself the first of the things that cause change? It is impossible. But when a thing that has moved itself changes another thing, and that other a third, and the motion thus spreads progressively through thousands upon thousands of things, will the primary source of all their motions be anything else than the movement of that which has moved itself?

CLIN. Excellently put, and we must assent to your argument.

ATH. Further, let us question and answer ourselves thus:—Supposing that the Whole of things were to unite and stand still,—as most of these thinkers[88] venture to maintain,—which of the motions mentioned would necessarily arise in it first? That motion, of course, which is self-moving; for it will never be shifted beforehand by another thing, since no shifting force exists in things beforehand. Therefore we shall assert that inasmuch as the self-moving motion is the starting-point of all motions and the first to arise in things at rest and to exist in things in motion, it is of necessity the most

[88] E.g. Anaxagoras, who taught, originally, "all things were together"; and the Eleatic School (Parmenides, etc.) asserted that the Real World is One and motionless.

ancient and potent change of all, while the motion which is altered by another thing and itself moves others comes second.

CLIN. Most true.

ATH. Now that we have come to this point in our discourse, here is a question we may answer.

CLIN. What is it?

ATH. If we should see that this motion had arisen in a thing of earth or water or fire, whether separate or in combination, what condition should we say exists in such a thing?

CLIN. What you ask me is, whether we are to speak of a thing as "alive" when it moves itself?

ATH. Yes.

CLIN. It is alive, to be sure.

ATH. Well then, when we see soul in things, must we not equally agree that they are alive?

CLIN. We must.

ATH. Now stop a moment, in Heaven's name! Would you not desire to observe three points about every object?

CLIN. What do you mean?

ATH. One point is the substance, one the definition of the substance, and one the name;[89] and, moreover, about everything that exists there are two questions to be asked.

CLIN. How two?

ATH. At one time each of us, propounding the name by itself, demands the definition; at another, propounding the definition by itself, he demands the name.

CLIN. Is it something of this kind we mean now to convey?

ATH. Of what kind?

CLIN. We have instances of a thing divisible into two halves, both in arithmetic and elsewhere; in arithmetic the name of this is "the even," and the definition is "a number divisible into two equal parts."

ATH. Yes, that is what I mean. So in either case it is the same object, is it not, which we describe, whether, when asked for the definition, we reply by giving the name, or, when asked for the name, we give the definition,—describing one and the same object by the name "even," and by the definition "a number divisible into two halves"?

[89] Cp. *Epistle* 7, 342 A, B.

CLIN. Most certainly.

ATH. What is the definition of that object which has for its name "soul"? Can we give it any other definition than that stated just now—"the motion able to move itself"?

CLIN. Do you assert that "self-movement" is the definition of that very same substance which has "soul" as the name we universally apply to it?

ATH. That is what I assert. And if this be really so, do we still complain that it has not been sufficiently proved that soul is identical with the prime origin and motion of what is, has been, and shall be, and of all that is opposite to these, seeing that it has been plainly shown to be the cause of all change and motion in all things?

CLIN. We make no such complaint; on the contrary, it has been proved most sufficiently that soul is of all things the oldest, since it is the first principle of motion.

ATH. Then is not that motion which, when it arises in one object, is caused by another, and which never supplies self-motion to anything, second in order—or indeed as far down the list as one cares to put it,—it being the change of a really soulless body?

CLIN. True.

ATH. Truly and finally, then, it would be a most veracious and complete statement to say that we find soul to be prior to body, and body secondary and posterior, soul governing and body being governed according to the ordinance of nature.

CLIN. Yes, most veracious.

ATH. We recollect, of course, that we previously agreed[90] that if soul could be shown to be older than body, then the things of soul also will be older than those of body.

CLIN. Certainly we do.

ATH. Moods and dispositions and wishes and calculations and true opinions and considerations and memories will be prior to bodily length, breadth, depth and strength, if soul is prior to body.

CLIN. Necessarily.

ATH. Must we then necessarily agree, in the next place, that soul is the cause of things good and bad, fair and foul, just and unjust, and all the opposites, if we are to assume it to be the cause of all things?

[90] 892 A, B.

CLIN. Of course we must.

ATH. And as soul thus controls and indwells in all things everywhere that are moved, must we not necessarily affirm that it controls Heaven also?

CLIN. Yes.

ATH. One soul, is it, or several? I will answer for you—"several." Anyhow, let us assume not less than two—the beneficent soul and that which is capable of effecting results of the opposite kind.

CLIN. You are perfectly right.

ATH. Very well, then. Soul drives all things in Heaven and earth and sea by its own motions, of which the names are wish, reflection, forethought, counsel, opinion true and false, joy, grief, confidence, fear, hate, love, and all the motions that are akin to these or are prime-working motions; these, when they take over the secondary motions of bodies, drive them all to increase and decrease and separation and combination,[91] and, supervening on these, to heat and cold, heaviness and lightness, hardness and softness, whiteness and blackness, bitterness and sweetness, and all those qualities which soul employs, both when it governs all things rightly and happily as a true goddess, in conjunction with reason, and when, in converse with unreason, it produces results which are in all respects the opposite. Shall we postulate that this is so, or do we still suspect that it may possibly be otherwise?

CLIN. By no means.

ATH. Which kind of soul, then, shall we say is in control of Heaven and earth and the whole circle? That which is wise and full of goodness, or that which has neither quality? To this shall we make reply as follows?

CLIN. How?

ATH. If, my good sir, we are to assert that the whole course and motion of Heaven and of all it contains have a motion like to the motion and revolution and reckonings of reason, and proceed in a kindred manner, then clearly we must assert that the best soul regulates the whole cosmos and drives it on its course, which is of the kind described.

CLIN. You are right.

ATH. But the bad soul, if it proceeds in a mad and disorderly way.

[91] Cp. 894 B, C.

CLIN. That also is right.

ATH. Then what is the nature of the motion of reason? Here, my friends, we come to a question that is difficult to answer wisely; consequently, it is fitting that you should now call me in to assist you with the answer.

CLIN. Very good.

ATH. In making our answer let us not bring on night, as it were, at midday, by looking right in the eye of the sun, as though with mortal eyes we could ever behold reason and know it fully; the safer way to behold the object with which our question is concerned is by looking at an image of it.

CLIN. How do you mean?

ATH. Let us take as an image that one of the ten motions which reason resembles; reminding ourselves of which[92] I, along with you, will make answer.

CLIN. You will probably speak admirably.

ATH. Do we still recollect thus much about the things then described, that we assumed that, of the total, some were in motion, others at rest?

CLIN. Yes.

ATH. And further, that, of those in motion, some move in one place, others move in several places?

CLIN. That is so.

ATH. And that, of these two motions, the motion which moves in one place must necessarily move always round some centre, being a copy of the turned wheels; and that this has the nearest possible kinship and similarity to the revolution of reason?

CLIN. How do you mean?

ATH. If we described them both as moving regularly and uniformly in the same spot, round the same things and in relation to the same things, according to one rule and system—reason, namely, and the motion that spins in one place (likened to the spinning of a turned globe),—we should never be in danger of being deemed unskilful in the construction of fair images by speech.

CLIN. Most true.

ATH. On the other hand, will not the motion that is never uniform or regular or in the same place or around or in relation to the

---

[92] Cp. 893 B ff.; the motion to which reason is likened is the first of the ten.

same things, not moving in one spot nor in any order or system or rule—will not this motion be akin to absolute unreason?

Clin. It will, in very truth.

Ath. So now there is no longer any difficulty in stating expressly that, inasmuch as soul is what we find driving everything round, we must affirm that this circumference of Heaven is of necessity driven round under the care and ordering of either the best soul or its opposite.

Clin. But, Stranger, judging by what has now been said, it is actually impious to make any other assertion than that these things are driven round by one or more souls endowed with all goodness.

Ath. You have attended to our argument admirably, Clinias. Now attend to this further point.

Clin. What is that?

Ath. If soul drives round the sum total of sun, moon and all other stars, does it not also drive each single one of them?

Clin. Certainly.

Ath. Then let us construct an argument about one of these stars which will evidently apply equally to them all.

Clin. About which one?

Ath. The sun's body is seen by everyone, its soul by no one. And the same is true of the soul of any other body, whether alive or dead, of living beings. There is, however, a strong suspicion that this class of object, which is wholly imperceptible to sense, has grown round all the senses of the body, and is an object of reason alone. Therefore by reason and rational thought let us grasp this fact about it,—

Clin. What fact?

Ath. If soul drives round the sun, we shall be tolerably sure to be right in saying that it does one of three things.

Clin. What things?

Ath. That either it exists everywhere inside of this apparent globular body and directs it, such as it is, just as the soul in us moves us about in all ways; or, having procured itself a body of fire or air (as some argue), it in the form of body pushes forcibly on the body from outside; or, thirdly, being itself void of body, but endowed with other surpassingly marvellous potencies, it conducts the body.

CLIN. Yes, it must necessarily be the case that soul acts in one of these ways when it propels all things.

ATH. Here, I pray you, pause. This soul,—whether it is by riding in the car of the sun,[93] or from outside, or otherwise, that it brings light to us all—every man is bound to regard as a god. Is not that so?

CLIN. Yes; everyone at least who has not reached the uttermost verge of folly.

ATH. Concerning all the stars and the moon, and concerning the years and months and all seasons, what other account shall we give than this very same,—namely, that, inasmuch as it has been shown that they are all caused by one or more souls, which are good also with all goodness, we shall declare these souls to be gods, whether it be that they order the whole heaven by residing in bodies, as living creatures, or whatever the mode and method? Is there any man that agrees with this view who will stand hearing it denied that "all things are full of gods"?[94]

CLIN. There is not a man, Stranger, so wrong-headed as that.

ATH. Let us, then, lay down limiting conditions for the man who up till now disbelieves in gods, O Megillus and Clinias, and so be quit of him.

CLIN. What conditions?

ATH. That either he must teach us that we are wrong in laying down that soul is of all things the first production, together with all the consequential statements we made,—or, if he is unable to improve on our account, he must believe us, and for the rest of his life live in veneration of the gods. Let us, then, consider whether our argument for the existence of the gods addressed to those who disbelieve in them has been stated adequately or defectively.

CLIN. Anything rather than defectively, Stranger.

ATH. Then let our argument have an end, in so far as it is addressed to these men. But the man who holds that gods exist, but pay no regard to human affairs,—him we must admonish. "My good sir," let us say, "the fact that you believe in gods is due probably to a divine kinship drawing you to what is of like nature, to honour it and recognise its existence; but the fortunes of evil and

[93] Cp. *Timaeus* 41 D, E, where the Creator is said to apportion a soul to each star, in which it rides "as though in a chariot."

[94] A dictum of Thales.

unjust men, both private and public,—which, though not really happy, are excessively and improperly lauded as happy by public opinion,—drive you to impiety by the wrong way in which they are celebrated, not only in poetry, but in tales of every kind. Or again, when you see men attaining the goal of old age, and leaving behind them children's children in the highest offices, very likely you are disturbed, when amongst the number of these you discover —whether from hearsay or from your own personal observation— some who have been guilty of many dreadful impieties, and who, just because of these, have risen from a small position to royalty and the highest rank; then the consequence of all this clearly is that, since on the one hand you are unwilling to hold the gods responsible for such things because of your kinship to them, and since on the other hand you are driven by lack of logic and inability to repudiate the gods, you have come to your present morbid state of mind, in which you opine that the gods exist, but scorn and neglect human affairs. In order, therefore, that your present opinion may not grow to a greater height of morbid impiety, but that we may succeed in repelling the onset of its pollution (if haply we are able) by argument, let us endeavour to attach our next argument to that which we set forth in full to him who utterly disbelieves in gods, and thereby to employ the latter as well." And do you, Clinias and Megillus, take the part of the young man in answering, as you did before; and should anything untoward occur in the course of the argument, I will make answer for you, as I did just now, and convey you across the stream.[95]

CLIN. A good suggestion! We will do our best to carry it out; and do you do likewise.

ATH. Well, there will probably be no difficulty in proving to this man that the gods care for small things no less than for things superlatively great. For, of course, he was present at our recent argument, and heard that the gods, being good with all goodness, possess such care of the whole as is most proper to themselves.

CLIN. Most certainly he heard that.

ATH. Let us join next in enquiring what is that goodness of theirs in respect of which we agree that they are good. Come now, do we say that prudence and the possession of reason are parts of goodness, and the opposites of these of badness?

[95] Cp. 892 D, E.

CLIN. We do say so.

ATH. And further, that courage is part of goodness, and cowardice of badness?

CLIN. Certainly.

ATH. And shall we say that some of these are foul, others fair?

CLIN. Necessarily.

ATH. And shall we say that all such as are mean belong to us, if to anyone, whereas the gods have no share in any such things, great or small?

CLIN. To this, too, everyone would assent.

ATH. Well then, shall we reckon neglect, idleness and indolence as goodness of soul? Or how say you?

CLIN. How could we?

ATH. As the opposite, then?

CLIN. Yes.

ATH. And the opposites of these as of the opposite quality of soul?

CLIN. Of the opposite quality.

ATH. What then? He who is indolent, careless and idle will be in our eyes what the poet described—"a man most like to sting-less drones"?

CLIN. A most true description.

ATH. That God has such a character we must certainly deny, seeing that he hates it; nor must we allow anyone to attempt to say so.

CLIN. We could not possibly allow that.

ATH. When a person whose duty it is especially to act and care for some object has a mind that cares for great things, but neglects small things, on what principle could we praise such a person without the utmost impropriety? Let us consider the matter in this way: the action of him who acts thus, be he god or man, takes one of two forms, does it not?

CLIN. What forms?

ATH. Either because he thinks that neglect of the small things makes no difference to the whole, or else, owing to laziness and indolence, he neglects them, though he thinks they do make a difference. Or is there any other way in which neglect occurs? For when it is impossible to care for all things, it will not in that case be neglect of great things or small when a person—be he god or common man—fails to care for things which he lacks the power and capacity to care for.

CLIN. Of course not.

ATH. Now to us three let these two men make answer, of whom both agree that gods exist, but the one asserts that they can be bribed, and the other that they neglect the small. First, you both assert that the gods know and hear and see all things, and that nothing of all that is apprehended by senses or sciences can escape their notice; do you assert that this is so, or what?

CLIN. That is what we assert.[96]

ATH. And further, that they can do all that can be done by mortal or immortal?

CLIN. They will, of course, admit that this also is the case.

ATH. And it is undeniable that all five of us agreed that the gods are good, yea, exceeding good.

CLIN. Most certainly.

ATH. Being, then, such as we agree, is it not impossible to allow that they do anything at all in a lazy and indolent way? For certainly amongst us mortals idleness is the child of cowardice, and laziness of idleness and indolence.

CLIN. Very true.

ATH. None, then, of the gods is neglectful owing to idleness and laziness, seeing that none has any part in cowardice.

CLIN. You are very right.

ATH. Further, if they do neglect the small and scant things of the All, they will do so either because they know that there is no need at all to care for any such things or—well, what other alternative is there except the opposite of knowing?

CLIN. There is none.

ATH. Shall we then assume, my worthy and excellent sir, that you assert that the gods are ignorant, and that it is through ignorance that they are neglectful when they ought to be showing care, —or that they know indeed what is needful, yet act as the worst of men are said to do, who, though they know that other things are better to do than what they are doing, yet do them not, owing to their being somehow defeated by pleasures or pains?

CLIN. Impossible.

[96] Here, and in what follows, Clinias is answering on behalf of the two misbelievers.

ATH. Do not human affairs share in animate nature, and is not man himself, too, the most god-fearing of all living creatures?

CLIN. That is certainly probable.

ATH. We affirm that all mortal creatures are possessions of the gods, to whom belongs also the whole heaven.

CLIN. Of course.

ATH. That being so, it matters not whether a man says that these things are small or great in the eyes of the gods; for in neither case would it behove those who are our owners to be neglectful, seeing that they are most careful and most good. For let us notice this further fact—

CLIN. What is it?

ATH. In regard to perception and power,—are not these two naturally opposed in respect of ease and difficulty?

CLIN. How do you mean?

ATH. It is more difficult to see and hear small things than great; but everyone finds it more easy to move, control and care for things small and few than their opposites.

CLIN. Much more.

ATH. When a physician is charged with the curing of a whole body, if, while he is willing and able to care for the large parts, he neglects the small parts and members, will he ever find the whole in good condition?

CLIN. Certainly not.

ATH. No more will pilots or generals or house-managers, nor yet statesmen or any other such persons, find that the many and great thrive apart from the few and small; for even masons say that big stones are not well laid without little stones.

CLIN. They cannot be.

ATH. Let us never suppose that God is inferior to mortal crafts-men who, the better they are, the more accurately and perfectly do they execute their proper tasks, small and great, by one single art, —or that God, who is most wise, and both willing and able to care, cares not at all for the small things which are the easier to care for— like one who shirks the labour because he is idle and cowardly,—but only for the great.

CLIN. By no means let us accept such an opinion of the gods, Stranger: that would be to adopt a view that is neither pious nor true at all.

ATH. And now, as I think, we have argued quite sufficiently with him who loves to censure the gods for neglect.

CLIN. Yes.

ATH. And it was by forcing him by our arguments to acknowledge that what he says is wrong. But still he needs also, as it seems to me, some words of counsel to act as a charm upon him.

CLIN. What kind of words, my good sir?

ATH. Let us persuade the young man by our discourse that all things are ordered systematically by Him who cares for the World-all with a view to the preservation and excellence of the Whole, whereof also each part, so far as it can, does and suffers what is proper to it. To each of these parts, down to the smallest fraction, rulers of their action and passion are appointed to bring about fulfilment even to the uttermost fraction; whereof thy portion also, O perverse man, is one, and tends therefore always in its striving towards the All, tiny though it be. But thou failest to perceive that all partial generation is for the sake of the Whole, in order that for the life of the World-all blissful existence may be secured,—it not being generated for thy sake, but thou for its sake. For every physician and every trained craftsman works always for the sake of a Whole, and strives after what is best in general, and he produces a part for the sake of a whole, and not a whole for the sake of a part; but thou art vexed, because thou knowest not how what is best in thy case for the All turns out best for thyself also, in accordance with the power of your common origin. And inasmuch as soul, being conjoined now with one body, now with another, is always undergoing all kinds of changes either of itself or owing to another soul, there is left for the draughts-player no further task,—save only to shift the character that grows better to a superior place, and the worse to a worse, according to what best suits each of them, so that to each may be allotted its appropriate destiny.

CLIN. In what way do you mean?

ATH. The way I am describing is, I believe, that in which supervision of all things is most easy for the gods. For if one were to shape all things, without a constant view to the Whole, by transforming them (as, for instance, fire into water), instead of merely converting one into many or many into one, then when things had shared in a first, or second, or even third generation,[97] they would

[97] This seems to refer to three stages of the soul's incarnation.

be countless in number in such a system of transformations; but as things are, the task before the Supervisor of the All is wondrous easy.

CLIN. How do you mean?

ATH. Thus:—Since our King saw that all actions involve soul, and contain much good and much evil, and that body and soul are, when generated, indestructible but not eternal,[98] as are the gods ordained by law (for if either soul or body had been destroyed, there would never have been generation of living creatures), and since He perceived that all soul that is good naturally tends always to benefit, but the bad to injure,—observing all this, He designed a location for each of the parts, wherein it might secure the victory of goodness in the Whole and the defeat of evil most completely, easily, and well. For this purpose He has designed the rule which prescribes what kind of character should be set to dwell in what kind of position and in what regions; but the causes of the generation of any special kind he left to the wills of each one of us men. For according to the trend of our desires and the nature of our souls, each one of us generally becomes of a corresponding character.

CLIN. That is certainly probable.

ATH. All things that share in soul change, since they possess within themselves the cause of change, and in changing they move according to the law and order of destiny; the smaller the change of character, the less is the movement over surface in space, but when the change is great and towards great iniquity, then they move towards the deep and the so-called lower regions, regarding which— under the names of Hades and the like—men are haunted by most fearful imaginings, both when alive and when disparted from their bodies. And whenever the soul gets a specially large share of either virtue or vice, owing to the force of its own will and the influence of its intercourse growing strong, then, if it is in union with divine virtue, it becomes thereby eminently virtuous, and moves to an eminent region, being transported by a holy road to another and a better region; whereas, if the opposite is the case, it changes to the opposite the location of its life's abode. "This is the just decree of the gods who inhabit Olympus," O thou child and stripling who

[98] Cp. *Timaeus* 42 B ff. where it is said that the soul of the good man returns at death to its native star, while that of the bad takes the form of a woman in its second, and that of a beast in its third incarnation.

thinkest thou art neglected by the gods,—the decree that as thou becomest worse, thou goest to the company of the worse souls, and as thou becomest better, to the better souls; and that, alike in life and in every shape of death, thou both doest and sufferest what it is befitting that like should do towards like. From this decree of Heaven neither wilt thou nor any other luckless wight ever boast that he has escaped; for this decree is one which the gods who have enjoined it have enjoined above all others, and meet it is that it should be most strictly observed. For by it thou wilt not ever be neglected, neither if thou shouldest dive, in thy very littleness, into the depths of the earth below, nor if thou shouldest soar up to the height of Heaven above; but thou shalt pay to the gods thy due penalty, whether thou remainest here on earth, or hast passed away to Hades, or art transported to a region yet more fearsome. And the same rule, let me tell thee, will apply also to those whom thou sawest growing to great estate from small after doing acts of impiety or other such evil,—concerning whom thou didst deem that they had risen from misery to happiness, and didst imagine, therefore, that in their actions, as in mirrors, thou didst behold the entire neglect of the gods, not knowing of their joint contribution and how it contributes to the All. And surely, O most courageous of men, thou canst not but suppose that this is a thing thou must needs learn. For if a man learns not this, he can never see even an outline of the truth, nor will he be able to contribute an account of life as regards its happiness or its unhappy fortune. If Clinias here and all our gathering of elders succeed in convincing thee of this fact, that thou knowest not what thou sayest about the gods, then God Himself of His grace will aid thee; but shouldest thou still be in need of further argument, give ear to us while we argue with the third unbeliever, if thou hast sense at all. For we have proved, as I would maintain, by fairly sufficient argument that the gods exist and care for men; the next contention, that the gods can be won over by wrongdoers, on the receipt of bribes, is one that no one should admit, and we must try to refute it by every means in our power.

CLIN. Admirably spoken: let us do as you say.

ATH. Come now, in the name of these gods themselves I ask—in what way would they come to be seduced by us, if seduced they were? Being what in their essence and character? Necessarily they must be rulers, if they are to be in continual control of the whole heaven.

CLIN. True.

ATH. But to which kind of rulers are they like? Or which are like to them, of those rulers whom we can fairly compare with them, as small with great? Would drivers of rival teams resemble them, or pilots of ships? Or perhaps they might be likened to rulers of armies; or possibly they might be compared to physicians watching over a war against bodily disease, or to farmers fearfully awaiting seasons of wonted difficulty for the generation of plants, or else to masters of flocks. For seeing that we have agreed among ourselves that the heaven is full of many things that are good, and of the opposite kind also, and that those not good are the more numerous, such a battle, we affirm, is undying, and needs a wondrous watchfulness,—the gods and daemons being our allies, and we the possession of the gods and daemons; and what destroys us is iniquity and insolence combined with folly, what saves us, justice and temperance combined with wisdom, which dwell in the animate powers of the gods, and of which some small trace may be clearly seen here also residing in us. But there are certain souls that dwell on earth and have acquired unjust gain which, being plainly bestial, beseech the souls of the guardians—whether they be watchdogs or herdsmen or the most exalted of masters—trying to convince them by fawning words and prayerful incantations that (as the tales of evil men relate) they can profiteer among men on earth without any severe penalty: but we assert that the sin now mentioned, of profiteering or "over-gaining," is what is called in the case of fleshly bodies "disease,"[99] in that of seasons and years "pestilence," and in that of States and polities, by a verbal change, this same sin is called "injustice."

CLIN. Certainly.

ATH. Such must necessarily be the account of the matter given by the man who says that the gods are always merciful to unjust men and those who act unjustly, provided that one gives them a share of one's unjust gains; it is just as if wolves were to give small

---

[99] Cp. *Republic* 609, *Symposium* 188 A ff., where the theory is stated that health depends upon the "harmony," or equal balance, of the constituent elements of the body ("heat" and "cold," "moisture" and "dryness,"); when any of these (opposite) elements is in excess disease sets in. So, too, in the "body politic," the excess of due measure by any element, or member, is injustice.

bits of their prey to watch-dogs, and they being mollified by the gifts were to allow them to go ravening among the flocks. Is not this the account given by the man who asserts that the gods are open to bribes?

CLIN. It is.

ATH. To which of the guardians aforementioned might a man liken the gods without incurring ridicule? Is it to pilots, who, when warped themselves by wine's "flow and flavour," overturn both ships and sailors?

CLIN. By no means.

ATH. And surely not to drivers ranged up for a race and seduced by a gift to lose it in favour of other teams?

CLIN. If that was the account you gave of them, it would indeed be a horrible comparison.

ATH. Nor, surely, to generals or physicians or farmers or herdsmen; nor yet to dogs charmed by wolves?

CLIN. Hush! That is quite impossible.

ATH. Are not all gods the greatest of all guardians, and over the greatest things?

CLIN. Yes, by far.

ATH. Shall we say that those who watch over the fairest things, and who are themselves eminently good at keeping watch, are inferior to dogs and ordinary men, who would never betray justice for the sake of gifts impiously offered by unjust men?

CLIN. By no means; it is an intolerable thing to say, and whoever embraces such an opinion would most justly be adjudged the worst and most impious of all the impious men who practice impiety in all its forms.

ATH. May we now say that we have fully proved our three propositions,—namely, that the gods exist, and that they are careful, and that they are wholly incapable of being seduced to transgress justice?

CLIN. Certainly we may; and in these statements you have our support.

ATH. And truly they have been made in somewhat vehement terms, in our desire for victory over those wicked men; and our desire for victory was due to our fear lest haply, if they gained the mastery in argument, they should suppose they had gained the right to act as they chose—those men who wickedly hold all those false notions about the gods. On this account we have been zealous to speak with special vigour; and if we have produced any good effect, however small, in the way of persuading the men to hate themselves and to feel some love for an opposite kind of character, then our prelude to the laws respecting impiety will not have been spoken amiss.

CLIN. Well, there is hope; and if not, at any rate no fault will be found with the lawgiver in respect of the nature of the argument.

ATH. After the prelude it will be proper for us to have a statement of a kind suitable to serve as the laws' interpreter, forewarning all the impious to quit their ways for those of piety. For those who disobey, this shall be the law concerning impiety:—If anyone commits impiety either by word or deed, he that meets with him shall defend the law by informing the magistrates, and the first magistrates who hear of it shall bring the man up before the court appointed to decide such cases as the laws direct; and if any magistrate on hearing of the matter fail to do this, he himself shall be liable to a charge of impiety at the hands of him who wishes to punish him on behalf of the laws. And if a man be convicted, the court shall assess one penalty for each separate act of impiety. Imprisonment shall be imposed in every case; and since there are three prisons in the State (namely, one public prison near the market for most cases, to secure the persons of the average criminals; a second, situated near the assembly-room of the officials who hold nightly assemblies,[100] and named the "reformatory"; and a third situated in the middle of the country, in the wildest and loneliest spot possible, and named after "retribution"), and since men are involved in impiety from the three causes which we have described, and from each such cause two forms of impiety result—consequently those who sin in respect of religion fall into six classes which require to be distinguished, as needing penalties that are neither equal nor similar. For while those who, though they utterly disbelieve in the existence of the gods, possess by nature a just character, both hate the evil and, because of their dislike of injustice, are incapable of being induced to commit unjust actions, and flee from unjust men and love the just, on the other hand, those who, besides holding that the world is empty of gods, are afflicted by incontinence in respect of pleasures and pains, and possess also powerful memories and sharp

[100] Cp. 909 A, 961 A ff.

wits—though both these classes share alike in the disease of atheism, yet in respect of the amount of ruin they bring on other people, the latter class would work more and the former less of evil. For whereas the one class will be quite frank in its language about the gods and about sacrifices and oaths, and by ridiculing other people will probably convert others to its views, unless it meets with punishment, the other class, while holding the same opinions as the former, yet being specially "gifted by nature" and being full of craft and guile, is the class out of which are manufactured many diviners and experts in all manner of jugglery; and from it, too, there spring sometimes tyrants and demagogues and generals, and those who plot by means of peculiar mystic rites of their own, and the devices of those who are called "sophists." Of these there may be many kinds; but those which call for legislation are two, of which the "ironic"[101] kind commits sins that deserve not one death only or two, while the other kind requires both admonition and imprisonment. Likewise also the belief that the gods are neglectful breeds two other kinds of impiety; and the belief in their being open to bribes, other two. These kinds being thus distinguished, those criminals who suffer from folly, being devoid of evil disposition and character, shall be placed by the judge according to law in the reformatory for a period of not less than five years, during which time no other of the citizens shall hold intercourse with them, save only those who take part in the nocturnal assembly,[102] and they shall company with them to minister to their souls' salvation by admonition; and when the period of their incarceration has expired, if any of them seems to be reformed, he shall dwell with those who are reformed, but if not, and if he be convicted again on a like charge, he shall be punished by death. But as to all those who have become like ravening beasts, and who, besides holding that the gods are negligent or open to bribes, despise men, charming the souls of many of the living, and claiming that they charm the souls of the dead, and promising to persuade the gods by bewitching them, as it were, with sacrifices, prayers and incantations,[103] and who try thus to wreck utterly not

---

[101] *I.e.* "hypocritical," hiding impiety under a cloak of religion.

[102] Cp. 908 A.

[103] Cp. 933 A, *Rep.* 364 B ff.

only individuals, but whole families and States for the sake of money,—if any of these men be pronounced guilty, the court shall order him to be imprisoned according to law in the mid-country gaol, and shall order that no free man shall approach such criminals at any time, and that they shall receive from the servants a ration of food as fixed by the Law-wardens. And he that dies shall be cast outside the borders without burial; and if any free man assist in burying him, he shall be liable to a charge of impiety at the hands of anyone who chooses to prosecute. And if the dead man leaves children fit for citizenship, the guardians of orphans shall take them also under their charge from the day of their father's conviction, just as much as any other orphans.

For all these offenders one general law must be laid down, such as will cause the majority of them not only to offend less against the gods by word and deed, but also to become less foolish, through being forbidden to trade in religion illegally. To deal comprehensively with all such cases the following law shall be enacted:—No one shall possess a shrine in his own house: when anyone is moved in spirit to do sacrifice, he shall go to the public places to sacrifice, and he shall hand over his oblations to the priests and priestesses to whom belongs the consecration thereof; and he himself, together with any associates he may choose, shall join in the prayers. This procedure shall be observed for the following reasons:—It is no easy task to found temples and gods, and to do this rightly needs much deliberation; yet it is customary for all women especially, and for sick folk everywhere, and those in peril or in distress (whatever the nature of the distress), and conversely for those who have had a slice of good fortune, to dedicate whatever happens to be at hand at the moment, and to vow sacrifices and promise the founding of shrines to gods and demi-gods and children of gods; and through terrors caused by waking visions or by dreams, and in like manner as they recall many visions and try to provide remedies for each of them, they are wont to found altars and shrines, and to fill with them every house and every village, and open places too, and every spot which was the scene of such experiences. For all these reasons their action should be governed by the law now stated; and a further reason is this—to prevent impious men from acting fraudulently in regard to these matters also, by setting up shrines and altars in private houses, thinking to propitiate the gods privily by sacrifices and vows, and thus increasing infinitely their own iniquity, whereby they make both themselves and those better men who allow them guilty in the eyes of the gods, so that the whole State reaps the consequences of their impiety in some degree—and deserves to reap them. The lawgiver himself, however, will not be blamed by the god; for this shall be the law laid down:—Shrines of the gods no one must possess in a private house; and if anyone is proved to possess and worship at any shrine other than the public shrines—be the possessor man or woman,—and if he is guilty of no serious act of impiety, he that notices the fact shall inform the Law-wardens, and they shall give orders for the private shrines to be removed to the public temples, and if the owner disobeys the order, they shall punish him until he removes them. And if anyone be proved to have committed an impious act, such as is not the venial offence of children, but the serious irreligion of grown men, whether by setting up a shrine on private ground, or on public ground, by doing sacrifice to any gods whatsoever, for sacrificing in a state of impurity he shall be punished with death. And the Law-wardens[104] shall judge what is a childish or venial offence and what not, and then shall bring the offenders before the court, and shall impose upon them the due penalty for their impiety.

[104] Cf. two passages from Book xii of the *Laws* on the *sine qua non* qualifications of these Law-wardens:

"While one should pardon the mass of the citizens if they merely follow the letter of the law, one must exclude from office those who are eligible for wardenship, unless they labour to grasp all the proofs there are about the existence of gods. Such exclusion from office consists in refusing ever to choose as a Law-warden, or to number among those approved for excellence, a man who is not divine himself, nor has spent any labour over things divine" (966 D).

"It is impossible for any mortal man to become permanently god-fearing if he does not grasp the two truths now stated,—namely, how that the soul is the oldest of all things that partake of generation and is immortal, and rules over all bodies,—and in addition to this, he must also grasp that reason which, as we have often affirmed, controls what exists among the stars, together with the necessary preliminary sciences; and he must observe also the connection therewith of musical theory, and apply it harmoniously to the institutions and rule of ethics; and he must be able to give a rational explanation of all that admits of rational explanation. He that is unable to master these sciences, in addition to the popular virtues, will never make a competent magistrate of the whole State, but only a minister to other magistrates" (967 D, E).—T. V. S.

MYTHS, TALES, ALLEGORIES, FIGURES

As Socrates' "voice" requires him in the "Phaedrus" to do penance for his light talk of Love, so the shade of Plato now exacts amends for the didactic form thus far followed in presenting him. Plato was a poet, so legend had it, before he met Socrates and became a philosopher; he was a poet to the end. That he was serious in his quest for truth no one has ever doubted; but that he loved beauty with a poignant pain no one can read him and deny. Beneath the requirements of logic, which he understood and respected, lay in him the call of life, which to deny would have been heavy sacrilege. The dialogue form lends itself to the enjoyment and the elaboration of scenery along paths of discourse cleared by logic. The Socratic "irony," the bluffing, the teasing, the raillery, the extravagance—these are all his minor acknowledgments that the field of significance far outruns the narrow realm of truth. His major acknowledgment of this insight is found in his allegories, tales, figures, and myths. When important issues impend, but the facts are not at hand in terms of which to delineate, much less to prove, their veritable configurations, Plato curtsies to his scientific censor with a smile and gives free rein to his richly informed subconscious in bodying forth shapes of clairvoyance none the less fruitful because admittedly dim. Plato had that sense of integrity rare among minds above the plodding which required him to know, and even to tell, when he was outtalking his information. Myths are his warnings to beware. But they are also his invitations to dare—to dare to make appear plausible what life requires us to treat "as if" true. Through this device he resurrects common sense long buried in proverbs or hidden in poetry; and enforces, at times almost like a prophet, moral insights that are sound but not scientific. The myths here presented run the gamut from the grotesque with Aristophanes to the loftily religious with Socrates, letting us pause between jollity and the final judgment to learn from Diotima, one of Plato's wise women, the never dying lessons of Love.

. . .

THE MYTH OF NATURAL INEQUALITY

Republic (Shorey trans.) 414C–415D ("Loeb Classical Library" series).

"How, then," said I [Socrates speaking; Glaucon answering], "might we contrive one of those opportune falsehoods of which we were just now speaking, so as by one noble lie to persuade if possible the rulers themselves, but failing that the rest of the city?" "What kind of a fiction do you mean?" said he. "Nothing unprecedented," said I, "but a sort of Phoenician tale, something that has happened ere now in many parts of the world, as the poets aver and have induced men to believe, but that has not happened and perhaps would not be likely to happen in our day and demanding no little persuasion to make it believable." "You act like one who shrinks from telling his thought," he said. "You will think that I have right good reason for shrinking when I have told," I said. "Say on," said he, "and don't be afraid." "Very well, I will. And yet I hardly know how to find the audacity of the words to speak and undertake to persuade first the rulers themselves and the soldiers and then the rest of the city, that in good sooth all our training and educating of them were things that they imagined and that happened to them as it were in a dream; but that in reality at that time they were down within the earth being moulded and fostered themselves while their weapons and the rest of their equipment were being fashioned. And when they were quite finished the earth as being their mother delivered them, and now as if their land were their mother and their nurse they ought to take thought for her and defend her against any attack and regard the other citizens as their brothers and children of the self-same earth." "It is not for nothing," he said, "that you were so bashful about coming out with your lie." "It was quite natural that I should be," I said; "but all the same hear the rest of the story. While all of you in the city are brothers, we will say in our tale, yet God in fashioning those of you who are fitted to hold rule mingled gold in their generation, for which reason they are the most precious—but in the helpers silver, and iron and brass in the farmers and other craftsmen. And as you are all akin, though for the most part you will breed after your kinds, it may sometimes happen that a golden father would beget a silver son and that a golden offspring would come from a silver sire and that the rest would in like manner be born of one another. So that the first and chief injunction that the god lays upon the rulers is that of nothing else are they to be such careful guardians and so intently observant as of the intermixture of these metals in the souls of their offspring, and if sons are born to them with an infusion of brass or iron they shall by no means give way to pity in their treatment of them, but shall assign to each the status due to his nature and thrust them out among the artizans or the farmers. And again, if from these there is born a son with unexpected gold or silver in his composition they shall honour such and bid them go up higher, some to the office of guardian, some to the assistance-ship, alleging that there is an oracle that the state shall then be overthrown when the man of iron or brass is its guardian. Do you see any way of getting them to believe this tale?" "No, not these themselves," he said, "but I do, their sons and successors and the rest of mankind who come after." "Well," said I, "even that would have a good effect in making them more inclined to care for the state and one another."

THE MYTH OF MORAL EQUALITY

Protagoras 320-23. Lamb translation ("Loeb Classical Library" series).

[*Socrates and Protagoras speaking*]

.... I, Protagoras, believe that virtue is not teachable: but when I hear you speak thus, I am swayed over, and suppose there is something in what you say, because I consider you to have gained experience in many things and to have learnt many, besides finding out some for yourself. So if you can demonstrate to us more explicitly that virtue is teachable, do not grudge us your demonstration.

No, Socrates, I will not grudge it you; but shall I, as an old man speaking to his juniors, put my demonstration in the form of a fable, or of a regular exposition?

Many of the company sitting by him instantly bade him treat his subject whichever way he pleased.

Well then, he said, I fancy the more agreeable way is for me to tell you a fable.

There was once a time when there were gods, but no mortal creatures. And when to these also came their destined time to be created, the gods moulded their forms within the earth, of a mixture made of earth and fire and the elements that are compounded of fire and earth. When they were about to bring these creatures to light, they charged Prometheus and Epimetheus to deal to each the equipment of his proper faculty. Epimetheus besought Prometheus that he might do the dealing himself: "And when I have dealt," he said, "you shall examine." Having thus persuaded him he dealt; and in dealing he attached strength without speed to some, while the weaker he equipped with speed; and some he armed, while devising for others, along with an unarmed condition, some different faculty for preservation. To those which he invested with smallness he dealt a winged escape or an underground habitation; those which he increased in largeness he preserved by this very means; and he dealt all the other properties on this plan of compensation. In contriving all this he was taking precaution that no kind should be extinguished; and when he had equipped them with avoidances of mutual destruction, he devised a provision against the seasons ordained by Heaven, in clothing them about with thick-set hair and solid hides, sufficient to ward off winter yet able to shield them also from the heats, and so that on going to their lairs they might find in these same things a bedding of their own that was native to each; and some he shod with hoofs, others with claws and solid, bloodless hides. Then he proceeded to furnish each of them with its proper food, some with pasture of the earth, others with fruits of trees, and others again with roots; and to a certain number for food he gave other creatures to devour: to some he attached a paucity in breeding, and to others, which were being consumed by these, a plenteous brood, and so procured survival of their kind. Now Epimetheus, being not so wise as he might be, heedlessly squandered his stock of properties on the brutes; he still had left unequipped the race of men, and was at a loss what to do with it. As he was casting about, Prometheus arrived to examine his distribution, and saw that whereas the other creatures were fully and suitably provided, man was naked, unshod, unbedded, unarmed; and already the destined day was come, whereon man like the rest should emerge from earth to light. Then Prometheus, in his perplexity as to what preservation he could devise for man, stole from Hephaestus and Athena wisdom in the arts together with fire —since by no means without fire could it be acquired or helpfully used by any—and he handed it there and then as a gift to man. Now although man acquired in this way the wisdom of daily life, civic wisdom he had not, since this was in the possession of Zeus; Prometheus could not make so free as to enter the citadel which is the dwelling-place of Zeus, and moreover the guards of Zeus were terrible: but he entered unobserved the building shared by Athena and Hephaestus for the pursuit of their arts, and stealing Hephaestus's fiery art and all Athena's also he gave them to man, and hence it is that man gets facility for his livelihood, but Prometheus, through Epimetheus' fault, later on (the story goes) stood his trial for theft.

And now that man was partaker of a divine portion,[105] he, in the first place, by his nearness of kin to deity, was the only creature that worshipped gods, and set himself to establish altars and holy images; and secondly, he soon was enabled by his skill to articulate speech and words, and to invent dwellings, clothes, sandals, beds, and the foods that are of the earth. Thus far provided, men dwelt separately in the beginning, and cities there were none; so that they were being destroyed by the wild beasts, since these were in all ways stronger than they; and although their skill in handiwork was sufficient aid in respect of food, in their warfare with the beasts it was defective; for as yet they had no civic art, which includes the art of war. So they sought to band themselves together and secure their lives by founding cities. Now as often as they were banded together they did wrong to one another through the lack of civic art, and thus they began to be scattered again and to perish. So Zeus, fearing that our race was in danger of utter destruction, sent Hermes to bring respect and right among men, to the end that there should be regulation of cities and friendly ties to draw them together. Then Hermes asked Zeus in what manner then was he to

[105] *I.e.* of arts originally apportioned to gods alone.

give men right and respect: "Am I to deal them out as the arts have
been dealt? That dealing was done in such wise that one man possessing medical art is able to treat many ordinary men, and so with
the other craftsmen. Am I to place among men right and respect
in this way also, or deal them out to all?" "To all," replied Zeus;
"let all have their share; for cities cannot be formed if only a few
have a share of these as of other arts. And make thereto a law of my
ordaining, that he who cannot partake of respect and right shall die
the death as a public pest." Hence it comes about, Socrates, that
people in cities, and especially in Athens, consider it the concern of
a few to advise on cases of artistic excellence or good craftsmanship,
and if anyone outside the few gives advice they disallow it, as you
say, and not without reason, as I think: but when they meet for a
consultation on civic art, where they should be guided throughout
by justice and good sense, they naturally allow advice from everybody, since it is held that everyone should partake of this excellence,
or else that states cannot be. This, Socrates, is the explanation of
it. And that you may not think you are mistaken, to show how all
men verily believe that everyone partakes of justice and the rest of
civic virtue, I can offer yet a further proof. In all other excellences,
as you say, when a man professes to be good at flute-playing or any
other art in which he has no such skill, they either laugh him to
scorn or are annoyed with him, and his people come and reprove
him for being so mad: but when justice or any other civic virtue is
involved, and they happen to know that a certain person is unjust,
if he confesses the truth about his conduct before the public, that
truthfulness which in the former arts they would regard as good
sense they here call madness. Everyone, they say, should profess
to be just, whether he is so or not, and whoever does not make some
pretension to justice is mad; since it is held that all without exception must needs partake of it in some way or other, or else not be of
human kind.

THE STORY OF THE INVISIBLE SHEPHERD

Republic (Shorey trans.) 359C–361D ("Loeb Classical Library" series).

. . . . [Let] "us grant [says Glaucon speaking to Socrates] to
each, the just and the unjust, licence and power to do whatever
he pleases, and then accompany them in imagination and see

whither his desire will conduct each. We should then catch the just man in the very act of resorting to the same conduct as the unjust man because of the self-advantage which every creature by its nature pursues as a good, while by the convention of law it is forcibly diverted to paying honour to 'equality.' The licence that I mean would be most nearly such as would result from supposing them to have the power which men say once came to the ancestor of Gyges the Lydian. They relate that he was a shepherd in the service of the ruler at that time of Lydia, and that after a great deluge of rain and an earthquake the ground opened and a chasm appeared in the place where he was pasturing; and they say that he saw and wondered and went down into the chasm; and the story goes that he beheld other marvels there and a hollow bronze horse with little doors, and that he peeped in and saw a corpse within, as it seemed, of more than mortal stature, and that there was nothing else but a gold ring on its hand, which he took off and went forth. And when the shepherds held their customary assembly to make their monthly report to the king about the flocks, he also attended wearing the ring. So as he sat there it chanced that he turned the collet of the ring towards himself, towards the inner part of his hand, and when this took place they say that he became invisible to those who sat by him and they spoke of him as absent; and that he was amazed, and again fumbling with the ring turned the collet outwards and became visible. On noting this he experimented with the ring to see if it possessed this virtue, and he found the result to be that when he turned the collet inwards he became invisible, and when outwards visible; and becoming aware of this, he immediately managed things so that he became one of the messengers who went up to the king, and on coming there he seduced the king's wife and with her aid set upon the king and slew him and possessed his kingdom. If now there should be two such rings, and the just man should put on one and the unjust the other, no one could be found, it would seem, of such adamantine temper as to persevere in justice and endure to refrain his hands from the possessions of others and not touch them, though he might with impunity take what he wished even from the market-place, and enter into houses and lie with whom he pleased, and slay and loose from bonds whomsoever he would, and in all other things conduct himself among mankind as the equal of a god. And in so acting he would do no differently from the other man, but both would pursue the same course. And yet this is a great proof, one might argue, that no one is just of his own will but only from constraint, in the belief that justice is not his personal good, inasmuch as every man, when he supposed himself to have the power to do wrong, does wrong. For that there is far more profit for him personally in injustice than in justice is what every man believes, and believes truly, as the proponent of this theory will maintain. For if anyone who had got such a licence within his grasp should refuse to do any wrong or lay his hands on others' possessions, he would be regarded as most pitiable and a great fool by all who took note of it, though they would praise him before one another's faces, deceiving one another because of their fear of suffering injustice. So much for this point.

"But to come now to the decision between our two kinds of life, if we separate the most completely just and the most completely unjust man, we shall be able to decide rightly, but if not, not. How, then, is this separation to be made? Thus: we must subtract nothing of his injustice from the unjust man or of his justice from the just, but assume the perfection of each in his own mode of conduct. In the first place, the unjust man must act as clever craftsmen do: a first-rate pilot or physician, for example, feels the difference between impossibilities and possibilities in his art and attempts the one and lets the others go; and then, too, if he does happen to trip, he is equal to correcting his error. Similarly, the unjust man who attempts injustice rightly must be supposed to escape detection if he is to be altogether unjust, and we must regard the man who is caught as a bungler. For the height of injustice is to seem just without being so. To the perfectly unjust man, then, we must assign perfect injustice and withhold nothing of it, but we must allow him, while committing the greatest wrongs, to have secured for himself the greatest reputation for justice; and if he does happen to trip, we must concede to him the power to correct his mistakes by his ability to speak persuasively if any of his misdeeds come to light, and when force is needed, to employ force by reason of his manly spirit and vigour and his provision of friends and money; and when we have set up an unjust man of this character, our theory must set the just man at his side—a simple and noble man, who, in the phrase of Aeschylus, does not wish to seem but be good. Then we must deprive him of the seeming. For if he is going to be thought just he will have honours and gifts because of that esteem. We cannot be sure in that case whether he is just for justice's sake or for the sake of the gifts and the honours. So we must strip him bare of everything but justice and make his state the opposite of his imagined counterpart. Though doing no wrong he must have the repute of the greatest injustice, so that he may be put to the test as regards justice through not softening because of ill repute and the consequences thereof. But let him hold on his course unchangeable even unto death, seeming all his life to be unjust though being just, that so, both men attaining to the limit, the one of injustice, the other of justice, we may pass judgement which of the two is the happier."

THE ALLEGORY OF THE CAVE

Republic (Davies and Vaughan trans.) vii. 514-18.

Imagine a number of men living in an underground cavernous chamber, with an entrance open to the light, extending along the entire length of the cavern, in which they have been confined, from their childhood, with their legs and necks so shackled, that they are obliged to sit still and look straight forwards, because their chains render it impossible for them to turn their heads round: and imagine a bright fire burning some way off, above and behind them, and an elevated roadway passing between the fire and the prisoners, with a low wall built along it, like the screens which conjurors put up in front of their audience, and above which they exhibit their wonders.

I have it, he replied.

Also figure to yourself a number of persons walking behind this wall, and carrying with them statues of men, and images of other animals, wrought in wood and stone and all kinds of materials, together with various other articles, which overtop the wall; and, as you might expect, let some of the passers-by be talking, and others silent.

You are describing a strange scene, and strange prisoners.

They resemble us, I replied. For let me ask you, in the first place, whether persons so confined could have seen anything of themselves or of each other, beyond the shadows thrown by the fire upon the part of the cavern facing them?

Certainly not, if you suppose them to have been compelled all their lifetime to keep their heads unmoved.

And is not their knowledge of the things carried past them equally limited?

Unquestionably it is.

And if they were able to converse with one another, do you not think that they would be in the habit of giving names to the objects which they saw before them?

Doubtless they would.

Again: if their prison-house returned an echo from the part facing them, whenever one of the passers-by opened his lips, to what, let me ask you, could they refer the voice, if not to the shadow which was passing?

Unquestionably they would refer it to that.

Then surely such persons would hold the shadows of those manufactured articles to be the only realities.

Without a doubt they would.

Now consider what would happen if the course of nature brought them a release from their fetters, and a remedy for their foolishness, in the following manner. Let us suppose that one of them has been released, and compelled suddenly to stand up, and turn his neck round and walk with open eyes towards the light; and let us suppose that he goes through all these actions with pain, and that the dazzling splendour renders him incapable of discerning those objects of which he used formerly to see the shadows. What answer should you expect him to make, if some one were to tell him that in those days he was watching foolish phantoms, but that now he is somewhat nearer to reality, and is turned towards things more real, and sees more correctly; above all, if he were to point out to him the several objects that are passing by, and question him, and compel him to answer what they are? Should you not expect him to be puzzled, and to regard his old visions as truer than the objects now forced upon his notice?

Yes, much truer.

And if he were further compelled to gaze at the light itself, would not his eyes, think you, be distressed, and would he not shrink and turn away to the things which he could see distinctly, and consider them to be really clearer than the things pointed out to him?

Just so.

And if some one were to drag him violently up the rough and steep ascent from the cavern, and refuse to let him go till he had drawn him out into the light of the sun, would he not, think you, be vexed and indignant at such treatment, and on reaching the light, would he not find his eyes so dazzled by the glare as to be incapable of making out so much as one of the objects that are now called true?

Yes, he would find it so at first.

Hence, I suppose, habit will be necessary to enable him to perceive objects in that upper world. At first he will be most successful in distinguishing shadows; then he will discern the reflections of men and other things in water, and afterwards the realities; and after this he will raise his eyes to encounter the light of the moon and stars, finding it less difficult to study the heavenly bodies and the heaven itself by night, than the sun and the sun's light by day.

Doubtless.

Last of all, I imagine, he will be able to observe and contemplate the nature of the sun, not as it *appears* in water or on alien ground, but as it *is* in itself in its own territory.

Of course.

His next step will be to draw the conclusion, that the sun is the author of the seasons and the years, and the guardian of all things in the visible world, and in a manner the cause of all those things which he and his companions used to see.

Obviously, this will be his next step.

What then? When he recalls to mind his first habitation, and the wisdom of the place, and his old fellow-prisoners, do you not think he will congratulate himself on the change, and pity them?

Assuredly he will.

And if it was their practice in those days to receive honour and commendations one from another, and to give prizes to him who had the keenest eye for a passing object, and who remembered best all that used to precede and follow and accompany it, and from these data divined most ably what was going to come next, do you fancy that he will covet these prizes, and envy those who receive honour and exercise authority among them? Do you not rather imagine that he will feel what Homer describes, and wish extremely

To drudge on the lands of a master,
Under a portionless wight,

and be ready to go through anything, rather than entertain those opinions, and live in that fashion?

For my own part, he replied, I am quite of that opinion. I believe he would consent to go through anything rather than live in that way.

And now consider what would happen if such a man were to descend again and seat himself on his old seat? Coming so suddenly out of the sun, would he not find his eyes blinded with the gloom of the place?

Certainly, he would.

And if he were forced to deliver his opinion again, touching the shadows aforesaid, and to enter the lists against those who had always been prisoners, while his sight continued dim, and his eyes unsteady,—and if this process of initiation lasted a considerable time,—would he not be made a laughingstock, and would it not be said of him, that he had gone up only to come back again with his eyesight destroyed, and that it was not worth while even to attempt the ascent? And if any one endeavoured to set them free and carry them to the light, would they not go so far as to put him to death, if they could only manage to get him into their power?

Yes, that they would.

Now this imaginary case, my dear Glaucon, you must apply in all its parts to our former statements, by comparing the region which the eye reveals, to the prisonhouse, and the light of the fire therein to the power of the sun: and if, by the upward ascent and the contemplation of the upper world, you understand the mounting of the soul into the intellectual region, you will hit the tendency of my own surmises, since you desire to be told what they are; though, indeed, God only knows whether they are correct. But, be that as it may, the view which I take of the subject is to the following effect. In the world of knowledge, the essential Form of Good is the limit of our inquiries, and can barely be perceived; but, when perceived, we cannot help concluding that it is in every case the source of all that is bright and beautiful,—in the visible world giving birth to light and its master, and in the intellectual world dispensing, immediately and with full authority, truth and reason;—and that whosoever would act wisely, either in private or in public, must set this Form of Good before his eyes.

To the best of my power, said he, I quite agree with you.

That being the case, I continued, pray agree with me on another point, and do not be surprised, that those who have climbed so high are unwilling to take a part in the affairs of men, because their souls are ever loath to desert that upper region. For how could it be otherwise, if the preceding simile is indeed a correct representation of their case?

True, it could scarcely be otherwise.

Well: do you think it a marvellous thing, that a person, who has just quitted the contemplation of divine objects for the study of human infirmities, should betray awkwardness, and appear very ridiculous, when with his sight still dazed, and before he has become sufficiently habituated to the darkness that reigns around, he finds himself compelled to contend in courts of law, or elsewhere, about the shadows of justice, or images which throw the shadows, and to enter the lists in questions involving the arbitrary suppositions entertained by those who have never yet had a glimpse of the essential features of justice?

No, it is anything but marvellous.

Right: for a sensible man will recollect that the eyes may be confused in two distinct ways and from two distinct causes,—that is to say, by sudden transitions either from light to darkness, or from darkness to light. And, believing the same idea to be applicable to the soul, whenever such a person sees a case in which the mind is perplexed and unable to distinguish objects, he will not laugh irrationally, but he will examine whether it has just quitted a brighter life, and has been blinded by the novelty of darkness, or whether it has come from the depths of ignorance into a more brilliant life, and has been dazzled by the unusual splendour; and not till then will he congratulate the one upon its life and condition, and compassionate the other; and if he chooses to laugh at it, such laughter will be less ridiculous than that which is raised at the expense of the soul that has descended from the light of a higher region.

You speak with great judgment.

Hence, if this be true, we cannot avoid adopting the belief, that the real nature of education is at variance with the account given of it by certain of its professors, who pretend, I believe, to infuse into the mind a knowledge of which it was destitute, just as sight might be instilled into blinded eyes.

True; such are their pretensions.

Whereas, our present argument shews us that there is a faculty residing in the soul of each person, and an instrument enabling each of us to learn; and that, just as we might suppose it to be impossible to turn the eye round from darkness to light without turning the whole body, so must this faculty, or this instrument, be wheeled round, in company with the entire soul, from the perishing world, until it be enabled to endure the contemplation of the real world and the brightest part thereof, which, according to us, is the Form of Good.

Here we note, but do not requote, two great myths from the "Symposium," which may well be read in this order:

THE MYTH OF SEX: THE SOUL'S PREDICAMENT (*Symposium* 189–93)

THE LESSON OF DIOTIMA: LOVE'S GENEALOGY (*Symposium* 201–12)

THE TALE OF ER: THE SOUL'S JUDGMENT

Republic (Davies and Vaughan trans.) x. 614–21 end.

Well, I will tell you a tale, not like that of Odysseus to Alcinous,[106] but of what once happened to a brave man, Er the son of Armenius, a native of Pamphylia, who, according to story, was killed in battle. When the bodies of the slain were taken up ten days afterwards for burial in a state of decomposition, Er's body was found to be still fresh. He was carried home, and was on the point of being interred, when, on the twelfth day after his death, as he lay on the funeral-pyre, he came to life again, and then proceeded to describe what he had seen in the other world. His story was, that when the soul had gone out of him, it travelled in company with many others, till they came to a mysterious place, in which were two gaps, adjoining one another, in the earth, and exactly opposite them two gaps above in the heaven. Between these gaps sate judges, who, after passing sentence, commanded the just to take the road to the right upwards through the heaven, and fastened in front of them some symbol of the judgment that had been given; while the

---

[106] That is, according to the commentators, not a long story.

unjust were ordered to take the road downwards to the left, and also carried behind them evidence of all their evil deeds. When he came to the place himself, he was told that he would have to carry to men a report of the proceedings of that other world; and he was admonished to listen, and watch everything that went on there. So he looked, and beheld the souls on one side taking their departure at one of the gaps in the heaven and the corresponding gap in the earth, after judgment had been passed upon them; while at the two other gaps he saw them arriving, squalid and dusty, or pure and bright, according as they ascended from earth, or descended from heaven. Each soul, as it arrived, wore a travel-stained appearance, and gladly went away into the meadow and there took up quarters, as people do when some great festival is pending. Greetings passed between all that were known to one another; and those who had descended from heaven were questioned about heaven by those who had risen out of the earth; while the latter were questioned by the former about earth. Those who were come from earth told their tale with lamentations and tears, as they bethought them of all the dreadful things that they had seen and suffered in their subterranean journey, which they said had lasted a thousand years: while those who were come from heaven described enjoyments and sights of marvellous beauty. It would take a long time, Glaucon, to repeat at length the many particulars of their stories: but, according to Er, the main points were the following. For every one of all the crimes, and all the personal injuries, committed by them, they suffered tenfold retribution when the turn for it came. The cycle of punishment recommenced every century, because the length of human life was estimated at a hundred years,—the object being to make them pay the penalty for each offence ten times over. Thus, all who had been guilty of a number of murders, or had betrayed and enslaved cities and armies, or had been accomplices in any other villainy, were intended to undergo tenfold sufferings for all and each of their offences; while, on the other hand, those who had done any charitable acts, and had shewn themselves just and holy, were meant to receive on the same principle their due reward. With regard to those whose death followed close upon their birth, he gave some particulars which need not be recorded. But, according to his narrative, the punishment for impiety, disobedience to parents, and the murder of near relations, was unusually severe;

and the reward for piety and obedience unusually great. For he was within hearing, he said, when one of the spirits asked another where Ardiaeus the Great was. Now this Ardiaeus had been sovereign in a city of Pamphylia, a thousand years before that time, and was said to have put his aged father and elder brother to death, besides committing a number of other wicked actions. The spirit to whom the question was addressed, replied, 'He is not come, and is not likely to come hither. For this, you must know, was one of the terrible sights that we beheld. When we were close to the aperture, and were on the point of ascending, after having undergone all our other sufferings, we suddenly came in sight of Ardiaeus and others, of whom the greater part, I think I may say, had been despots; though it is true there were also a few private persons, who had once been reckoned among enormous criminals. These people, when they thought themselves sure of ascending immediately, were repulsed by the aperture, which bellowed whenever one of these incurable sinners, or anybody who had not fully expiated his offences, attempted to ascend. Thereupon certain fierce and fiery-looking men, who were in attendance and understood the meaning of the sound, seized some of them by the waist and carried them off; but Ardiaeus and others were bound, hand and foot and head, and thrown down, and flayed with scourges, and dragged out by the wayside, and carded, like wool, upon thorn-bushes; and those who were passing by at the time were informed why they were put to this torture, and that they were being carried away in order to be flung into Tartarus. We had already gone through a great variety of alarms, but none of them were equal to the terror that then seized us, lest that sound should be uttered when any of us tried to go up; and most glad we all were to ascend, when it was not heard.' This will convey an idea of the penalties and the tortures; while the rewards were precisely the opposite. When seven days had elapsed since the arrival of the spirits in the meadow, they were compelled to leave the place, when their time came, and set out on the eighth day, and travel three days, till they arrived on the fourth at a place, from whence they looked down upon a straight pillar of light, stretching across the whole heaven and earth, more like the rainbow than anything else, only brighter and clearer. This they reached, when they had gone forward a day's journey; and, arriving at the centre of the light, they saw that its extremities were fastened by chains to the sky. For this light binds the sky together, like the hawser that strengthens a trireme, and thus holds together the whole revolving universe. To the extremities is fastened the distaff of Necessity, by means of which all the revolutions of the universe are kept up. The shaft and hook of this distaff are made of steel; the whorl is a compound of steel and other materials. The nature of the whorl may be thus described. In shape it is like an ordinary whorl; but from Er's account we must picture it to ourselves under the form of a large hollow whorl, scooped out right through, into which a similar, but smaller, whorl is nicely inserted, like those boxes which fit into one another. In the same way a third whorl is inserted within the second, a fourth within the third, and so on to four more. For in all, there are eight whorls, inserted into one another,—each concentric circle shewing its rim above the next outer, and all together forming one solid whorl embracing the shaft, which is passed right through the centre of the eighth. The first and outermost whorl has the broadest rim; the sixth has the next broadest; then comes the fourth; then the eighth; then the seventh; then the fifth; then the third; and the second has the narrowest rim. The rim of the greatest whorl exhibits a variety of colours; that of the seventh is most brilliant; that of the eighth derives its colour from the reflected light of the seventh; that of the second and that of the fifth are similar, but of a deeper colour than the others; the third has the palest colour; the fourth is rather red; and the sixth is almost as pale as the third. Now the distaff as a whole spins round with uniform velocity; but while the whole revolves, the seven inner circles travel slowly round in the opposite direction; and of them the eighth moves quickest, and after it the seventh, sixth and fifth, which revolve together: the fourth, as it appeared to them, completes its revolution with a velocity inferior to the last-mentioned; the third ranks fourth in speed; and the second, fifth. The distaff spins round upon the knees of Necessity. Upon each of its circles stands a siren, who travels round with the circle, uttering one note in one tone; and from all the eight notes there results a single harmony. At equal distances around sit three other personages, each on a throne. These are the daughters of Necessity, the Fates, Lachesis, Clotho, and Atropos; who, clothed in white robes, with garlands on their heads, chant to the music of the sirens, Lachesis the events of the past, Clotho those of the present, Atropos those of the future.

Clotho with her right hand takes hold of the outermost rim of the distaff, and twirls it altogether, at intervals; and Atropos with her left hand twirls the inner circles in like manner; while Lachesis takes hold of each in turn with either hand. Now the souls, immediately on their arrival, were required to go to Lachesis. An interpreter first of all marshalled them in order, and then having taken from the lap of Lachesis a number of lots and plans of life, mounted a high pulpit, and spoke as follows: 'Thus saith the maiden Lachesis, the daughter of Necessity. Ye short-lived souls, a new generation of men shall here begin the cycle of its mortal existence. Your destiny shall not be allotted to you, but you shall choose it for yourselves. Let him who draws the first lot be the first to choose a life, which shall be his irrevocably. Virtue owns no master: he who honours her shall have more of her, and he who slights her, less. The responsibility lies with the chooser. Heaven is guiltless.' Having said this, he threw the lots down upon the crowd; and each spirit took up the one which fell by his side, except Er himself, who was forbidden to do so. Each, as he took up his lot, saw what number he had drawn. This done, the plans of life, which far outnumbered the souls that were present, were laid before them on the ground. They were of every kind. There were lives of all living things, and among them every sort of human life. They included sovereignties, of which some were permanent, and others were abruptly terminated and ended in poverty and exile and beggary. There were also lives of famous men, renowned either for beauty of person and feature, for bodily strength and skill in games, or else for high birth and the merits of ancestors; and in the same way there were lives of undistinguished men, and likewise lives of celebrated and uncelebrated women. But no settled character of soul was included in them, because with the change of life, the soul inevitably becomes changed itself. But in every other respect the materials were very variously combined,—wealth appearing here, and poverty there; disease here, and health there; and here again a mean between these extremes. This, my dear Glaucon, is apparently the moment when everything is at stake with a man; and for this reason, above all others, it is the duty of each of us diligently to investigate and study, to the neglect of every other subject, that science which may haply enable a man to learn and discover, who will render him so instructed as to be able to discrimi-

nate between a good and an evil life, and according to his means to
choose, always and everywhere, that better life, by carefully calculating the influence which the things just mentioned, in combination or in separation, have upon real excellence of life; and who will
teach him to understand what evil or good is wrought by beauty
tempered with poverty or wealth, and how the result is affected by
the state of soul which enters into the combination; and what is the
consequence of blending together such ingredients as high or
humble birth, private or public life, bodily strength or weakness,
readiness or slowness of apprehension, and everything else of the
kind, whether naturally belonging to the soul or accidentally acquired by it;—so as to be able to form a judgment from all these
data combined, and, with an eye steadily fixed on the nature of the
soul, to choose between the good and the evil life, giving the name
of evil to the life which will draw the soul into becoming more unjust, and the name of good to the life which will lead it to become
more just, and bidding farewell to every other consideration. For
we have seen that in life and in death it is best to choose thus.
With iron resolution must he hold fast this opinion when he enters
the future world, in order that, there as well as here, he may escape
being dazzled by wealth and similar evils; and may not plunge into
usurpations or other corresponding courses of action, to the inevitable detriment of others, and to his own still heavier affliction;
but may know how to select that life which always steers a middle
course between such extremes, and to shun excess on either side
to the best of his power, not only in this life, but also in that which is
to come. For, by acting thus, he is sure to become a most happy
man.

To return; the messenger from the other world reported that on
the same occasion the Interpreter spoke to this effect: 'Even the
last comer, if he chooses with discretion and lives strenuously, will
find in store for him a life that is anything but bad, with which he
may well be content. Let not the first choose carelessly, or the last
despond.' As soon as he had said these words, the one who had
drawn the first lot advanced, and chose the most absolute despotism he could find; but so thoughtless was he, and greedy, that he
had not carefully examined every point before making his choice; so
that he failed to remark that he was fated therein, amongst other
calamities, to devour his own children. Therefore, when he had

studied it at his leisure, he began to beat his breast and bewail his choice; and, disregarding the previous admonitions of the Interpreter, he laid the blame for his misfortune not upon himself, but upon Fortune and Destiny, and upon any body sooner than himself. He was one of those who had come from heaven, and had lived during his former life under a well-ordered constitution, and hence a measure of virtue had fallen to his share through the influence of habit, unaided by philosophy. Indeed, according to Er's account, more than half the persons similarly deluded, had come from heaven; which is to be explained by the fact of their never having felt the discipline of trouble. For the majority of those who came from the earth did not make their choice in this careless manner, because they had known affliction themselves, and had seen it in others. On this account, and also through the chances of the lot, most of the souls exchanged an evil destiny for a good, or a good destiny for an evil. But if a man were always to study wisdom soundly, whenever he entered upon his career on earth, and if it fell to his lot to choose anywhere but among the very last, there is every probability, to judge by the account brought from the other world, that he would not only be happy while on earth, but also that he would travel from this world to the other and back again, not along a rough and subterranean, but along a smooth and heavenly road. It was a truly wonderful sight, he said, to watch how each soul selected its life,—a sight, at once melancholy, and ludicrous, and strange. The experience of their former life generally guided the choice. Thus he saw the soul, which had once been that of Orpheus, choosing the life of a swan, because from having been put to death by women, he detested the whole race so much, that he would not consent to be conceived and born of a woman. And he saw the soul of Thamyras choosing the life of a nightingale. He saw also a swan changing its nature, and selecting the life of a man; and its example was followed by other musical animals. The soul that drew the twentieth lot chose a lion's life. It was the soul of Ajax the son of Telamon, who shrunk from becoming a man, because he recollected the decision respecting the arms of Achilles. He was followed by the soul of Agamemnon, who had been also taught by his sufferings to hate mankind so bitterly, that he adopted in exchange an eagle's life. The soul of Atalanta, which had drawn one of the middle lots, beholding the great honours attached to the life of an athlete, could not resist the temptation to take it up. Then he saw the soul of Epeus the son of Panopeus, assuming the nature of a skilful work-woman. And in the distance, among the last, he saw the soul of the buffoon Thersites putting on the exterior of an ape. It so happened that the soul of Odysseus had drawn the last lot of all. When he came up to choose, the memory of his former sufferings had so abated his ambition, that he went about a long time looking for a quiet retired life, which with great trouble he discovered lying about, and thrown contemptuously aside by the others. As soon as he saw it, he chose it gladly, and said that he would have done the same, if he had even drawn the first lot. In like manner some of the other animals passed into men, and into one another,—the unjust passing into the wild, and the just into the tame: and every kind of mixture ensued.

Now, when all the souls had chosen their lives in the order of the lots, they advanced in their turn to Lachesis, who dispatched with each of them the Destiny he had selected, to guard his life and satisfy his choice. This Destiny first led the soul to Clotho in such a way as to pass beneath her hand and the whirling motion of the distaff, and thus ratified the fate which each had chosen in the order of precedence. After touching her, the same Destiny led the soul next to the spinning of Atropos, and thus rendered the doom of Clotho irreversible. From thence the souls passed straightforward under the throne of Necessity. When the rest had passed through it, Er himself also passed through; and they all travelled into the plain of Forgetfulness, through dreadful suffocating heat, the ground being destitute of trees and of all vegetation. As the evening came on, they took up their quarters by the bank of the river of Indifference, whose water cannot be held in any vessel. All persons are compelled to drink a certain quantity of the water; but those who are not preserved by prudence drink more than the quantity: and each, as he drinks, forgets everything. When they had gone to rest, and it was now midnight, there was a clap of thunder and an earthquake; and in a moment the souls were carried up to their birth, this way and that, like shooting stars. Er himself was prevented from drinking any of the water; but how, and by what road, he reached his body, he knew not: only he knew that he suddenly opened his eyes at dawn, and found himself laid out upon the funeral-pyre.

And thus, Glaucon, the tale was preserved, and did not perish; and it may also preserve us, if we will listen to its warnings; in which case we shall pass prosperously across the river of Lethe, and not defile our souls. Indeed, if we follow my advice, believing the soul to be immortal, and to possess the power of entertaining all evil, as well as all good, we shall ever hold fast the upward road, and devotedly cultivate justice combined with wisdom; in order that we may be loved by one another and by the gods, not only during our stay on earth, but also when, like conquerors in the games collecting the presents of their admirers, we receive the prizes of virtue; and, in order that both in this life and during the journey of a thousand years which we have described, we may never cease to prosper.

THE MYTH OF DEATH: THE SOUL'S PURGATION

Gorgias 523–27. Lamb translation ("Loeb Classical Library" series).

Soc. Give ear then, as they say, to a right fine story, which you will regard as a fable, I fancy, but I as an actual account; for what I am about to tell you I mean to offer as the truth. By Homer's account, Zeus, Poseidon, and Pluto divided the sovereignty amongst them when they took it over from their father. Now in the time of Cronos there was a law concerning mankind, and it holds to this very day amongst the gods, that every man who has passed a just and holy life departs after his decease to the Isles of the Blest, and dwells in all happiness apart from ill; but whoever has lived unjustly and impiously goes to the dungeon of requital and penance which, you know, they call Tartarus. Of these men there were judges in Cronos' time, and still of late in the reign of Zeus—living men to judge the living upon the day when each was to breathe his last; and thus the cases were being decided amiss. So Pluto and the overseers from the Isles of the Blest came before Zeus with the report that they found men passing over to either abode undeserving. Then spake Zeus: "Nay," said he, "I will put a stop to these proceedings. The cases are now indeed judged ill; and it is because they who are on trial are tried in their clothing, for they are tried alive. Now many," said he, "who have wicked souls are clad in fair bodies and ancestry and wealth, and at their judgement appear many witnesses to testify that their lives have been just. Now, the judges are confounded not only by their evidence but at the same time by being clothed themselves while they sit in judgement, having their own soul muffled in the veil of eyes and ears and the whole body. Thus all these are a hindrance to them, their own habiliments no less than those of the judged. Well, first of all," he said, "we must put a stop to their foreknowledge of their death; for this they at present foreknow. However, Prometheus has already been given the word to stop this in them. Next they must be stripped bare of all those things before they are tried; for they must stand their trial dead. Their judge also must be naked, dead, beholding with very soul the very soul of each immediately upon his death, bereft of all his kin and having left behind on earth all that fine array, to the end that the judgement may be just. Now I, knowing all this before you, have appointed sons of my own to be judges; two from Asia, Minos and Rhadamanthus, and one from Europe, Aeacus. These, when their life is ended, shall give judgement in the meadow at the dividing of the road, whence are the two ways leading, one to the Isles of the Blest, and the other to Tartarus. And those who come from Asia shall Rhadamanthus try, and those from Europe, Aeacus; and to Minos I will give the privilege of the final decision, if the other two be in any doubt; that the judgement upon this journey of mankind may be supremely just."

This, Callicles, is what I have heard and believe to be true; and from these stories, on my reckoning, we must draw some such moral as this: death, as it seems to me, is actually nothing but the disconnexion of two things, the soul and the body, from each other. And so when they are disconnected from one another, each of them keeps its own condition very much as it was when the man was alive, the body having its own nature, with its treatments and experiences all manifest upon it. For instance, if anyone's body was large by nature or by feeding or by both when he was alive, his corpse will be large also when he is dead; and if he was fat, it will be fat too after his death, and so on for the rest; or again, if he used to follow the fashion of long hair, long-haired also will be his corpse. Again, if anyone had been a sturdy rogue, and bore traces of his stripes in scars on his body, either from the whip or from other wounds, while yet alive, then after death too his body has these marks visible upon it; or if anyone's limbs were broken or distorted in life, these same effects are manifest in death. In a word, whatever sort of bodily appearance a man had acquired in life, that is manifest also after his death either wholly or in the main for some time. And so it seems to me that the same is the case with the soul too, Callicles: when a man's soul is stripped bare of the body, all its natural gifts, and the experiences added to that soul as the result of his various pursuits, are manifest in it. So when they have arrived in presence of their judge, they of Asia before Rhadamanthus, these Rhadamanthus sets before him and surveys the soul of each, not knowing whose it is; nay, often when he has laid hold of the Great King or some other prince or potentate, he perceives the utter unhealthiness of his soul, striped all over with the scourge, and a mass of wounds, the work of perjuries and injustice; where every act has left its smirch upon his soul, where all is awry through falsehood and imposture, and nothing straight because of a nurture that knew not truth: or, as the result of an unbridled course of fastidiousness, insolence, and incontinence, he finds the soul full fraught with disproportion and ugliness. Beholding this he sends it away in dishonour straight to the place of custody, where on its arrival it is to endure the sufferings that are fitting. And it is fitting that every one under punishment rightly inflicted on him by another should either be made better and profit thereby, or serve as an example to the rest, that others seeing the sufferings he endures may in fear amend themselves. Those who are benefited by the punishment they get from gods and men are they who have committed remediable offences; but still it is through bitter throes of pain that they receive their benefit both here and in the nether world; for in no other way can there be riddance of iniquity. But of those who have done extreme wrong and, as a result of such crimes, have become incurable, of those are the examples made; no longer are they profited at all themselves, since they are incurable, but others are profited who behold them undergoing for their transgressions the greatest, sharpest, and most fearful sufferings evermore, actually hung up as examples there in the infernal dungeon, a spectacle and a lesson to such of the wrongdoers as arrive from time to time. Among them I say Archelaus also will be found, if what Polus tells us is true, and every other despot of his sort. And I think, moreover, that most of these examples have come from despots and kings and potentates and public administrators; for these, since they have a free hand, commit the greatest and most impious offences. Homer also testifies to this; for he has represented kings and potentates as those who are punished everlastingly in the nether world—Tantalus and Sisyphus and Tityus; but Thersites, or any other private person who was wicked, has been portrayed by none as incurable and therefore subjected to heavy punishment; no doubt because he had not a free hand, and therefore was in fact happier than those who had. For in fact, Callicles, it is among the powerful that we find the specially wicked men. Still there is nothing to prevent good men being found even among these, and it deserves our special admiration when they are; for it is hard, Callicles, and deserving of no slight praise, when a man with a perfectly free hand for injustice lives always a just life. The men of this sort are but few; for indeed there have been, and I expect there yet will be, both here and elsewhere, men of honour and excellence in this virtue of administering justly what is committed to their charge. One in fact there has been whose fame stands high among us and throughout the rest of Greece, Aristeides, son of Lysimachus; but most of those in power, my excellent friend, prove to be bad. So, as I was saying, whenever the judge Rhadamanthus has to deal with such an one, he knows nothing else of him at all, neither who he is nor of what descent, but only that he is a wicked person; and on perceiving this he sends him away to Tartarus, first setting a mark on him to show whether he deems it a curable or an incurable case; and when the man arrives there he suffers what is fitting. Sometimes, when he discerns another soul that has lived a holy life in company with truth, a private man's or any other's—especially, as I claim, Callicles, a philosopher's who has minded his own business and not been a busybody in his lifetime—he is struck with admiration and sends it off to the Isles of the Blest. And exactly the same is the procedure of Aeacus: each of these two holds a rod in his hand as he gives judgement; but Minos sits as supervisor, distinguished by the golden sceptre that he holds, as Odysseus in Homer tells how he saw him—

> Holding a golden sceptre, speaking dooms to the dead.

Now for my part, Callicles, I am convinced by these accounts, and I consider how I may be able to show my judge that my soul is in the best of health. So giving the go-by to the honours that most men seek I shall try, by inquiry into the truth, to be really good in as high a degree as I am able, both in my life and, when I come to die, in my death. And I invite all other men likewise, to the best of my power, and you particularly I invite in return, to this life and this contest, which I say is worth all other contests on this earth; and I make it a reproach to *you*, that you will not be able to deliver yourself when your trial comes and the judgement of which I told you just now; but when you go before your judge, the son of Aegina, and he grips you and drags you up, you will gape and feel dizzy there no less than I do here, and some one perhaps will give you, yes, a degrading box on the ear, and will treat you with every kind of contumely.

THE FIGURE OF THE CHARIOTEER: THE SOUL'S CAREER

Phaedrus 246–57. Fowler translation ("Loeb Classical Library" series).

Socrates. To tell what it [the soul] really is would be a matter for utterly superhuman and long discourse, but it is within human power to describe it briefly in a figure; let us therefore speak in that way. We will liken the soul to the composite nature of a pair of winged horses and a charioteer. Now the horses and charioteers of the gods are all good and of good descent, but those of other races are mixed; and first the charioteer of the human soul drives a pair, and secondly one of the horses is noble and of noble breed, but the other quite the opposite in breed and character. Therefore in our case the driving is necessarily difficult and troublesome. Now we must try to tell why a living being is called mortal or immortal. Soul, considered collectively, has the care of all that which is soul-less, and it traverses the whole heaven, appearing sometimes in one form and sometimes in another; now when it is perfect and fully winged, it mounts upward and governs the whole world; but the soul which has lost its wings is borne along until it gets hold of something solid, when it settles down, taking upon itself an earthly body, which seems to be self-moving, because of the power of the soul within it; and the whole, compounded of soul and body, is called a living being, and is further designated as mortal. It is not immortal by any reasonable supposition, but we, though we have never seen or rightly conceived a god, imagine an immortal being which has both a soul and a body which are united for all time. Let that, however, and our words concerning it, be as is pleasing to God; we will now consider the reason why the soul loses its wings. It is something like this.

The natural function of the wing is to soar upwards and carry that which is heavy up to the place where dwells the race of the gods. More than any other thing that pertains to the body it partakes of the nature of the divine. But the divine is beauty, wisdom, goodness, and all such qualities; by these then the wings of the soul are nourished and grow, but by the opposite qualities, such as vileness and evil, they are wasted away and destroyed. Now the great leader in heaven, Zeus, driving a winged chariot, goes first, arranging all things and caring for all things. He is followed by an army of gods and spirits, arrayed in eleven squadrons; Hestia alone remains in the house of the gods. Of the rest, those who are included among the twelve great gods and are accounted leaders, are assigned each to his place in the army. There are many blessed sights and many ways hither and thither within the heaven, along which the blessed gods go to and fro attending each to his own duties; and whoever wishes, and is able, follows, for jealousy is excluded from the celestial band. But when they go to a feast and a banquet, they proceed steeply upward to the top of the vault of heaven, where the chariots of the gods, whose well matched horses obey the rein, advance easily, but the others with difficulty; for the horse of evil nature weighs the chariot down, making it heavy and pulling toward the earth the charioteer whose horse is not well trained. There the utmost toil and struggle await the soul. For those that are called immortal, when they reach the top, pass outside and take their place on the outer surface of the heaven, and when they have taken their stand, the revolution carries them round and they behold the things outside of the heaven.

But the region above the heaven was never worthily sung by any earthly poet, nor will it ever be. It is, however, as I shall tell; for I must dare to speak the truth, especially as truth is my theme. For the colourless, formless, and intangible truly existing essence, with which all true knowledge is concerned, holds this region and is visible only to the mind, the pilot of the soul. Now the divine intelligence, since it is nurtured on mind and pure knowledge, and the intelligence of every soul which is capable of receiving that which befits it, rejoices in seeing reality for a space of time and by gazing upon truth is nourished and made happy until the revolution brings it again to the same place. In the revolution it beholds absolute justice, temperance, and knowledge, not such knowledge as has a beginning and varies as it is associated with one or another of the things we call realities, but that which abides in the real eternal absolute; and in the same way it beholds and feeds upon the other eternal verities, after which, passing down again within the heaven, it goes home, and there the charioteer puts up the horses at the manger and feeds them with ambrosia and then gives them nectar to drink.

Such is the life of the gods; but of the other souls, that which best follows after God and is most like him, raises the head of the charioteer up into the outer region and is carried round in the revolution, troubled by the horses and hardly beholding the realities; and another sometimes rises and sometimes sinks, and, because its horses are unruly, it sees some things and fails to see others. The other souls follow after, all yearning for the upper region but unable to reach it, and are carried round beneath, trampling upon and colliding with one another, each striving to pass its neighbour. So there is the greatest confusion and sweat of rivalry, wherein many are lamed, and many wings are broken through the incompetence of the drivers; and after much toil they all go away without gaining a view of reality, and when they have gone away they feed upon opinion. But the reason of the great eagerness to see where the plain of truth is, lies in the fact that the fitting pasturage for the best part of the soul is in the meadow there, and the wing on which the soul is raised up is nourished by this. And this is a law of Destiny, that the soul which follows after God and obtains a view of any of the truths is free from harm until the next period, and if it can always attain this, is always unharmed; but when, through inability to follow, it fails to see, and through some mischance is filled with forgetfulness and evil and grows heavy, and when it has grown heavy, loses its wings and falls to the earth, then it is the law that this soul shall never pass into any beast at its first birth, but the soul that has seen the most shall enter into the birth of a man who is to be a philosopher or a lover of beauty, or one of a musical or loving nature, and the second soul into that of a lawful king or a warlike ruler, and the third into that of a politician or a man of business or a financier, the fourth into that of a hard-working gymnast or one who will be concerned with the cure of the body, and the fifth will lead the life of a prophet or someone who conducts mystic rites; to the sixth, a poet or some other imitative artist will be united, to the seventh, a craftsman or a husbandman, to the eighth, a sophist or a demagogue, to the ninth, a tyrant.

Now in all these states, whoever lives justly obtains a better lot, and whoever lives unjustly, a worse. For each soul returns to the place whence it came in ten thousand years; for it does not regain its wings before that time has elapsed, except the soul of him who has been a guileless philosopher or a philosophical lover; these, when for three successive periods of a thousand years they have chosen such a life, after the third period of a thousand years become winged in the three thousandth year and go their way; but the rest, when they have finished their first life, receive judgment, and after the judgment some go to the places of correction under the earth and pay their penalty, while the others, made light and raised up into a heavenly place by justice, live in a manner worthy of the life they led in human form. But in the thousandth year both come to draw lots and choose their second life, each choosing whatever it wishes. Then a human soul may pass into the life of a beast, and a soul which was once human, may pass again from a beast into a man. For the soul which has never seen the truth can never pass into human form. For a human being must understand a general conception formed by collecting into a unity by means of reason the many perceptions of the senses; and this is a recollection of those things which our soul once beheld, when it journeyed with God and, lifting its vision above the things which we now say exist, rose up into real being. And therefore it is just that the mind of the philosopher only has wings, for he is always, so far as he is able, in communion through memory with those things the communion with which causes God to be divine. Now a man who employs such memories rightly is always being initiated into perfect mysteries and he alone becomes truly perfect; but since he separates himself from human interests and turns his attention toward the divine, he is rebuked by the vulgar, who consider him mad and do not know that he is inspired.

All my discourse so far has been about the fourth kind of madness, which causes him to be regarded as mad, who, when he sees the beauty on earth, remembering the true beauty, feels his wings growing and longs to stretch them for an upward flight, but cannot do so, and, like a bird, gazes upward and neglects the things below. My discourse has shown that this is, of all inspirations, the best and of the highest origin to him who has it or who shares in it, and that he who loves the beautiful, partaking in this madness, is called a lover. For, as has been said, every soul of man has by the law of nature beheld the realities, otherwise it would not have entered into a human being, but it is not easy for all souls to gain from earthly things a recollection of those realities, either for those which had but a brief view of them at that earlier time, or for those which, after falling to earth, were so unfortunate as to be turned toward unrighteousness through some evil communications and to have forgotten the holy sights they once saw. Few then are left which retain an adequate recollection of them; but these when they see here any likeness of the things of that other world, are stricken with amazement and can no longer control themselves; but they do not understand their condition, because they do not clearly perceive. Now in the earthly copies of justice and temperance and the other ideas which are precious to souls there is no light, but only a few, approaching the images through the darkling organs of sense, behold in them the nature of that which they imitate, and these few do this with difficulty. But at that former time they saw beauty shining in brightness, when, with a blessed company—we following in the train of Zeus, and others in that of some other god—they saw the blessed sight and vision and were initiated into that which is rightly called the most blessed of mysteries, which we celebrated in a state of perfection, when we were without experience of the evils which awaited us in the time to come, being permitted as initiates to the sight of perfect and simple and calm and happy apparitions, which we saw in the pure light, being ourselves pure and not entombed in this which we carry about with us and call the body, in which we are imprisoned like an oyster in its shell.

So much, then, in honour of memory, on account of which I have now spoken at some length, through yearning for the joys of that other time. But beauty, as I said before, shone in brilliance among those visions; and since we came to earth we have found it shining most clearly through the clearest of our senses; for sight is the sharpest of the physical senses, though wisdom is not seen by it, for wisdom would arouse terrible love, if such a clear image of it were granted as would come through sight, and the same is true of the other lovely realities; but beauty alone has this privilege, and therefore it is most clearly seen and loveliest. Now he who is not newly initiated, or has been corrupted, does not quickly rise from this world to that other world and to absolute beauty when he sees its namesake here, and so he does not revere it when he looks upon it, but gives himself up to pleasure and like a beast proceeds to lust and begetting; he makes licence his companion and is not afraid or ashamed to pursue pleasure in violation of nature. But he who is newly initiated, who beheld many of those realities, when he sees a godlike face or form which is a good image of beauty, shudders at first, and something of the old awe comes over him, then, as he gazes, he reveres the beautiful one as a god, and if he did not fear to be thought stark mad, he would offer sacrifice to his beloved as to an idol or a god. And as he looks upon him, a reaction from his shuddering comes over him, with sweat and unwonted heat; for as the effluence of beauty enters him through the eyes, he is warmed; the effluence moistens the germ of the feathers, and as he grows warm, the parts from which the feathers grow, which were before hard and choked, and prevented the feathers from sprouting, become soft, and as the nourishment streams upon him, the quills of the feathers swell and begin to grow from the roots over all the form of the soul; for it was once all feathered.

Now in this process the whole soul throbs and palpitates, and as in those who are cutting teeth there is an irritation and discomfort in the gums, when the teeth begin to grow, just so the soul suffers when the growth of the feathers begins; it is feverish and is uncomfortable and itches when they begin to grow. Then when it gazes upon the beauty of the boy and receives the particles which flow thence to it (for which reason they are called yearning), it is moistened and warmed, ceases from its pain and is filled with joy; but when it is alone and grows dry, the mouths of the passages in which the feathers begin to grow become dry and close up, shutting in the sprouting feathers, and the sprouts within, shut in with the yearning, throb like pulsing arteries, and each sprout pricks the passage in which it is, so that the whole soul, stung in every part, rages with pain; and then again, remembering the beautiful one, it rejoices. So, because of these two mingled sensations, it is greatly troubled by its strange condition; it is perplexed and maddened, and in its madness it cannot sleep at night or stay in any one place by day, but it is filled with longing and hastens wherever it hopes to see the beautiful one. And when it sees him and is bathed with the waters of yearning, the passages that were sealed are opened, the soul has respite from the stings and is eased of its pain, and this pleasure which it enjoys is the sweetest of pleasures at the time. Therefore the soul will not, if it can help it, be left alone by the beautiful one, but esteems him above all others, forgets for him mother and brothers and all friends, neglects property and cares not for its loss, and despising all the customs and proprieties in which it formerly took pride, it is ready to be a slave and to sleep wherever it is allowed, as near as possible to the beloved; for it not only reveres him who possesses beauty, but finds in him the only healer of its greatest woes. Now this condition, fair boy, about which I am speaking, is called Love by men, but when you hear what the gods call it, perhaps because of your youth you will laugh. But some of the Homeridae, I believe, repeat two verses on Love from the spurious poems of Homer, one of which is very outrageous and not perfectly metrical. They sing them as follows:

"Mortals call him winged Love, but the immortals call him The Winged One, because he must needs grow wings."

You may believe this, or not; but the condition of lovers and the cause of it are just as I have said.

Now he who is a follower of Zeus, when seized by Love can bear a heavier burden of the winged god; but those who are servants of Ares and followed in his train, when they have been seized by Love and think they have been wronged in any way by the beloved, become murderous and are ready to sacrifice themselves and the beloved. And so it is with the follower of each of the other gods; he lives, so far as he is able, honouring and imitating that god, so long as he is uncorrupted, and is living his first life on earth, and in that way he behaves and conducts himself toward his beloved and toward all others. Now each one chooses his love from the ranks of the beautiful according to his character, and he fashions him and adorns him like a statue, as though he were his god, to honour and worship him. The followers of Zeus desire that the soul of him whom they love be like Zeus; so they seek for one of philosophical and lordly nature, and when they find him and love him, they do all they can to give him such a character. If they have not previously had experience, they learn then from all who can teach them anything; they seek after information themselves, and when they search eagerly within themselves to find the nature of their god, they are successful, because they have been compelled to keep their eyes fixed upon the god, and as they reach and grasp him by memory they are inspired and receive from him character and habits, so far as it is possible for a man to have part in God. Now they consider the beloved the cause of all this, so they love him more than before, and if they draw the waters of their inspiration from Zeus, like the bacchantes, they pour it out upon the beloved and make him, so far as possible, like their god. And those who followed after Hera seek a kingly nature, and when they have found such an one, they act in a corresponding manner toward him in all respects; and likewise the followers of Apollo, and of each of the gods, go out and seek for their beloved a youth whose nature accords with that of the god, and when they have gained his affection, by imitating the god themselves and by persuasion and education they lead the beloved to the conduct and nature of the god, so far as each of them can do so; they exhibit no jealousy or meanness toward the loved one, but endeavour by every means in their power to lead him to the likeness of the god whom they honour. Thus the desire of the true lovers, and the initiation into the mysteries of love, which they teach, if they accomplish what they desire in the way I describe, is beautiful and brings happiness from the inspired lover to the loved one, if he be captured; and the fair one who is captured is caught in the following manner:—

In the beginning of this tale I divided each soul into three parts, two of which had the form of horses, the third that of a charioteer. Let us retain this division. Now of the horses we say one is good and the other bad; but we did not define what the goodness of the one and the badness of the other was. That we must now do. The horse that stands at the right hand is upright and has clean limbs; he carries his neck high, has an aquiline nose, is white in colour, and has dark eyes; he is a friend of honour joined with temperance and modesty, and a follower of true glory; he needs no whip, but is guided only by the word of command and by reason. The other, however, is crooked, heavy, ill put together, his neck is short and thick, his nose flat, his colour dark, his eyes grey and bloodshot; he is the friend of insolence and pride, is shaggy-eared and deaf, hardly obedient to whip and spurs. Now when the charioteer beholds the love-inspiring vision, and his whole soul is warmed by the sight, and is full of the tickling and prickings of yearning, the horse that is obedient to the charioteer, constrained then as always by modesty, controls himself and does not leap upon the beloved; but the other no longer heeds the pricks or the whip of the charioteer, but springs wildly forward, causing all possible trouble to his mate and to the charioteer, and forcing them to approach the beloved and propose the joys of love. And they at first pull back indignantly and will not be forced to do terrible and unlawful deeds; but finally, as the trouble has no end, they go forward with him, yielding and agreeing to do his bidding. And they come to the beloved and behold his radiant face.

And as the charioteer looks upon him, his memory is borne back to the true nature of beauty, and he sees it standing with modesty upon a pedestal of chastity, and when he sees this he is afraid and falls backward in reverence, and in falling he is forced to pull the reins so violently backward as to bring both horses upon their haunches, the one quite willing, since he does not oppose him, but the unruly beast very unwilling. And as they go away, one horse in his shame and wonder wets all the soul with sweat, but the other, as soon as he is recovered from the pain of the bit and the fall, before he has fairly taken breath, breaks forth into angry reproaches, bitterly reviling his mate and the charioteer for their cowardice and lack of manhood in deserting their post and breaking their agreement; and again, in spite of their unwillingness, he urges them forward and hardly yields to their prayer that he postpone the matter to another time. Then when the time comes which they have agreed upon, they pretend that they have forgotten it, but he reminds them; struggling, and neighing, and pulling he forces them again with the same purpose to approach the beloved one, and when they are near him, he lowers his head, raises his tail, takes the bit in his teeth, and pulls shamelessly. The effect upon the charioteer is the same as before, but more pronounced; he falls back like a racer from the starting-rope, pulls the bit backward even more violently than before from the teeth of the unruly horse, covers his scurrilous tongue and jaws with blood, and forces his legs and haunches to the ground, causing him much pain. Now when the bad horse has gone through the same experience many times and has ceased from his unruliness, he is humbled and follows henceforth the wisdom of the charioteer, and when he sees the beautiful one, he is overwhelmed with fear; and so from that time on the soul of the lover follows the beloved in reverence and awe.

Now the beloved, since he receives all service from his lover, as if he were a god, and since the lover is not feigning, but is really in love, and since the beloved himself is by nature friendly to him who serves him, although he may at some earlier time have been prejudiced by his schoolfellows or others, who said that it was a disgrace to yield to a lover, and may for that reason have repulsed his lover, yet, as time goes on, his youth and destiny cause him to admit him to his society. For it is the law of fate that evil can never be a friend to evil and that good must always be friend to good. And when the lover is thus admitted, and the privilege of conversation and intimacy has been granted him, his good will, as it shows itself in close intimacy, astonishes the beloved, who discovers that the friendship of all his other friends and relatives is as nothing when compared with that of his inspired lover. And as this intimacy continues and the lover comes near and touches the beloved in the gymnasia and in their general intercourse, then the fountain of that stream which Zeus, when he was in love with Ganymede, called "desire" flows copiously upon the lover; and some of it flows into him, and some, when he is filled, overflows outside; and just as the wind or an echo rebounds from smooth, hard surfaces and returns whence it came, so the stream of beauty passes back into the beautiful one through the eyes, the natural inlet to the soul, where it reanimates the passages of the feathers, waters them and makes the feathers begin to grow, filling the soul of the loved one with love. So he is in love, but he knows not with whom; he does not understand his own condition and cannot explain it; like one who has caught a disease of the eyes from another, he can give no reason for it; he sees himself in his lover as in a mirror, but is not conscious of the fact. And in the lover's presence, like him he ceases from his pain, and in his absence, like him he is filled with yearning such as he inspires, and love's image, requited love, dwells within him; but he calls it, and believes it to be, not love, but friendship. Like the lover, though less strongly, he desires to see his friend, to touch him, kiss him, and lie down by him; and naturally these things are soon brought about. Now as they lie together, the unruly horse of the lover has something to say to the charioteer, and demands a little enjoyment in return for his many troubles; and the unruly horse of the beloved says nothing, but teeming with passion and confused emotions he embraces and kisses his lover, caressing him as his best friend; and when they lie together, he would not refuse his lover any favour, if he asked it; but the other horse and the charioteer oppose all this with modesty and reason.

If now the better elements of the mind, which lead to a well ordered life and to philosophy, prevail, they live a life of happiness and harmony here on earth, self controlled and orderly, holding in subjection that which causes evil in the soul and giving freedom to that which makes for virtue; and when this life is ended they are light and winged, for they have conquered in one of the three truly Olympic contests. Neither human wisdom nor divine inspiration can confer upon man any greater blessing than this. If however they live a life less noble and without philosophy, but yet ruled by the love of honour, probably, when they have been drinking, or in some other moment of carelessness, the two unruly horses, taking the souls off their guard, will bring them together and seize upon and accomplish that which is by the many accounted blissful; and when this has once been done, they continue the practice, but infrequently, since what they are doing is not approved by the whole mind. So these two pass through life as friends, though not such friends as the others, both at the time of their love and afterwards, believing that they have exchanged the most binding pledges of love, and that they can never break them and fall into enmity. And at last, when they depart from the body, they are not winged, to be sure, but their wings have begun to grow, so that the madness of love brings them no small reward; for it is the law that those who have once begun their upward progress shall never again pass into darkness and the journey under the earth, but shall live a happy life in the light as they journey together, and because of their love shall be alike in their plumage when they receive their wings.

These blessings, so great and so divine, the friendship of a lover will confer upon you, dear boy; but the affection of the non-lover, which is alloyed with mortal prudence and follows mortal and parsimonious rules of conduct, will beget in the beloved soul the narrowness which the common folk praise as virtue; it will cause the soul to be a wanderer upon the earth for nine thousand years and a fool below the earth at last. There, dear Love, thou hast my recantation, which I have offered and paid as beautifully and as well as I could, especially in the poetical expressions which I was forced to employ on account of Phaedrus. Pardon, I pray, my former words and accept these words with favour; be kind and gracious to me; do not in anger take from me the art of love which thou didst give me, and deprive me not of sight, but grant unto me to be even more than now esteemed by the beautiful. And if in our former discourse Phaedrus and I said anything harsh against thee, blame Lysias, the father of that discourse, make him to cease from such speeches, and turn him, as his brother Polemarchus is turned, toward philosophy, that his lover Phaedrus may no longer hesitate, as he does now, between two ways, but may direct his life with all singleness of purpose toward love and philosophical discourses.

PHOENIX BOOKS *Titles in print*

THE UNIVERSITY OF CHICAGO PRESS